AF477103

DORSET
THEN AND NOW
FROM THE AIR

DORSET
THEN AND NOW
FROM THE AIR

GORDON LE PARD

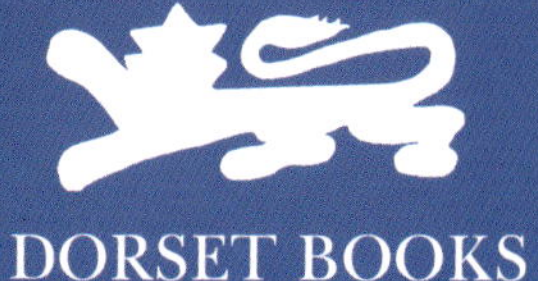

DORSET BOOKS

First published in Great Britain in 2011

British Library Cataloguing-in-Publication Data
A CIP record for this title is available from the British Library

ISBN 978 1 871164 81 7

DORSET BOOKS
Dorset Books is a partnership between
Dorset County Council and Halsgrove
Halsgrove House,
Ryelands Business Park,
Bagley Road, Wellington, Somerset TA21 9PZ
Tel: 01823 653777 Fax: 01823 216796
email: sales@halsgrove.com

Part of the Halsgrove group of companies.
Information on all Halsgrove titles is available at: www.halsgrove.com

Printed in China by Everbest Printing Co Ltd

CONTENTS

Abbotsbury 9
Arne 10
Ashmore 11
Badbury Rings 12
Ballard Down 14
Beaminster 15
Bere Regis 16
Blackdown North 18
Blackdown South – Bronkham Hill 19
Blandford Forum 20
Blandford Forum North 22
Bokerley Dyke and Pentridge 24
Bottlebush Down 25
Bournemouth Pier 26
Bournemouth Station 28
Bovington 29
Bradford Peverell and the Aqueduct 30
Bridport 31
Broadwindsor 32
Bulbarrow Hill and Rawlsbury Camp 34
Burton Bradstock 36
Cerne Abbas 38
Charlton Down 39
Charmouth and Black Ven 40
Chideock 41
Christchurch and Hengistbury Head 42
Christchurch Harbour Entrance 44
Compton Abbas 46
Corfe Castle 47
Cranborne 48
Cranborne Common 49
Creech 50
Creekmoor 52
Dorchester South 54
Dorchester West 56
Durlston 57
East Howe and Kinson 58
Edmondsham 59
Eggardon Hill 60
Ferndown 62
Ferrybridge 64
Fleet Narrows 66

Gillingham 67
Hod Hill 68
Holes Bay 69
Holton Heath 70
Kimmeridge 72
Kingcombe 73
Kingston Lacy 74
Kingston Maurward 76
Knowlton and Wimborne St Giles .78
Lyme Regis 80
Lyscombe Bottom 81
Maiden Castle 82
Maiden Newton 83
Marnhull 84
Marshwood Vale 86
Melbury Park 88
Milborne St Andrew 90
Milton Abbas 92
Oakley Down 94
Osmington White Horse 95
Parkstone 96
Piddlehinton 98
Pilsdon 100
Poole 102
Poole Harbour – South West Corner 104
Portland Bill 106
Portland Harbour and Sandsfoot Castle 108
Portland Verne 110
Rampisham Down Radio Masts 112
Sandbanks 113
Shaftesbury 114
Sherborne 116
Shillingstone 117
Spetisbury 118
Stoborough Heath 120
Stourton Caundle and Stock Gaylard 122
Sturminster Newton 124
Tarrant Rushton 126
Throop 127
Tyneham 128
Verwood 130
Wareham 132
Warmwell – Crossways 133
West Bay 134
West Moors 136
West Stafford Watermeadows 138
Weymouth 139
Whitchurch Canonicorum 140
Wimborne Minster 142
Woodlands 143
Worth Matravers 144

INTRODUCTION

Aerial photography began over a hundred years ago. At first these photographs, taken from balloons and later primitive aircraft, were little more than curiosities. It was during the First World War that aerial photography was really developed as a tool; the photography of enemy troops and installations became an essential part of military planning. After the war it was archaeology that was to take aerial photography forward. In 1928 O.G.S. Crawford (who had been an observer in the RFC during the war) and Alexander Keiller produced the first serious study of aerial photography and archaeology, *Wessex from the Air.* Nine of the sites illustrated in the book came from Dorset. Indeed the link between aerial photography and archaeology became so entrenched in the popular imagination that, during the early days of the Second World War, applicants for positions in aerial photographic interpretation were surprised to be asked to identify a flint tool! It being considered by the military that the only persons who knew about aerial photography were archaeologists!

It wasn't just the RAF who took aerial photographs, the Luftwaffe did too, and in 1940, as the Germans were planning their invasion of Britain, a good deal of Southern England was photographed. The invasion plans came to nothing, but the photographs survived and were captured towards the end of the war. They were a revelation and it was realised how useful these pictures could be for a wide range of purposes. However the Germans had only been concerned about planning for the invasion so the coverage was understandably incomplete.

This led to the initiation of a remarkable project. The RAF was commissioned to photograph the whole country! Using the aircraft and equipment developed during the war this was undertaken within two years. In 1947 Dorset was photographed. The quality of the pictures is very high and, for the first time, a complete picture of the county appears. The value of these pictures was immediately recognised, and as the decades passed, similar surveys were undertaken to update these images.

This coverage allows the numerous changes that have taken place in the county to be seen. Nothing has remained unchanged, and it is these changes that make the photographs so interesting. In the towns there is almost uniform growth: they grow outwards along the main roads, as various housing developments and estates are built. In the immediate post war period housing developments were laid out in the same way as they had been in the 1930s, with geometric forms such as semicircles imposed on grids. From the 1960s, such developments tended to eschew the geometric for a more sinuous, almost organic form, of curving cul de sacs and irregular plots. On some of the 1947 photographs the beginnings of this process can be seen in new roads and the first buildings of the new estates.

But it is not just in the growth of new houses that towns have altered. In 1947 every town, and most villages, were surrounded by blocks of allotments, relics of the *Dig for Victory* campaign. As the decades pass these shrink and the land, which tended to be owned by the local authority, turned over for more and more housing, until the end of the twentieth century when a renewed interest in vegetable growing seems to have arrested this change.

Changes in transport are another area which the photographs show well. In 1947 the county is criss-crossed by a network of railways. During the 1960s much of this vanished and the railway lines and the sites of the stations put to other uses. Though in one case, the branch line from Wareham to Swanage, the line closed and then reopened, as it was redeveloped as the Swanage Railway in the 1980s.

If railways have declined roads have developed, new main roads cross the countryside, and bypass or even cut through the older towns.

One of the biggest areas of change has been in the growth of the leisure industry. In resort towns such as Bournemouth and Weymouth new facilities have been built, and along the coast huge caravan and mobile home parks have been developed to provide low cost holiday accommodation. The massive increase in car ownership has led to the construction of the numerous car parks throughout the county for the use of visitors.

Agriculture has also changed over the years, intensification and the use of larger farm machinery has led to the removal of hedgerows and other field boundaries in many places. On the other hand the numerous remaining hedgerows are now more likely to contain hedgerow trees, which are far more common today than they were 60 years ago. In 1947 many villages had small orchards around them, but these have almost all disappeared. There has not, however, been a similar decline in other woodland, indeed woodland has increased extensively throughout the county. Many hedgerows are now thick with trees, old railway lines are linear woodlands as are some small fields and field margins. In virtually every photograph in this book woodland has increased, perhaps one of the most unexpected changes to have taken place, and been recorded in these aerial photographs.

About the photographs

When the RAF came to take the photographs in 1947 they naturally used the equipment that had been developed during the Second World War, for taking aerial reconnaissance photographs. Although the pilots did their best to align the photographs north south, in several cases the photographs are not exactly orientated, whilst the modern photographs are: the photograph of Portland Bill is a clear example. The modern photographs cover the same area as those of 1947, or indeed a little bit more; to compare the two you will need to find a fixed point in both photographs, a road or distinctively shaped field for example, and work from there.

An apology

I must apologise to all those people who will be upset not to find their village or favourite spot in Dorset included amongst these photographs. I just hope they will enjoy the photographs of the rest of the county showing the amazing mixture of continuity and change which makes Dorset such a fascinating place.

Acknowledgements

The 1947 photographs are currently held by Dorset County Council, whilst the modern photographs were taken for Dorset County Council and are their copyright. I must therefore thank the County Council for allowing me to make full and free use of these pictures. Finally I must of course acknowledge the skill and professionalism of the pilots of 1947 who took these remarkable photographs.

Abbotsbury 1947 photograph reference 2475-4275, centred on grid reference SY 575 849

The ancient town of Abbotsbury has hardly grown in the past sixty years, though there are some new houses to the east of the town. The surrounding landscape is only slightly altered, most of the field boundaries have survived but, as is common in Dorset, woodland has spread. In 1947 traces of the Second World War were still evident, for example the line of tank traps across Chesil Beach at the junction with the Fleet Lagoon can clearly be seen – these still exist today.

The greatest change has come about through the increase in tourism, the principle industry of Abbotsbury today. There are large car parks in the village, by the Swannery at the southern edge of the photograph and the Sub Tropical Gardens towards the west of the picture.

One aspect of the visitor attractions is the use made of the historic features. In the centre of the picture in the medieval chapel of St Catherine, which stands on a pointed hill which has been shaped by a series of medieval terraced fields. Towards the bottom of the picture, on the landward side of the Fleet the rare Duck Decoy can be seen: it is a square pond with extensions at each corner, called 'pipes' where ducks are trapped, once for food now for study.

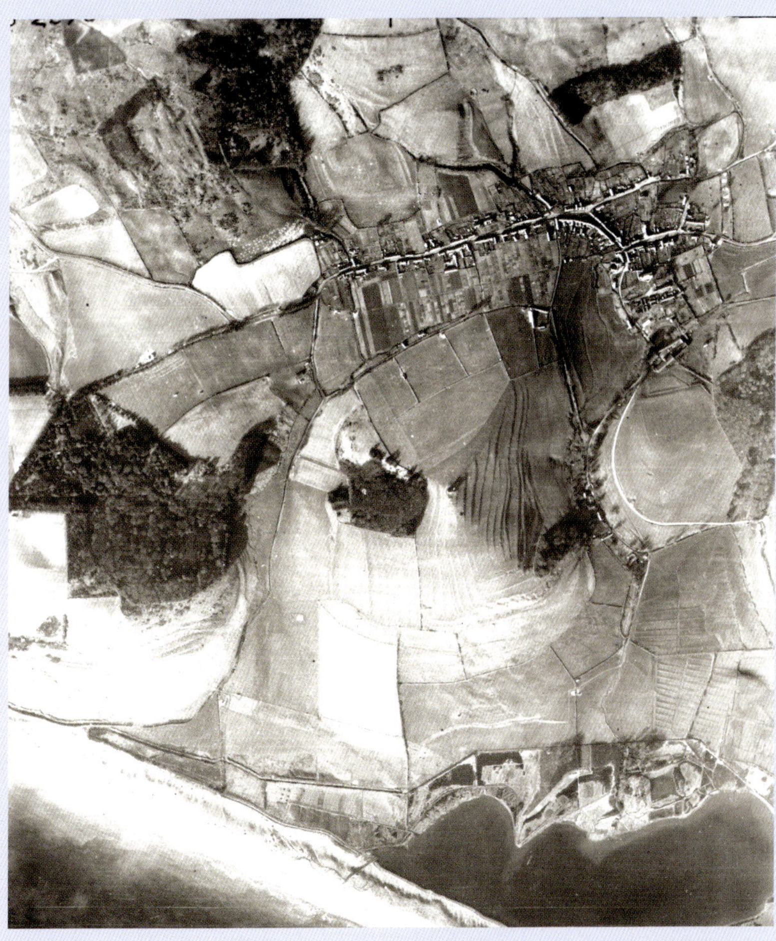

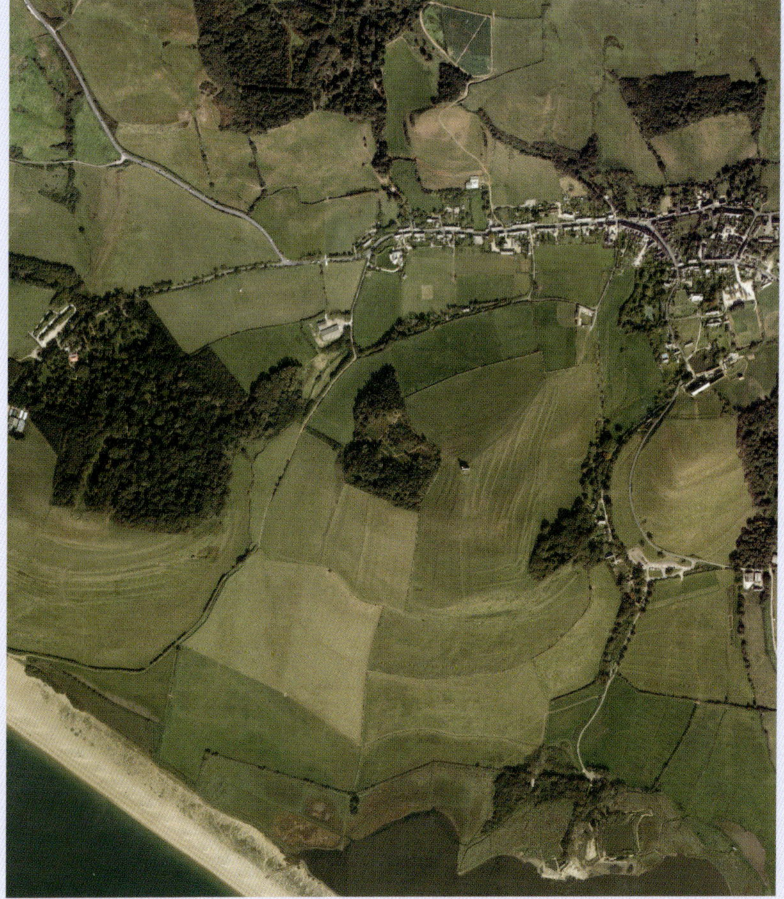

Arne

1947 photograph reference 1934-3046, centred on grid reference SY 976 889

On the 1947 photograph the most obvious feature is the group of about fifty landing craft moored along the shore of Arne Bay. These had been used during the Second World War; perhaps some of them may have been used on D-Day, but they were now surplus to requirement and were awaiting disposal. Two of them were used, in a more unconventional fashion, as harbour works. They were sunk to protect the new developing port at Hamworthy: they are still there.

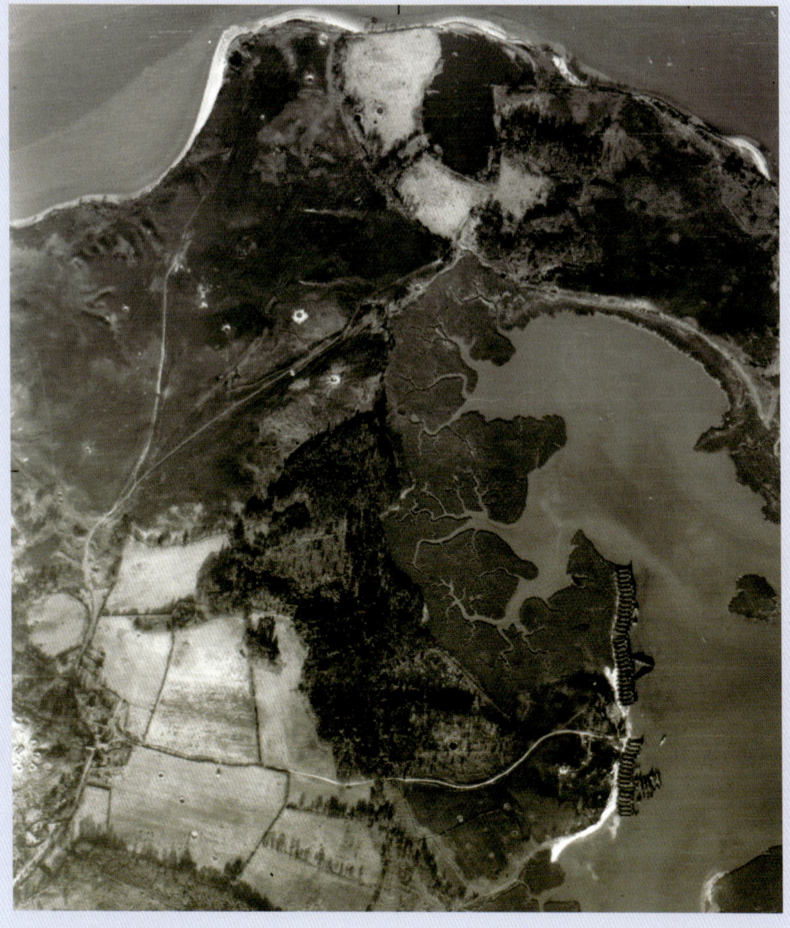

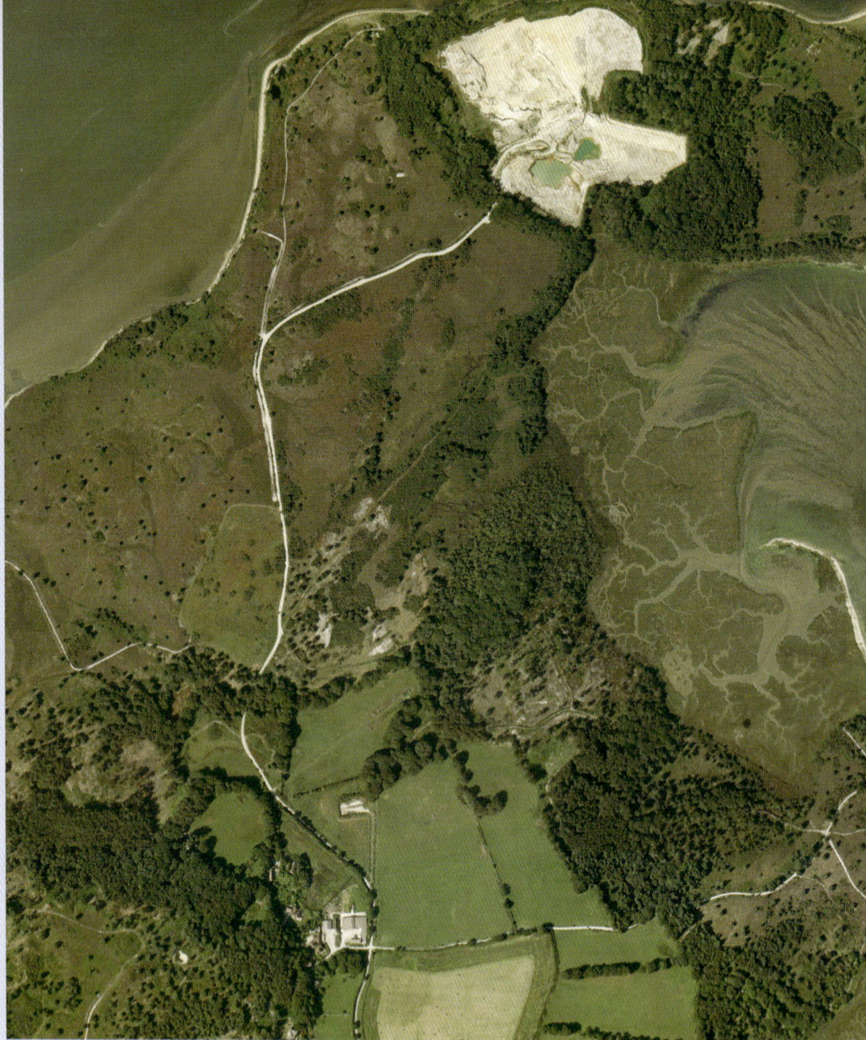

Across the heathland can be seen a series of pale circles, which are bomb craters. In 1940 Arne was made to resemble Poole, at night and from the air. Pale lights were shone to make the area look like a town under blackout. When a bombing raid began any fires started in Poole were extinguished as fast as possible, then fires were started on Arne to look like burning buildings; later waves of bombers would drop their bombs on the open heath and not the town. These bomb decoys worked and every crater here means lives saved and buildings undamaged.

Today the clearest change is the large ball-clay pit to the north, but elsewhere change has been very slight, most notably in the spread of trees. Loss of grazing on the heathland has enabled pine trees to spread away from their original plantations, though here trees are being kept in check, as much of the area is a nature reserve.

Ashmore Centred on grid reference ST 913 178

The village of Ashmore is famous for being the highest village in Dorset: unlike every other old village in the county Ashmore is situated on top of a hill. The village is centred on an ancient pond, the 'Ash-mere' from which the village got its name. The pond can clearly be seen at the centre of the village in both photographs. It has always been very difficult to get to Ashmore which is probably the reason it has not grown very much in the late twentieth century. Other villages have grown to provide accommodation for people who work away from the village in adjacent towns, but because of the difficulty of getting to any of the nearer towns, this has not happened here.

The surrounding countryside is remarkably unaltered over the sixty years since the 1947 photograph was taken, there has been only a little growth of woodland and virtually all the field boundaries are intact.

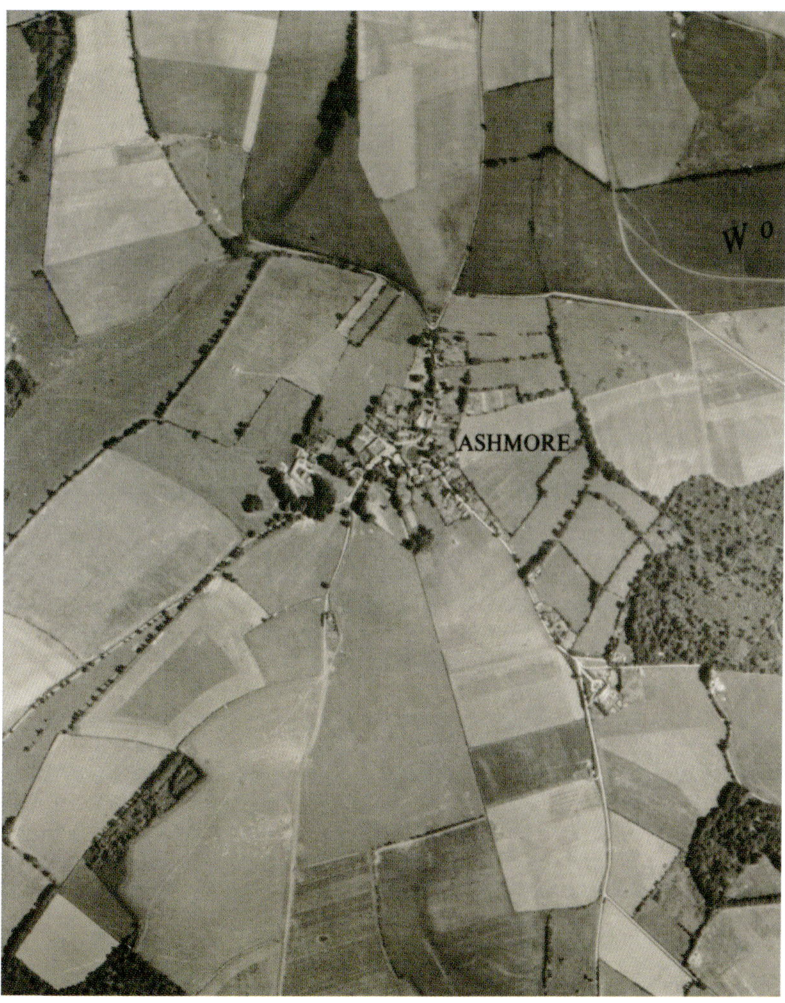

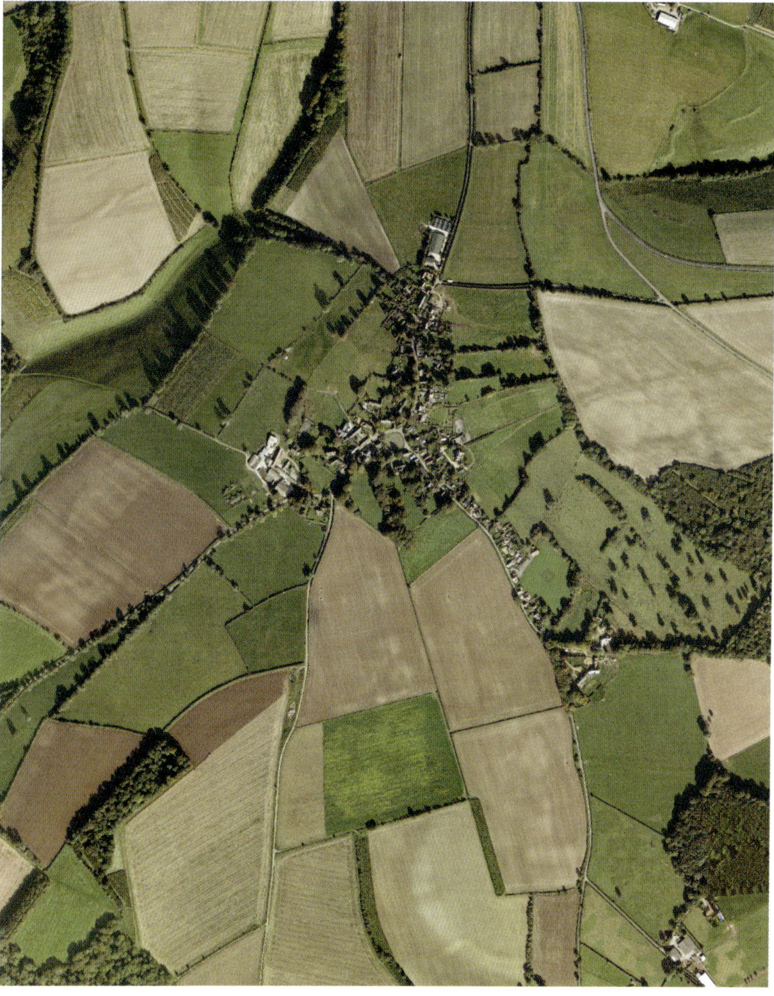

Badbury Rings 1947 photograph reference 1934-4195, centred on grid reference ST 970 024

This Iron Age hill fort was one of the first archaeological sites to be photographed from the air. It was a key site in the pioneering classic, *Wessex from the Air*. These early photographs revealed unexpected details of the hill fort, the Roman road and the Roman settlement. Indeed the Roman road is clearly visible just above the Rings in the 1947 picture. Also visible are the radiating tracks within the woodland of the hill fort, which were linked to a Victorian viewpoint in the middle of the Rings.

Today the area around the hill fort is remarkably unchanged. The hedgerows are still maintained, the principle difference is the large car park beside the Rings, part of the massive growth in the leisure industry during the late twentieth century.

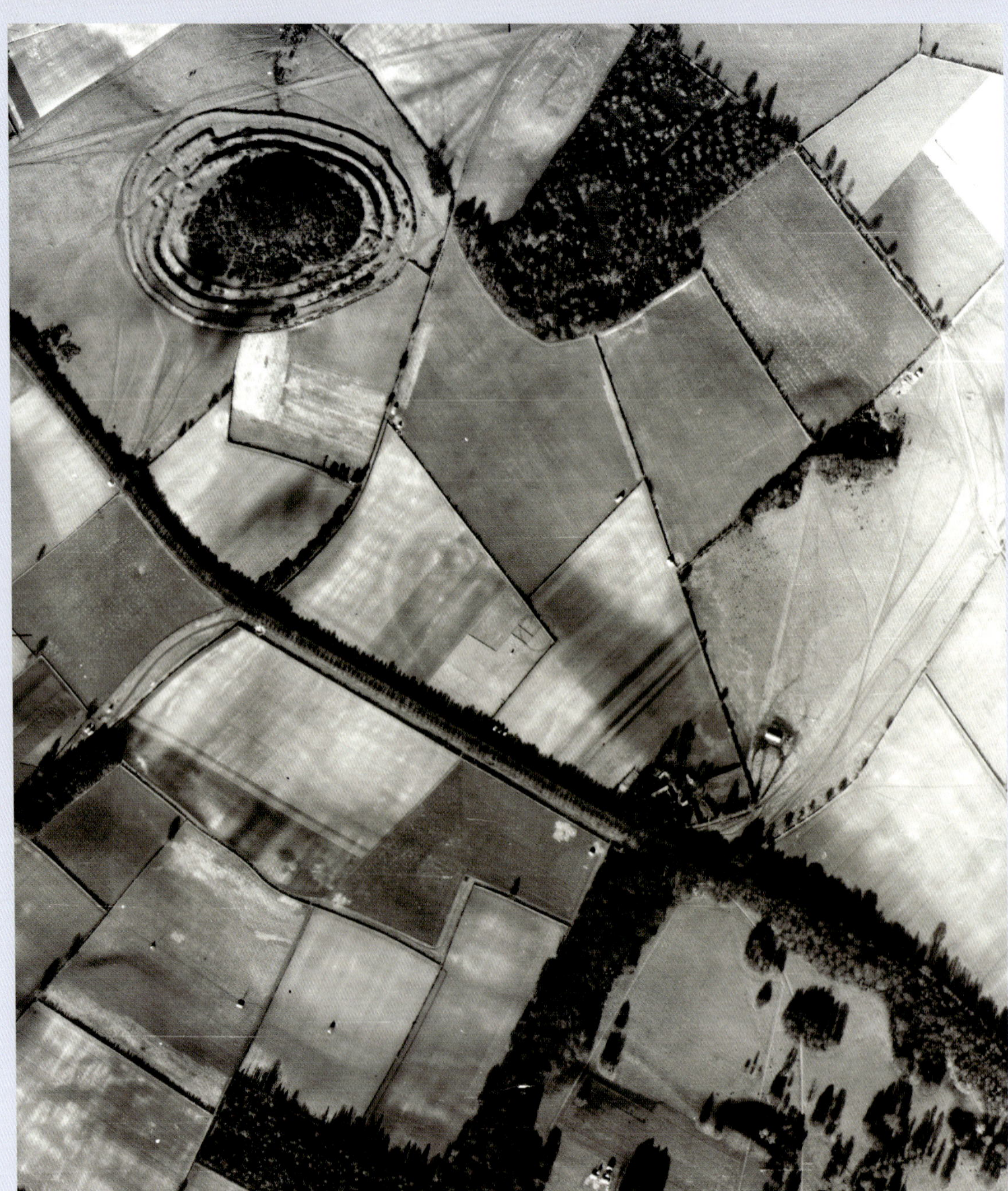

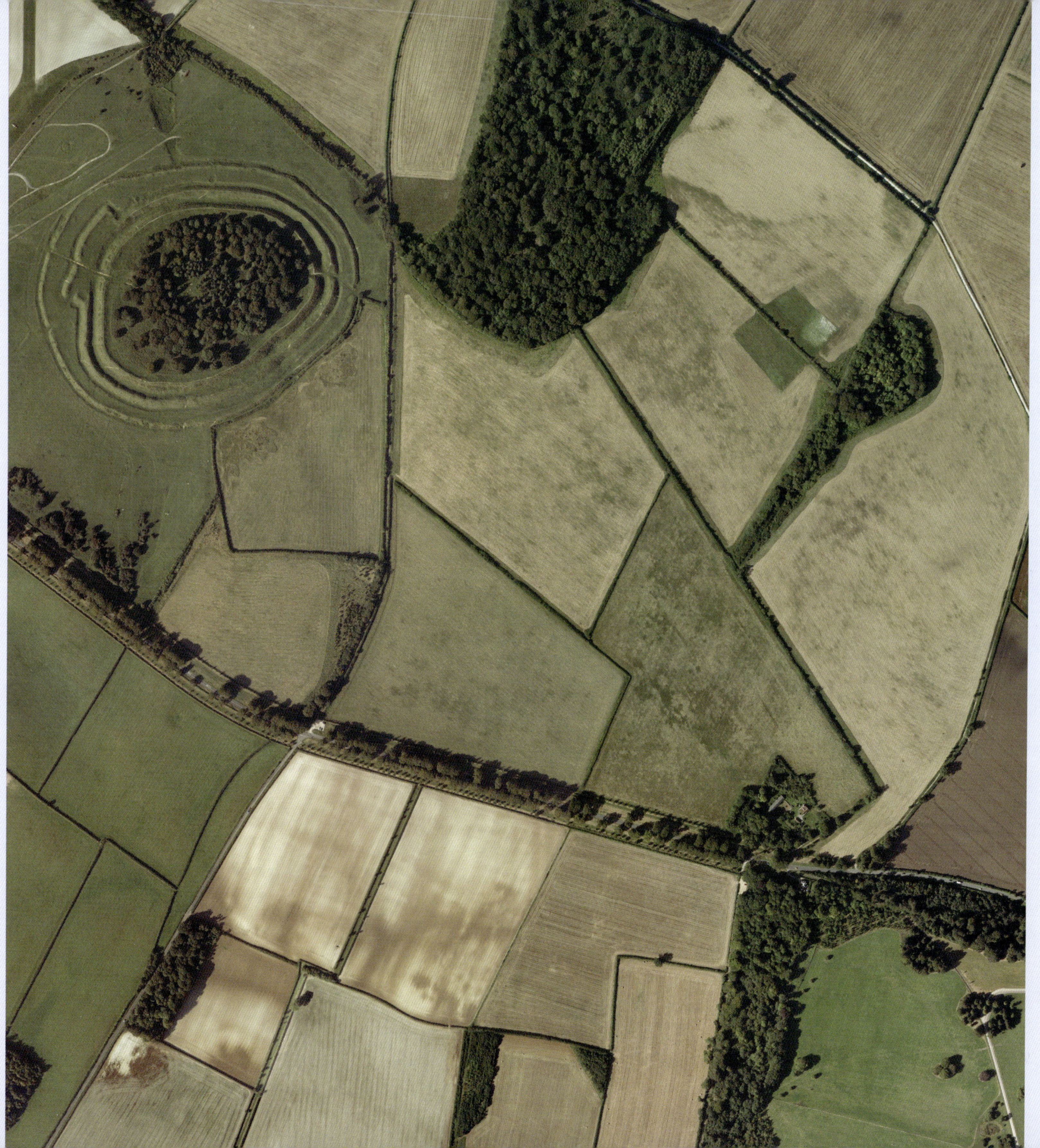

Ballard Down 1947 photograph reference 1821-2396, centred on grid reference SZ 027 811

These pictures show the mixture of continuity and change that is typical of so much of the Dorset countryside.

The area is crossed by the ridge of the Purbeck Hills. To the south the town of Swanage has spread northwards. In 1947 there were a number of small housing estates, and another one was in the process of being built. The development has not been as extensive as around other Dorset towns, because the land attracted protection early on. It was declared part of an Area of Outstanding Natural Beauty in 1957, Heritage Coast in 1981 whilst the adjacent coastline became a natural World Heritage Site in 2001. This has probably also been one of the reasons that the field boundaries are similarly unchanged, though in several places the fields have changed usage from pasture or arable to bearing a crop of caravans.

Along the Purbeck Hills the most obvious change is the spread of woodland, due to the decline in grazing, particularly by rabbits since the spread of the terrible disease myxomatosis in the 1950s & '60s.

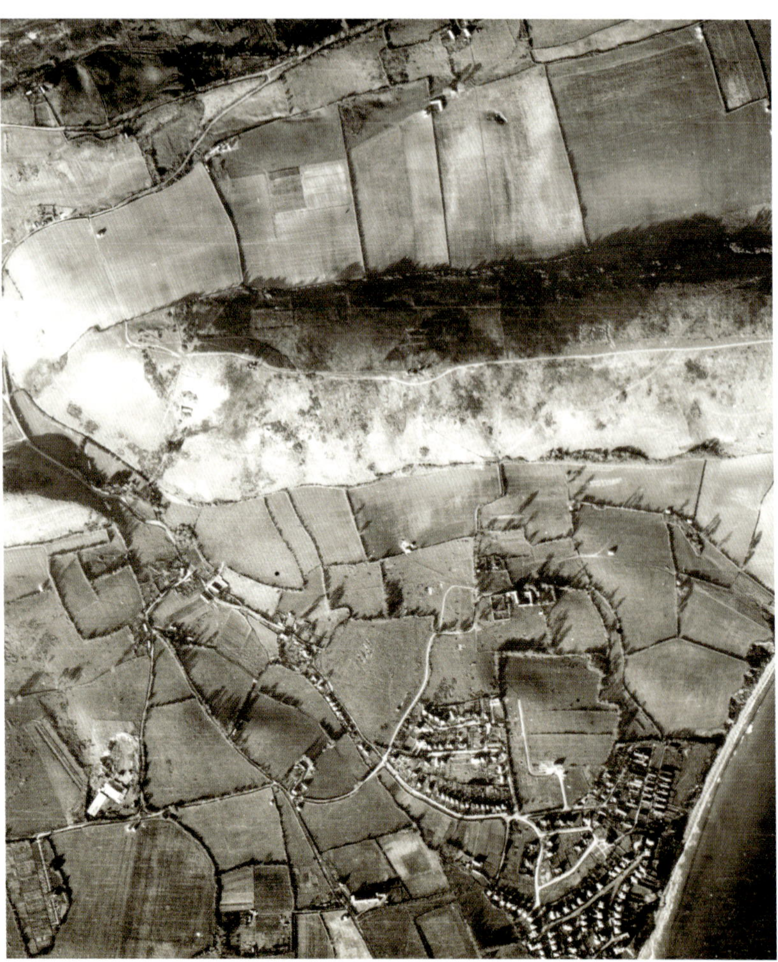

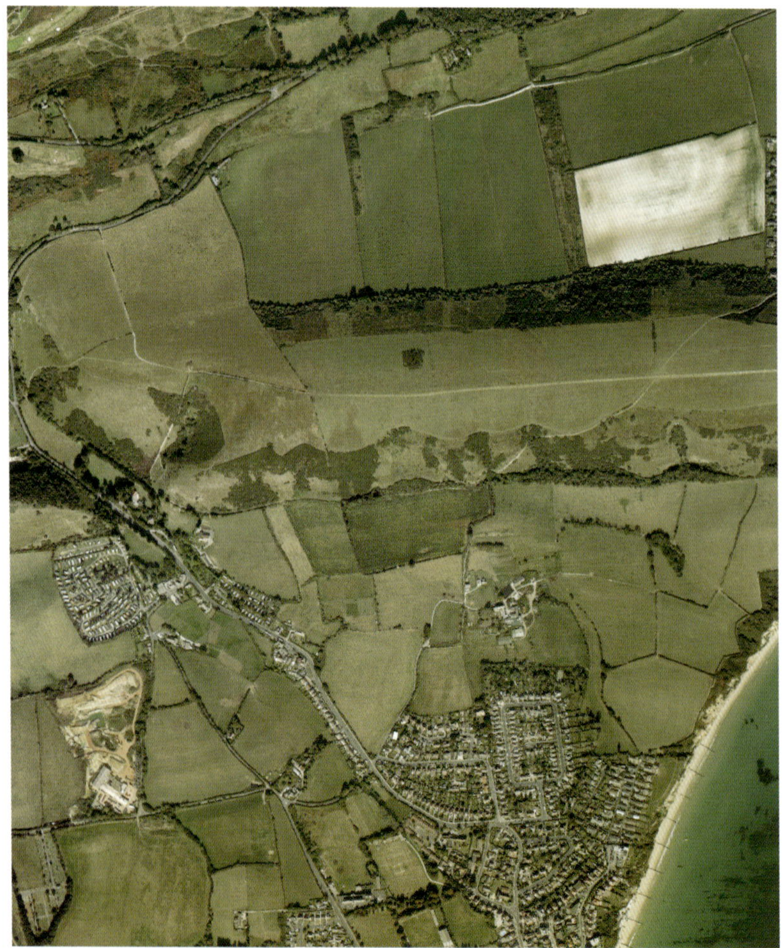

Beaminster 1947 photograph reference 1974-3342, centred on grid reference ST 478 022

The town of Beaminster grew slowly in the nineteenth century because it was never connected to the railway. In 1947 the town was still very small, based around the roads that run out of the market square. To the west of the town was a large military camp which became the focus for later development.

Today the town has spread extensively, along the roads to the north and east and especially on the western side of the town, where larger estates and light industry can be found.

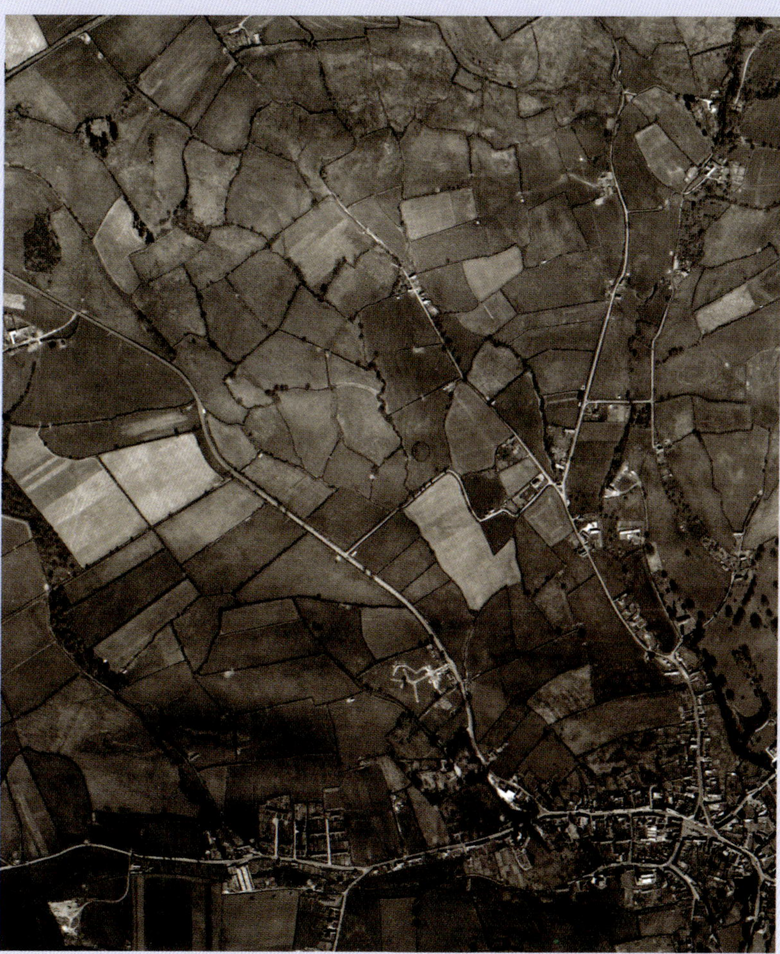

Away from the town the pattern of fields has changed little, most of the field boundaries still exist, but woodland has spread extensively, with small woods and dense rows of hedgerow trees.

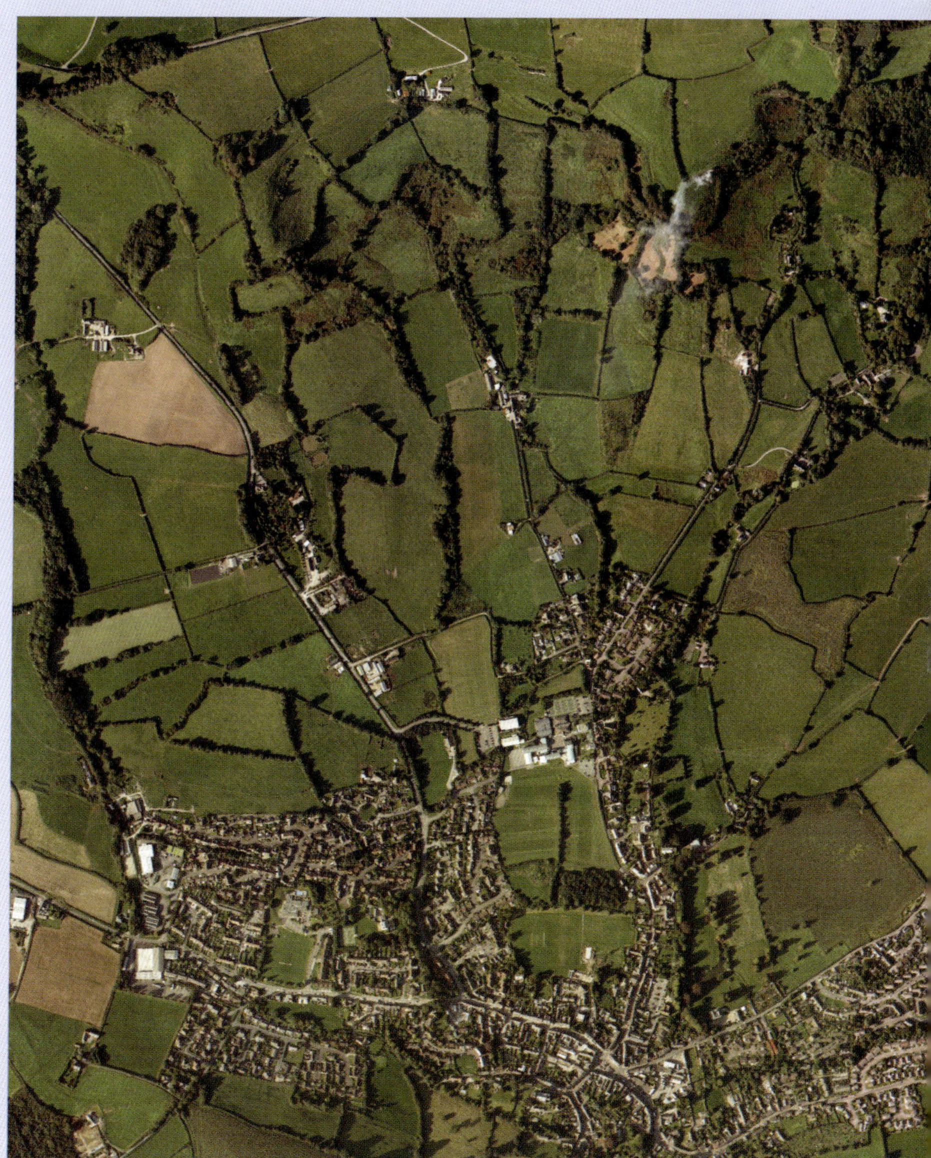

Bere Regis 1947 photograph reference 1974-1349, centred on grid reference SY 847 955

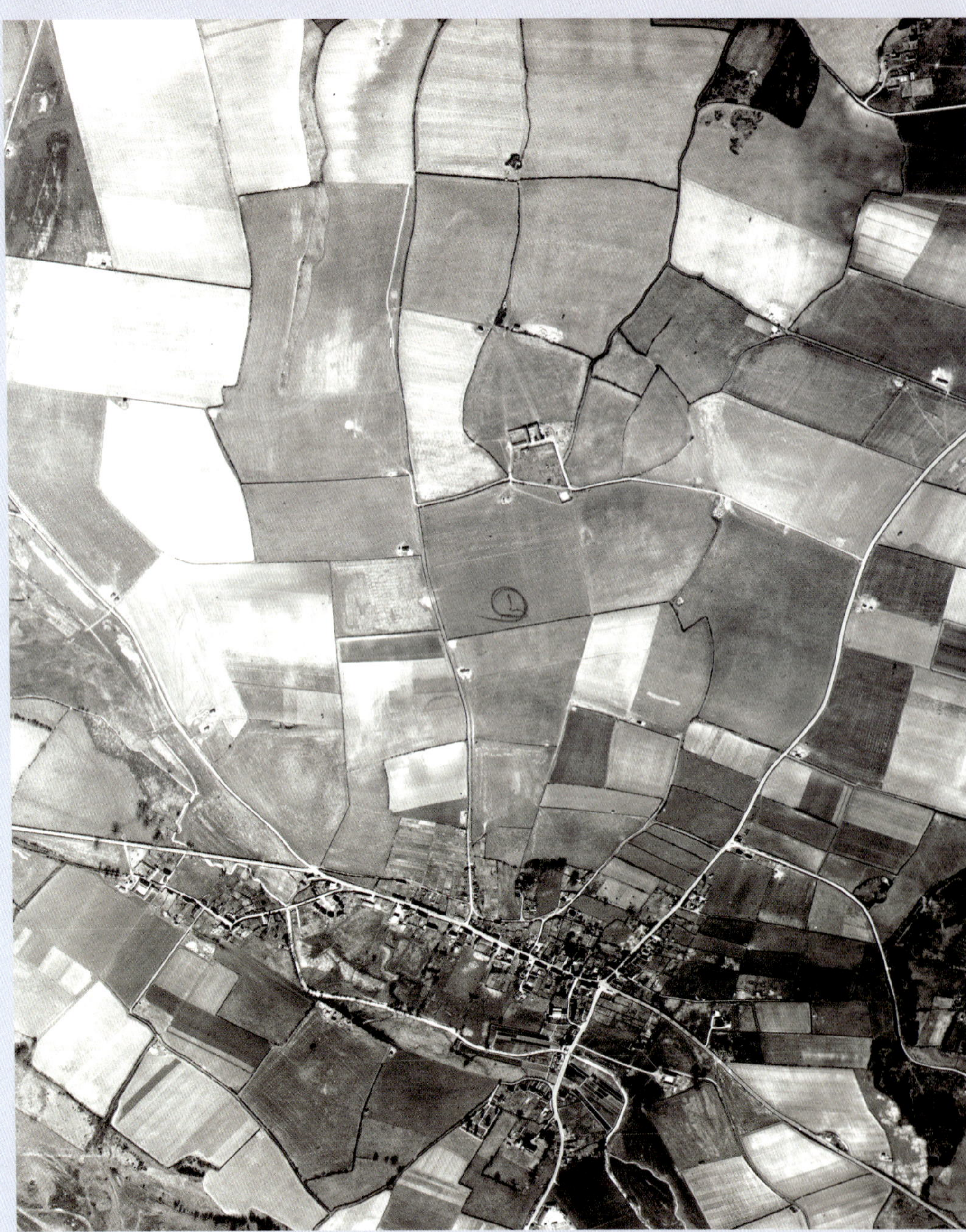

The village of Bere Regis grew around a major crossroads. By 1947 a second street ran parallel to the main east-west road and the housing was virtually confined to these roads. As well as the houses there were several areas of allotments, to the north and east of the town and between the two streets.

Today the village has grown comparatively little, there has been infilling between the two roads, and along short, minor roads leading off them. One of the areas of allotments has survived, but others have been returned to agriculture. The most obvious change however, has been the building of the Bere Regis by–pass to the north and east, taking the main east west traffic out of the narrow village streets.

Close to the village were a number of small fields which may have been formed by early enclosure of medieval strips. Away from the village the fields were quite large. Today the small fields have vanished and the large fields are even larger. The landscape has remained very open with only limited growth of woodland.

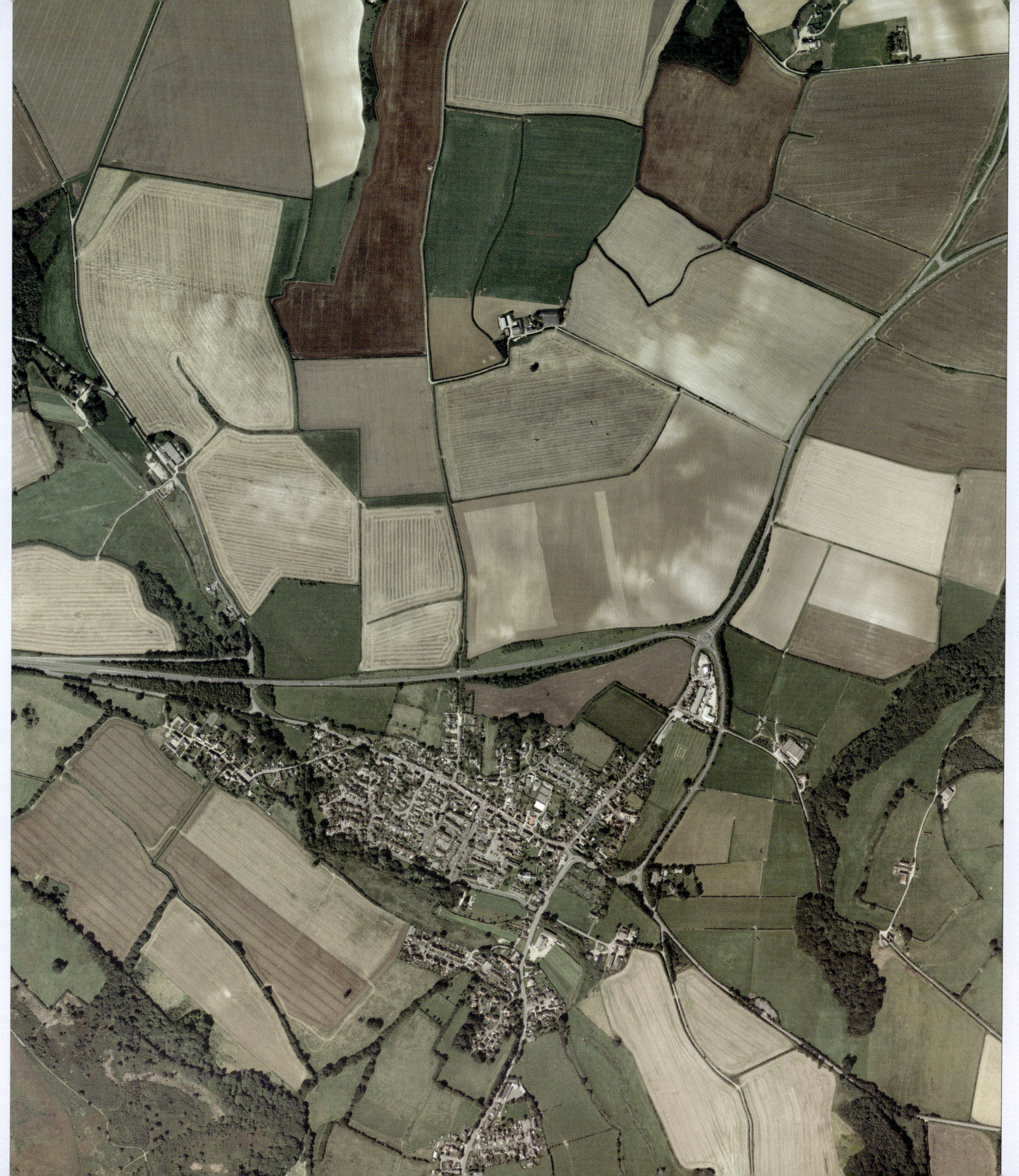

Blackdown North 1947 photograph reference 1934-3096, centred on grid reference SY 616 886

At the south of the photographs the tall tower of the Hardy Monument can be seen. To the north of this, in 1947, was a large area of heathland with a few patches of trees. Beyond to the north east were large arable fields, though open downland covered a good deal of the land, particularly to the north-west. This was covered with a network of prehistoric fields, visible as faint rectangles on the photograph.

Today much of the heathland has been covered with pine plantations. At one time these covered even more of it, but they have been felled, and some of the woodland in the photographs is also likely to be felled in the near future, as an attempt is made to restore the heathland to preserve its unique wildlife.

The large arable fields have been made larger by the removal of field boundaries. These large fields have spread over the downland destroying many of the ancient fields, which now only survive on the steeper land which it is too difficult to plough.

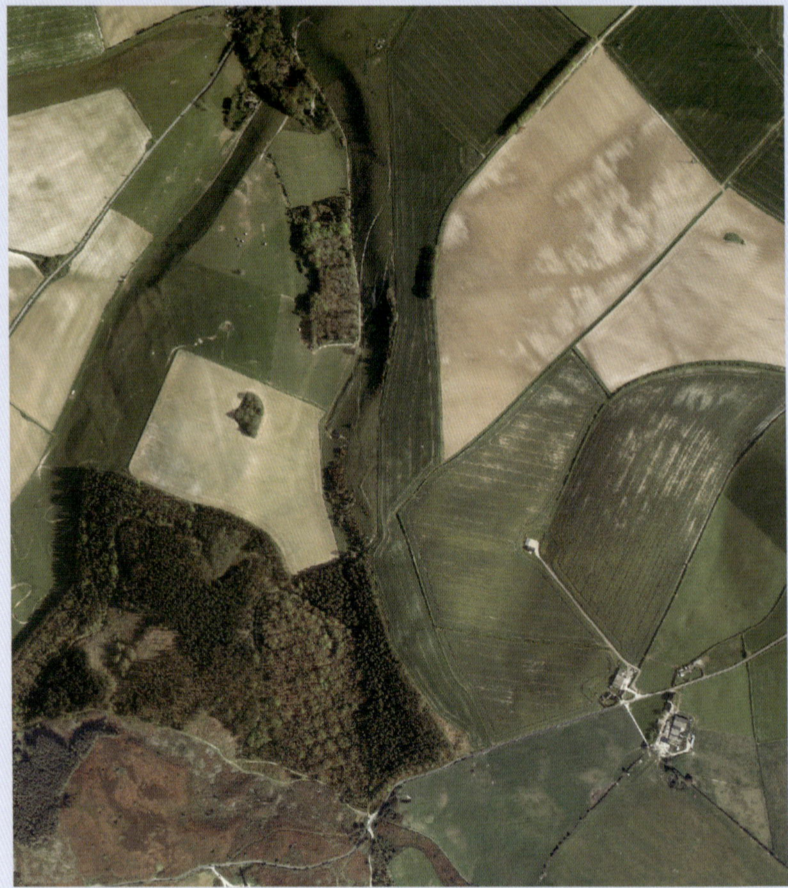

Blackdown South – Bronkham Hill

1947 photograph reference 1821-1067, centred on grid reference SY 622 865

These two photographs look remarkably similar, though there have been some interesting changes in the last sixty years.

In the north-west corner of the pictures is Blackdown. Whilst the Hardy Monument lies just off the edge of the picture the old gravel pits that lie just to the south can clearly be seen. On the north-east side lies Bronkham Hill. This is dotted with hollows: whilst they look like old quarry workings or bomb craters, both of which can be found elsewhere in the county, these are 'Dolines' or 'Sink Holes'. They are a natural phenom-

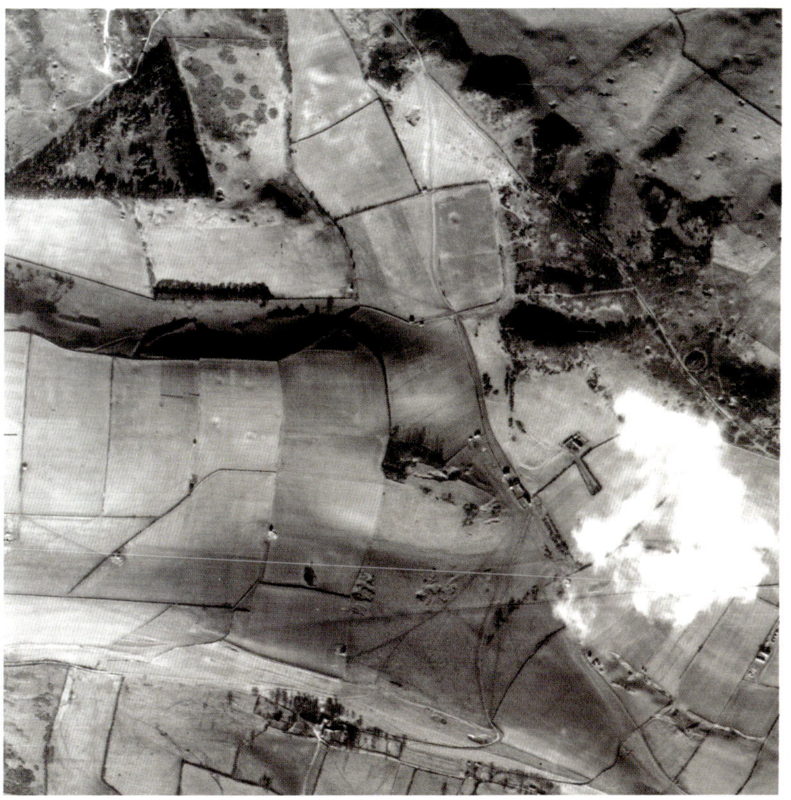

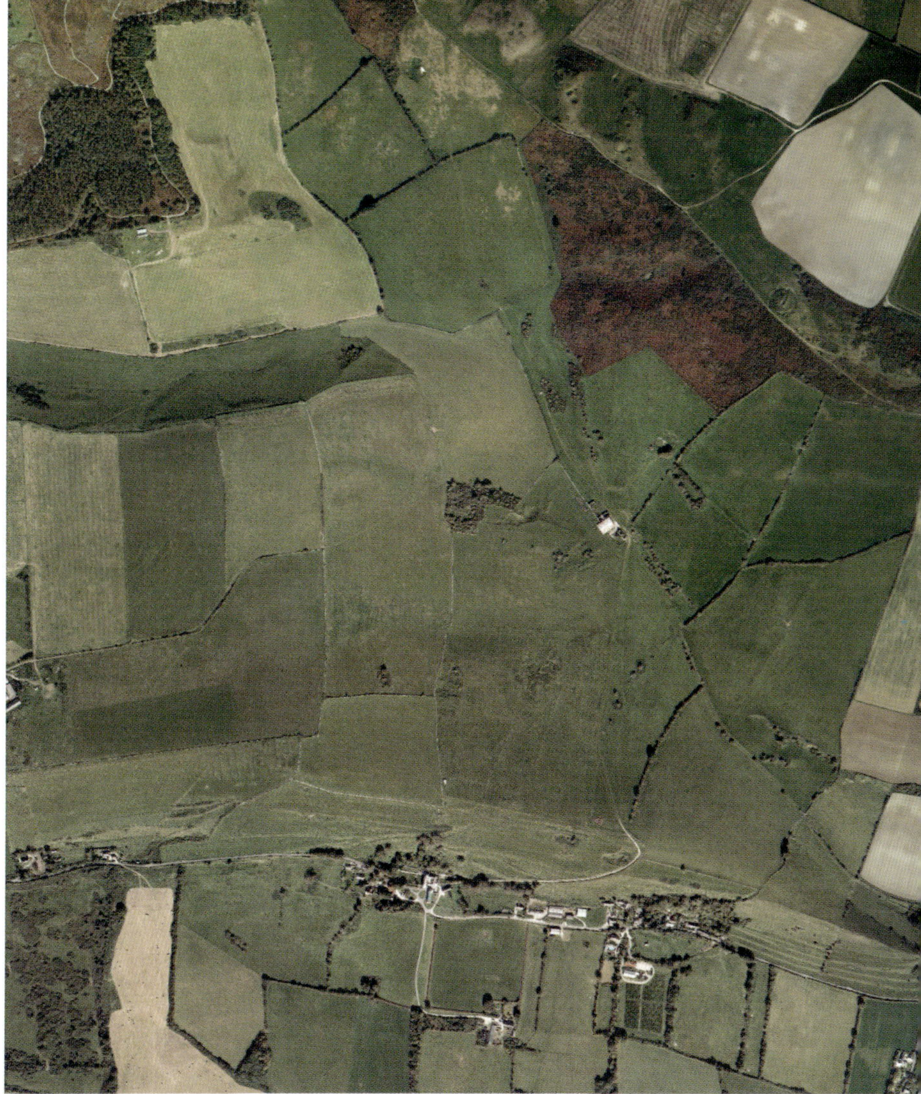

enon caused when the underlying chalk is dissolved by percolating water, forming a cave. This collapses causing the land above to sink creating a doline. This process is still continuing.

Since 1947 the downland of Bronkham has been partly enclosed and converted to arable, whist some of Blackdown is more densely wooded. In the centre of the 1947 photograph are a number of farm buildings; today these have all gone, they have either vanished from the map or are visible as ruins. There is only one large, recent, building in the happily named Hell Bottom, surrounded by roofless ruins. This is evidence of changes in agricultural methods. Easy transport has led to a concentration of activity in and around the farm, rather than scattered across the fields.

Blandford Forum 1947 photograph reference 1934-5159, centred on grid ST 891 071

In the middle of the nineteenth century the railway had come to Blandford Forum, passing close to the eastern boundary of the town. Nineteenth-century development has clustered around the railway station and this is reflected in the 1947 photograph. The railway line snakes down the picture and through the town, the old town lies to the west of the line, the later extension to the east.

However even in 1947 hints of the massive expansion that was to come can be seen. The cemetery, of distinctive triangular shape, had been placed to the east of the town, as though awaiting the town to come to it. There is even a new cul-de-sac under construction, the pale crook shape clearly visible towards the middle of the photograph

Today the railway has gone, its course visible by a thin line of woodland, the town has spread over much of the picture, and an industrial estate covers the 1947 allotments, though it is interesting to note how the housing developments have been fitted into the pre-existing fields, their boundaries fossilised in the layout of the modern town.

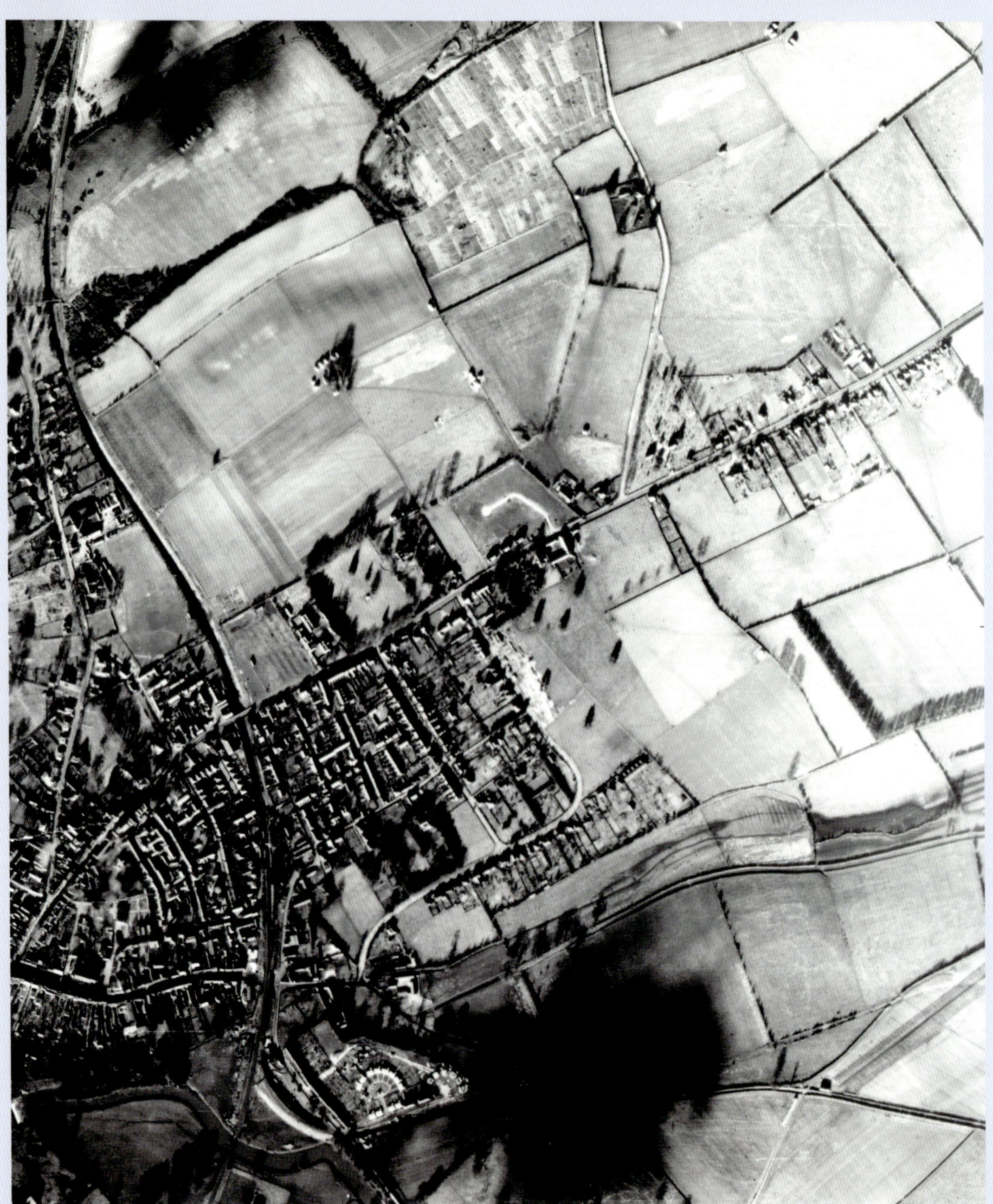

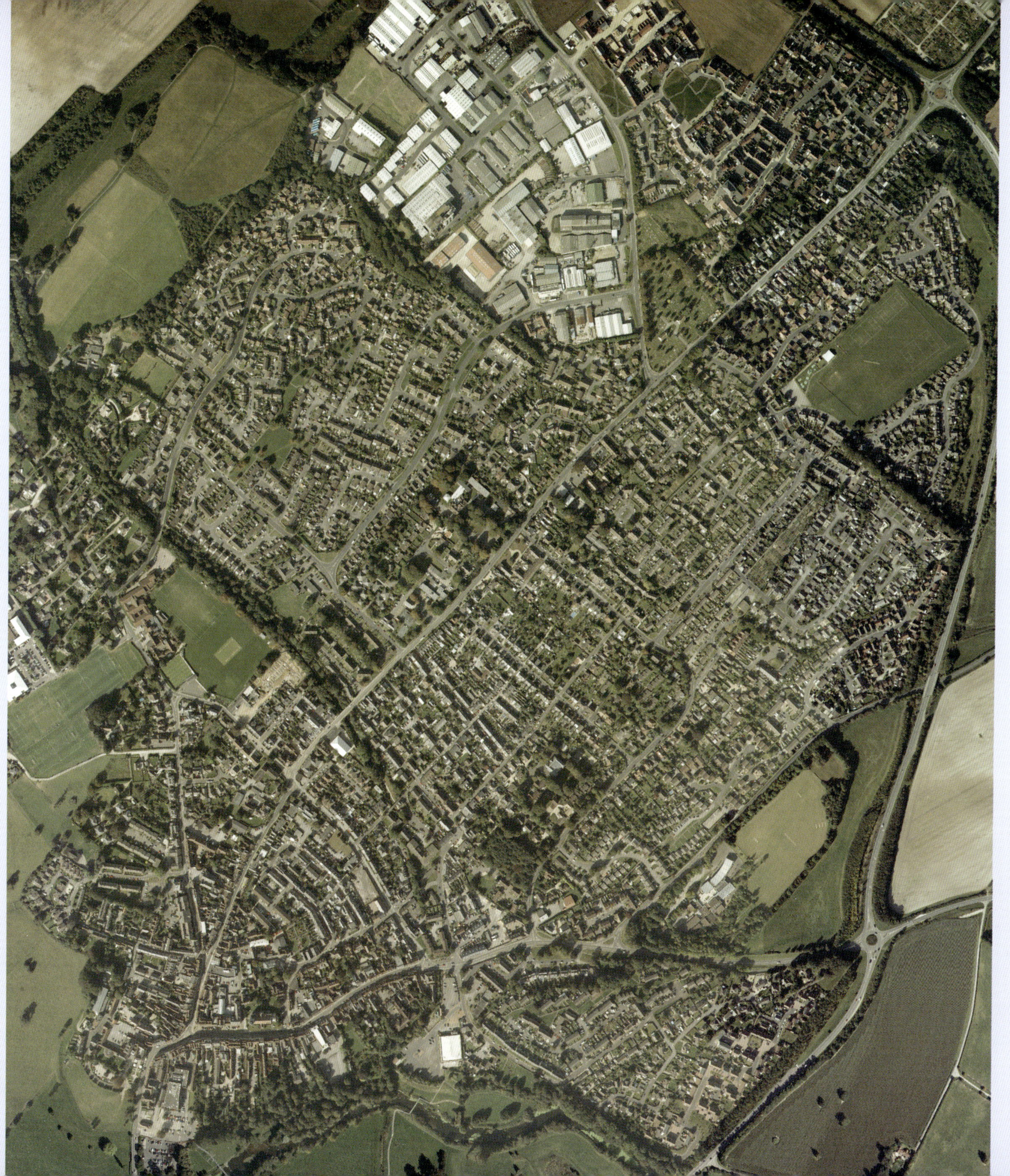

Blandford Forum North

1947 photograph reference 1934-2159, centred on grid reference ST 889 088

These photographs, of the land to the north of Blandford Forum, show many of the changes that have taken place in Dorset over the past sixty years.

The open farmland has become more open, as hedgerows have been removed primarily to allow larger machines to operate on arable fields. This is clearly seen in the northern part where large fields have been made larger.

To the south, in 1947, one of the fields had been given over to allotments, used by the people of Blandford: the quilted effect is very obvious. Then, in 1977 the Blandford by-pass was built. Inside the line of the by-pass development has spread, the allotments are now an industrial estate and new housing has been built.

During the building of the by-pass extensive areas of prehistoric settlement were discovered. On the modern photograph faint traces of the regular prehistoric fields can be seen.

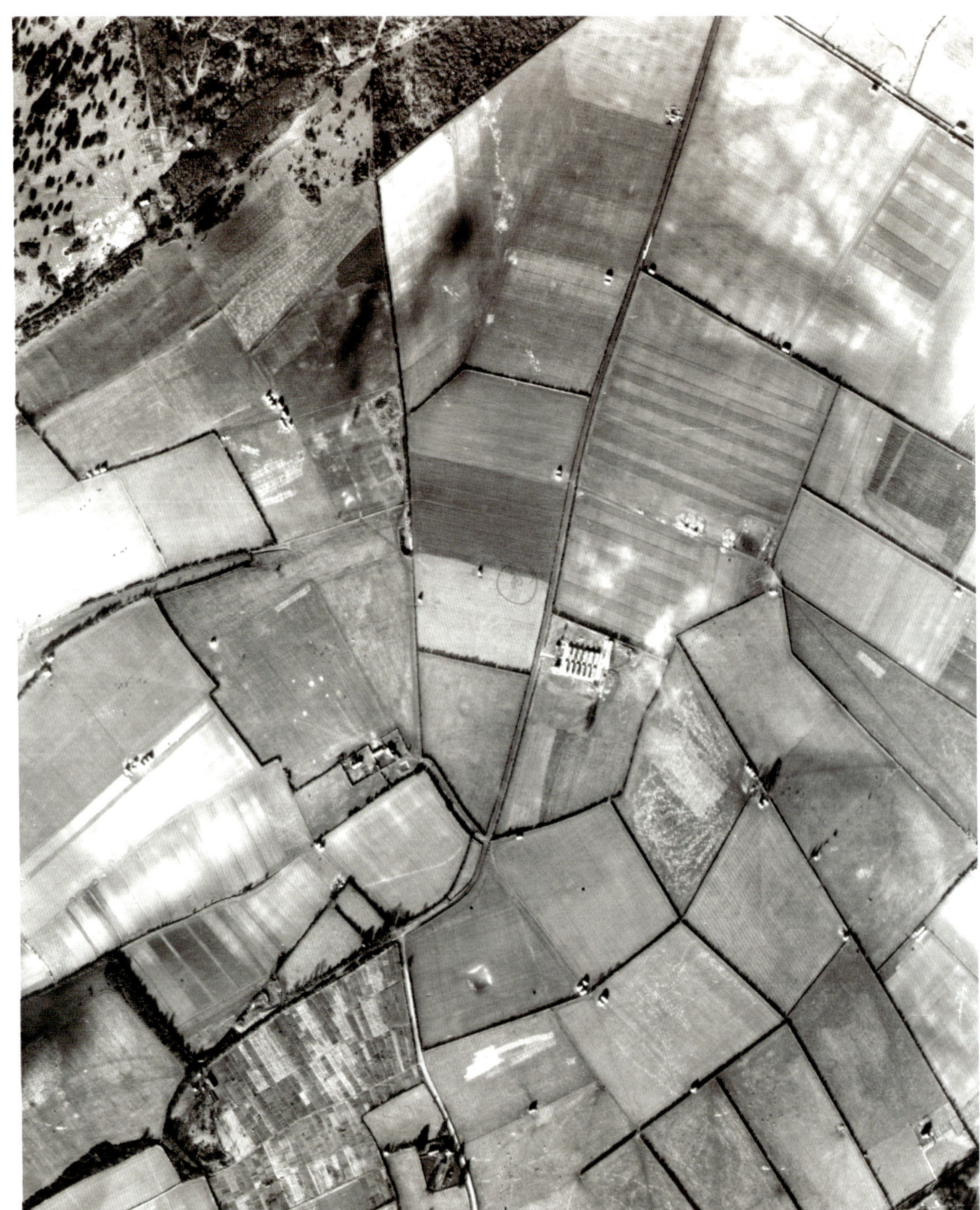

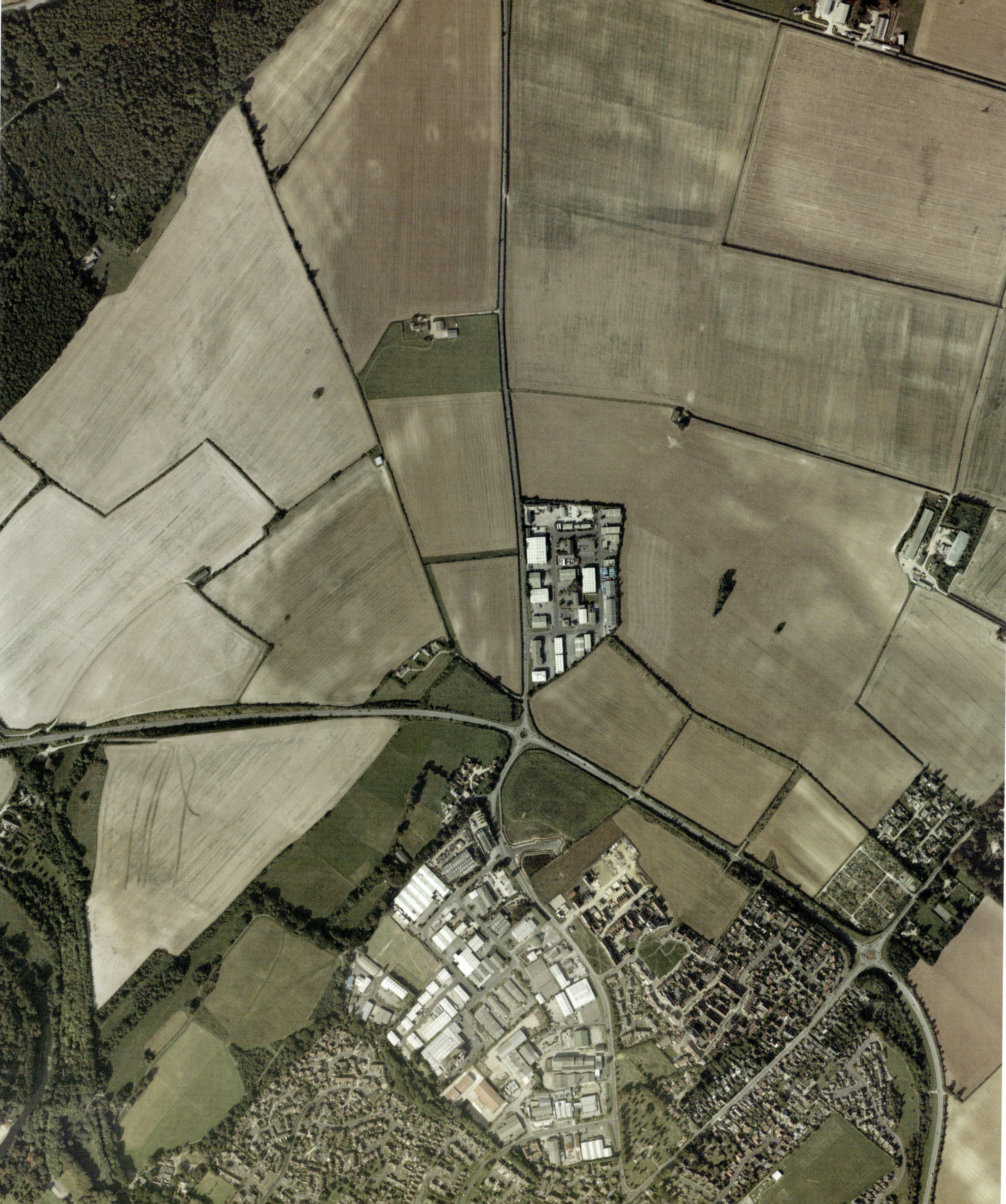

Bokerley Dyke and Pentridge

1947 photograph reference 2038-1060, centred on grid reference SU 030 185

Running across the photograph from east to west is Bokerely Dyke. It is clearer on the 1947 photograph because, at the time the photograph was taken, the sunlight was falling obliquely across the landscape. Bokerely Dyke forms one of the oldest political boundaries in the world. It was built to protect late Roman and British Dorset from Saxon attacks in the fourth century; in the fifth century it was the boundary between Britain, to the west, and England to the east. Today it marks the boundary between Dorset and Hampshire.

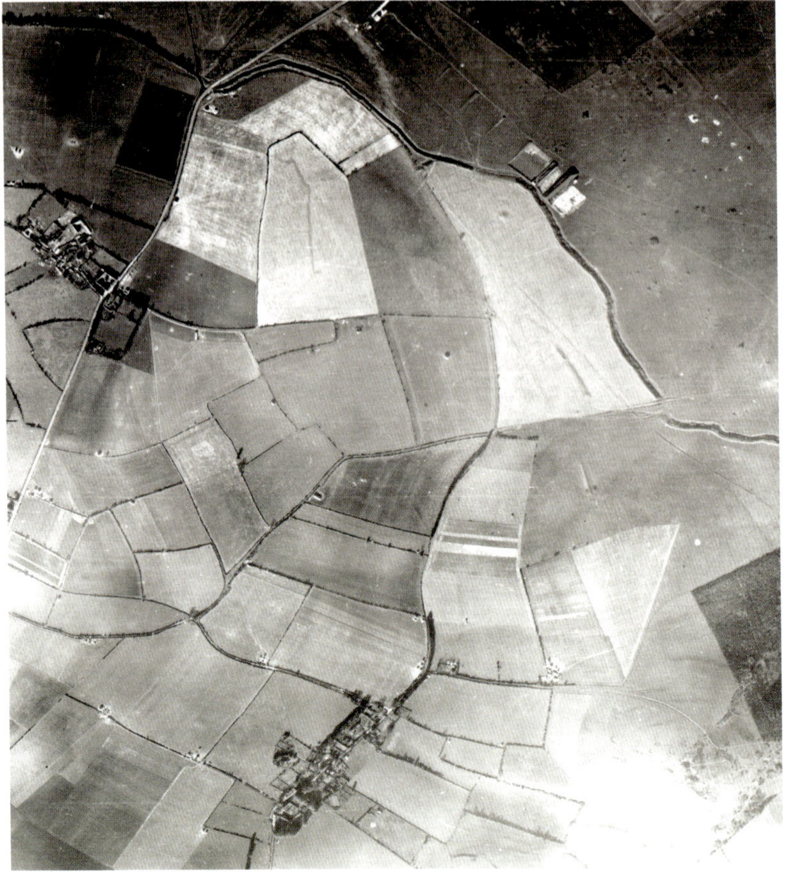

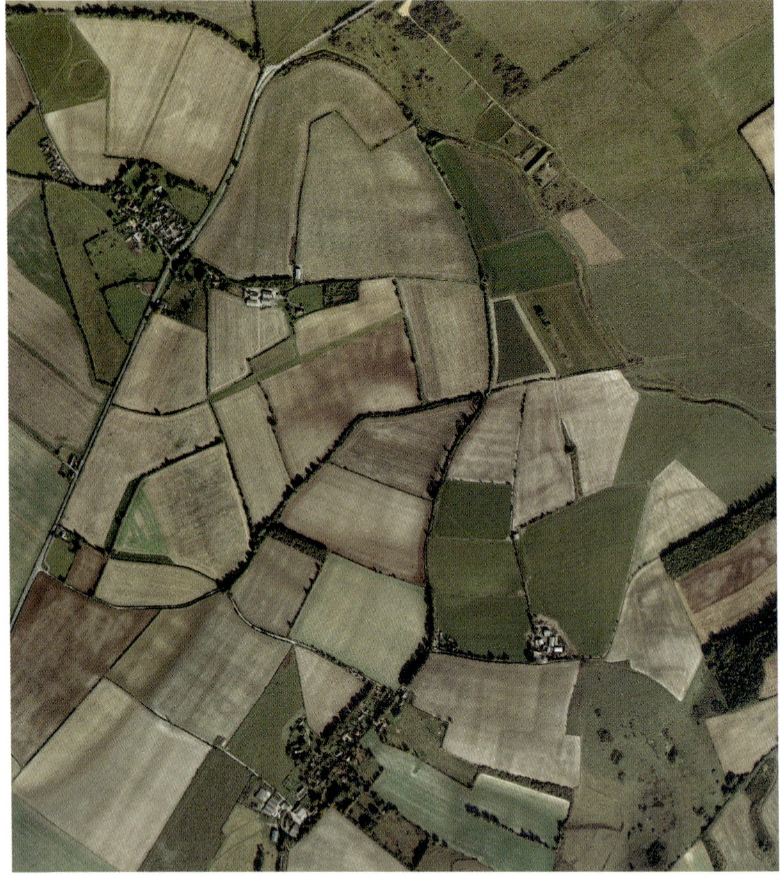

Just on the Hampshire side are the remains of a rifle range. In 1947 this had just gone out of use. Today the grass covered mounds of the Second World War are as much a part of a landscape as the Roman Bokerely Dyke.

In the south east of the pictures is the village of Pentridge, a tiny village which consists of a row of houses and a church. It has hardly grown in the sixty years between the photographs, probably because of its isolated position. It is at the end of a minor road that leads eastwards from the A354. Originally it lay on the main road from Salisbury that crossed Cranborne Chase. The route of this road can still be seen on the photographs in the form of field boundaries. In 1756 the road to Salisbury was turnpiked, and the new road followed the course of the old Roman Road effectively by-passing Pentridge, creating the isolation that exists today.

Bottlebush Down 1947 photograph reference 2038-3052, centred on grid reference SU 011 158

These photographs illustrate the reasons that archaeologists have found aerial photographs so useful, and why they have been using such photographs, almost from the invention of the aeroplane.

The fields here are full of archaeology that would not be visible on the ground. In the 1947 photograph dozens of small circles can be seen, these are known as 'ring ditches' and are usually all that remains of Bronze Age round barrows of which the mound has been ploughed away. Other lines mark ditches and enclosures, most of which are probably prehistoric, the most famous and important of these can be seen alongside the dark mass of woodland in the 1947 picture. Here there is a large rectangular shape, which is the Dorset Cursus, a huge enigmatic Neolithic Monument, nearly six thousand years old, the use of which is still a mystery.

Virtually none of these features can be seen on the modern photograph. This does not mean that they have been completely destroyed by more recent ploughing, rather that the photographs were taken at different times of the year. On the modern picture growing crops have obscured them, however these conditions can make other features more visible. What you see on an aerial photograph can depend on the season, the crops in the field, the weather and the time of day. This is why archaeologists are still discovering sites on aerial photographs.

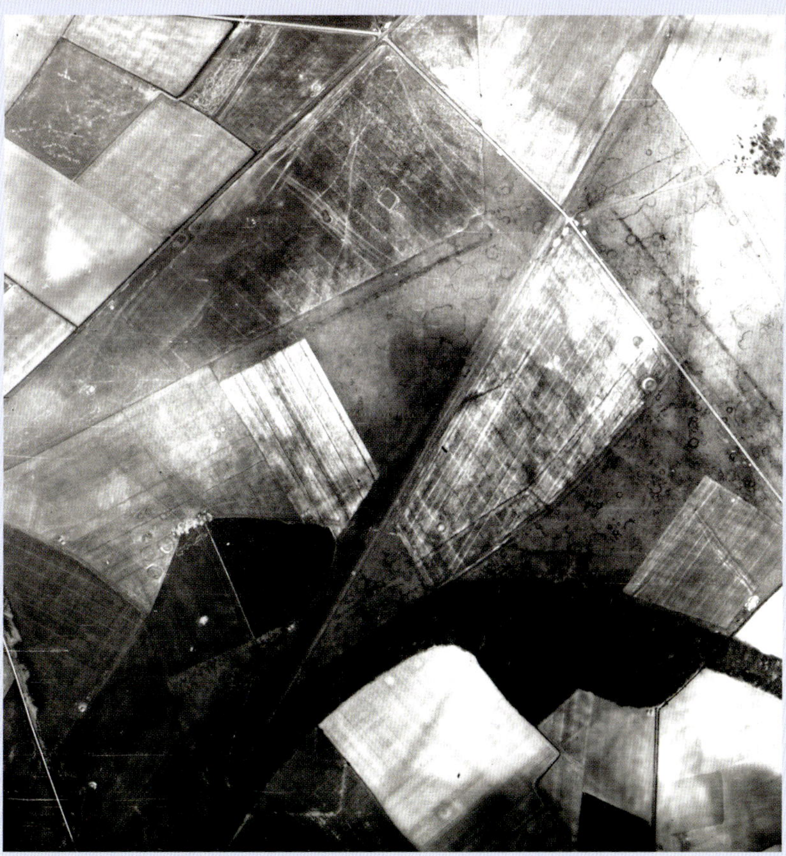

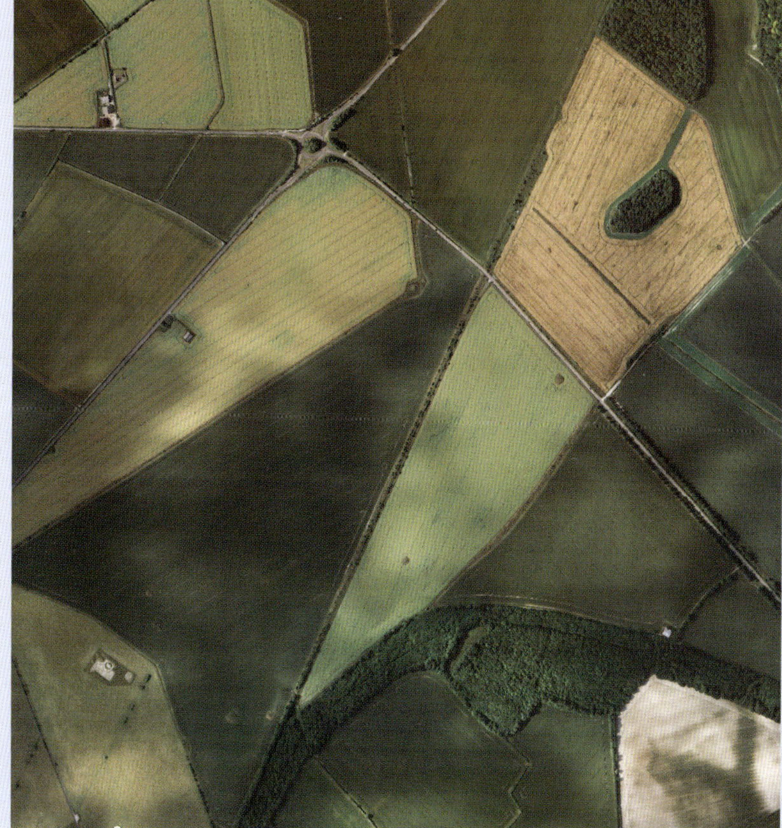

Bournemouth Pier 1947 photograph reference 1934-3030, centred on grid reference SZ 089 903

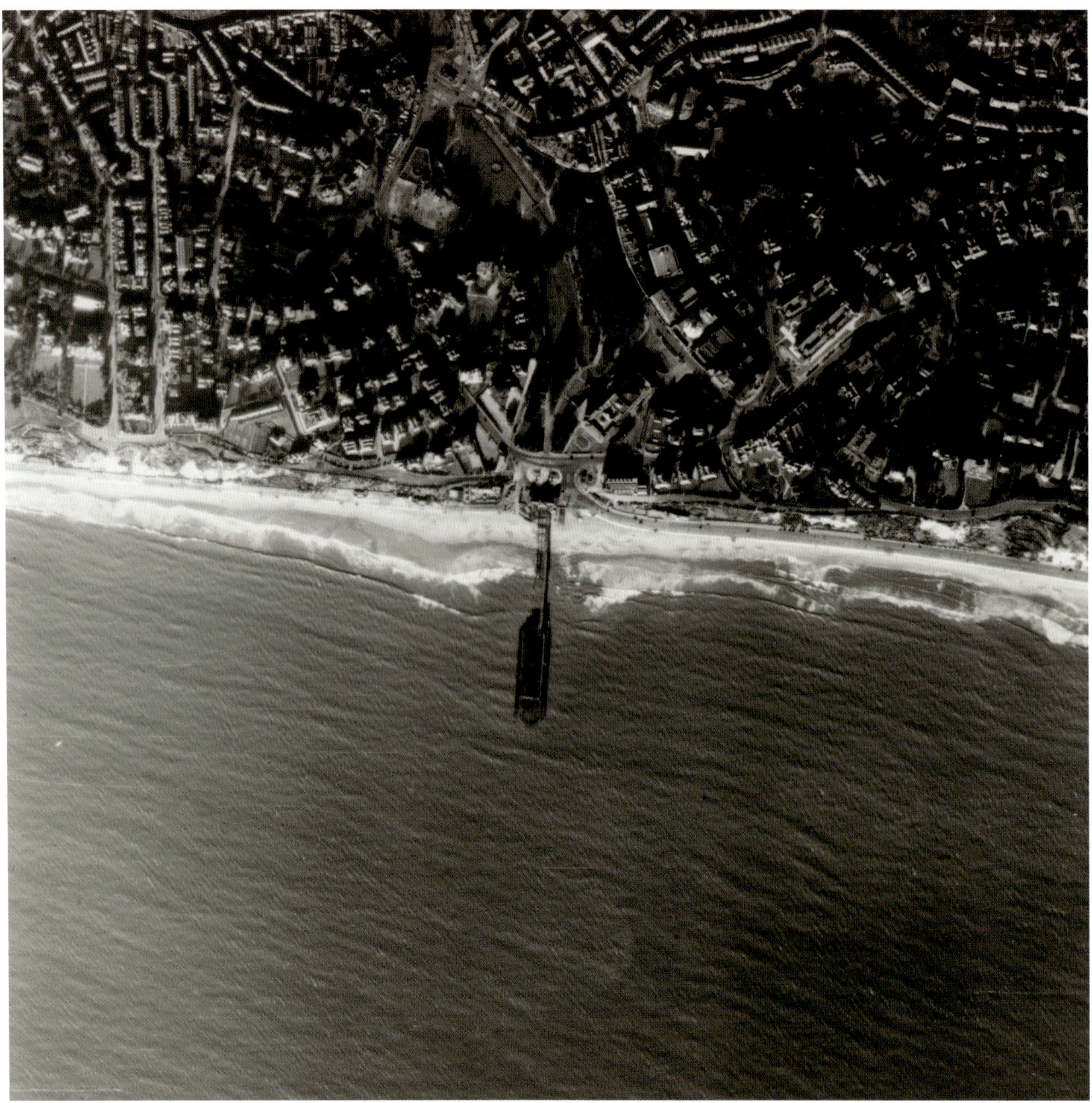

The pier has been the focus of Bournemouth as a seaside resort since 1856 when it was first built. However in 1947 it was unusable. In order to prevent it being used by the Germans as a landing stage, like most British piers, it had been cut. The gap was still in place two years after the war had ended. Inland the coast was fully developed, the only open space was the Pleasure Gardens.

Today, happily, the pier has been rebuilt, unlike many others and is still an important feature of the sea front. In addition new facilities have been built, notably the Bournemouth International Centre immediately to the west of the pier head. Inland new shops have been built around the square.

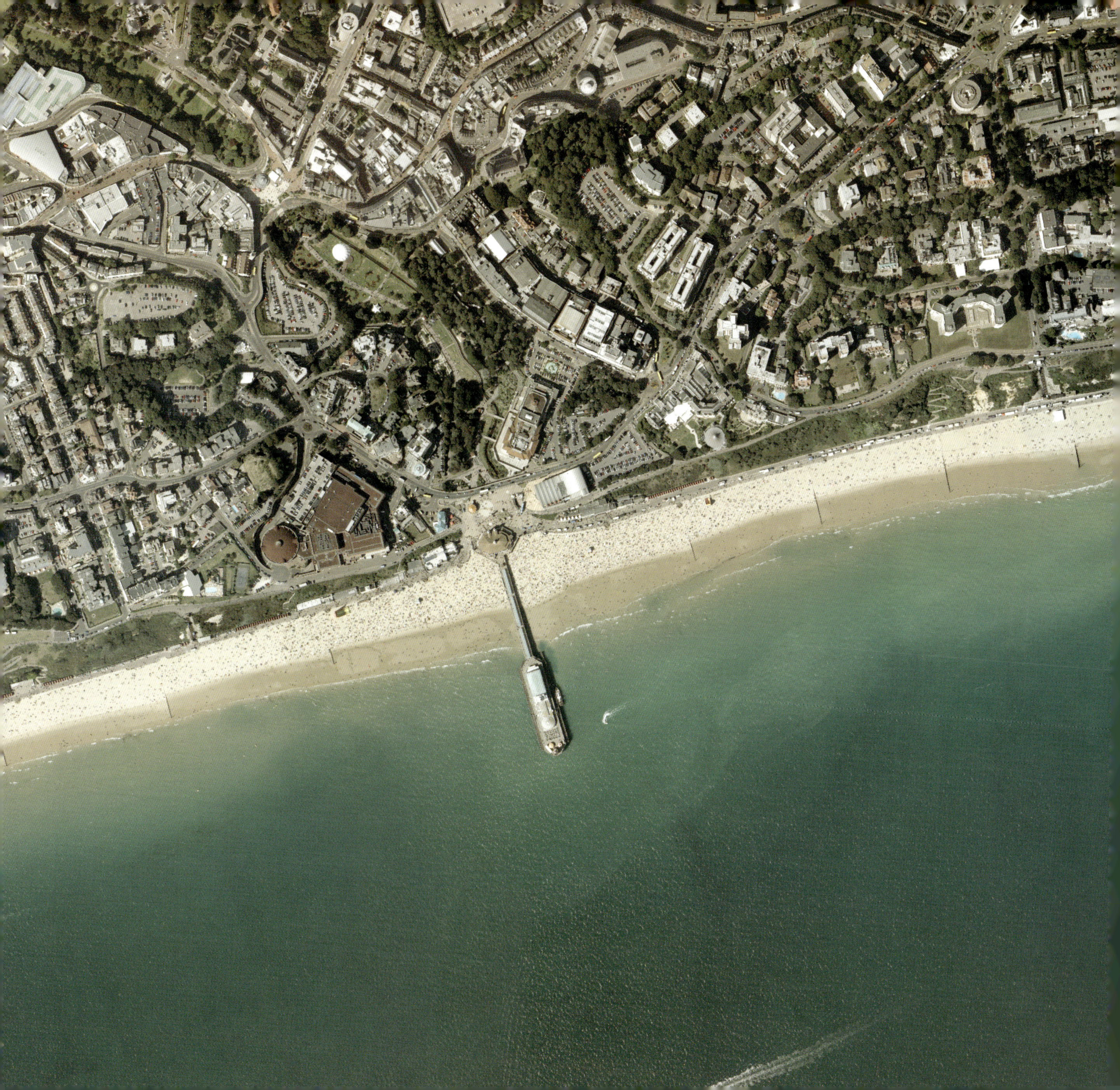

Bournemouth Station 1947 photograph reference 1934-5028, centred on grid reference SZ 095 924

In 1947 the land around Bournemouth Station had been fully developed, the only open areas were the sports field at Dene Park and Bournemouth Cemetery. These areas have remained essentially unchanged, however the main difference has come about because of the need to get motor traffic in and out of the centre of the town. A major road, the Wessex Way, has been cut through the houses. It is easy to find streets that have been cut in two – this would have had the effect of separating formerly near neighbours.

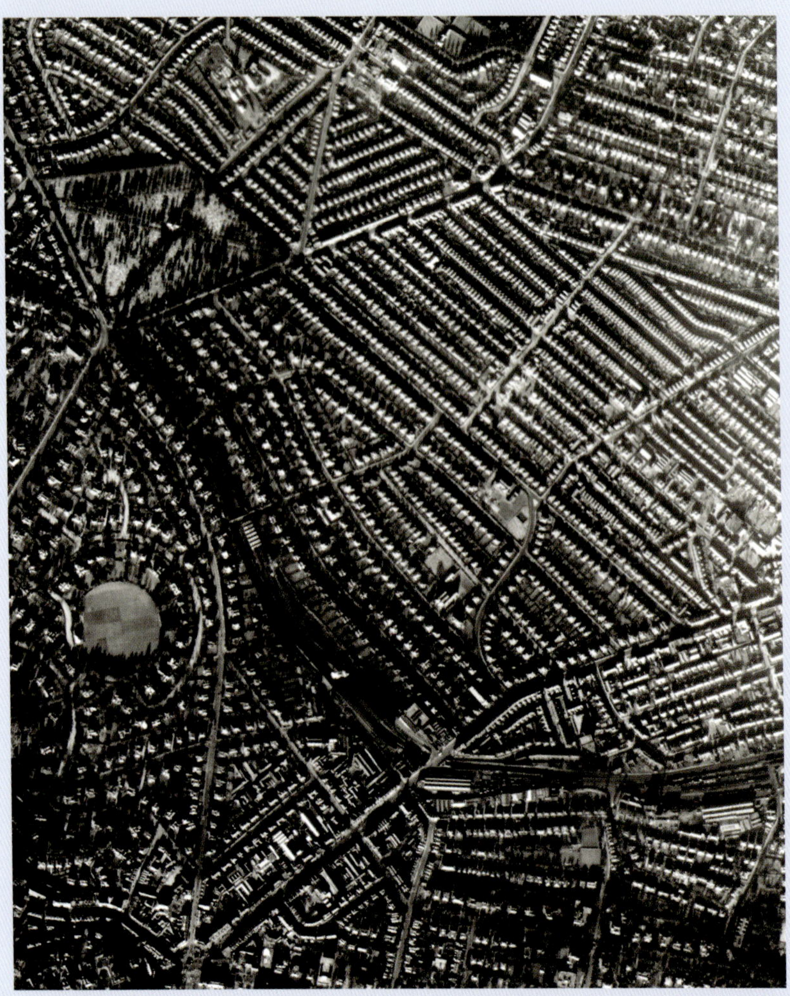

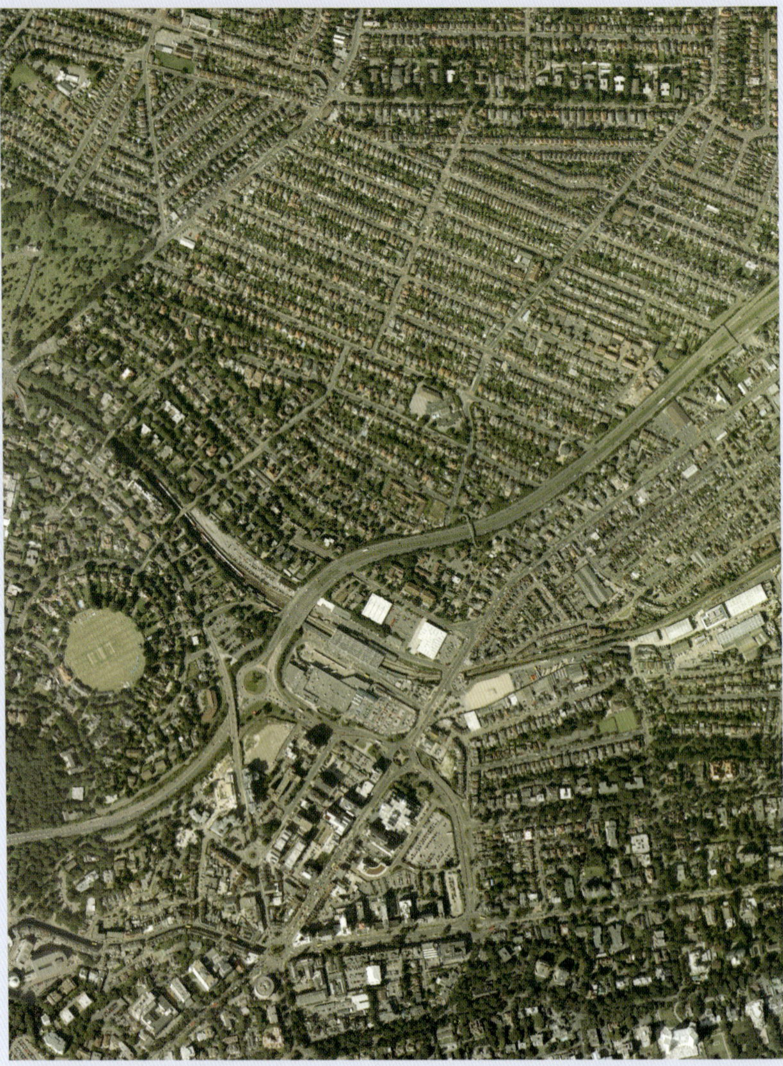

Around the station what were once residential areas have changed. Now surrounded by major roads they have ceased to be desirable places to live and have been given over to offices and commercial premises. The people have moved out, to the spreading edges of the town or the growing villages.

Bovington 1947 photograph reference 1934-5065, centred on grid reference SY 835 899

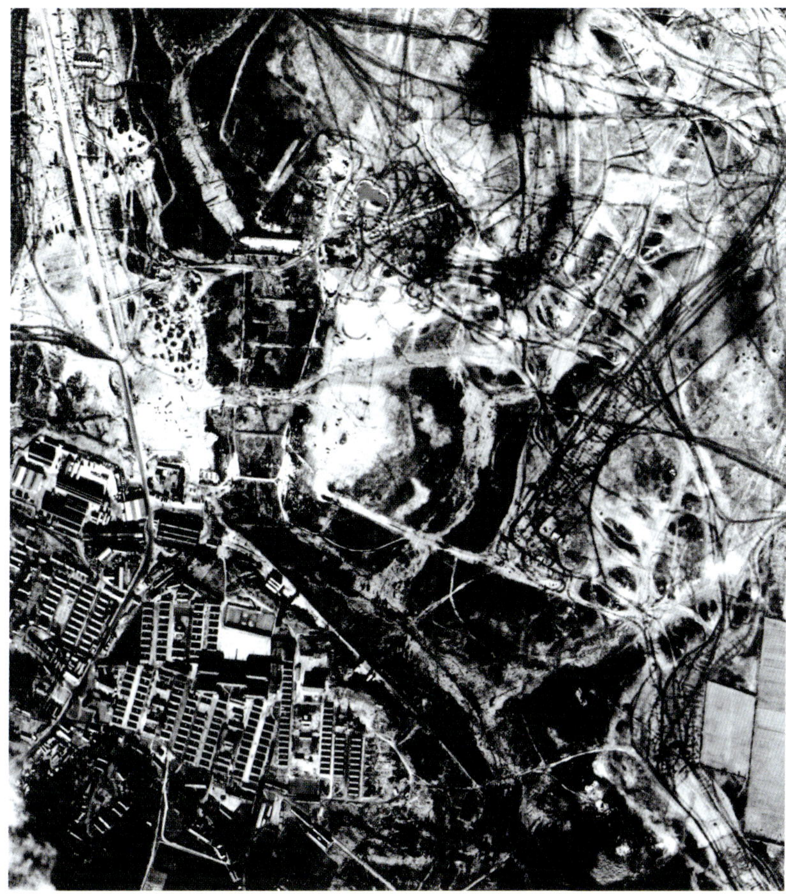

Tanks came to Bovington Heath during the First World War, and research and development continued there throughout the Second World War. The effect of this is clearly visible on the photograph with a mass of chaotic tracks covering the heathland to the north of Bovington Camp. The tanks developed here were vital, particularly for the invasion of Europe, and there were little or no restrictions on what the military could do with the land.

The modern photograph shows a changed, but not different, situation. Unlike many military installations Bovington has continued to operate, and still plays an important role as armoured vehicles are still vital to modern armed forces. The camp is now a more permanent structure with accommodation of different types as well as workshops and testing facilities. To the north the heathland has recovered in many places and the tracks are laid out in a more regular pattern for planned testing and training. Woodland has spread over the heathland, but large areas are still kept clear, partly for military reasons but also for nature conservation. The Army is proud of the care it gives to the wildlife in its training establishments, and the protection of the Dorset heathland is only one example.

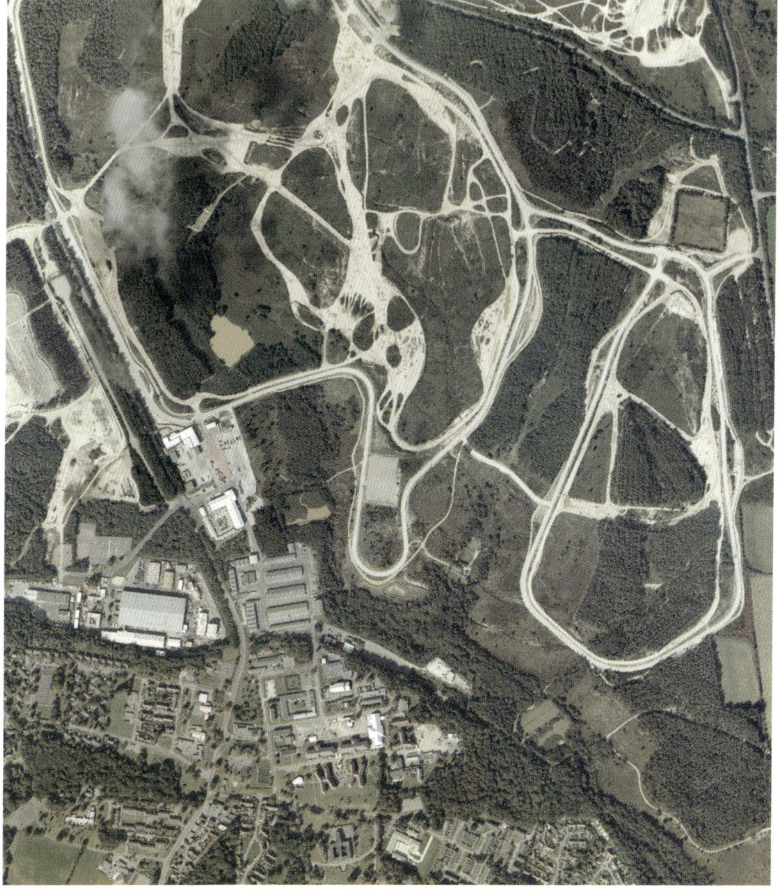

Bradford Peverell and the Aqueduct

1947 photograph reference 1934-2088, centred on grid reference SY 666 916

These photographs of land to the north west of Dorchester show the mixture of change and continuity that is typical of much of Dorset's landscape. Over most of the area there is little change, there has been some loss of field boundaries and some downland has been ploughed, whilst a few houses have been built in the small village of Bradford Peverell. However the south-east corner of the area has changed completely. The

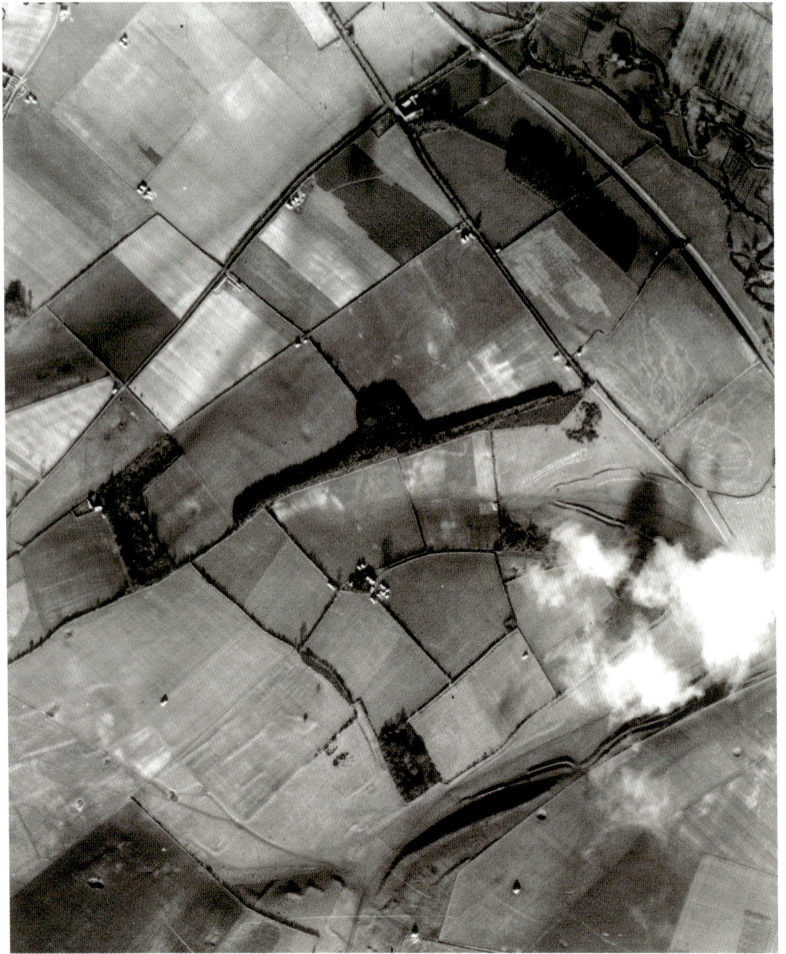

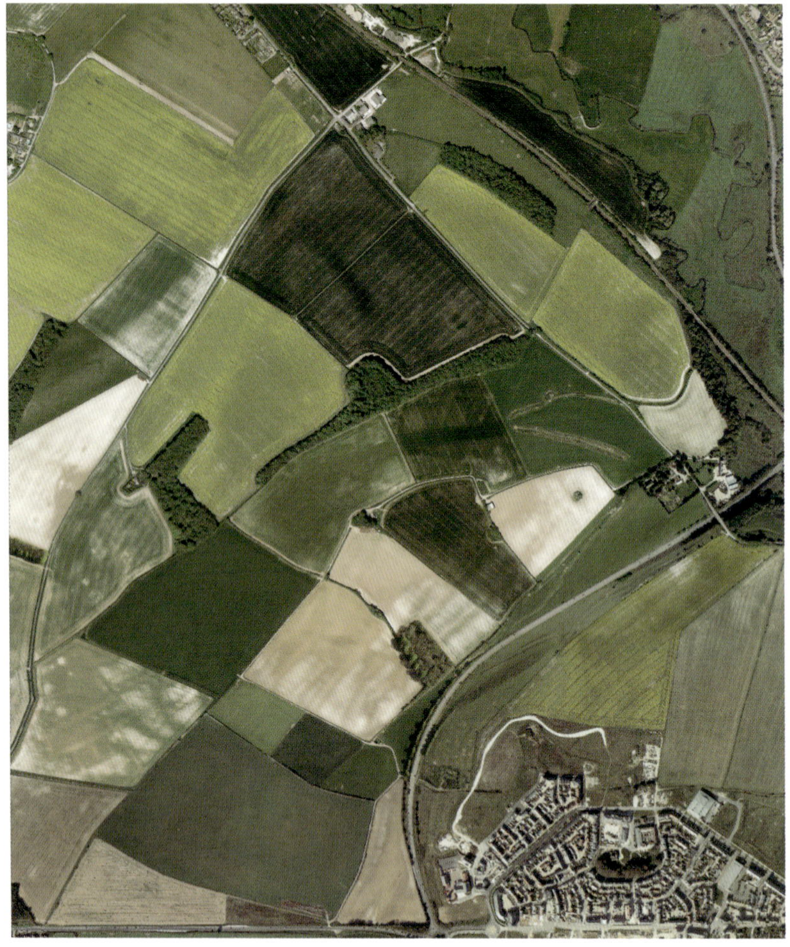

Dorchester by-pass (built 1988) has cut through the landscape and the developing townscape of the Poundbury suburb is creeping over the land. It is probably only the steepness of the slope that is restricting development here.

The area is also rich in archaeology, though there are marked differences in how this has fared over the past sixty years. In the south east, in 1947, extensive areas of prehistoric fields, marked by low rectangular banks, can clearly be seen. Today they have almost vanished as the land has been ploughed for decades. In contrast the curving bank and ditch of the Roman Aqueduct are prominent features of the eastern side of the pictures. These have been well protected as they are unique archaeological features, although the adjacent land has been tightly ploughed.

Bridport 1947 photograph reference 2431-3165, centred on grid reference SY 470 931

The aerial photograph of Bridport in 1947 showed the ancient layout of the town, along three main streets East, West and South. There had been some development along secondary roads to the north as well as in the suburb of Allington to the west.

The railway passed to the east of the town, with a large station well to the north-west of the main settlement. In Allington, on the north-west edge of the 1947 photograph is a newly-built estate showing the typical geometric form of a development of the interwar period.

On the northern side of the town is Downe Hall, a small country house on the very edge of the town. As with many country houses its gardens are enclosed by a belt of trees for privacy.

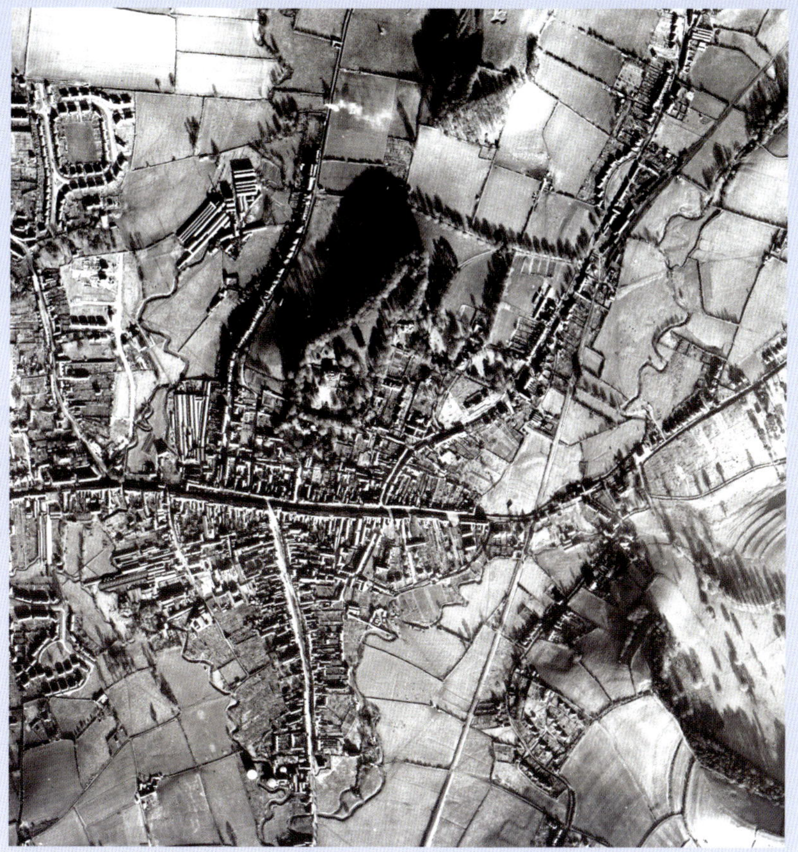

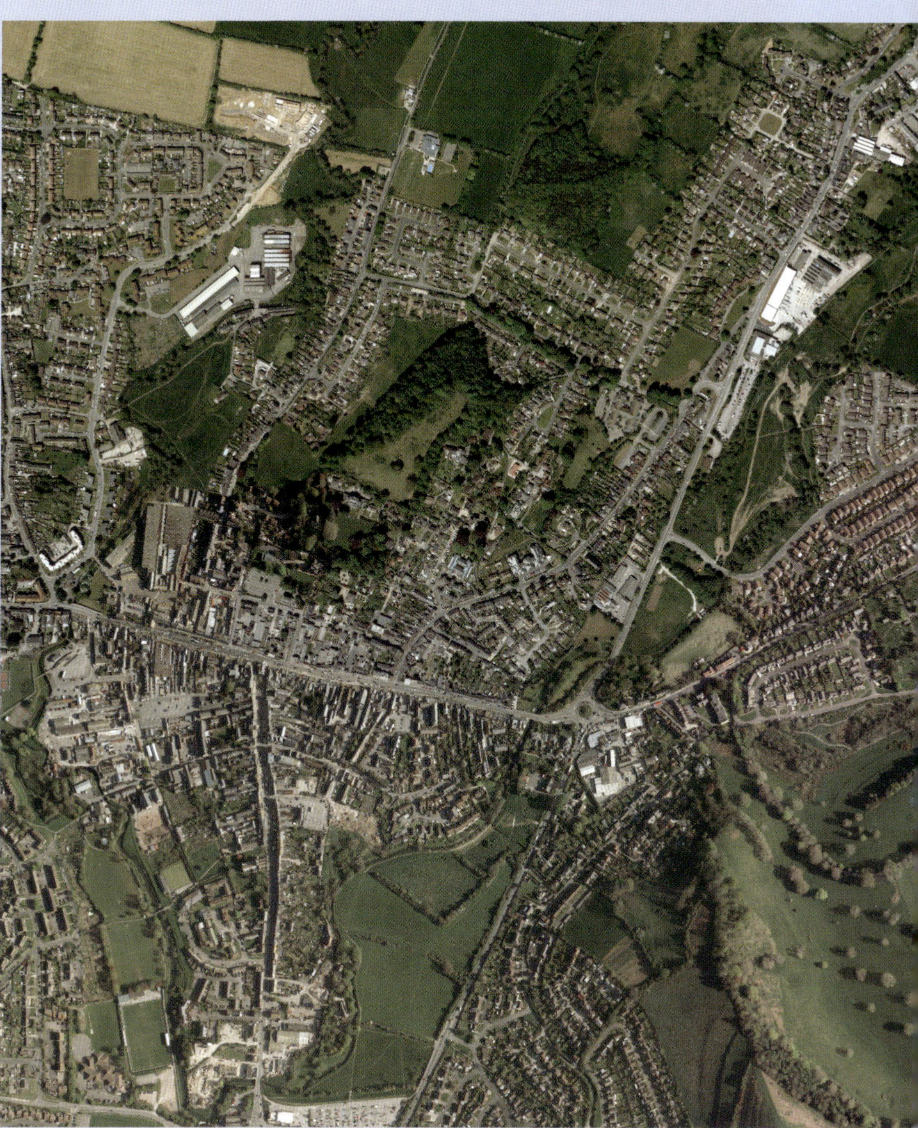

Today estates have spread between the roads that formed the old town of Bridport, and the railway has gone though its loss has had little effect. The railway line, which crossed the photograph from top to bottom, has mostly been reused for the Bridport by-pass that now takes the west-bound traffic that once made Bridport such a bottleneck.

Broadwindsor 1947 photograph reference 1974-3337, centred on grid reference ST 445 030

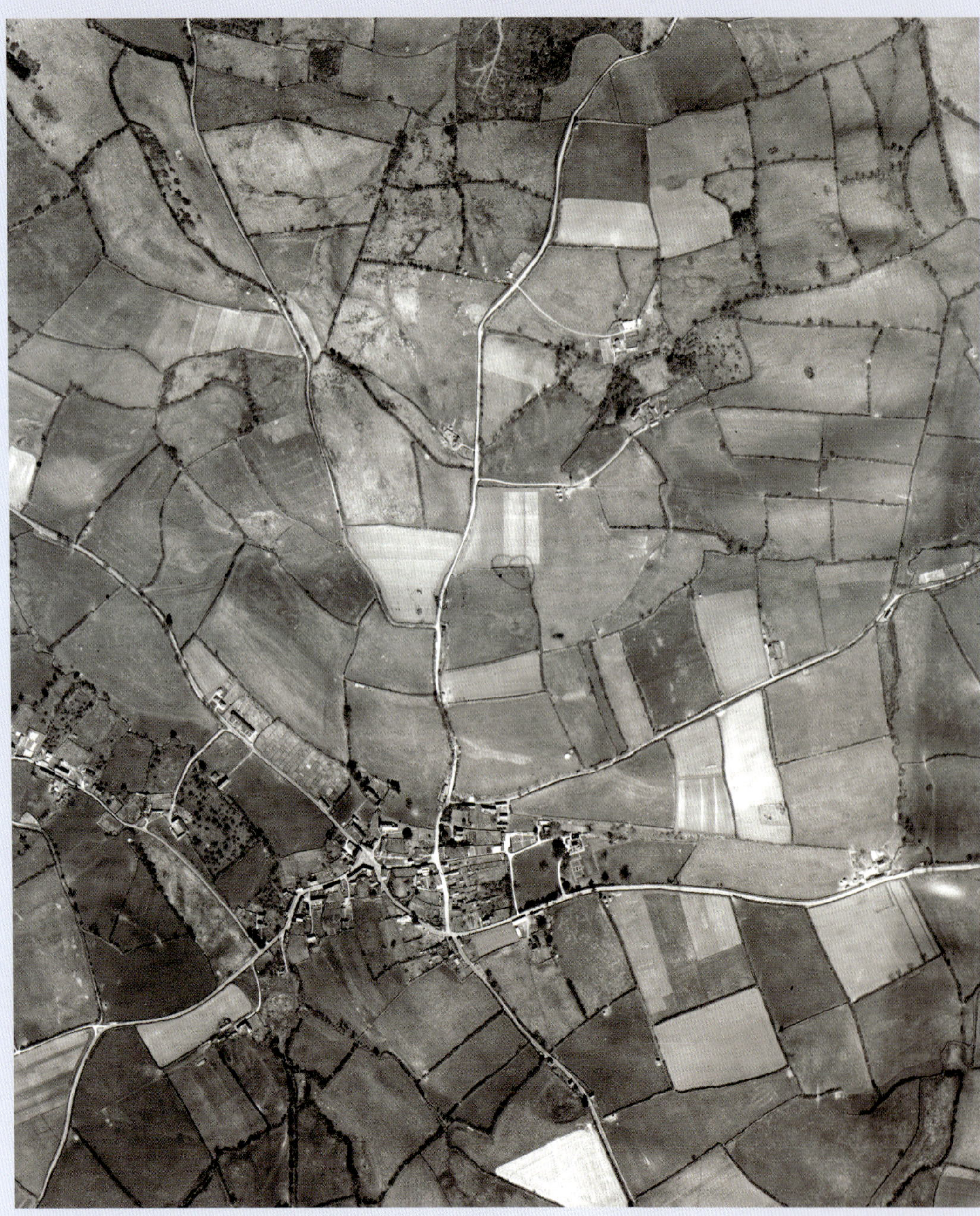

The two pictures of the village Broadwindsor in western Dorset reflect the changes that have happened to many small Dorset villages during the late twentieth century. Whist the original layout of the village is essentially unaltered, a number of new houses have been inserted. This has happened in two ways: individual houses have been fitted into gaps between existing buildings, the process of infill, whilst small estates, groups of houses, have been built around the village, often filling and fitting into pre-existing fields.

Around, and within, the village there has been extensive tree growth – trees in gardens and along the hedges, small woodlands in field corners and small woods, so there are probably far fewer open views around Broadwindsor today than there were in 1947.

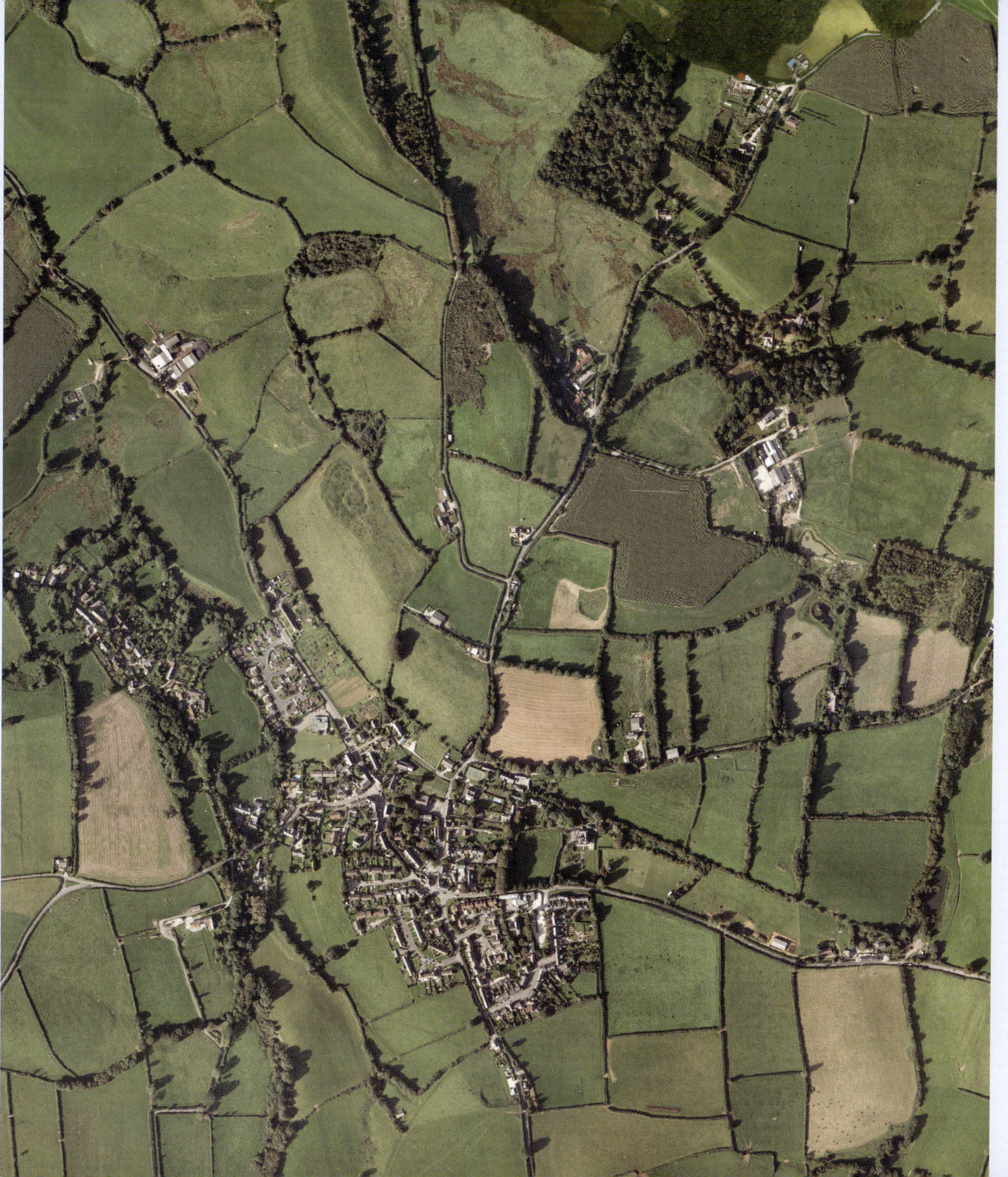

Bulbarrow Hill and Rawlsbury Camp

1947 photograph reference 1934-2176, centred on grid reference ST 768 057

Bulbarrow Hill is one of the finest viewpoints in Dorset, with magnificent views looking northwards towards the Blackmore Vale.

Towards the centre of the photograph is the small Iron Age hill fort of Rawlsbury Camp, clearer in the 1947 picture than in today's; indeed the 1947 photograph is particularly good at revealing the rural archaeology of the area. Immediately south of the hill fort are faint rectangular shapes that probably indicate the presence of Iron Age fields, perhaps contemporary with the hill fort. Further south the fields contain rows of thin lines, this is 'ridge and furrow', traces of medieval strip fields, which can also be found on other fields in the photograph. Finally to the east of the hill fort are thin snaking marks on the top of the hill: these are diggings, either for chalk, or for the thin layer of gravel that covered the hill tops.

Today these features are still there, but are less easily seen. Woodland has spread along the hedgerows and across some of the open downland, but the views from Bulbarrow Hill are still magnificent.

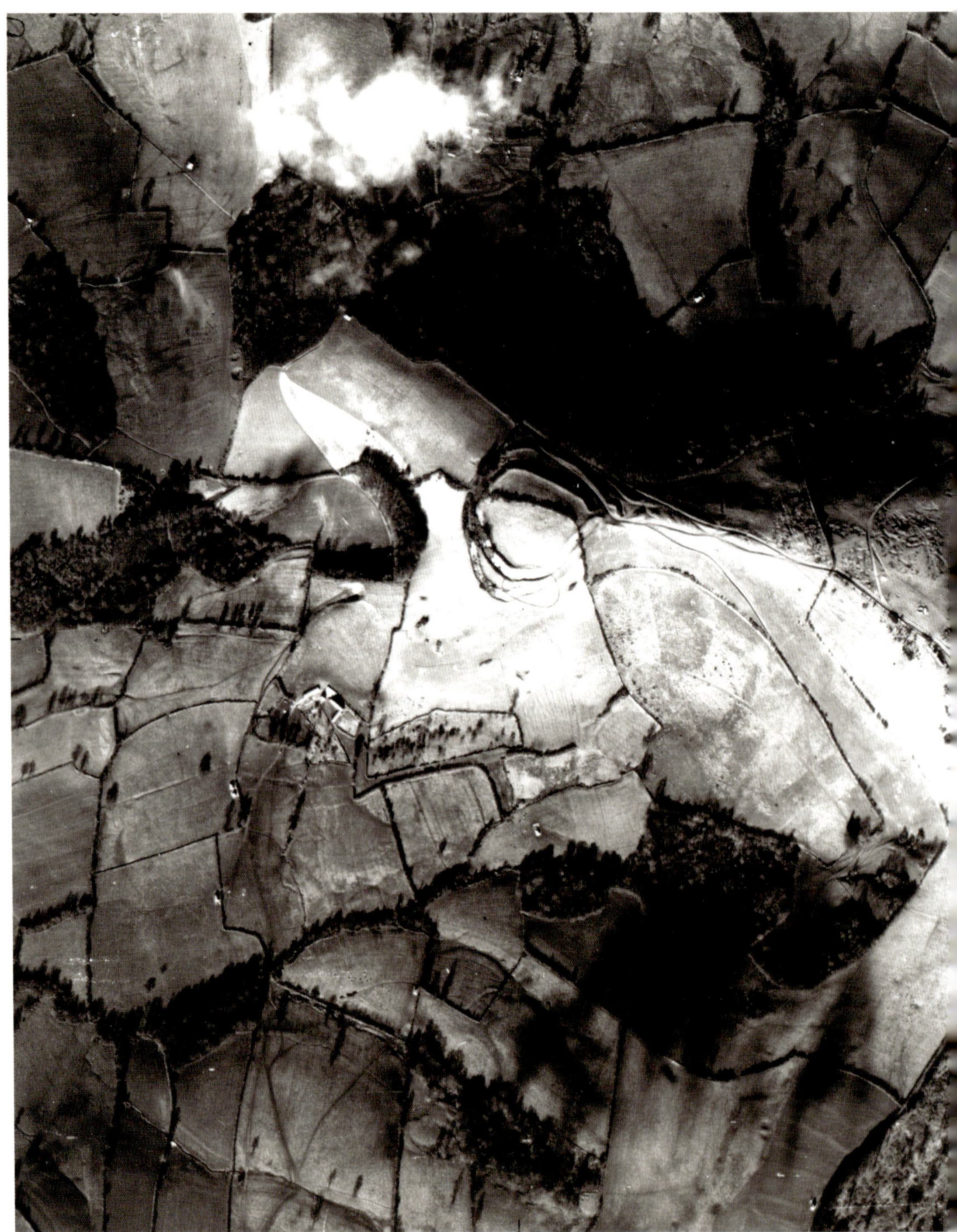

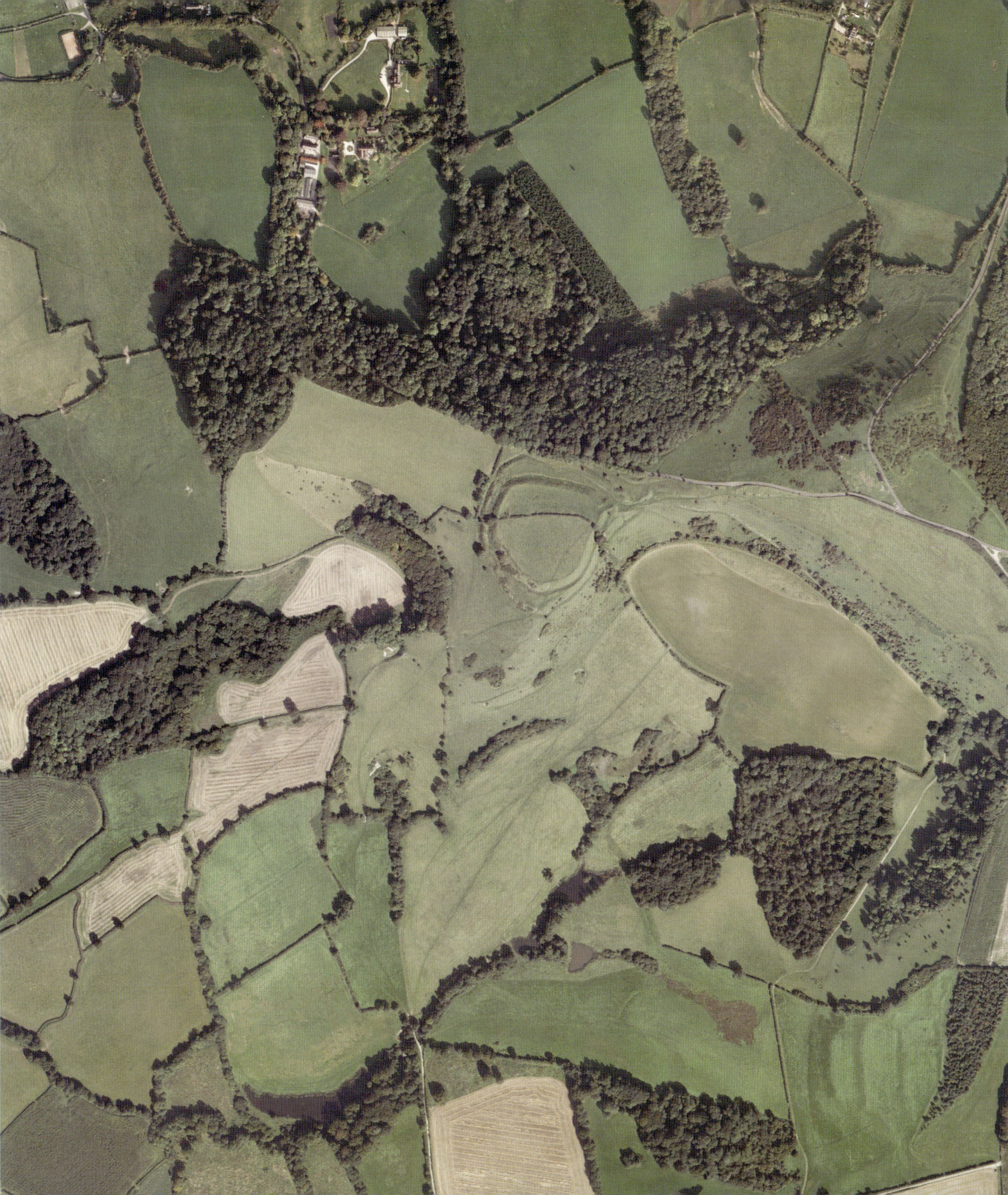

Burton Bradstock 1947 photograph reference 2475-3072, centred on grid reference SY 484 896

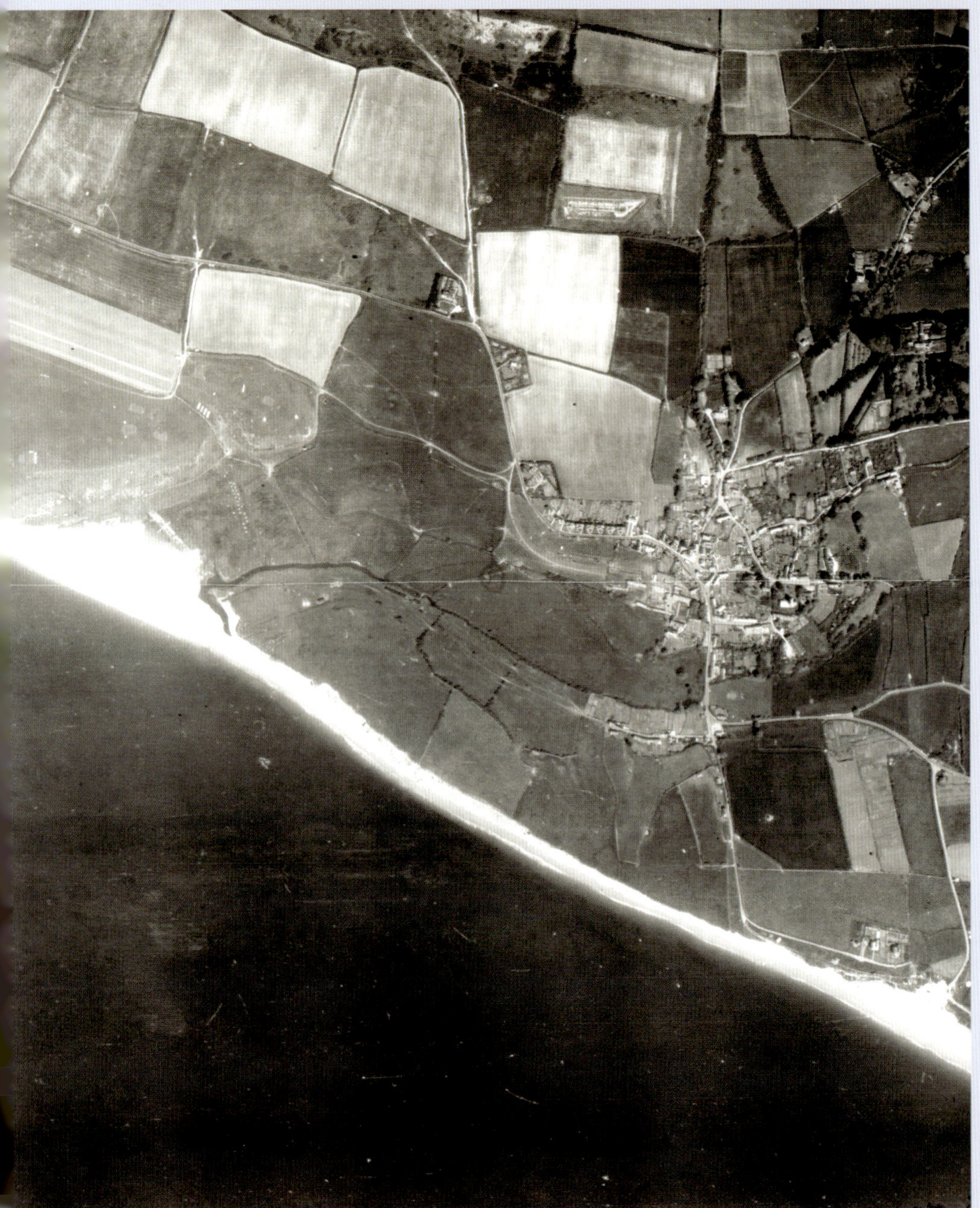

Though it is not particularly obvious these photographs of the land around Burton Bradstock show a remarkable transformation over sixty years, from war to peace, from a landscape dominated by military needs to one where recreation dominates.

Early in the Second World War Burton Bradstock had been heavily defended against the possibility of German landings, whilst by 1944 it was the temporary home to many American troops in the months preceding D-Day, when the cliffs were used extensively for training.

Along the coast, from east to west, can be seen many small features, mostly pill boxes and gun emplacements, whilst at Freshwater, on the western edge of the picture a large number of white dots are visible slightly inland. These are tank traps or 'dragon's teeth', rows of concrete blocks which crossed the valley and were intended to delay any German vehicles. From later in the war are temporary buildings, both along the valley that runs from Freshwater back towards Burton Bradstock and in woodland to the south east of the village. These were used as accommodation for troops but, at the time of the photograph, had been taken over as temporary housing whilst others had been turned into a chicken farm.

Today the concrete dragon's teeth have gone, to be used in the protection of West Bay harbour, and their place taken by an extensive caravan site, with a golf course to the west. To the east there is a small car park for visitors, run by the National Trust, for it was along this part of the coast that, it is said, a senior member of the National Trust was walking one day and was horrified by the spread of development. He vowed to do so something to protect Britain's coastline and which led to 'Enterprise Neptune' and the National Trust becoming one of the principal coastal landowners in the country.

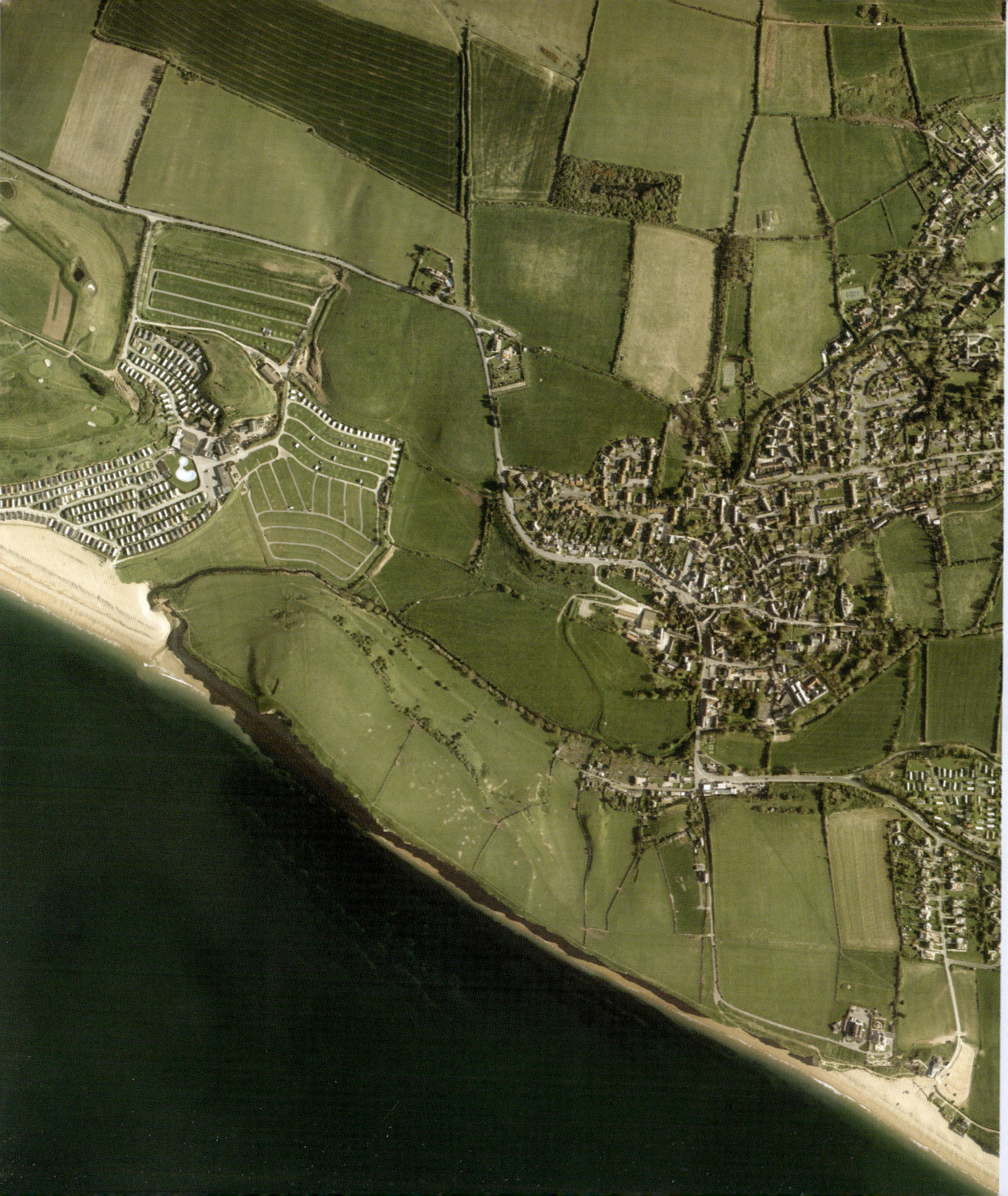

Cerne Abbas 1947 photograph reference 1974-2376, centred on grid reference ST 663 009

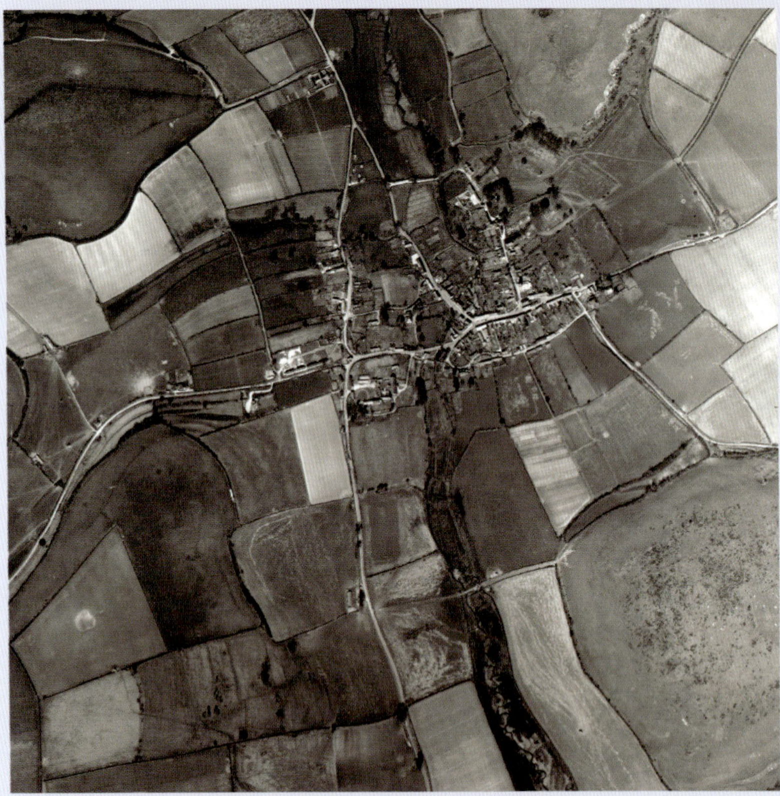

The most famous feature of Cerne Abbas is, of course, the Giant; but if you look on the 1947 photograph you will be hard put to find it, the fence around the site is far more clearly visible. For many years people have tried to censor the Giant, but without success, the people of Dorset being much too attached to the old gentleman to allow anything to be done to him. But in 1939 he was covered up in the cause of national security. The Cerne Giant, along with all the other hill figures in the country was covered over, as it was feared that their unique shapes could provide German aircraft with easily recognisable landmarks.

Today the Giant is clear again, as are the ancient fields which can be seen in the south western section of the photographs. These are medieval terraced fields, usually called lynchets, which were created to allow the sloping sides of the hills to be ploughed. Woodland has spread over some of the downland and some of the hedgerows have thickened into thin woods.

The village too has grown with new estates within (on land that was allotments in 1947) and outside to the south. Whilst to the north of the village there is an isolated cruciform building in 1947. This had been built as the workhouse in 1836, and after a period of disuse it was redeveloped into houses and flats, as has happened frequently in towns but less often in the wider countryside.

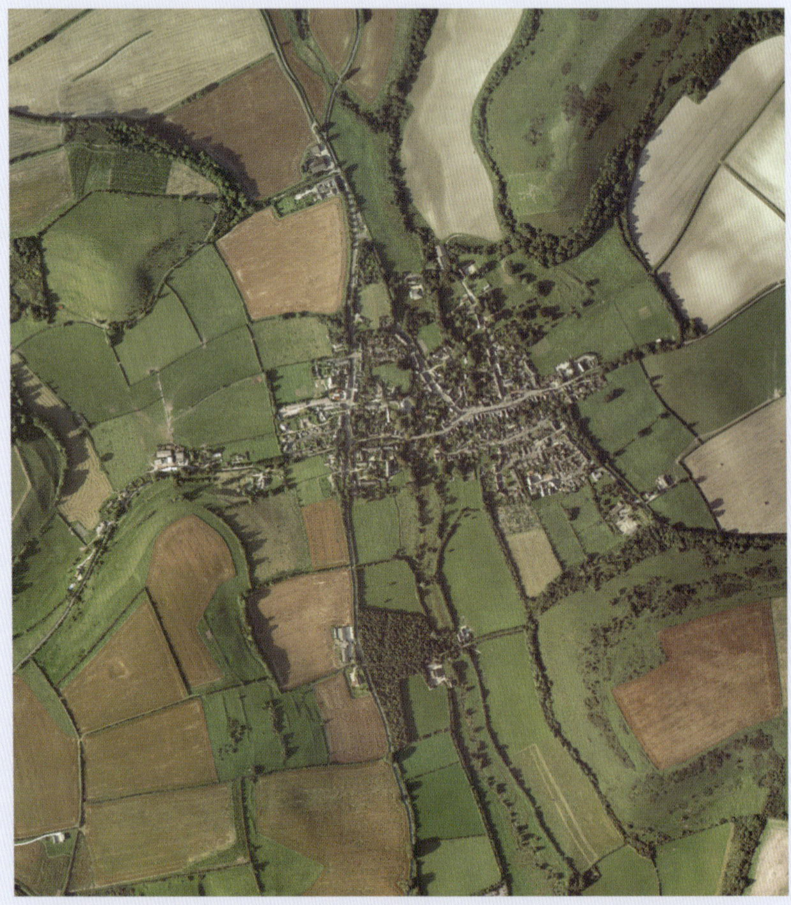

Charlton Down 1947 photograph reference 2475-3190, centred on grid reference SY 684 952

In 1947 this area, to the north of Dorchester, was seen as fairly remote, one minor road ran through large fields and patches of open downland. It was in this open countryside that the Dorset County Asylum was built in 1863; in 1947 the Herrison Hospital was still in operation treating mental illnesses. The buildings together with some temporary buildings erected during the war can be seen in the south-west corner, surrounded by trees with extensive areas of allotments.

Today this area has changed totally, there has been some loss of field boundaries and the surviving patches of downland have been ploughed, incidentally destroying some ancient field boundaries that could be seen in 1947 on the eastern side of the picture. The hospital closed in 1992 and subsequently the buildings have been restored and form the core of a new 'village', Charlton Down. This differs from other developments in the county in the large number of mature trees, which were originally planted in the grounds of the hospital.

The hospital cricket ground, the circular feature to the south of the hospital survives, happily still used for its original purpose on most weekends during the summer.

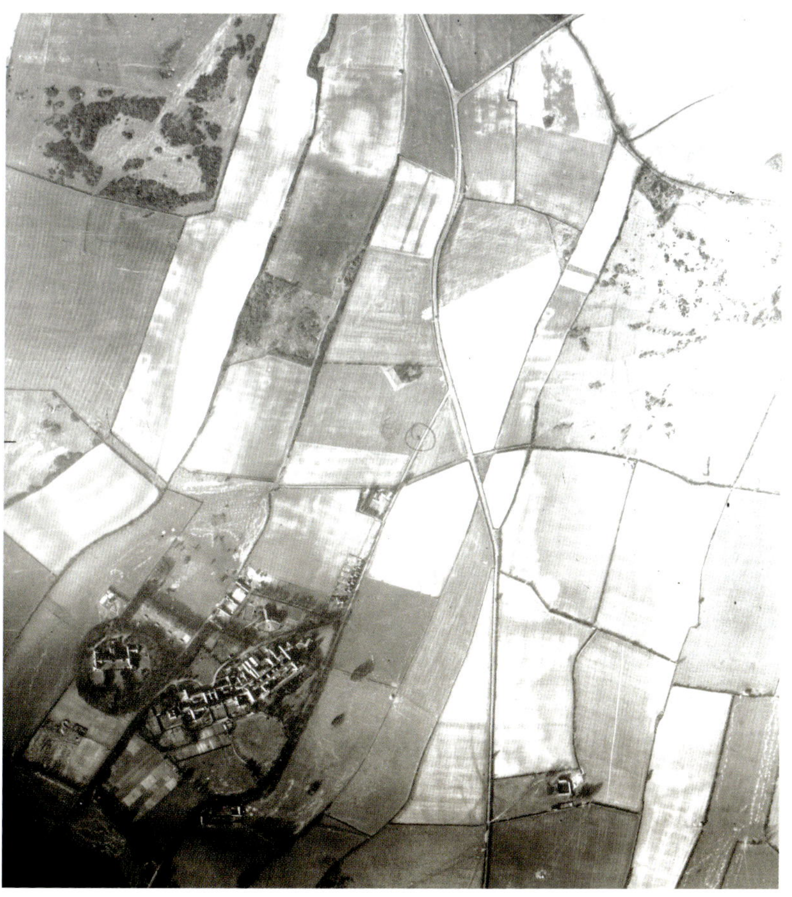

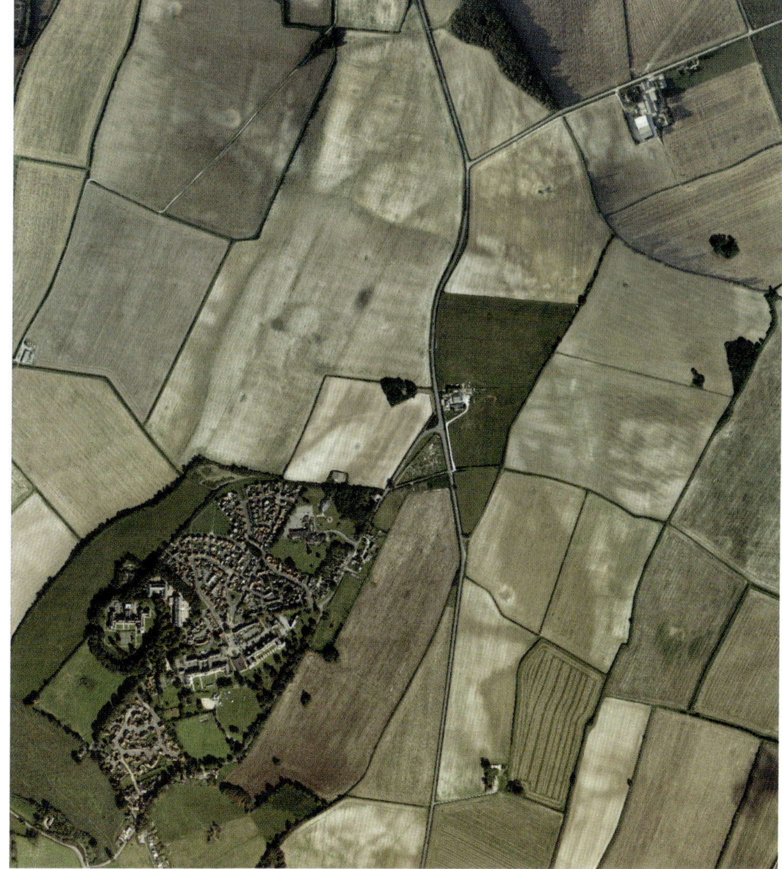

Charmouth and Black Ven

1947 photograph reference 2475-4318, centred on grid reference SY 355 936

Here the changes are as much due to natural causes as they are to man-made events. To the west of the village lies the massive mud slide of Black Ven. Since 1947 it is clear that the cliff has retreated, farmland has crumbled into the sea, and fields affected have been abandoned. This process had been going on for many years before this date, evidence for which can be seen in the form of two roads, running west from Charmouth which seem to run into the broken ground above Black

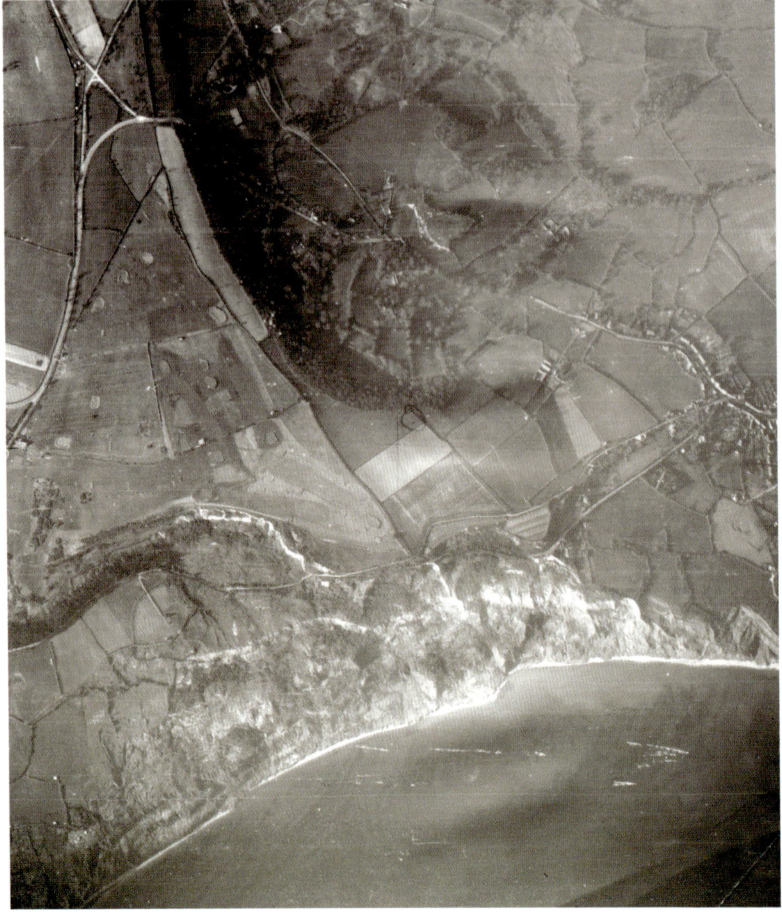

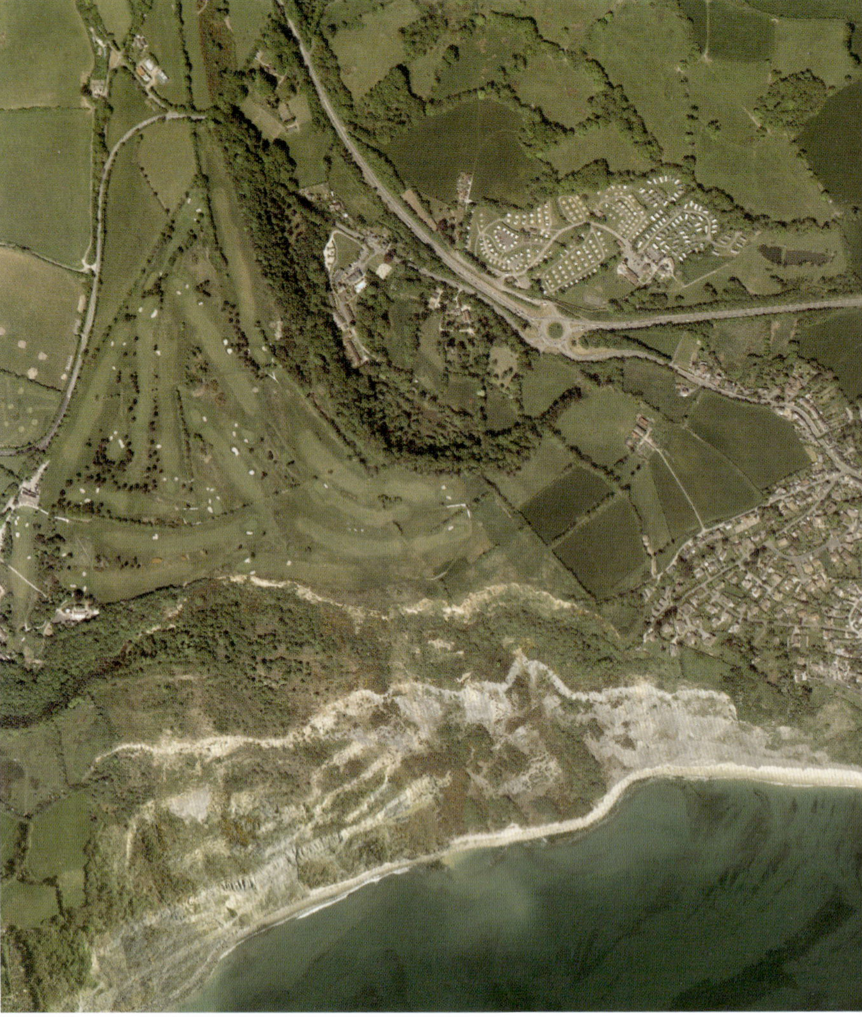

Ven and vanish. These are earlier versions of the coast road from Charmouth to Lyme Regis. Today the road runs well inland, and it will be many years before this road is threatened.

Charmouth has grown, as most villages have, though some of the houses seem to have been built dangerously close to the cliff edge. Inland the importance of visitors and recreation to the county can be seen in the large caravan park and the golf course. The latter was there in 1947 but has had to alter its shape as the southern edge of the course has continued to fall into the sea.

Chideock 1947 photograph reference 2431-4061, centred on grid reference SY 422 934

The countryside around the village of Chideock was very well wooded in 1947, with the result that there has been less significant woodland growth here than in other parts of the county. Indeed, although there has been some increase in the size of woods, and others have developed there may well have been a net loss here as many well-wooded hedgerows have been removed.

Growth in the village has been limited to estates on the edges, to the north, south and east.

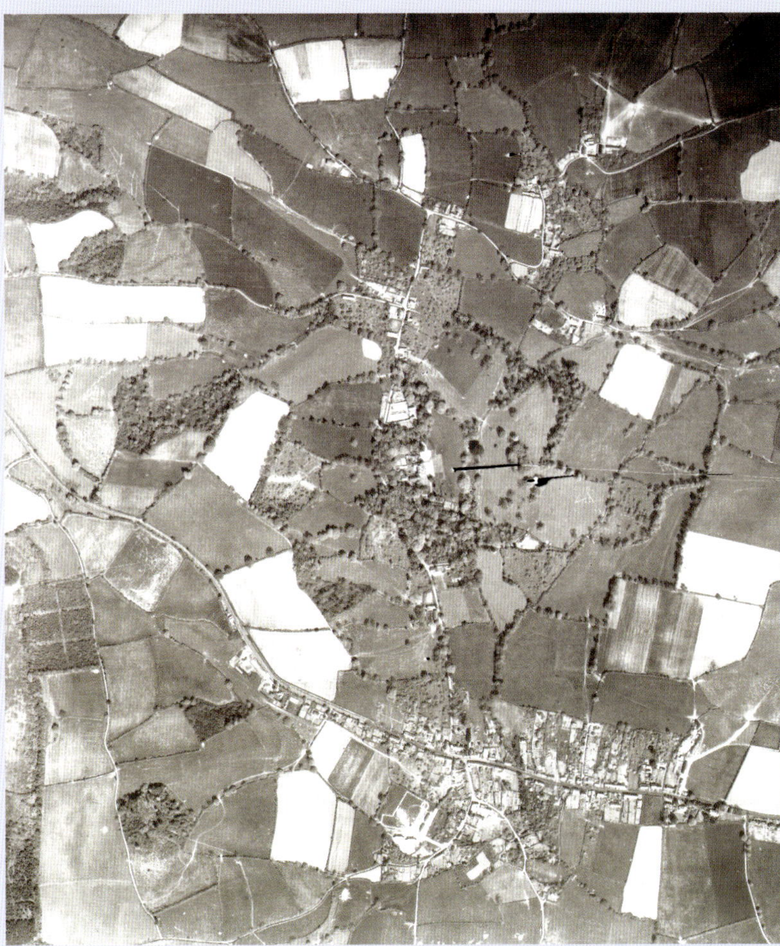

Immediately to the north of the village, and clearer on the modern photograph than on that of 1947, is a square earthwork, which is all that remains of Chideock Castle, rendered useless after the civil war and demolished thereafter.

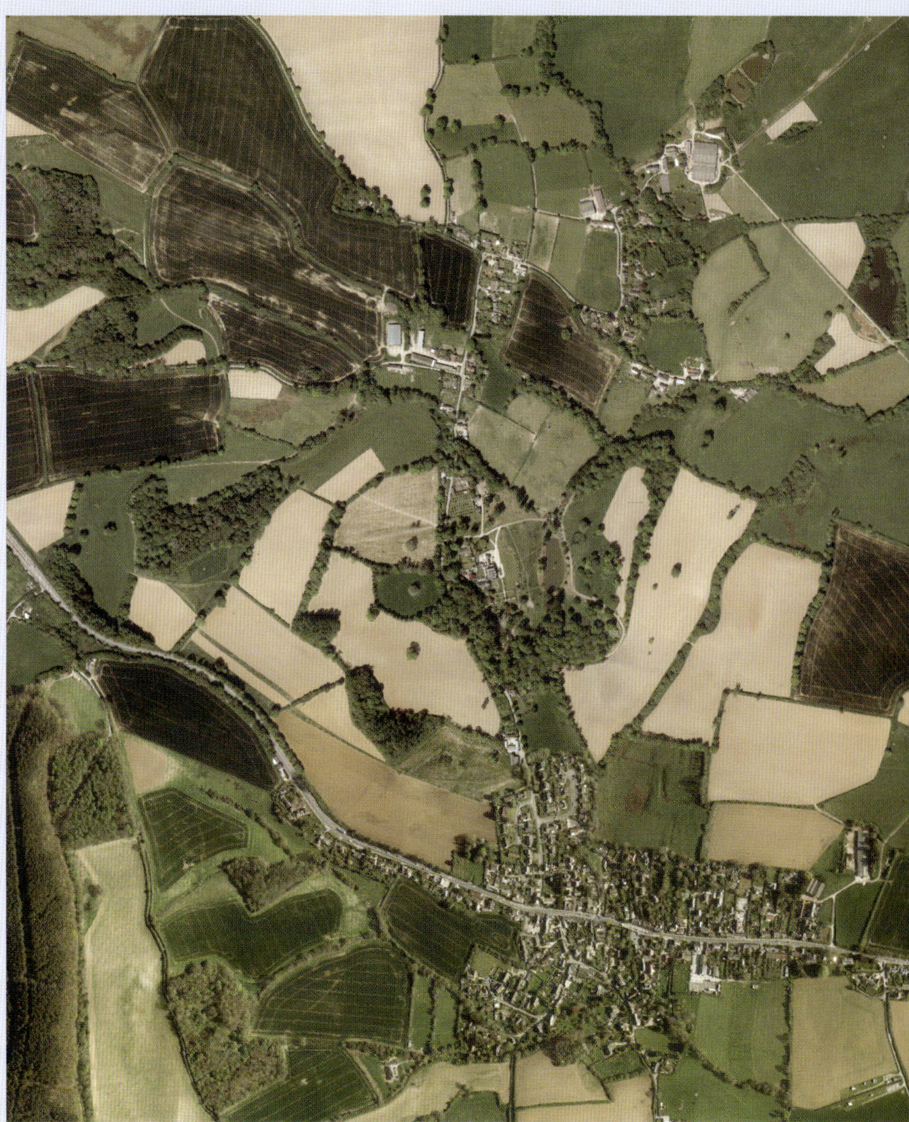

Christchurch and Hengistbury Head

1947 photograph reference 1934-3020, centred on grid reference SZ 158 919

Two thousand years ago one of the principle ports in the south of England lay on Hengistbury Head, towards the south of the photographs. The massive bank and ditch that protected the port, the 'Double Dykes' is clearly visible on both pictures.

In 1947 Christchurch, towards to the north of the picture was still a small town; there had been some expansion northward, but around the great priory church there was little change. To the west of Hengistbury Head housing was encroaching, but only a few terraces had been built in what were still open fields, which seem to have been ploughed as part of the wartime need for home grown food.

Today buildings have spread over the area. Now the open area west of the Double Dykes is protected as the approach to the site. Large car parks have been built as Hengistbury Head is a very popular tourist attraction. Around Christchurch almost every available area has been built on, only the playing fields, or land that is too marshy for development remain untouched. Leisure in the form of marinas, or even an estate where houses have built around a central pool for their owners' boats, has become extremely important.

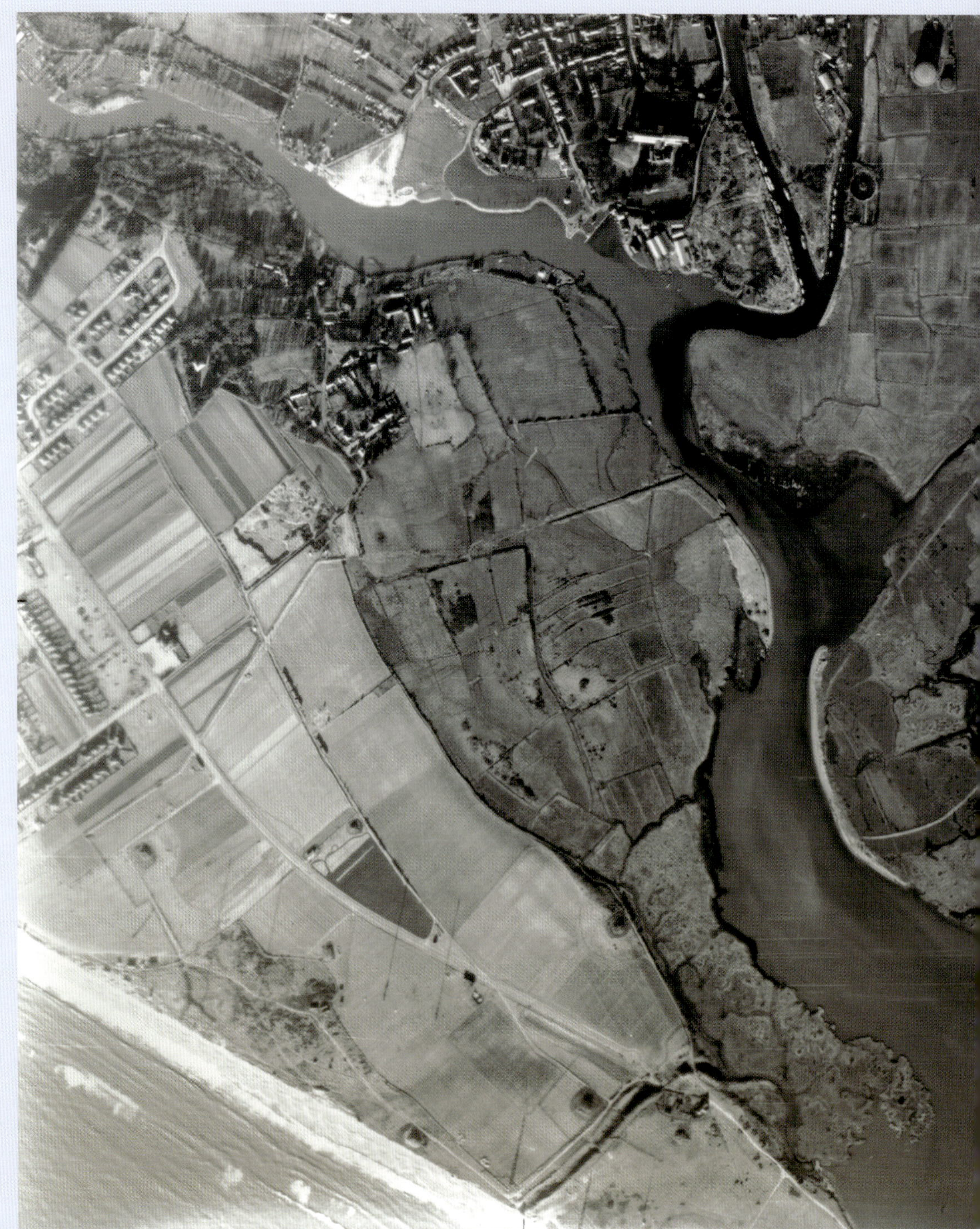

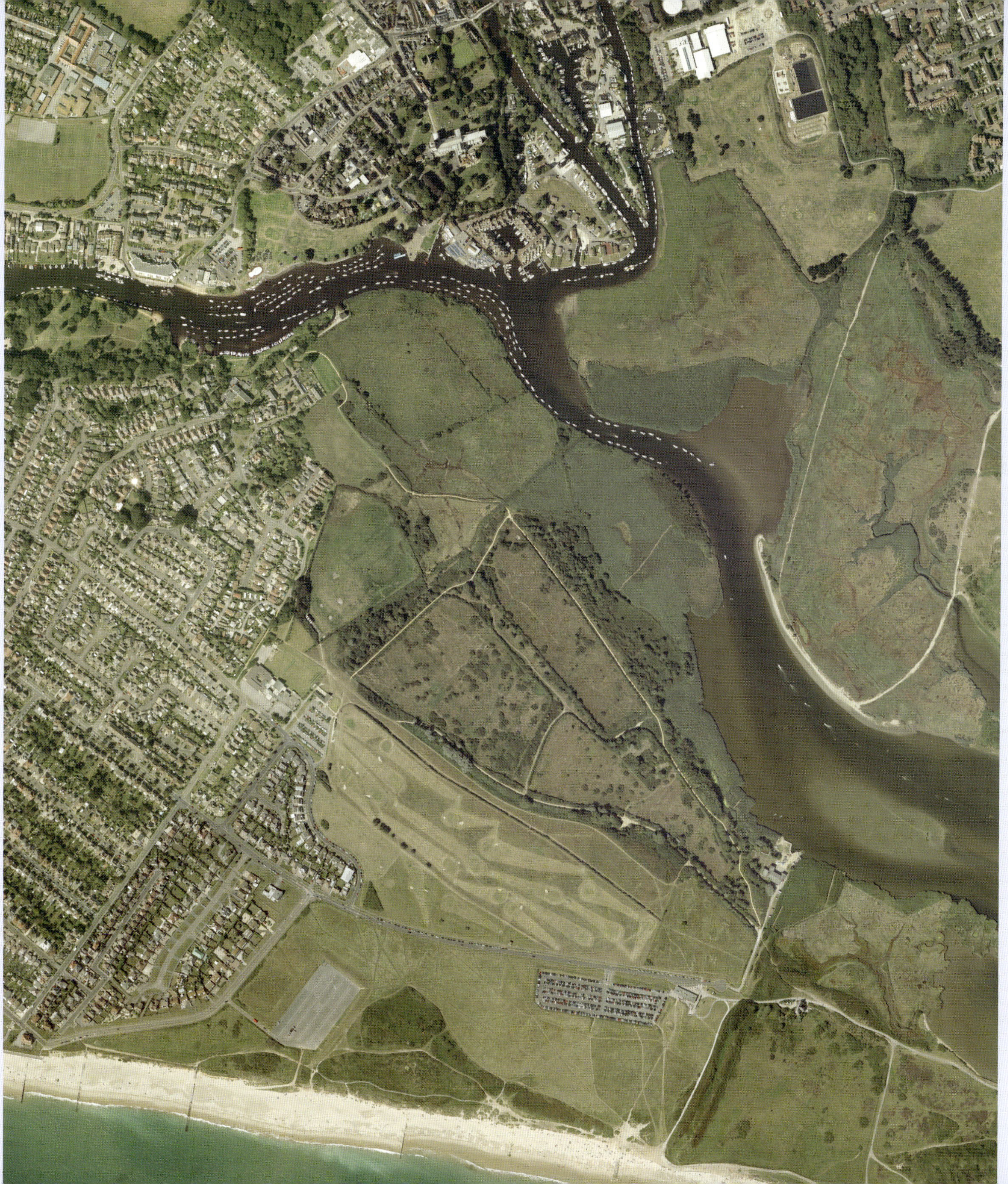

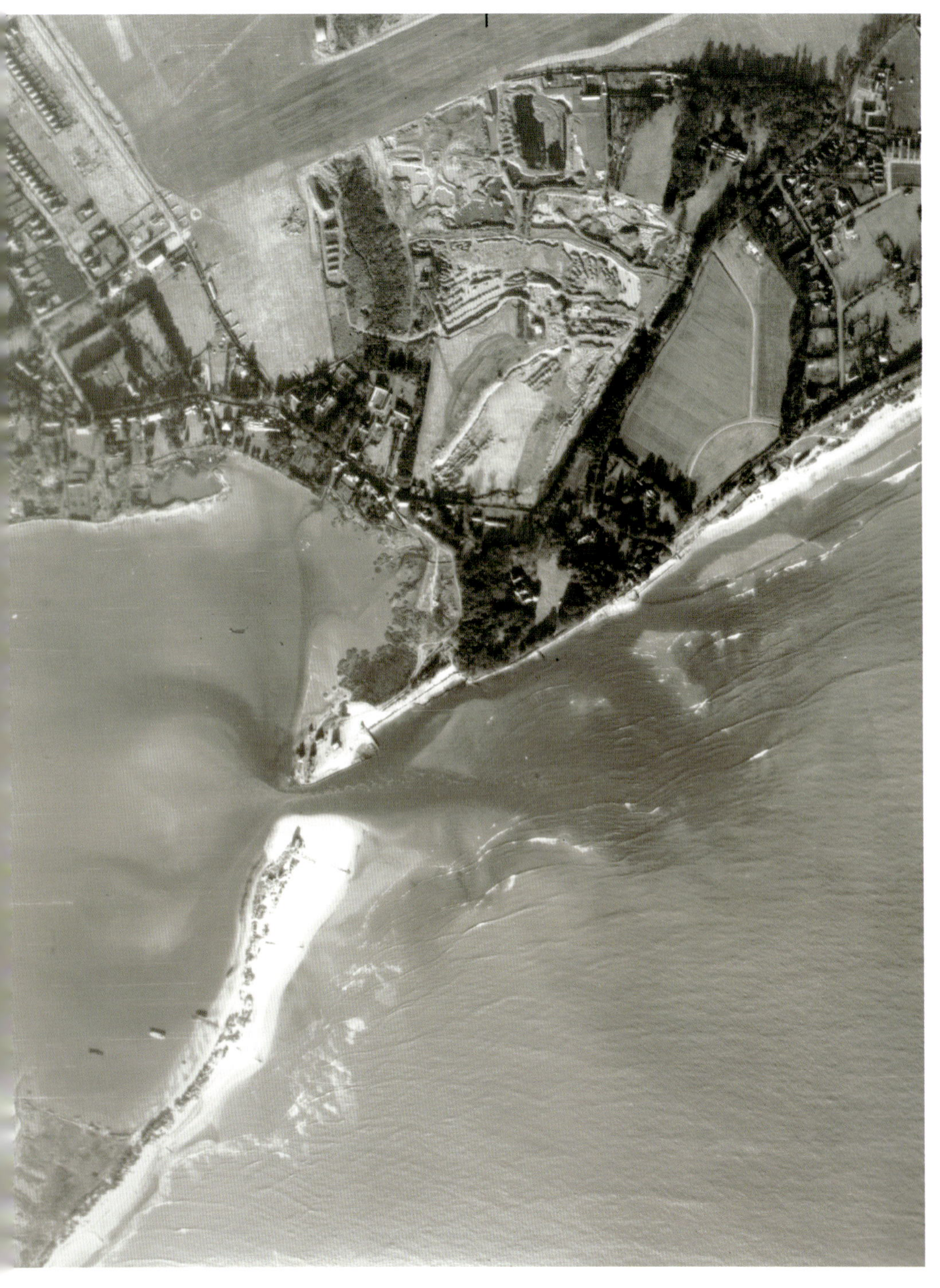

Christchurch Harbour Entrance

1947 photograph reference 1934-3016, centred on grid reference SZ 183 918

What was a remote spot in 1947 has changed considerably today. The settlement of Mudeford, to the north of the harbour entrance has grown considerably covering a gravel pit, playing field as well as the former Christchurch Airfield, which can be seen to the top of the 1947 photograph. This was a pre-war aerodrome which was taken over by the military during World War Two. The airfield continued in use after the war and finally closed in 1966.

Leisure activities have had a massive impact on the area. Mudeford Spit, on the northern side of the entrance has grown with a car park being built on reclaimed land. It also has the newest lifeboat station in the county, opened in 1981. It is intended to deal with any problems arising from the large number of leisure craft in the area, a large number of which can be seen scattered over the waters of the harbour.

On the southern side of the entrance are rows of beach huts. These had existed before the war but were all removed in 1939 as it was thought they might provide cover for the enemy if the Germans landed. As soon as the war ended they were rebuilt, at first providing the base for cheap holidays, although now they are very desirable properties and a beach hut on the Dorset coast can sell for more than a house elsewhere in the country!

These photographs also show the reason that archaeologists are always looking at aerial photographs, one picture can show features that are not visible on another. On the modern picture a dark line can be seen running into the sea. These are the remains of Clarendon's Pier, a harbour work constructed in 1666. It was there in 1947 but the tide wasn't right when the photograph was taken.

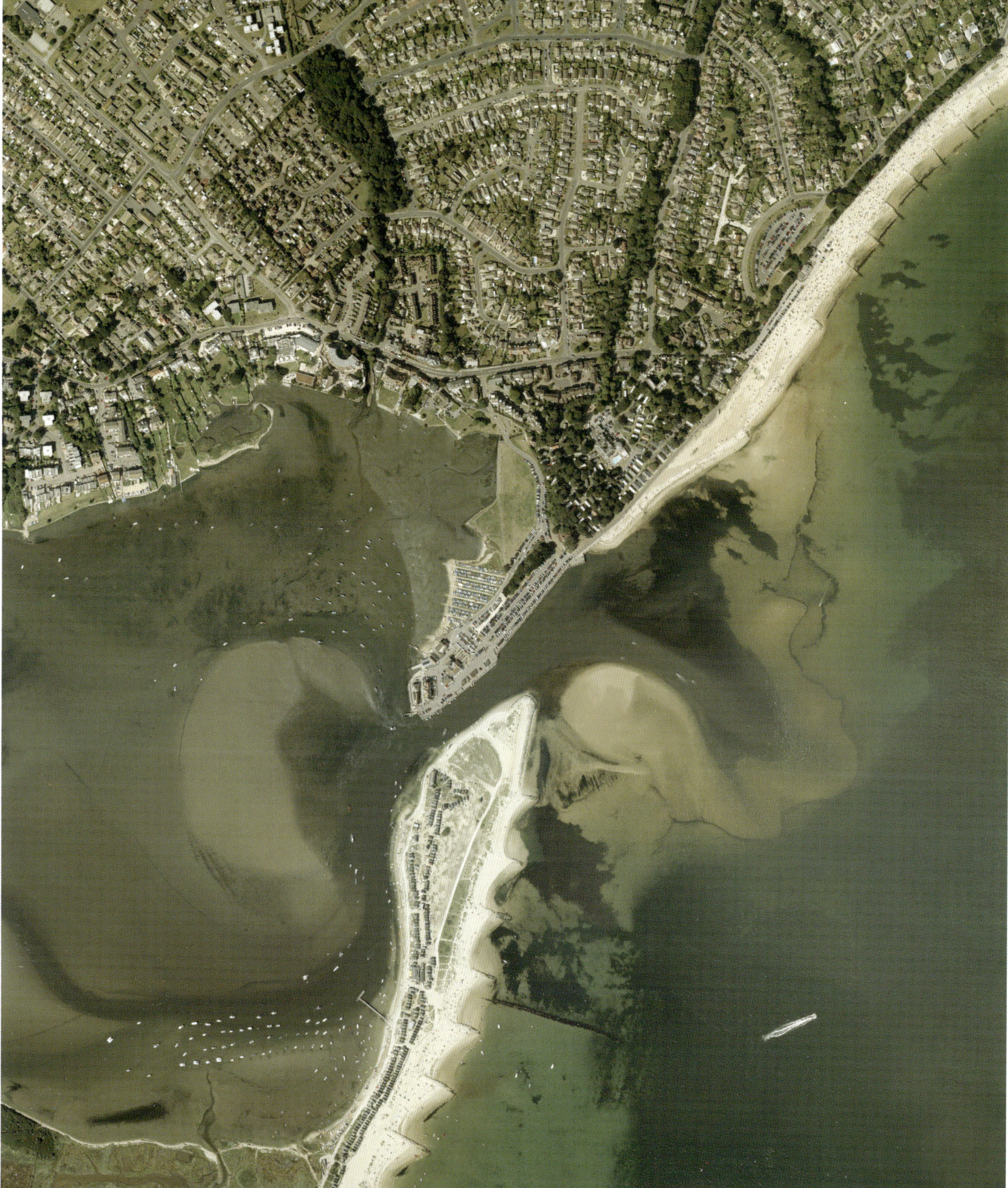

Compton Abbas Centred on grid reference ST 881 187

In 1947 the eastern portion of the village of Compton Abbas lay in a fold of the downs which were criss-crossed with ancient earthworks. To the south on Fontmell Down there is a cross ridge dyke, a prehistoric bank and ditch which crosses the down and probably marks an ancient land division. To the north on Melbury Hill is an ancient field system whilst on top of the hill is a curious circular earthwork, which is seen more easily on the modern photograph. This remarkable earthwork marks the site of a beacon erected in 1588 as part of the warning system against the Spanish Armada. Despite having been photographed only a few years after the end of the Second World War this is the only military feature visible.

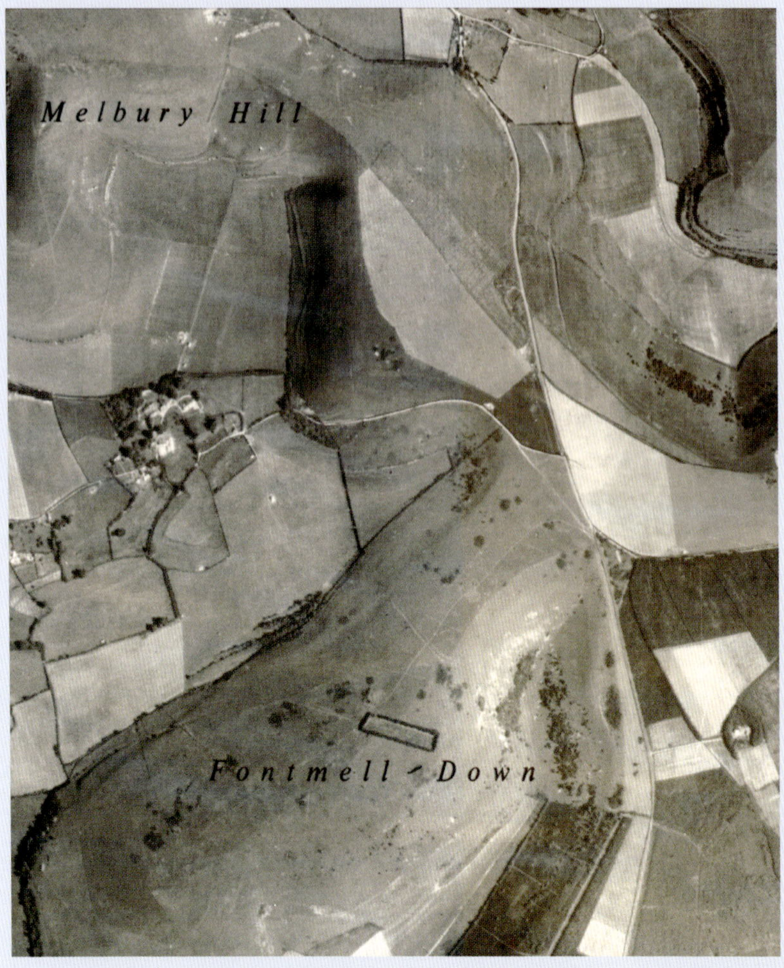

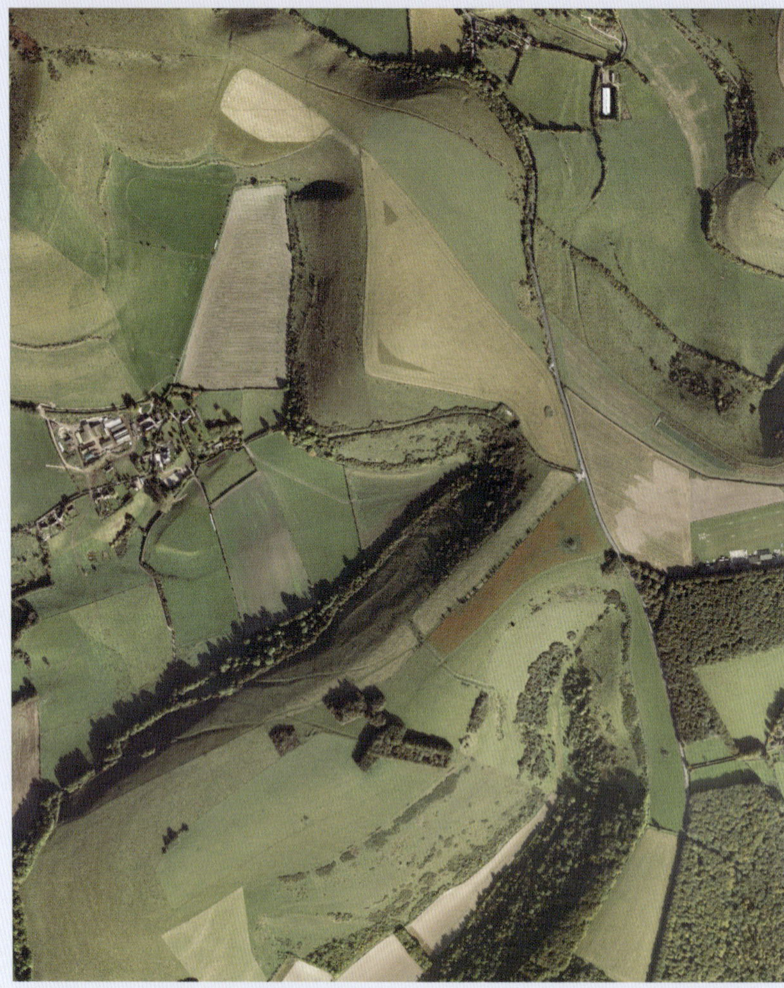

The modern photograph shows how woodland has spread, especially at the base of the downs. One unusual addition to the landscape has been the development of Compton Abbas Airfield. In other places airfields of 1947 have disappeared, here we have an airfield which has developed since 1947 and is now an accepted part of the local landscape.

Corfe Castle 1947 photograph reference 1821-2408, centred on grid reference SY 960 819

Corfe Castle itself has changed very little, the only differences are due to the work carried out to protect the ancient building. The village too has changed comparatively little. New estates have grown to the east and west of the main north-south road, and in one case a line of houses visible in 1947 has been extended.

The 1947 picture showed a landscape with considerable evidence of the important medieval town that Corfe Castle was, together with its turbulent history. Around the village, particularly beside the road that runs south west, are small fields with clear remains of the medieval strip fields, whist at the south-west corner of the picture lies Corfe Common, still an open area. Immediately south west of the Castle can be seen the earthwork of The Rings, which marks the site of a siege castle, originally built during the civil wars of Stephen and Matilda in the twelfth century, and reused during the later civil war between the king and parliament which led to the destruction of Corfe Castle itself.

Woodland has spread extensively, along the old stone walls, around the common and north of the Castle, where it has covered the old clay workings.

The changes to transport have been unusual here, as between the two photographs the railway has gone and returned, closed in 1972, then reopened as the Swanage Railway. What has disappeared is the light industrial line that can be seen north of the Purbeck Hills, snaking from west to east across the 1947 image. This served the clay pits, part of which is now a large car park for the use of people coming to the use the railway.

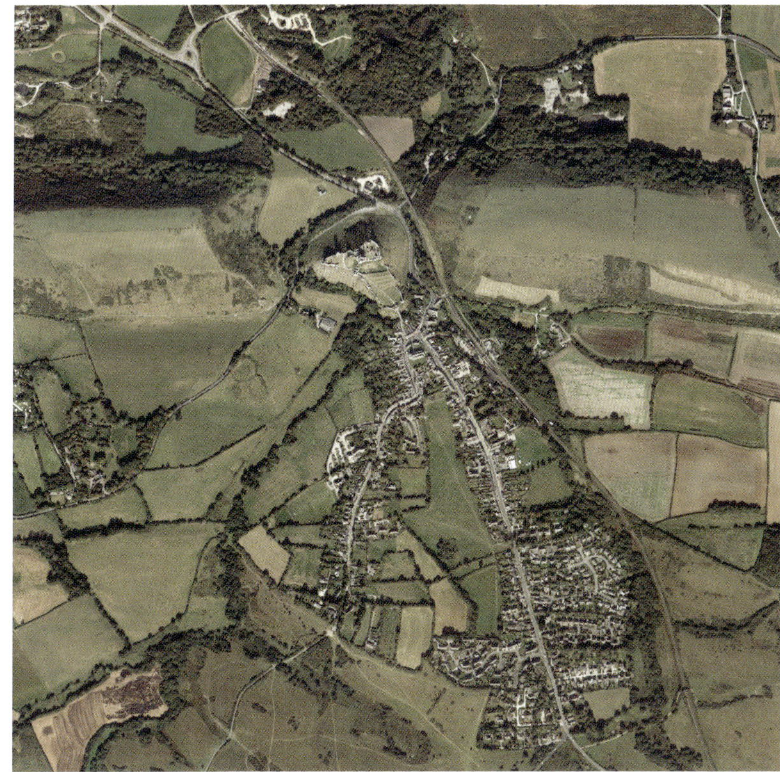

Cranborne 1947 photograph reference 1845-4061, centred on grid reference SU 057 140

Cranborne is now a moderately large village, but was once a small town. In the sixty years since the first photograph was taken the village has grown far less than similar settlements. There has been some infill in the form of small estates or groups of houses mostly on the western side of the village. Unusually these developments did not include the allotments, a large field on the northern side of the village was clearly used as allotments in 1947, but today the field has reverted to agriculture. The fields are also relatively unchanged, with little evidence of hedgerow removal.

Woodland has spread, as is common in the county, but not as much as elsewhere. The wood on the eastern side of the picture shows clear evidence of management, areas have been felled and then either

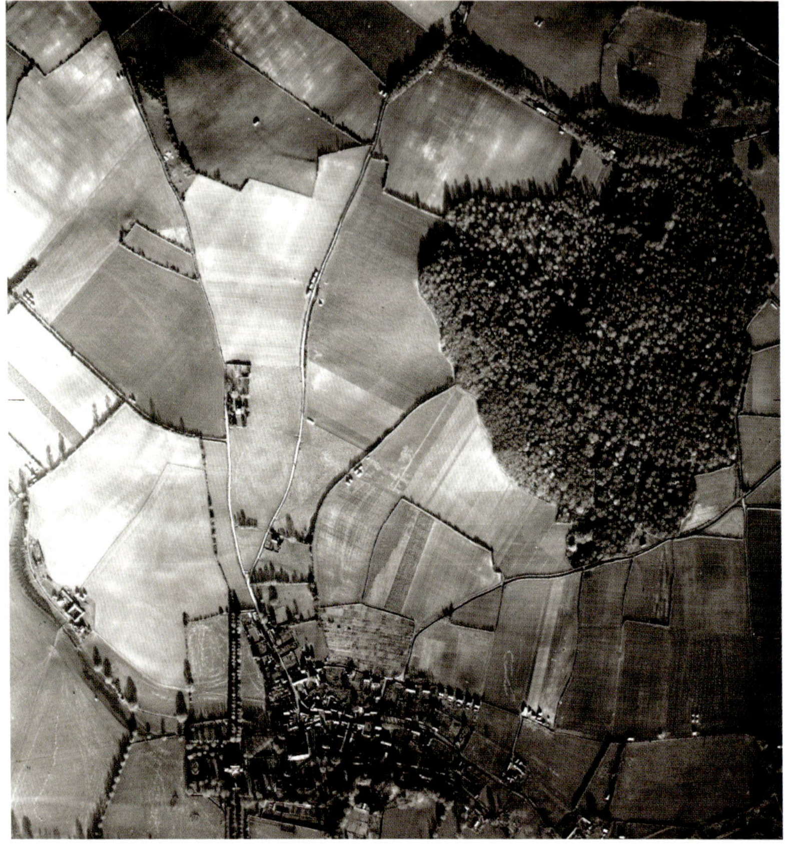

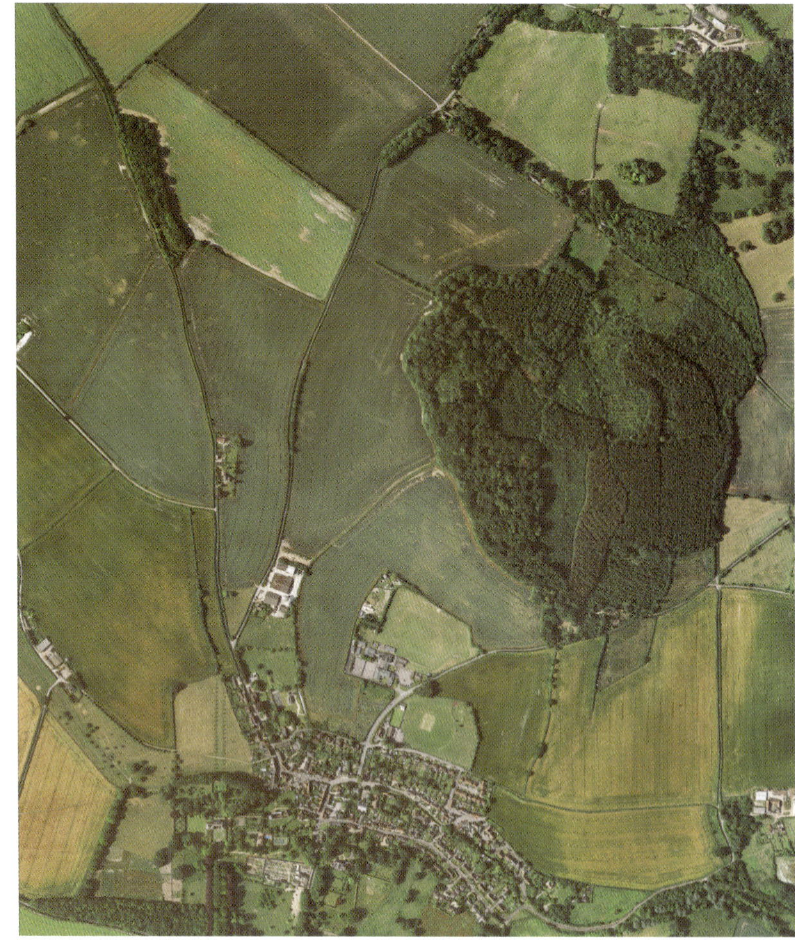

replanted or allowed to regenerate. Dutch elm disease in the 1970s had a serious impact in this part of the county; the avenue to the north of Cranborne manor, in the south west of the picture was a casualty and has clearly been replanted.

The other major change can be seen in a field to the north of the village. This is Cranborne Middle School, a large school with a very unusual feature, for in the northern corner is a fully functioning Iron Age farm, the Cranborne Ancient Technology Centre, a very effective and popular teaching aid.

Cranborne Common 1947 photograph reference 1845-3055, centred on grid reference SU 092 112

In 1947 Cranborne Common was still essentially heathland, there were virtually no trees and the open heathland still bore traces of ancient trackways. The railway crossed the heathland but, apart from this, the area had probably not changed very much for several hundred years. The heathland was fringed by a network of small fields with occasional areas of woodland.

Today the landscape has completely changed, the railway has gone though most of the heathland north of the old line has now been turned into small fields. Much of the rest of the heathland is now pine plantation, and other areas of woodland have developed over and around many of the small fields.

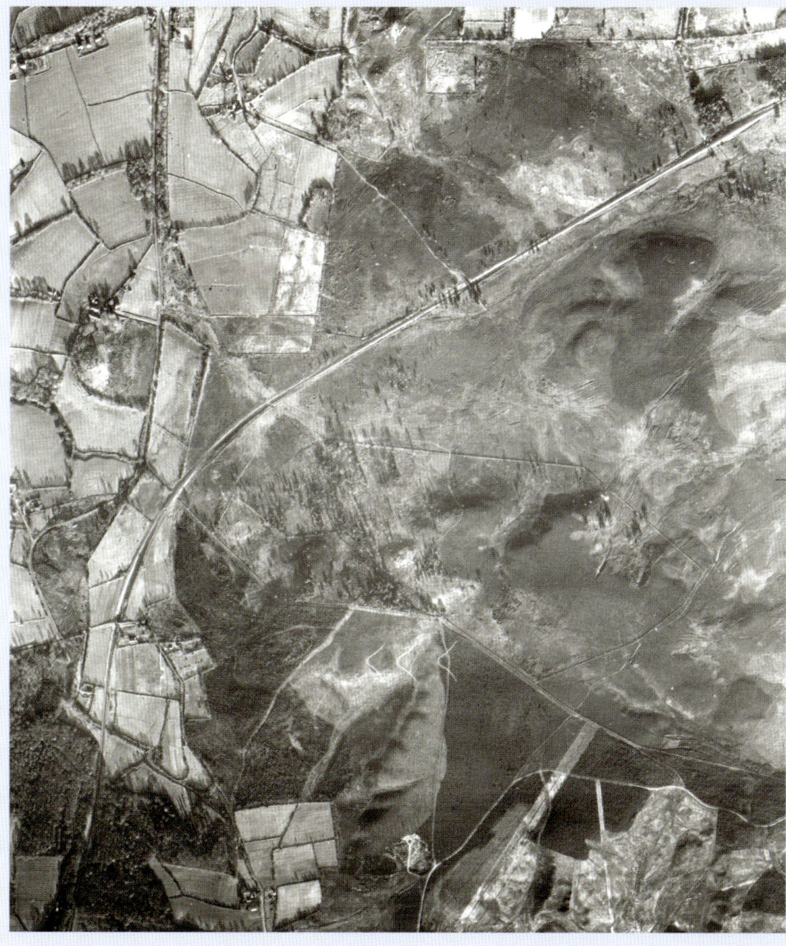

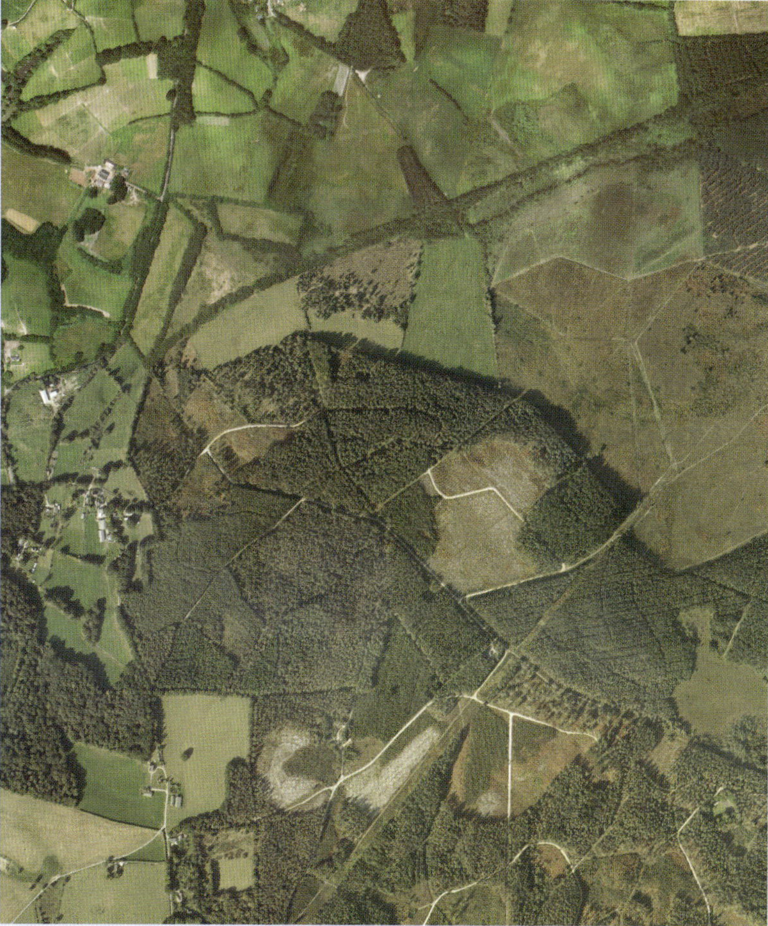

Creech 1947 photograph reference 1821-2418, centred on grid reference SY 908 821

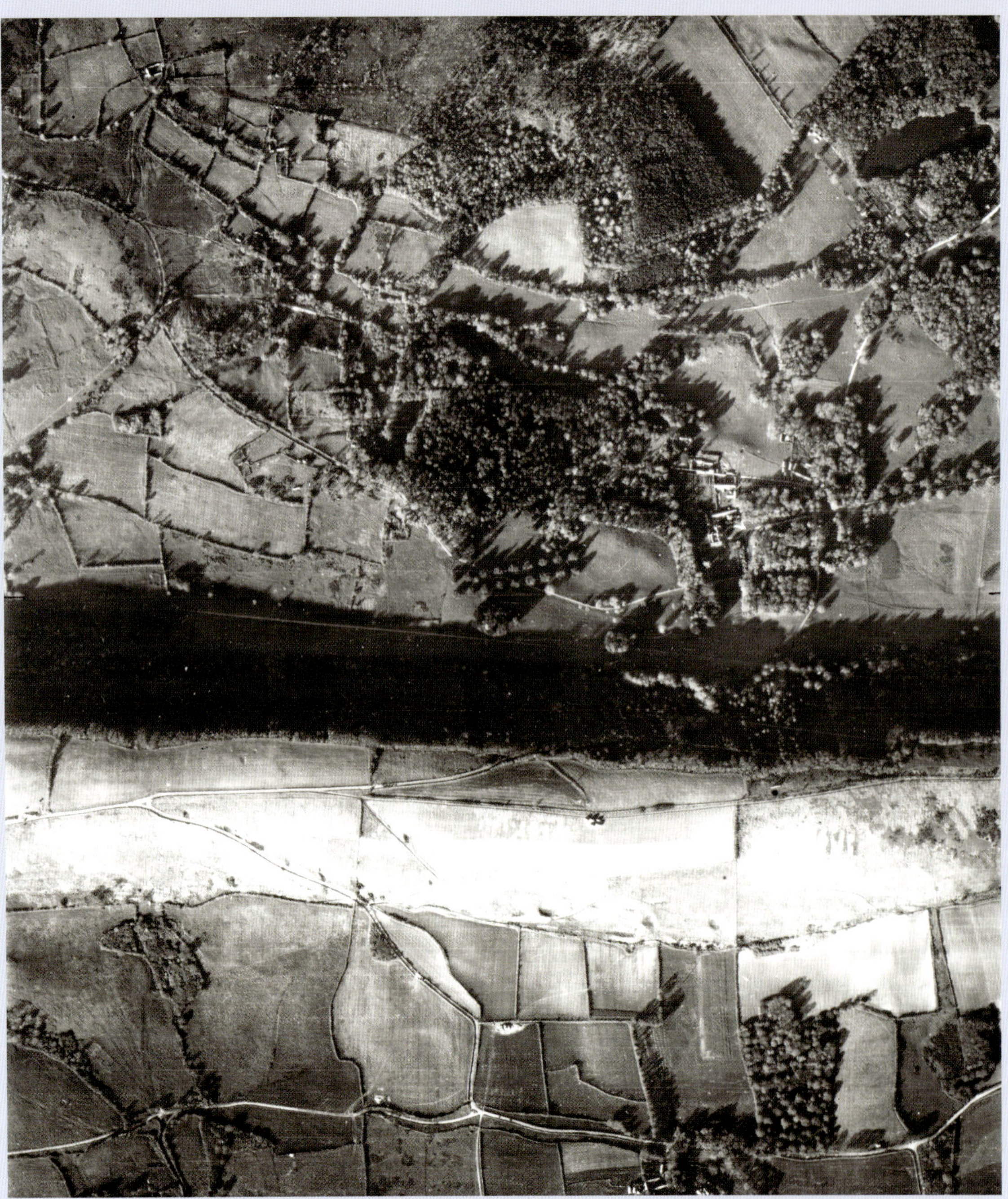

Creech on the Isle of Purbeck shows comparatively little change, but what there is, is interesting.

The picture is crossed from east to west by the massive ridge of the Purbeck Hills, most clearly shown on the 1947 photograph. To the north lies the large house of Creech Grange, surrounded by its park and garden. Here change has been superficial, woodland has spread across some small fields and other distinct areas have lost their integrity as trees have fallen. Some of the heathland has been planted with trees and other areas are now under cultivation, but the landscape is essentially intact.

The same is true south of the ridge, a few hedges have gone, and woodland has spread in a few areas, but it is on the hills that there has been the greatest change.

Halfway along the ridge is a large car park for people wishing to admire the view or walk to the strange monument of Creech Arch, clearly visible on the 1947 photograph. This is an 'eye catcher', a folly built on the hill top to provide an interesting view from Creech Grange in the valley below. It is less easy to see on the modern photograph as the woodland has spread up the hill from the north and now almost encloses the arch. To the south scrub has spread over the downland and in some places is turning into woodland.

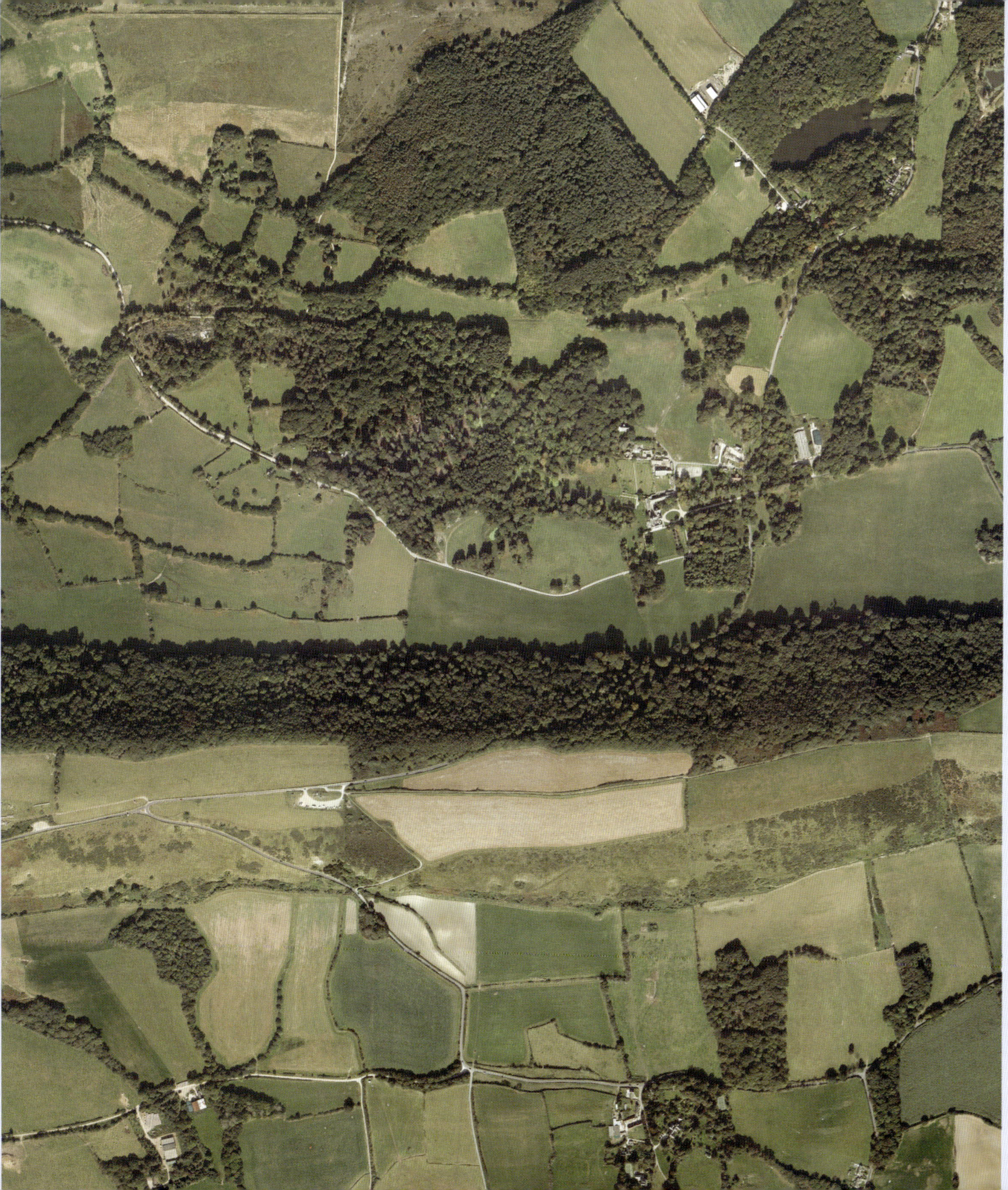

Creekmoor 1947 photograph reference 1934-4041, centred on grid reference SY 998 942

In 1947 this area was essentially rural, although the railway lines from Wimborne to Poole and to Dorchester, crossed the heathland and scattered farmland. Alongside the line to Poole a factory had been built served by its own siding, and there were a few short terraces of housing, probably homes for the factory workers. Almost as dominant is the line of the Roman road that runs in a straight line down the western side of the picture, which once linked the Roman Fort at Hamworthy with Lake Farm, just outside Wimborne, where there was a military supply base.

Today all has changed. The factory is still there, but is now the centre of a large industrial estate, served by a major road that runs along the line of the old railway. The few small terraces have expanded into a major housing development that has covered most of the farmland and spread onto the heathland.

The branch of the railway that ran to Dorchester is now a footpath, and is as clear on the modern photograph as the Roman road. The Dorset landscape has absorbed the railway as it did the road two thousand years earlier.

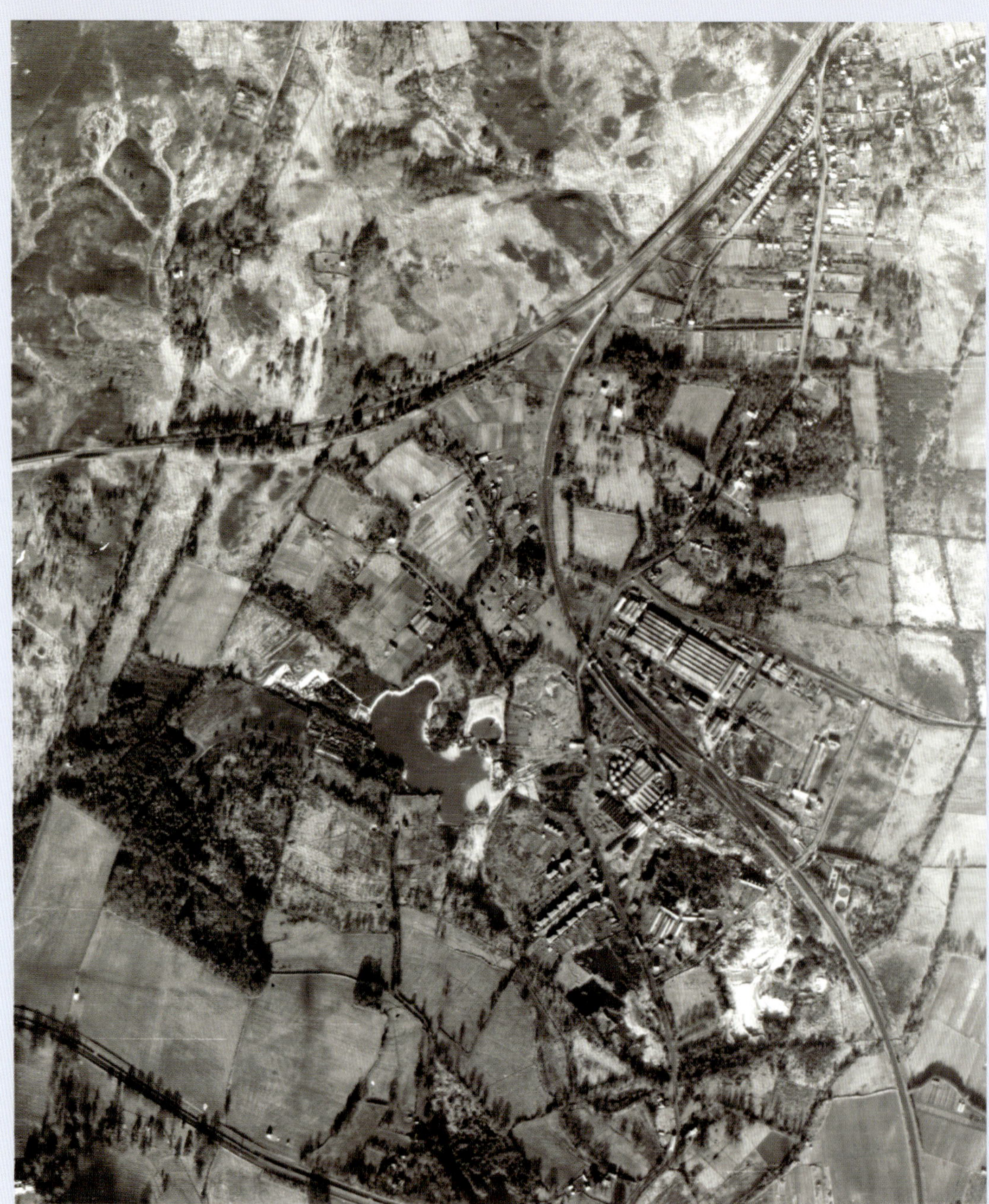

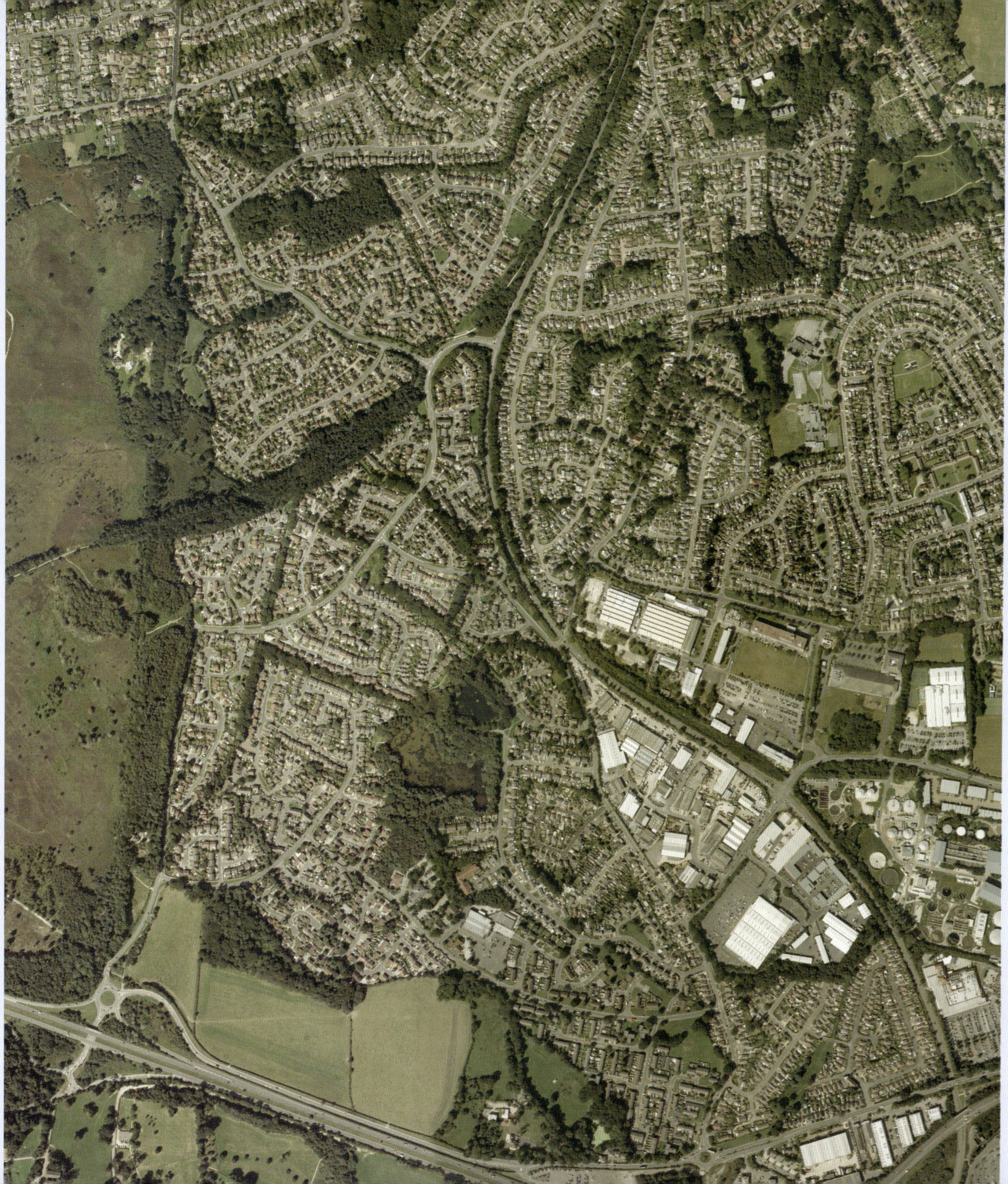

Dorchester South 1947 photograph reference 1934-5085, centred on grid reference SY 688 895

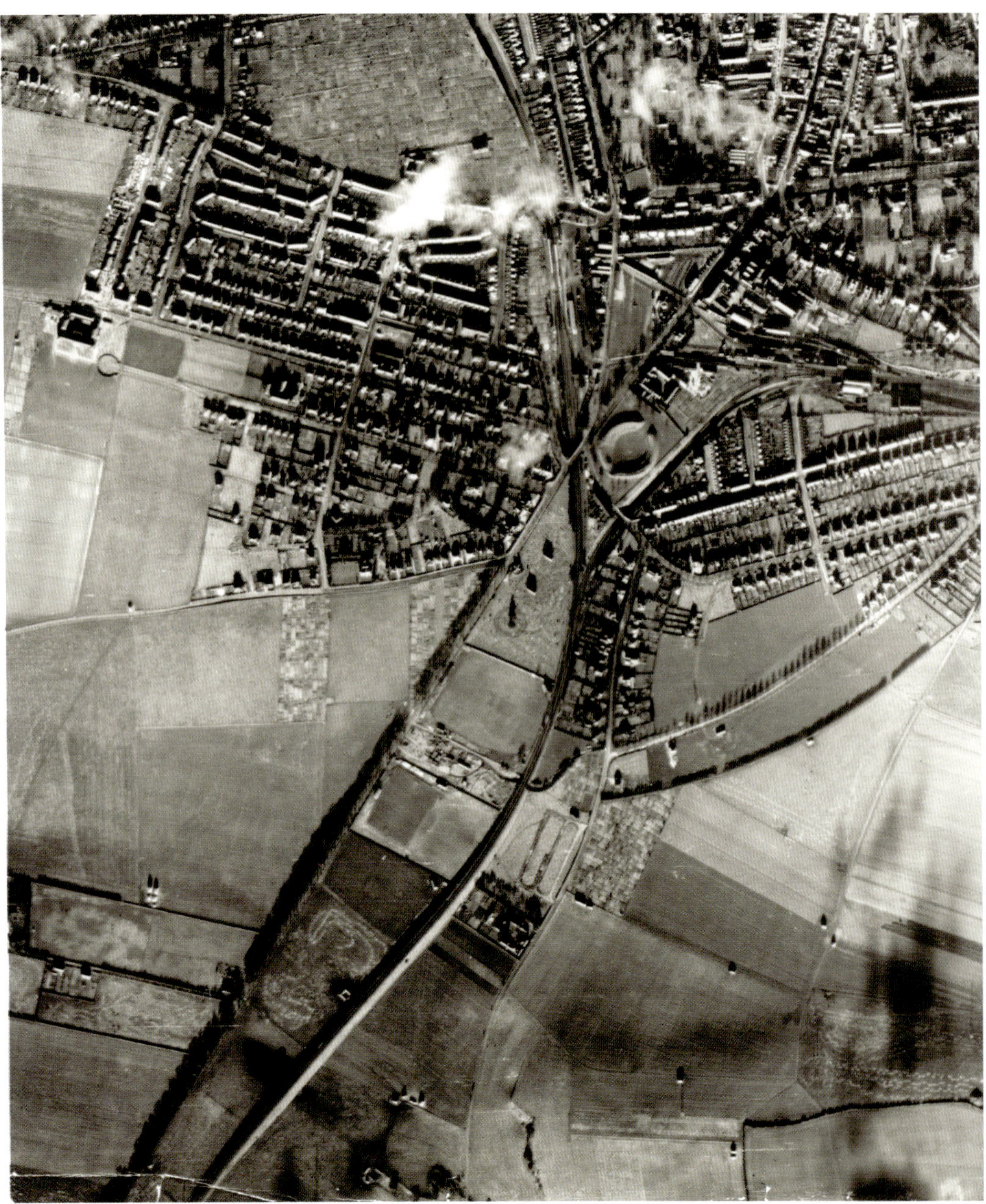

The growth of the county town has been prodigious, and these photographs confirm this. In 1947 the town still effectively ended at the ancient amphitheatre of Maumbury Rings. Its position between the two railway lines bears out the story of how it was saved. When the railway came to Dorchester in the 1840s the Great Western Railway Company wanted to cut through the Rings in building the railway to Weymouth. This led to massive protests in Dorchester. Eventually the company gave in and the Rings were saved. However the men who had led the campaign had enjoyed their time together so much that they formed a club, and so the Dorset Natural History and Archaeological Society, Dorset's first scientific and conservation organisation, was formed together with the County Museum.

In 1947 the campaign to 'Dig for Victory', still had an influence. To the north of the photograph are massive allotments, now the site of the County Hospital.

Running round the south is the Dorchester by-pass. For many years the town of Wareham had been confined within the ancient Saxon walls, now the town of Dorchester is confined within the line of the by-pass, the new city walls.

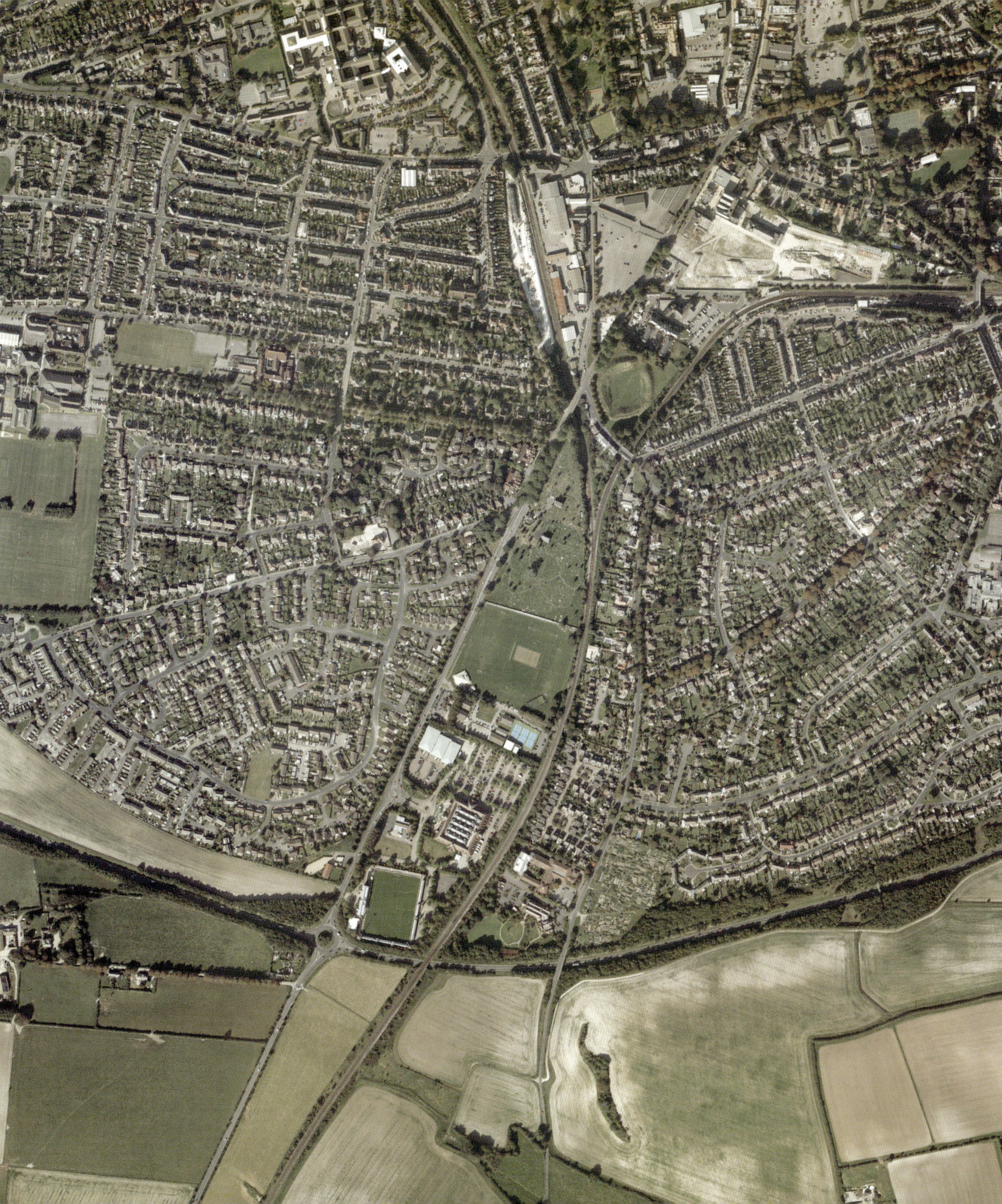

Dorchester West 1947 photograph reference 1934-5087, centred on grid reference SY 672 899

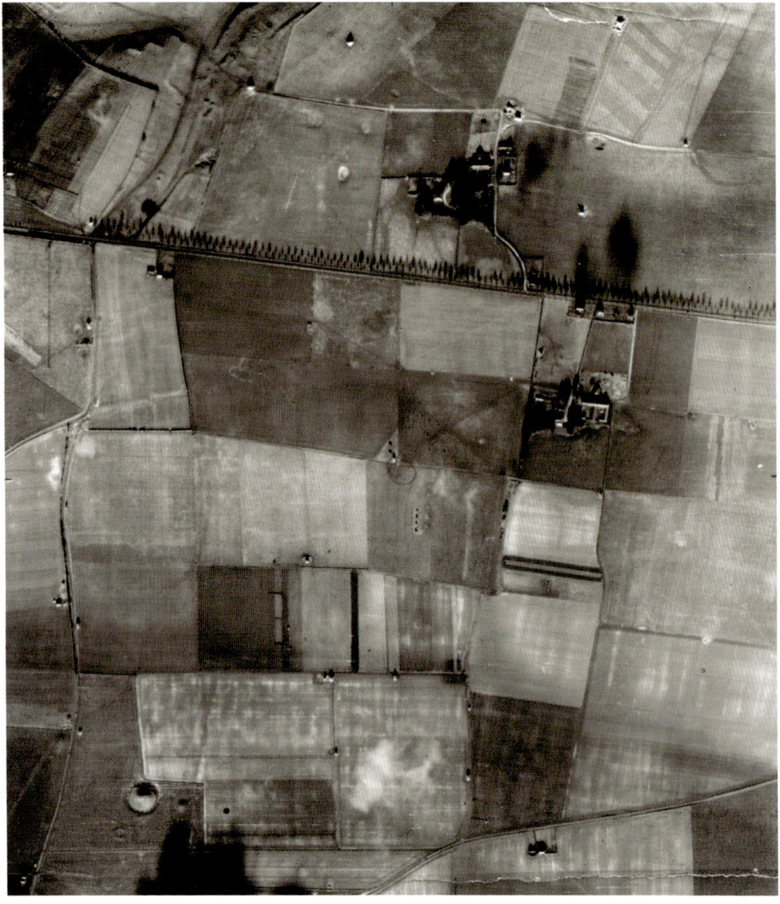

These two pictures are so completely different that, at first glance, one might think that an error has been made and they do not represent the same area of the county. But, amazing as it seems, they do.

To the west of Dorchester, in 1947, there were a few farms off the tree-lined road that ran westwards, following the line of the ancient Roman Road towards Bridport. The farmland was a fairly modern feature, dating from 1874 when the open fields that surrounded Dorchester were enclosed by the Duchy of Cornwall. In contrast the prominent barrows, prehistoric burial mounds, are the only distinctive feature of the southern part of the pictures.

Since 1947 changes have been massive, beginning in 1988 when the Dorchester by-pass was built. This has effectively split the area in two. Outside the line of the by-pass there have been minor changes to the field pattern but nothing substantial, however within the line the new suburb of Poundbury has grown, houses and business have been built. These, unlike many developments elsewhere in the county, have not respected the old field lines but have been imposed on the landscape – only the line of the Roman Road has remained. As time progresses it is likely that much of the currently undeveloped land inside the by-pass will be built over. Change will continue here into the foreseeable future.

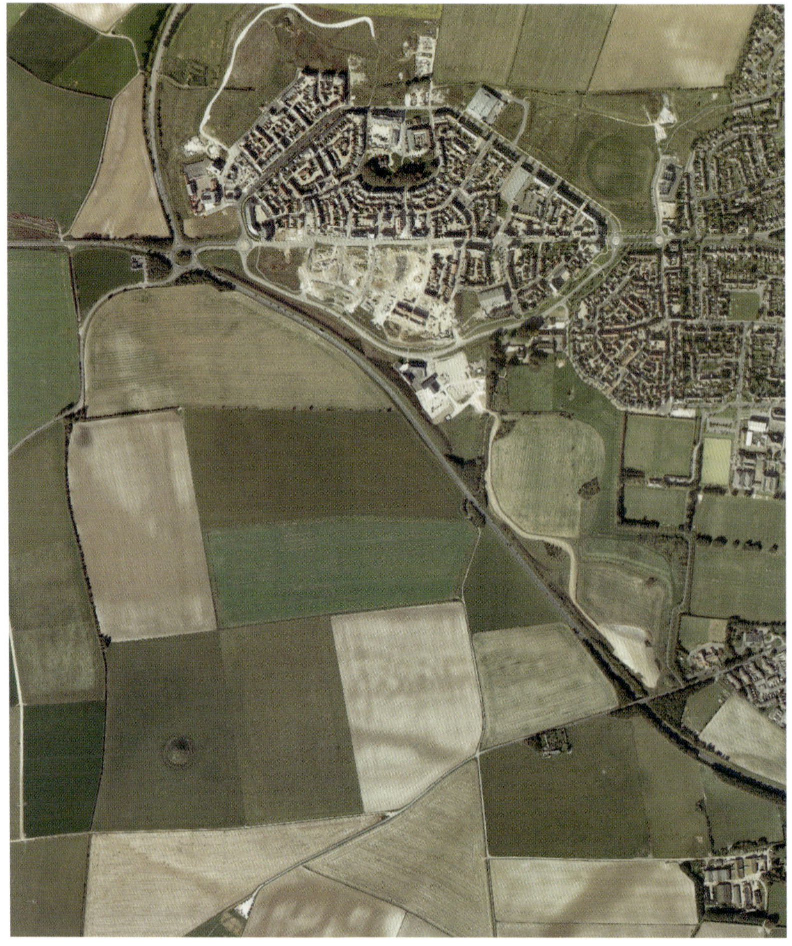

Durlston 1947 photograph reference 1821-3392, centred on grid reference SZ 028 770

The changes on Durlston Head, south of Swanage, have been superficially slight. Woodland has spread over some of the fields and downland, but field boundaries are essentially unchanged and the town of Swanage has expanded very little.

The reason for this is mainly linked to quarrying, the principle industry in the area. Quarries can be seen on both of the pictures. The large quarry to the north of the 1947 picture is now, in part, a mobile home park, but within the modern park are sealed shafts. This is the unfortunate legacy of the industry. Much of the stone was quarried from short shafts, called 'quarrs', which have left much of the land unstable; the dimples visible on the 1947 photographs are some of these shafts. This is one of the reasons why the town of Swanage has not spread south, and also why the field pattern is unchanged. The principle reason that field boundaries were removed was to allow larger machinery to be used. But here it is unwise to take heavy machinery on some of the fields. Also the fields are bounded by stone walls which are harder to remove. Indeed the fields still preserve medieval strip fields, some clearly visible on both the 1947 and modern pictures.

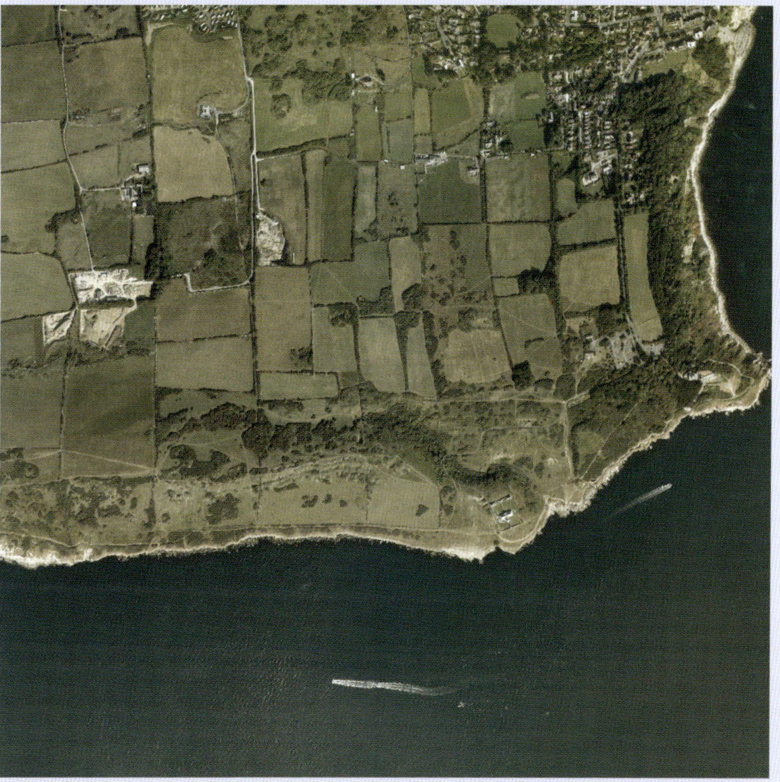

Immediately to the west of the headland, on the modern photograph, can be seen the car park and visitor centre of Durlston Country Park. These modern features seem to have predecessors on the 1947 picture; in fact these are the remains of a massive radar installation which was deliberately removed at the end of World War Two. The equipment was no longer needed but was still too secret to be abandoned.

East Howe and Kinson 1947 photograph reference 1934-4030, centred on grid reference SZ 069 954

The settlements of East Howe and Kinson are some of the small villages that lie on the northern edge of Bournemouth. At one time they were separate, but now they are little more than names designating areas of the wider town of Bournemouth.

In 1947 that process was not yet complete and, although development was spreading northwards, the villages still had a discreet identity. The photograph shows regular terraces of houses approaching the older more organic settlement in the north. Between the houses there are fields and areas of unenclosed heathland.

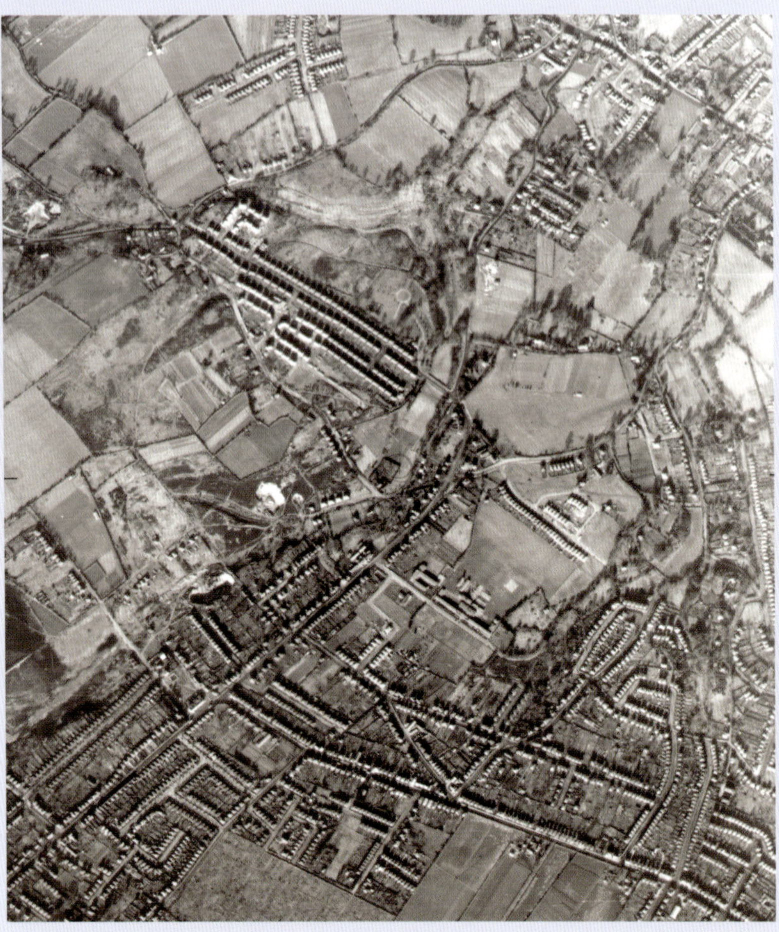

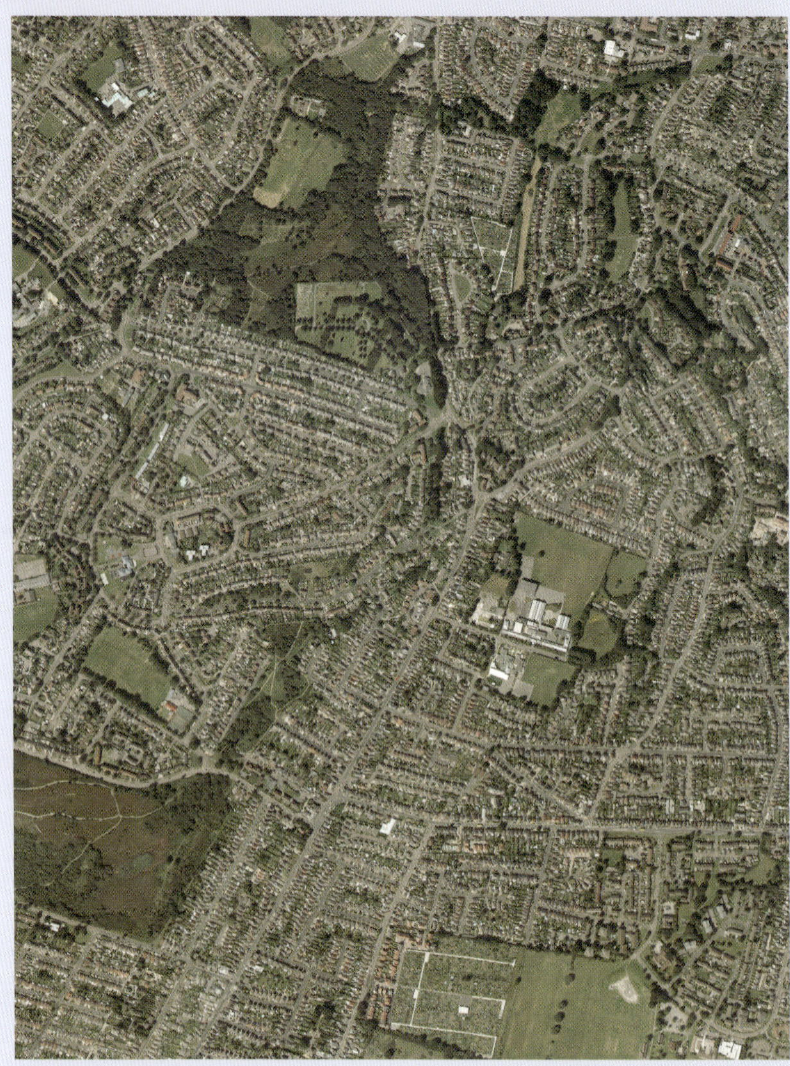

Today most of the land has been developed, the difference between the earlier terraces with their regular layout, and the more modern developments with a curving or sinuous form can clearly be seen. The undeveloped land is either public open space, cemeteries or playing fields; interestingly the allotments visible to the south in the 1947 photograph still remain in use.

Edmondsham 1947 photograph reference 1845-3060, centred on grid reference SU 064 122

The village of Edmondsham, towards the south of the photographs, has undergone few changes. A few houses have been added, to extend the village street, but not many. There have been few changes to the field boundaries. Here, on the edge of Cranborne Chase, fields tended to be large so there was little incentive to remove hedges to make it easier to work modern farm machinery.

Just to the west of the village lies Edmondsham House. In 1947 the park was under cultivation, part of the wartime (and post war) need to grow as much food as possible. Today that need no longer exists and, unlike some other county houses, the land has been returned to parkland.

To the north of the park is Castle Hill Wood, a large area of managed woodland. By 1947 several large areas had recently been felled, timber being in short supply after the war and desperately needed for the reconstruction that was going on all over the country. Some areas had been replanted and the different ages of the blocks is clearly visible. Today the trees are reaching maturity and the differences between the blocks is less easy to see.

In the north-west corner of the woodland are the earthworks of the Norman Cranborne Castle. This 'Motte and Bailey' castle is now hidden in the woodland.

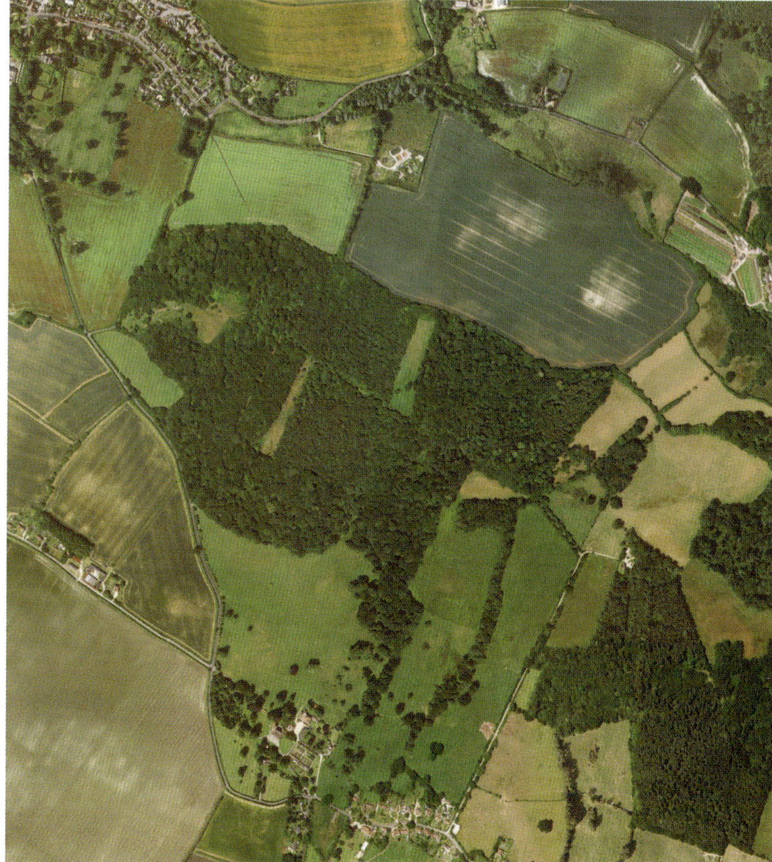

Eggardon Hill 1947 photograph reference 2475-3041, centred on grid reference SY 544 950

Eggardon is one of the more famous hill forts in western Dorset, standing on a prominent ridge overlooking Powerstock Common.

In 1947 the land to the north consisted of small hedged fields with numerous hedgerow trees, and also several areas of woodland. On the eastern side of the photograph there was chalk downland divided into large fields. At the road junction just east of Eggardon is a prominent Disc Barrow, which consists of a small mound surrounded at a little distance by a ditch and bank, dating to the early Bronze Age.

Today the land to the north is essentially unchanged, the field pattern is more or less the same though the woodland has spread. On the downland however the large fields have been enlarged by the removal of hedgerows. Eggardon Camp and the Disc Barrow are unchanged, since they are protected ancient monuments.

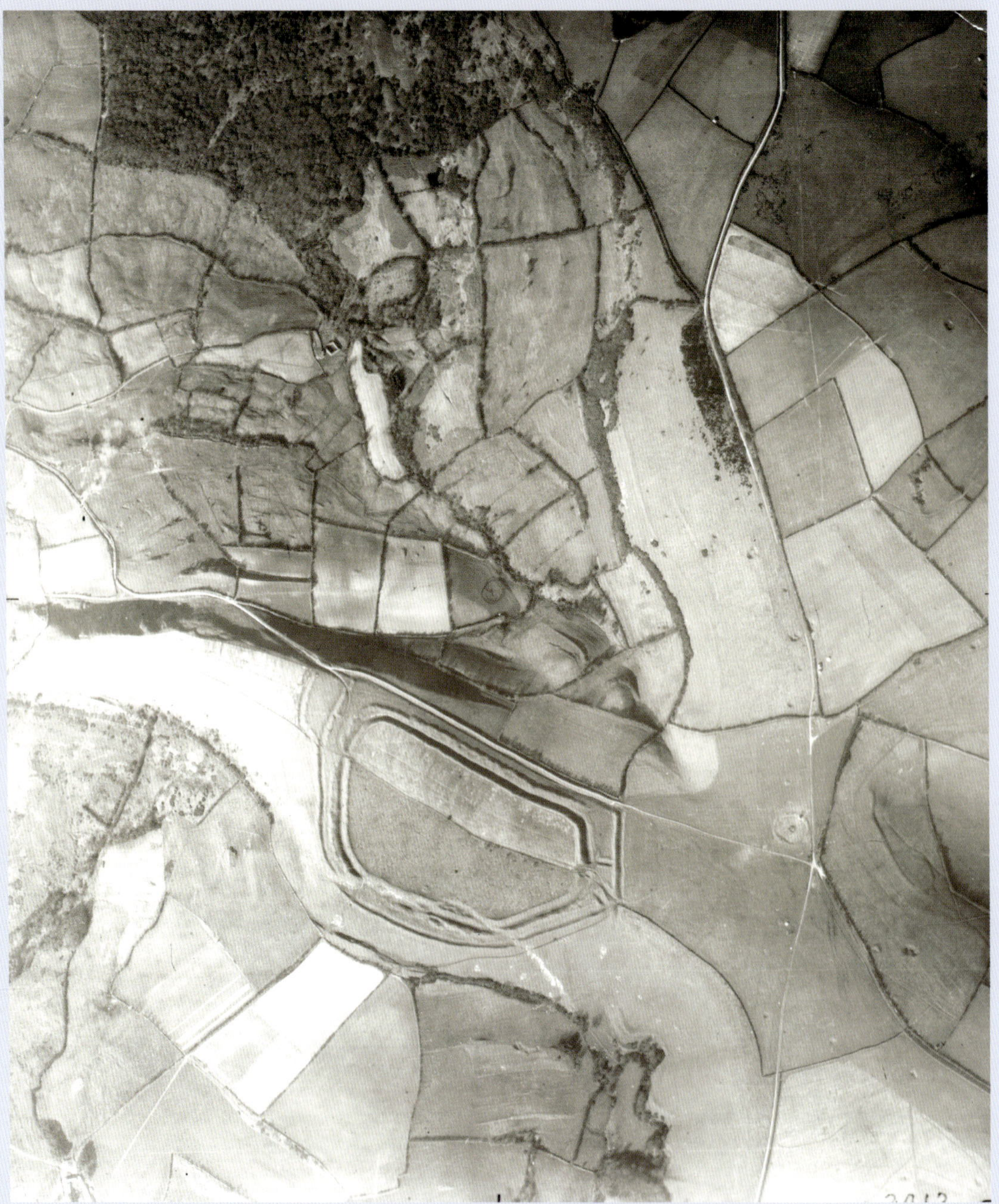

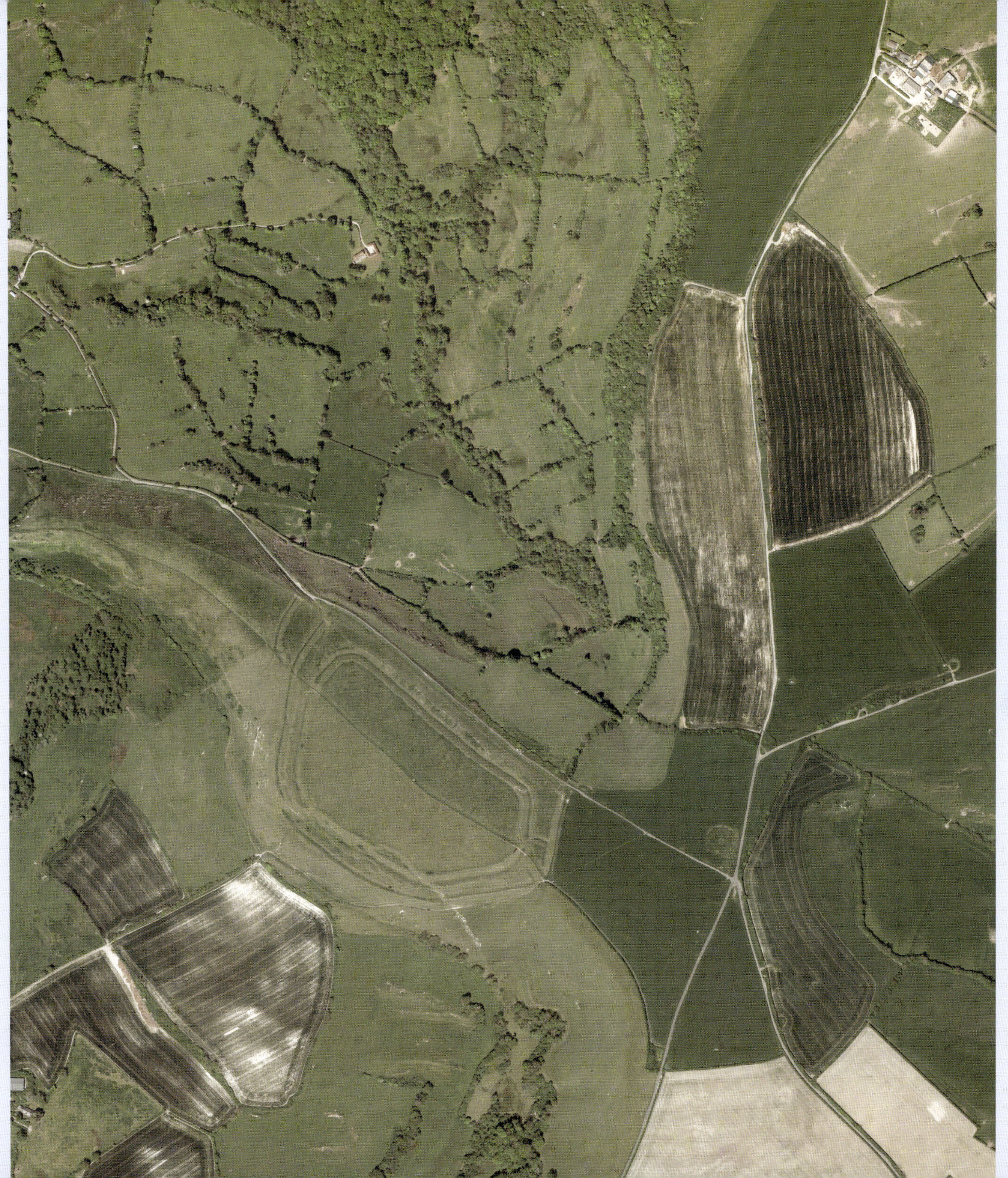

Ferndown 1947 photograph reference 1845-1019, centred on grid reference SZ 072 998

Ferndown on the eastern edge of Dorset has grown considerably in the past sixty years. The settlement had begun with a series of speculative houses built in a grid fashion. These houses can be seen lining the straight roads on the northern edge of the 1947 photograph. Just to the south and east of these houses was unenclosed heathland with a few small paddocks.

Today Ferndown has grown both by infilling between the original houses and building on the heathland to the south and east. The western heathland is now a mixture of small fields, woodlands and areas of protected heathland. The heathland of eastern Dorset is extremely important for its wildlife and many of the surviving areas are cared for.

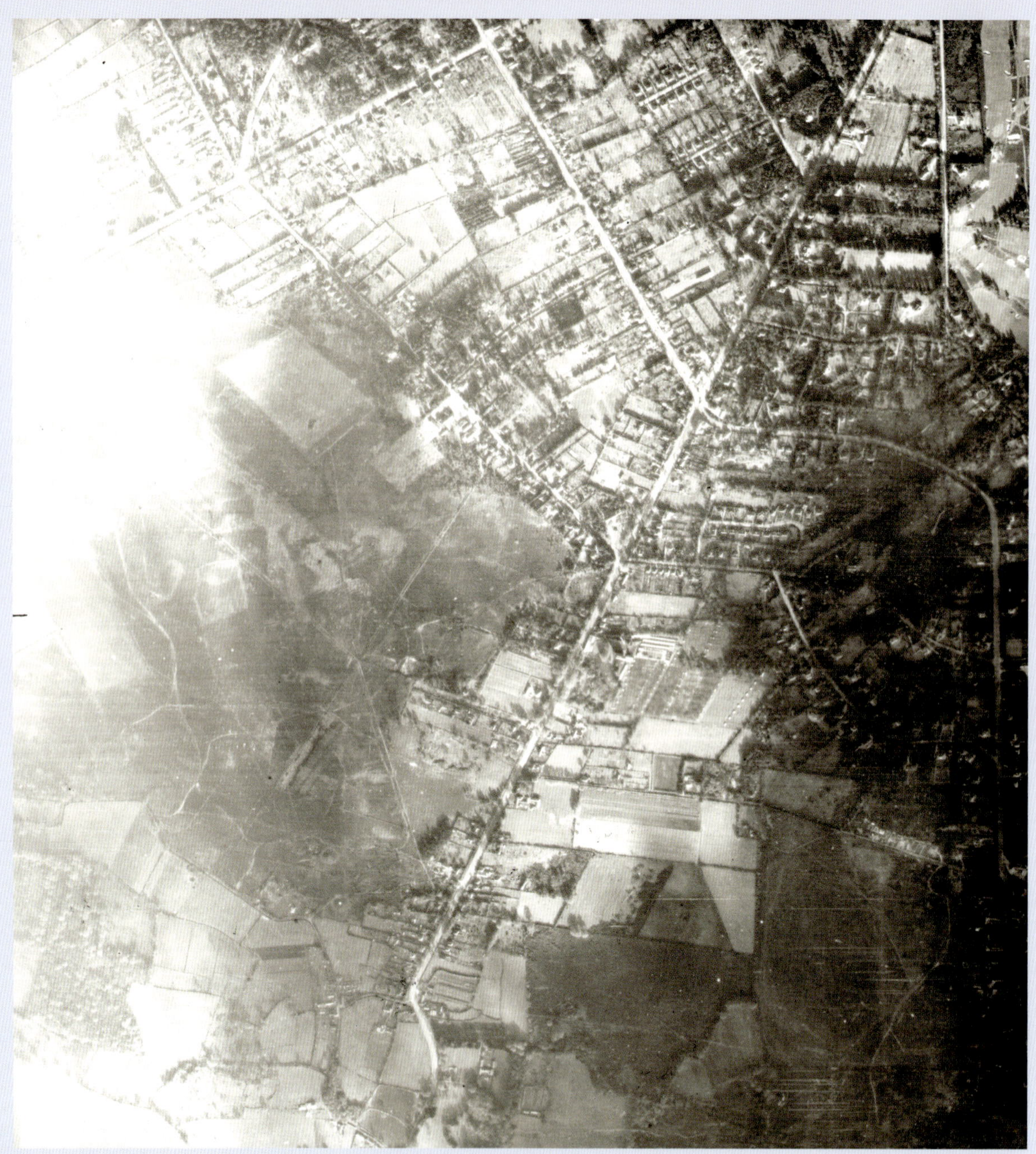

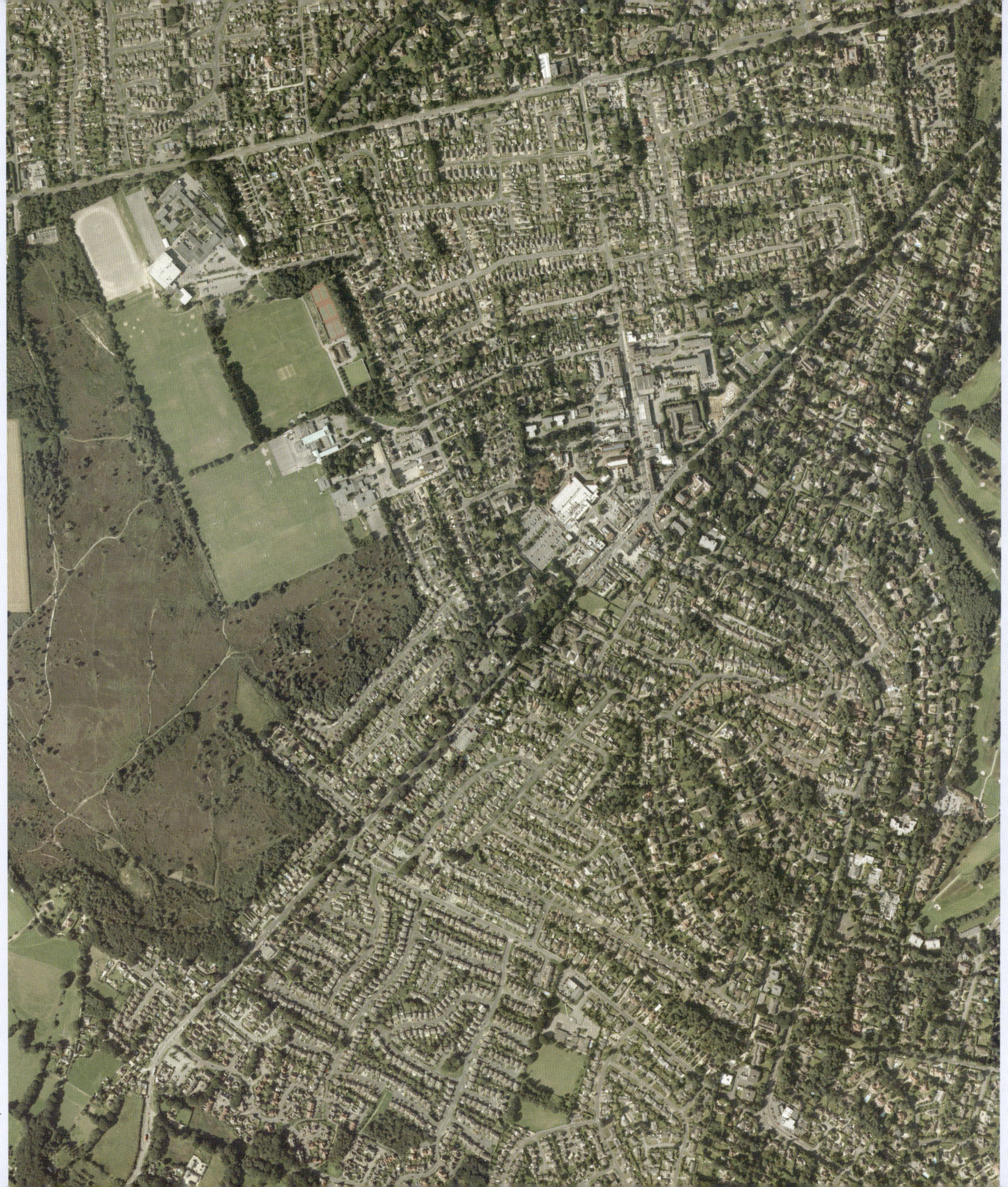

Ferrybridge 1947 photograph reference 1821-3428, centred on grid reference SY 673 753

In 1947 this was an industrial and, above all, military area. Today leisure activities dominate the landscape.

Starting at the northern end in 1947, the large buildings beside the road were the Whitehead Torpedo works, the world's first torpedo factory and, in 1947, still in full production. Running out into the harbour is the long torpedo pier, used for testing and experimentation. The few houses were accommodation for the workers. Understandably it was not a favoured place to live, especially as, to the west of the road was Weymouth's isolation hospital. This spot was chosen as a suitable place to treat people with seriously infectious diseases and build weapons.

Today the torpedo factory is just a memory, commemorated on two memorial stones within a housing estate whilst the isolation hospital forms the central block of a holiday camp!

The road and railway crossed the entrance to the Fleet Lagoon. The railway finally closed in 1965, and in 1972 a new road bridge was built south of the original crossing and a new entrance to the Fleet was cut. This was done so that the road link to Portland was never completely closed.

Beside the road, as it runs towards Portland a large car park can be seen on the modern photograph. This serves the Chesil Beach Centre, and unlike most visitor car parks this is visible on the 1947 photograph – indeed it was larger then than it is today. It was built in 1944 for parking vehicles prior to their departure for France in the months following D-Day as the allies consolidated their gains in liberated Europe.

Finally as Portland is reached the area was dominated, in 1947, by the oil tanks of the Mere Tank Farm. Today these have all gone to be replaced by the National Sailing Academy and its associated facilities.

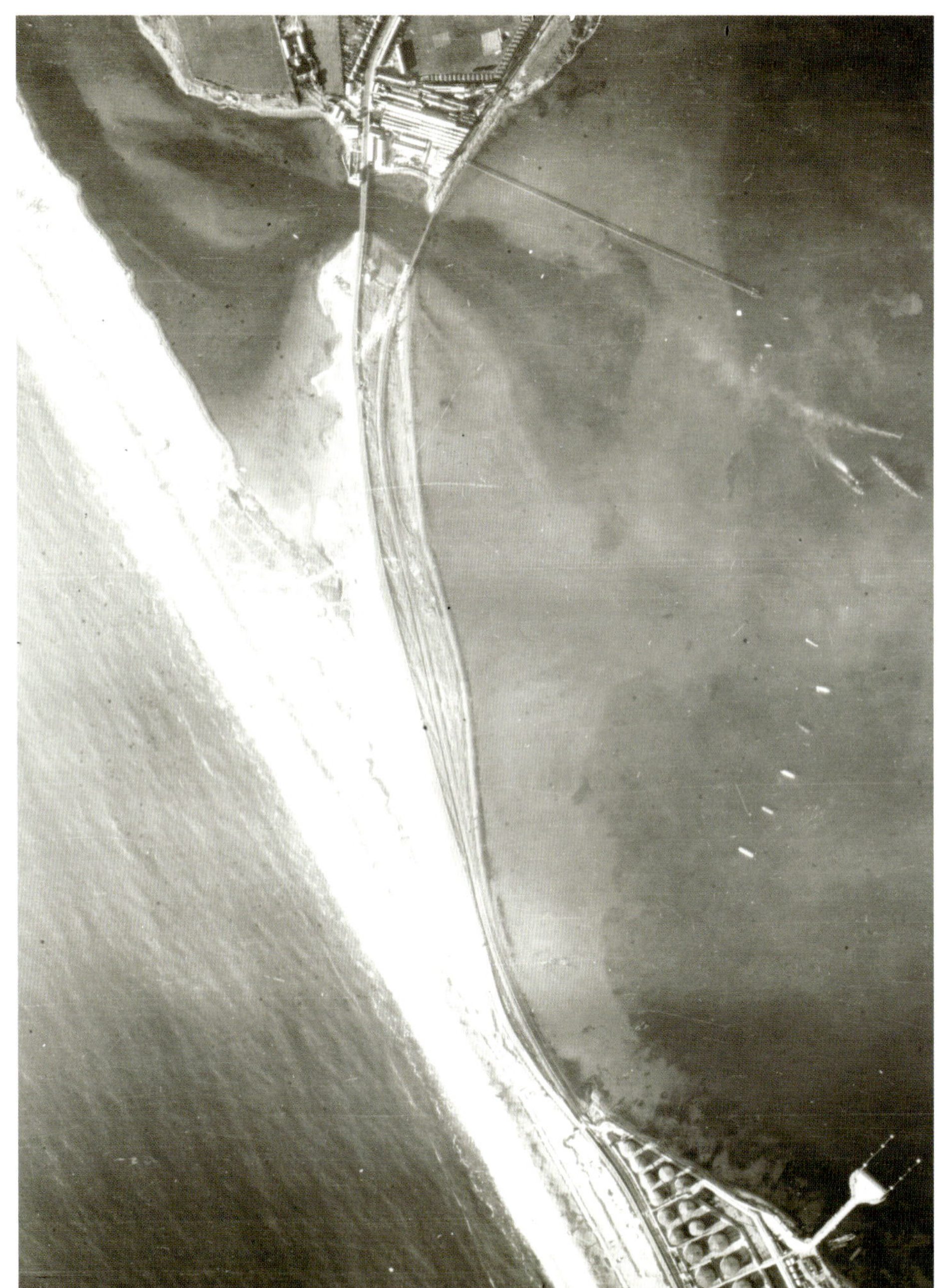

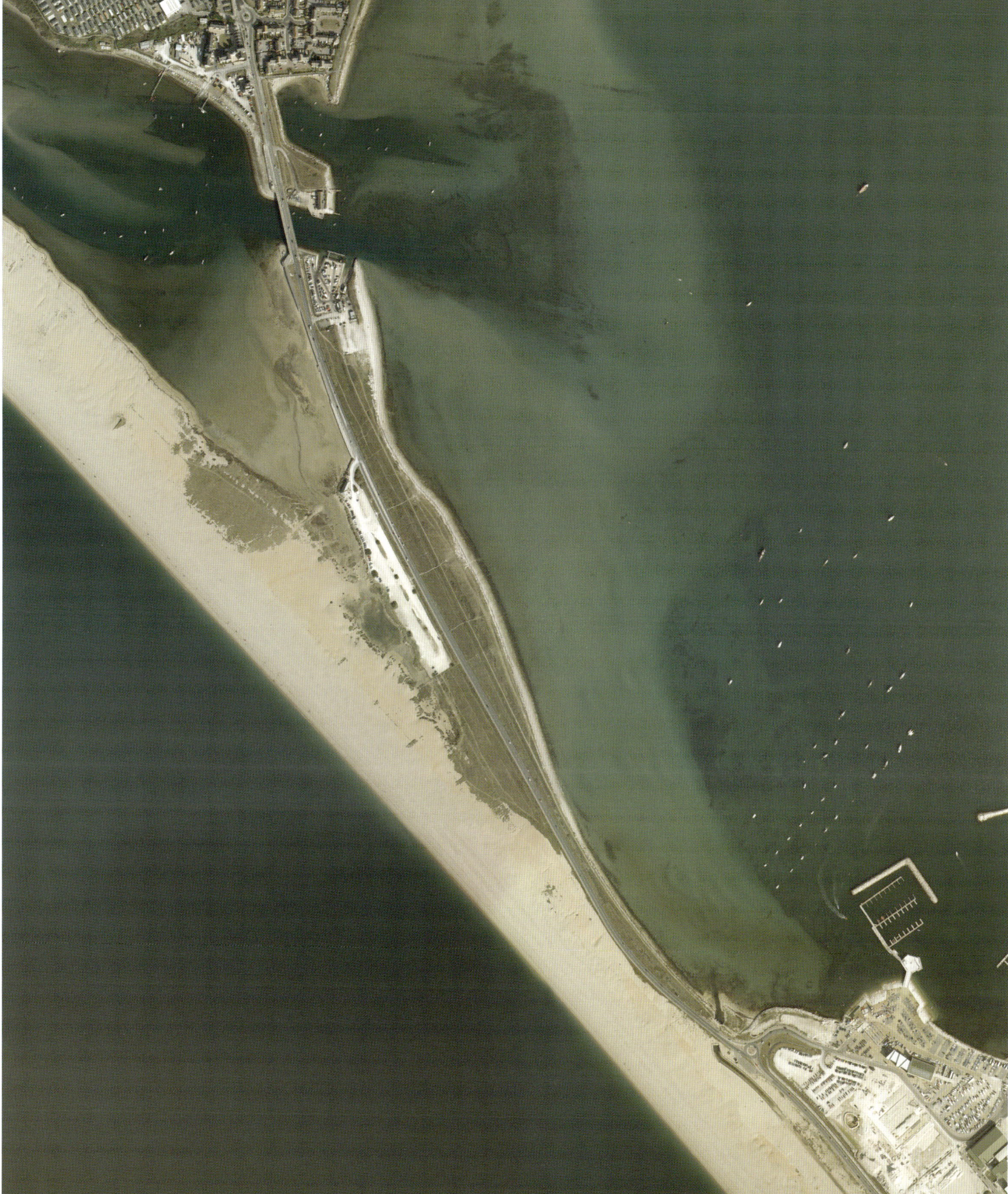

Fleet Narrows 1947 photograph reference 1821-5450, centred on grid reference SY 657 776

The Fleet Narrows lie towards the south-eastern end of the Fleet. Here the Fleet narrows to only a few hundred metres.

In 1947 a small army camp had been built in order to train soldiers in the construction of Bailey bridges, which were temporary bridges that could be used to replace damaged bridges. Inland there was a large accommodation area just marked out by its roads. On the eastern side of the photograph can be seen housing including some under construction. The fields particularly those close to the Fleet show evidence of ancient fields in the form of roughly parallel lines.

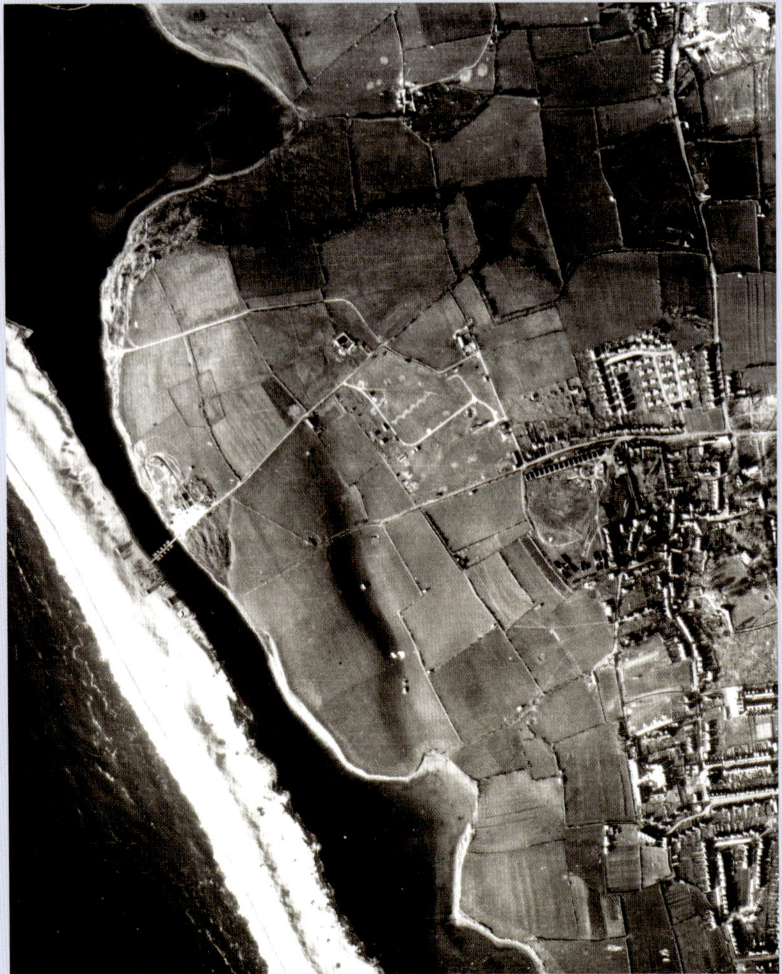

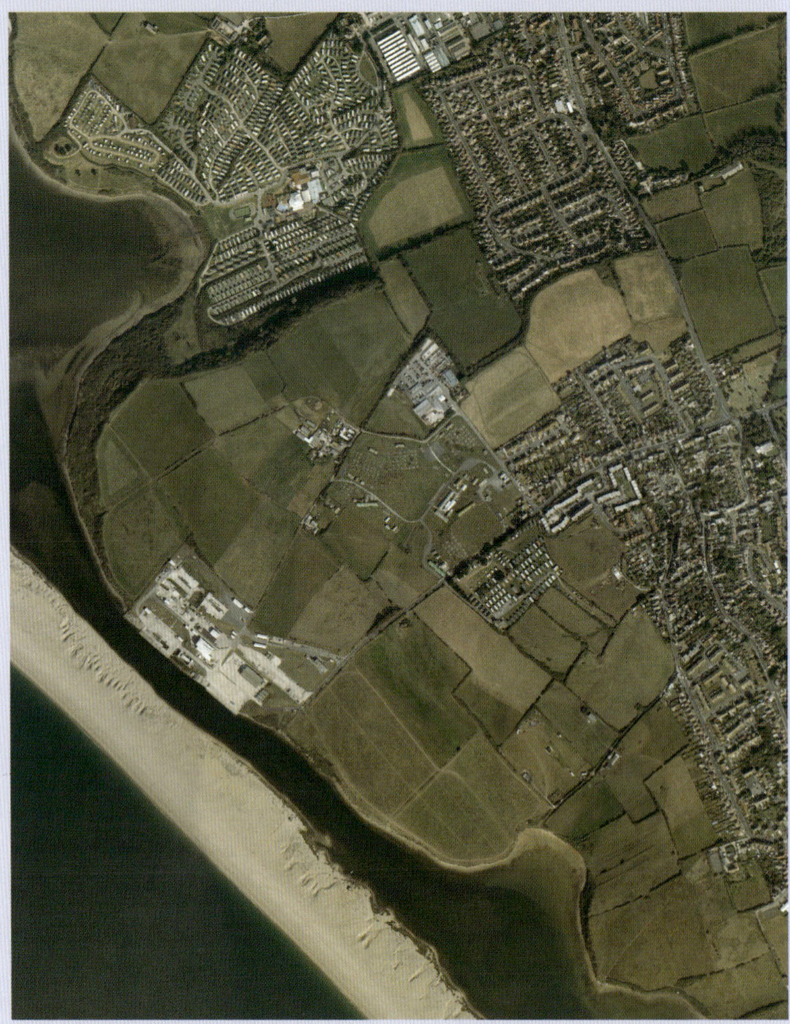

Today the housing has spread and the bridging camp is a permanent fixture. Holiday accommodation is now one of the main activities in the area with large camps of caravans and mobile homes to the north and south.

Gillingham 1947 photograph reference 2038-1091, centred on grid reference ST 812 267

The town of Gillingham, on the northern edge of the county has grown substantially in the late twentieth century.

Unlike many Dorset towns it has not lost its railway, indeed large industrial estates have grown up alongside the line. A by-pass, built in 1990, circles the historic core of the town, and provides access to the large developments to the north and west. Unlike Dorchester where the by-pass is providing a barrier to development, here it seems to have encouraged development on that side of Gillingham.

The development on the southern edge of the town now circles around 'King's Court Palace', clearly visible as a rectangular earthwork just south of the railway line. This was a medieval hunting lodge, used by several medieval kings and queens when they came to hunt in Gillingham Forest.

Away from the suburban development of Gillingham, the field pattern is essentially unchanged, apart from the growth of some hedgerow trees, in some cases turning the hedges into thin, linear, woodlands.

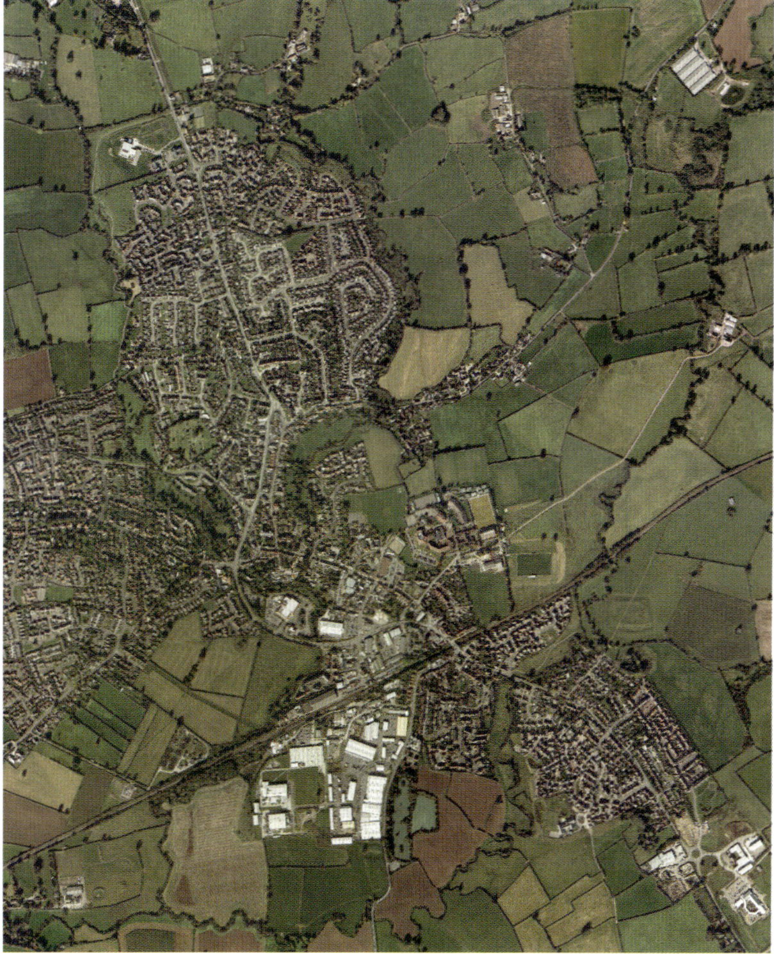

Hod Hill 1947 photograph reference 1934-4161, centred on grid reference ST 867 100

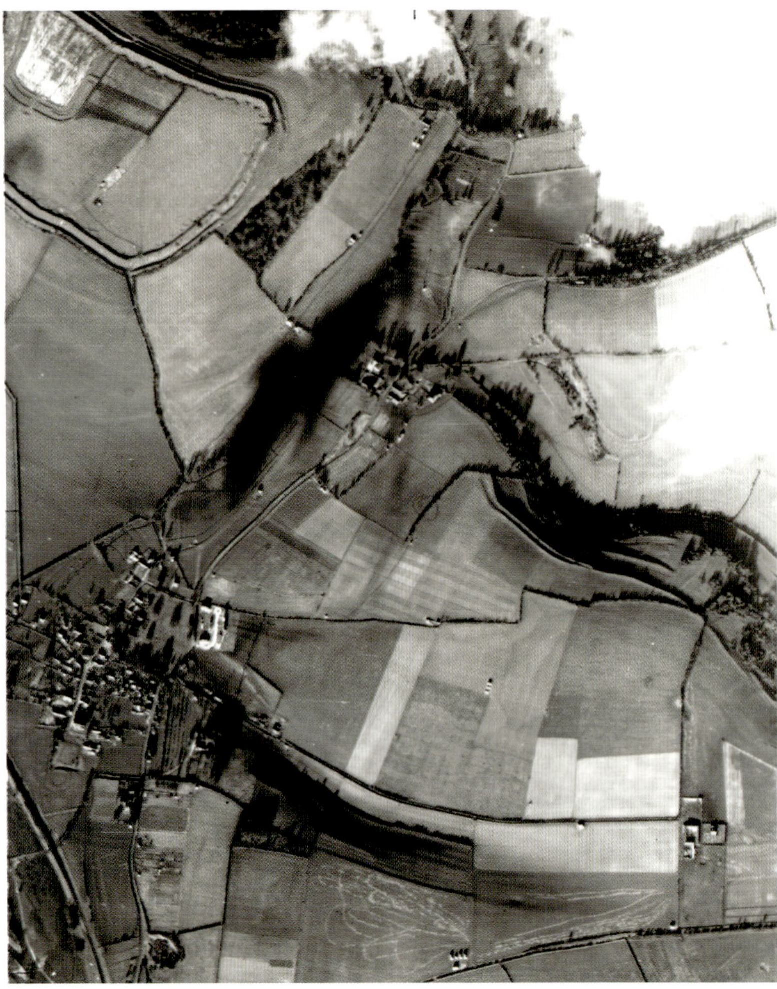

The north-west corner of both photographs is dominated by the rectangular shape of Hod Hill, a massive Iron Age hill fort with, remarkably, a Roman Fort in the north-west corner. Today the forts are under grass and very strongly protected, but this has not always been the case. In 1947 the Roman Fort was being ploughed with the result that the lines of the streets in the fort can clearly be seen. The damaged done by this ploughing led a few years later to a series of excavations of the hill fort by Sir Ian Richmond which provided a remarkable insight into the history of the hill, the people who lived there and how it was eventually conquered by the Romans.

On the slopes below the hill, and indeed over much of the picture, small areas of wood have spread, and there has been some loss of field boundaries. The village of Stourpaine has grown, with infill within the village as well as growth alongside the road to the south, though the railway line that ran beside the village has long since closed.

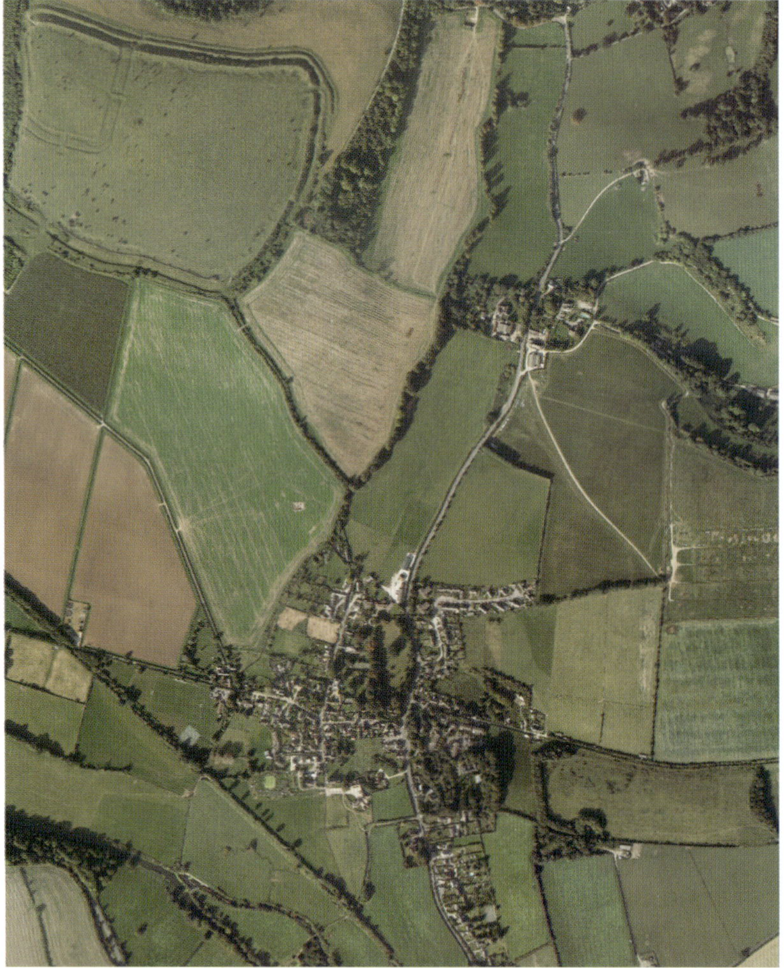

Holes Bay 1947 photograph reference 1934-2042, centred on grid reference SY 997 922

In 1947 Holes Bay, to the north of Poole was fairly quiet, few vessels used it and the only disturbance came from the long causeway and viaduct that carried the railway line from Poole to Dorchester.

Today the situation is completely different. The railway remains and it has helped protect the northern part of the bay from disturbance. Upton House in the north-west corner is now a country park, woodland has been encouraged within the grounds and along the shores of the bay to reduce the disturbance to wildlife. Pergin's Island, apart from being more wooded, is virtually unaltered.

South of the railway the changes have been considerable. Large areas of the marshland have been reclaimed and are now part of Hamworthy. Cobbs Quay has grown into a massive marina spreading out into the bay, and the channels cut to serve the leisure craft have substantially altered the form and layout of the mudflats.

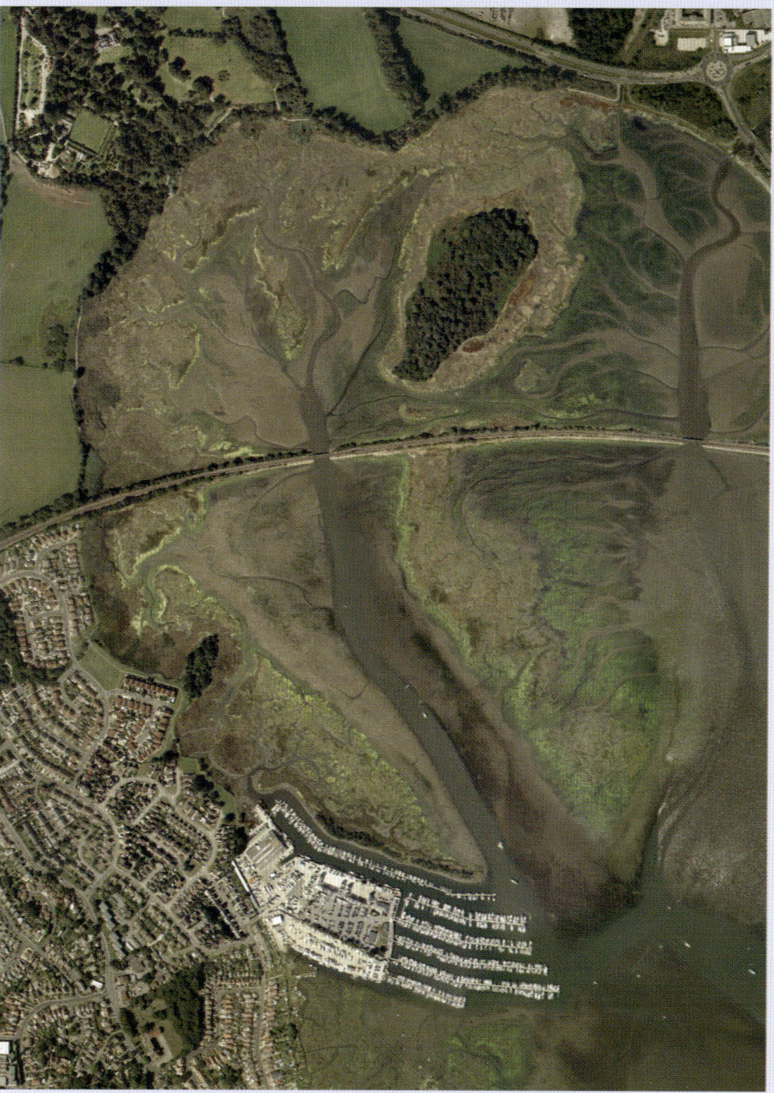

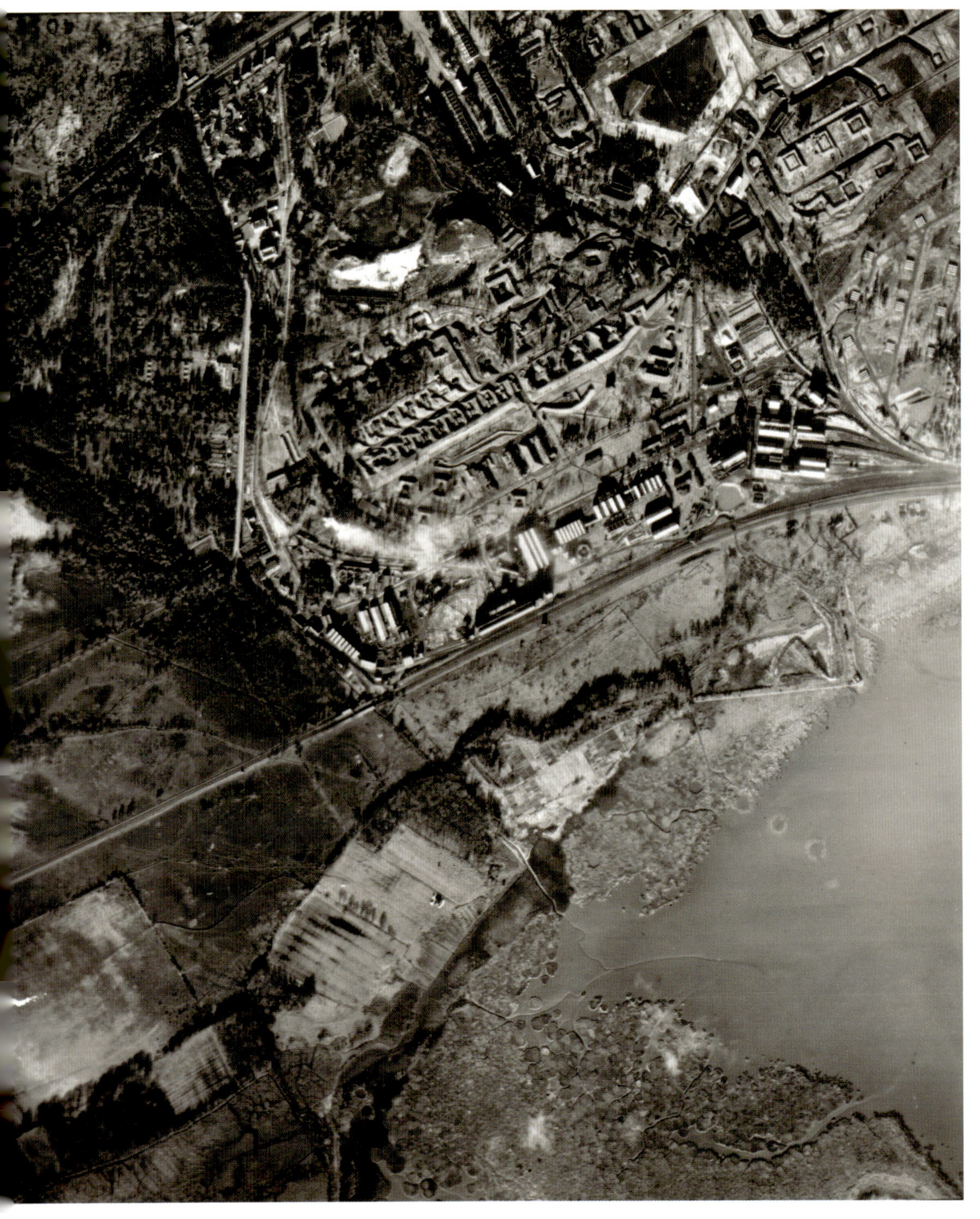

Holton Heath

1947 photograph reference 1934-5049, centred on grid reference SY 947 904

Holton Heath, on the north western shore of Poole Harbour, is an area where an industry has disappeared since the Second World War. The buildings visible in the 1947 photograph formed one of the largest cordite factories in the country. The factory was dispersed over a wide area of heathland as the dangers of an accidental explosion were always present, particularly as the manufacturing process involved nitro-glycerine.

This area had been chosen because it was remote from habitation yet lay on a main railway line. However its proximity to Poole, as well as its military importance, meant that it was always in danger of attack by enemy aircraft. In order to protect the factory it was defended by a series of anti-aircraft guns, some of which were mounted on remarkable concrete towers, one of which is visible on the extreme west of the photograph.

Today the factory has almost entirely disappeared, part of the site is now an industrial estate whilst the rest has returned to heathland, indeed part is now a National Nature Reserve. The concrete anti-aircraft tower has been designated as a Scheduled Monument (the term Scheduled Ancient Monument is no longer used as features from the Second World War or later cannot be reasonably described as ancient).

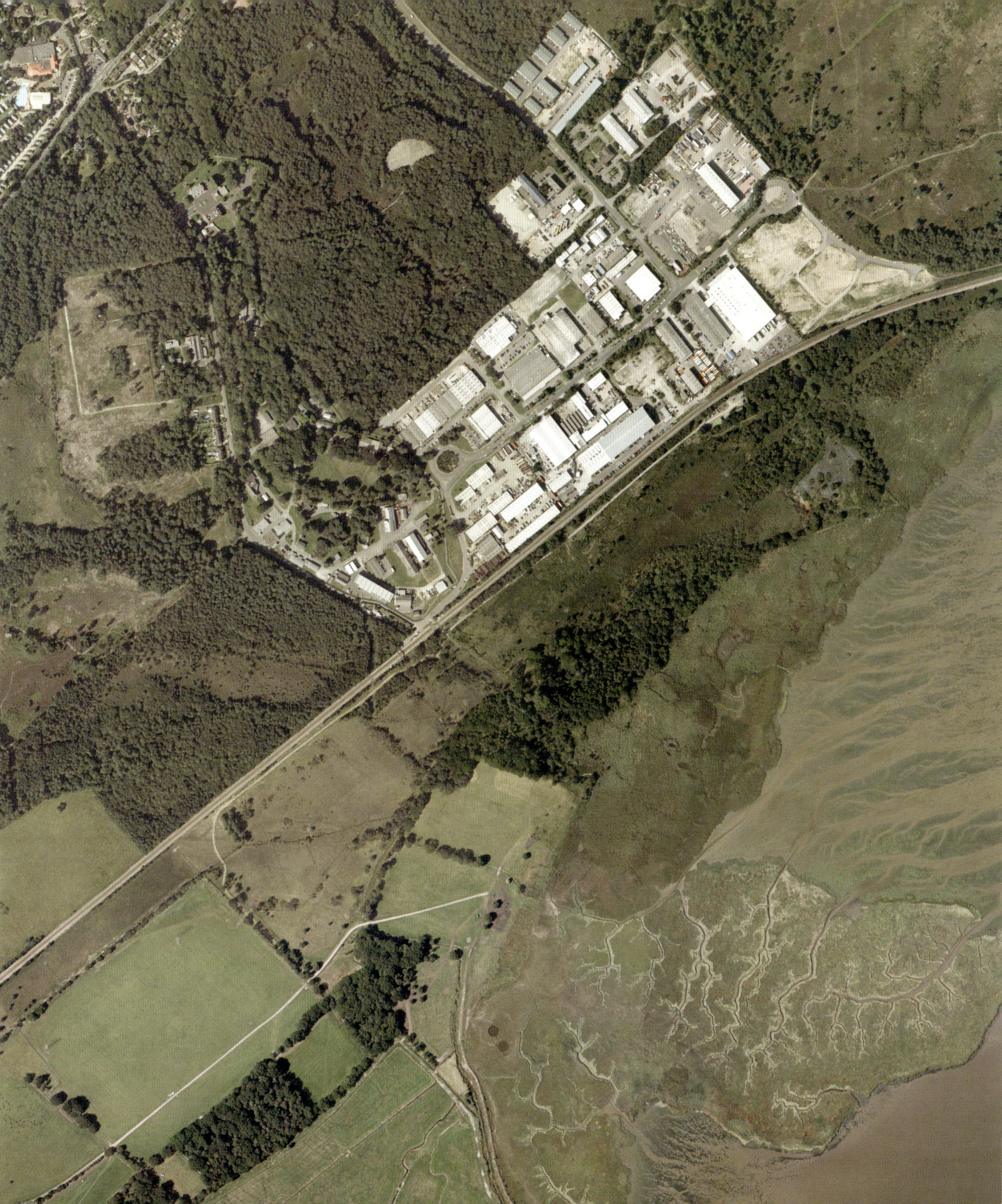

Kimmeridge 1947 photograph reference 1821-3413, centred on grid reference SY 918 782

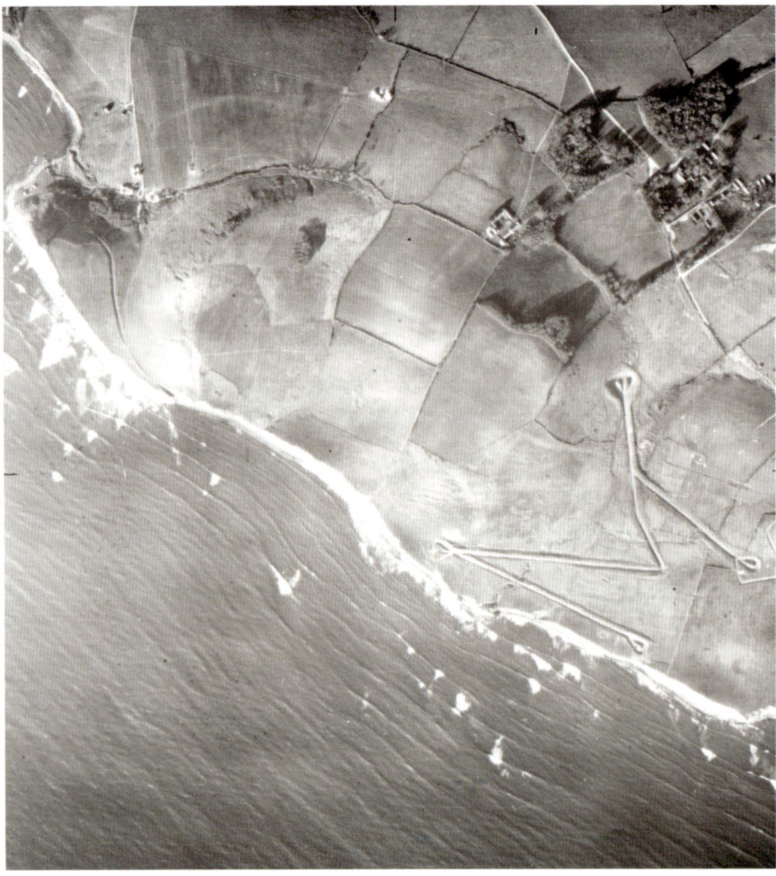

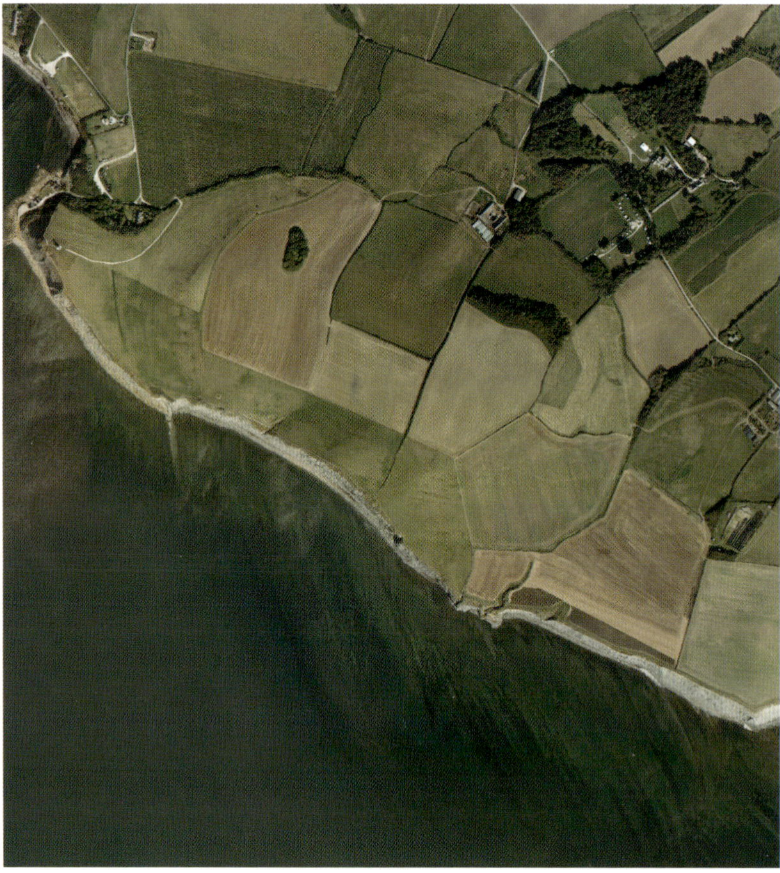

The countryside to the south-east of Kimmeridge Bay is, superficially, remarkably unchanged in the past sixty years.

The main change is the disappearance of the most obvious feature on the 1947 photograph, the curious M-shaped earthwork on the eastern edge of the picture. This was the track bed of an unusual military railway. The engines were completely automatic and carried a gunnery target. By altering a series of controls alongside the track the train could be made to alter direction and speed in a seemingly random manner. This provided the trainee gunners with a more complex, and realistic, target to aim at.

The remains of another old railway line can be seen on the western edge of the picture, just above the cliff edge. This was all that was left of an industrial railway that carried oil shale from one of the nineteenth century mines to a quay in Kimmeridge Bay. All traces of both railways have now vanished.

As with many places along the coast a car park has been beside above the bay, whilst in 2008 Clavell Tower, a folly on the cliff to the south-east of the bay, was carefully moved inland and restored to prevent an iconic coastal landmark from being lost to the sea.

Kingcombe 1947 photograph reference 1974-3390, centred on grid reference SY 546 998

Kingcombe in central Dorset is a tiny hamlet just to the west of Toller Porcorum. In 1947 the landscape consisted of a series of small fields and areas of woodland.

The area appears to be unchanged, with only the substantial growth of woodland in the southern part of the photograph suggesting any

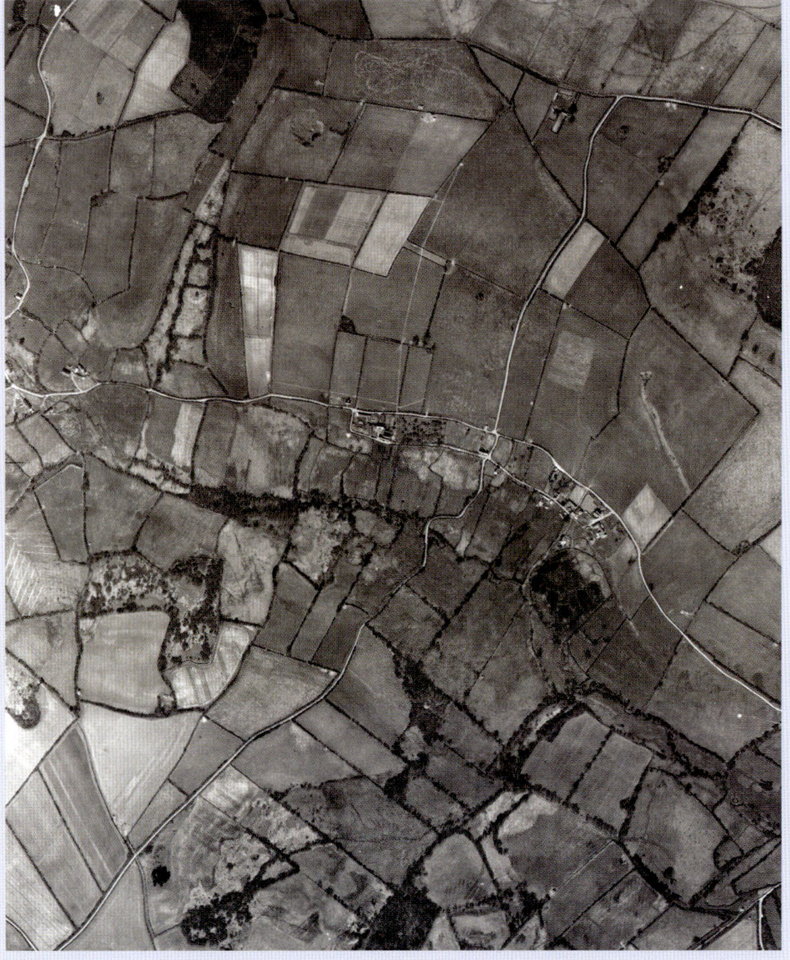

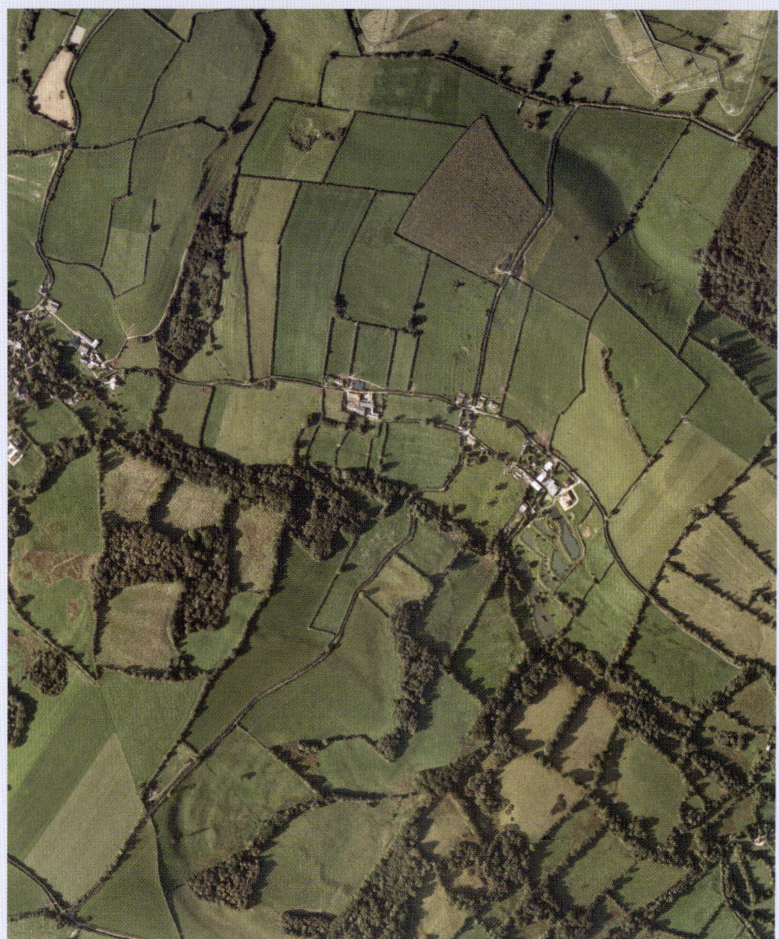

alteration. This area includes the Kingcombe nature reserve. A few years ago the farm came up for sale and it was realized that this particular area had not been managed intensively and was very rich in farmland plants that had become very rare elsewhere. The difference between the low management regime, almost unmanaged land, of the farm and the more intensively managed land elsewhere is easily seen.

Kingston Lacy

1947 photograph reference 1934-1112, centred on grid reference ST 981 014

The great country house, surrounded by its parkland, can seem to be an unchanging fixture in the middle of the changing countryside. However as these pictures show the reality can sometimes be very different.

Kingston Lacy park, as with many other great houses, is surrounded by a dense shelter belt of trees to give privacy to the house and its occupants. Over the past sixty years the belt of trees seems essentially unchanged as, remarkably, do the fields that surround it.

Within the park, however, the changes have been substantial. In 1947 there was a massive military hospital in the eastern part, though the house, towards the centre of the picture, was unaltered. Sixty years later the hospital has completely gone, and many of the trees in the park have gone too. They were badly affected by a series of severe gales in the late twentieth century; today many have been replanted as the estate now belongs to the National Trust. Whilst the house and gardens are being carefully maintained, there is a huge car park in the grounds to cater for the large number of visitors that come every year.

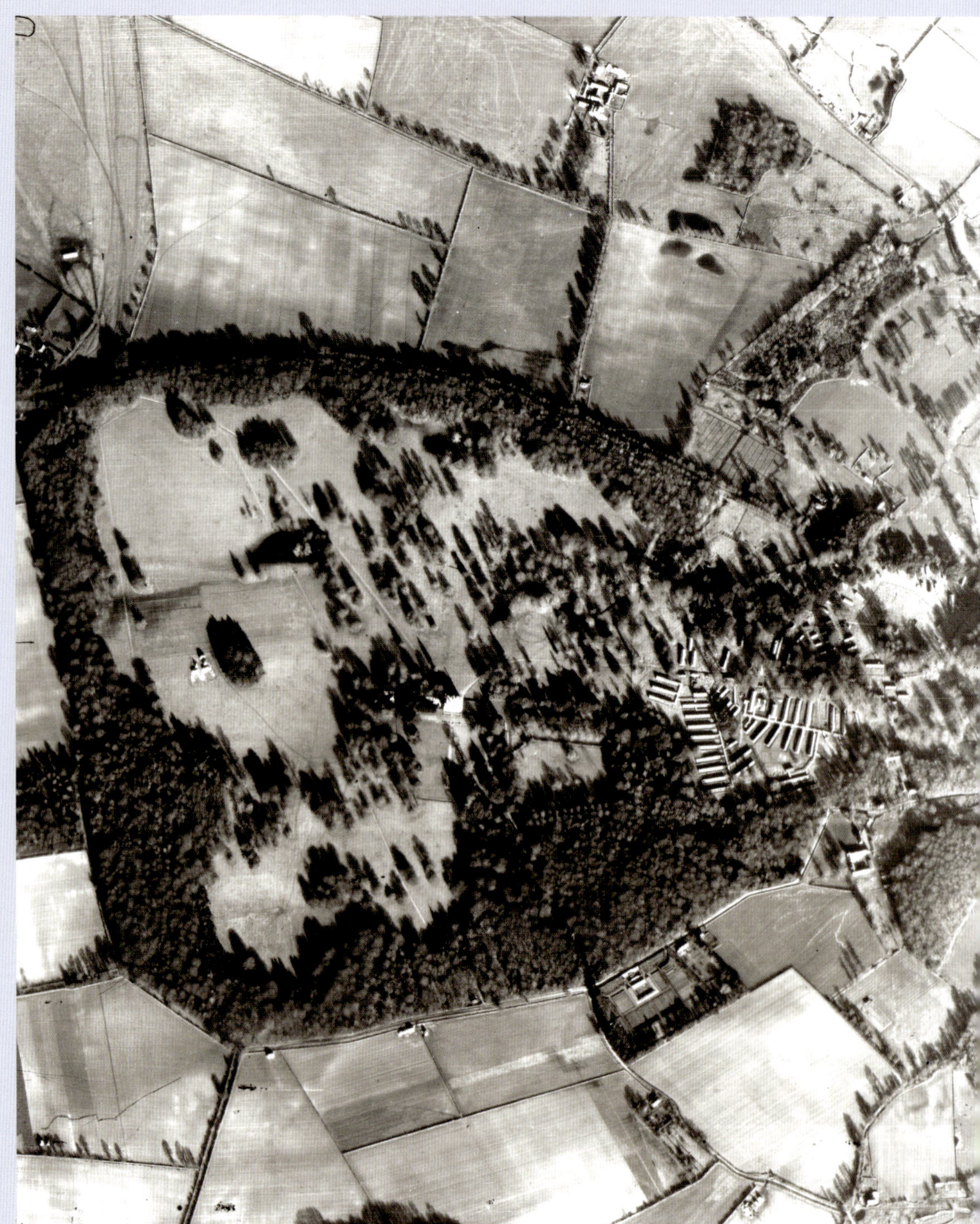

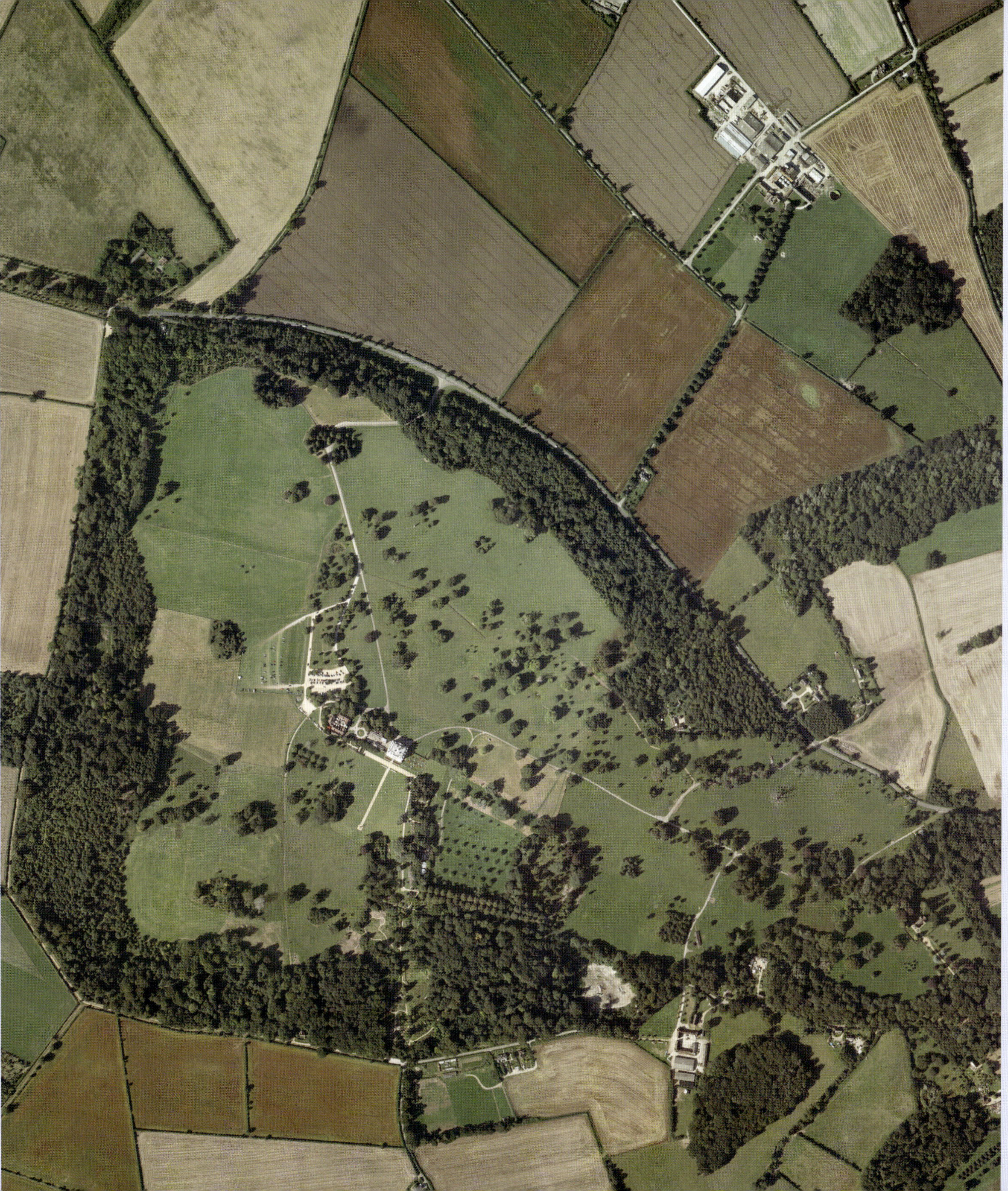

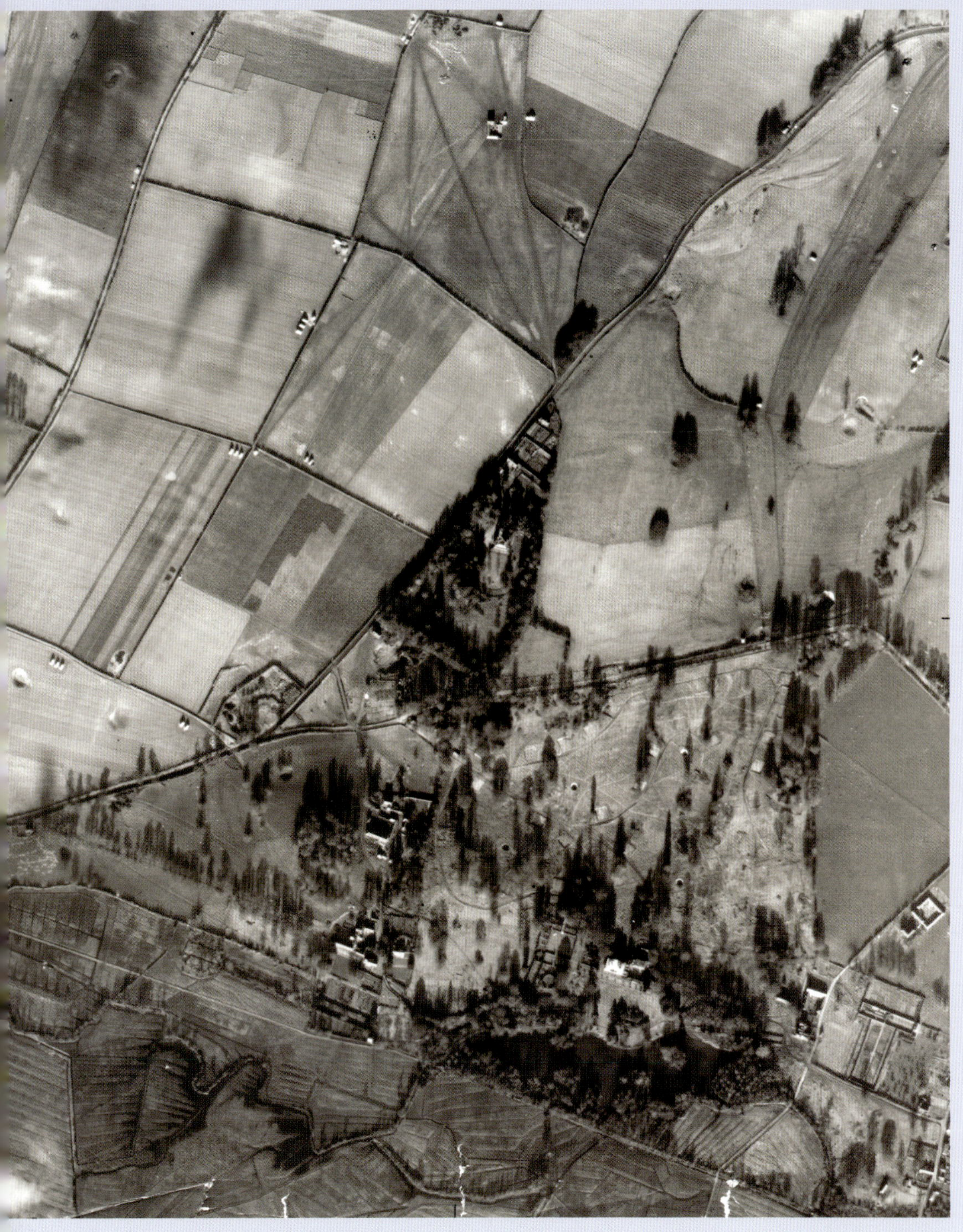

Kingston Maurward

1947 photograph reference 1934-2081, centred on grid reference SY 719 913

Kingston Maurward is another great country house that has changed considerably, but here the changes have been even more dramatic.

During the Second World War Kingston Maurward was taken over by the American army, and the park was used for storing fuel. Some of the buildings in the park, visible on the 1947 photograph, were probably connected with this.

Shortly after this photograph was taken, the house was purchased by the County Council for use as an agricultural college. Kingston Maurward College has thrived, the gardens are beautifully maintained (by horticultural students) and a fine avenue has been developed north of the house. Within the park numerous additional buildings have been built to serve the college.

In the fields to the south of the house there are numerous traces of an old water meadow system.

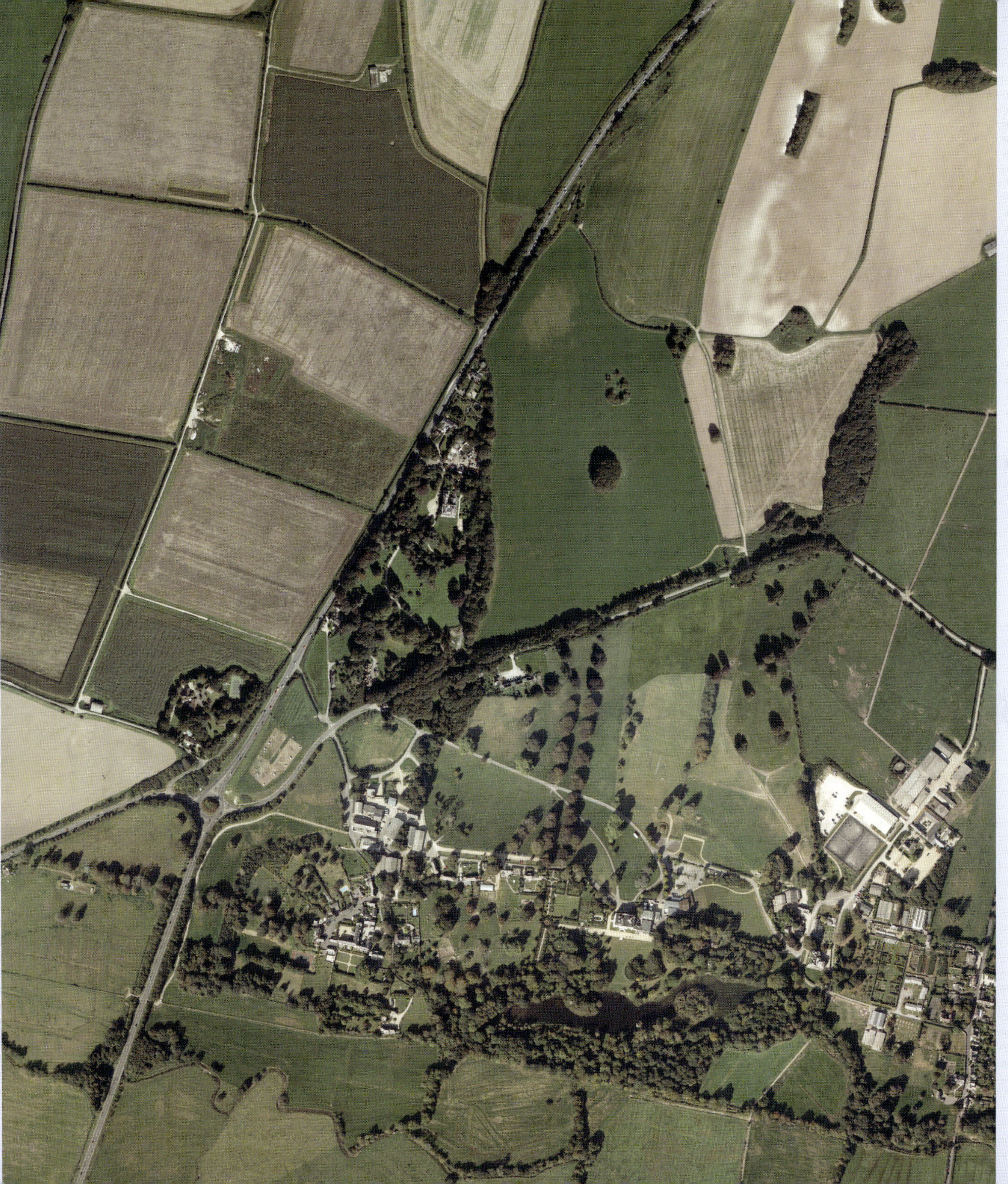

Knowlton and Wimborne St Giles

1947 photograph reference 1845-6039, centred on grid reference SU 033 106

There are two areas of particular interest in these pictures.

In the south-west corner lies the remarkable ancient site of Knowlton. Here the ruins of a Norman church can be found inside a prehistoric 'henge', a circular earthwork consisting of a bank with a ditch inside it, of Neolithic date, about 3000BC. Other henges once existed in the area, as do many barrows, indeed aerial photography has revealed a huge complex of prehistoric monuments around the henge.

The henge has remained virtually unaltered since 1947, as it has long been a protected monument. The large fields around the henge have changed little, as they were big in 1947 and so there was not the need to remove hedgerows to make them accessible to modern machinery.

The greatest change has taken place to the north. In 1947 this area was taken up by the park of Wimborne St Giles. The park was surrounded by its shelter belt of trees, large areas of parkland surrounded the house with its formal gardens, and a fine avenue ran eastwards from the house. The house had been used by an evacuated school during the Second World War, and this had not seriously affected the buildings and park. Sadly the house fell on bad times after the war, part of the park was given over to agriculture, the gardens fell into disuse, and the avenue was neglected. Only recently has an attempt been made to restore the house and its grounds. Perhaps when a photograph is taken of this area in sixty years' time the house will once again stand proud in its park.

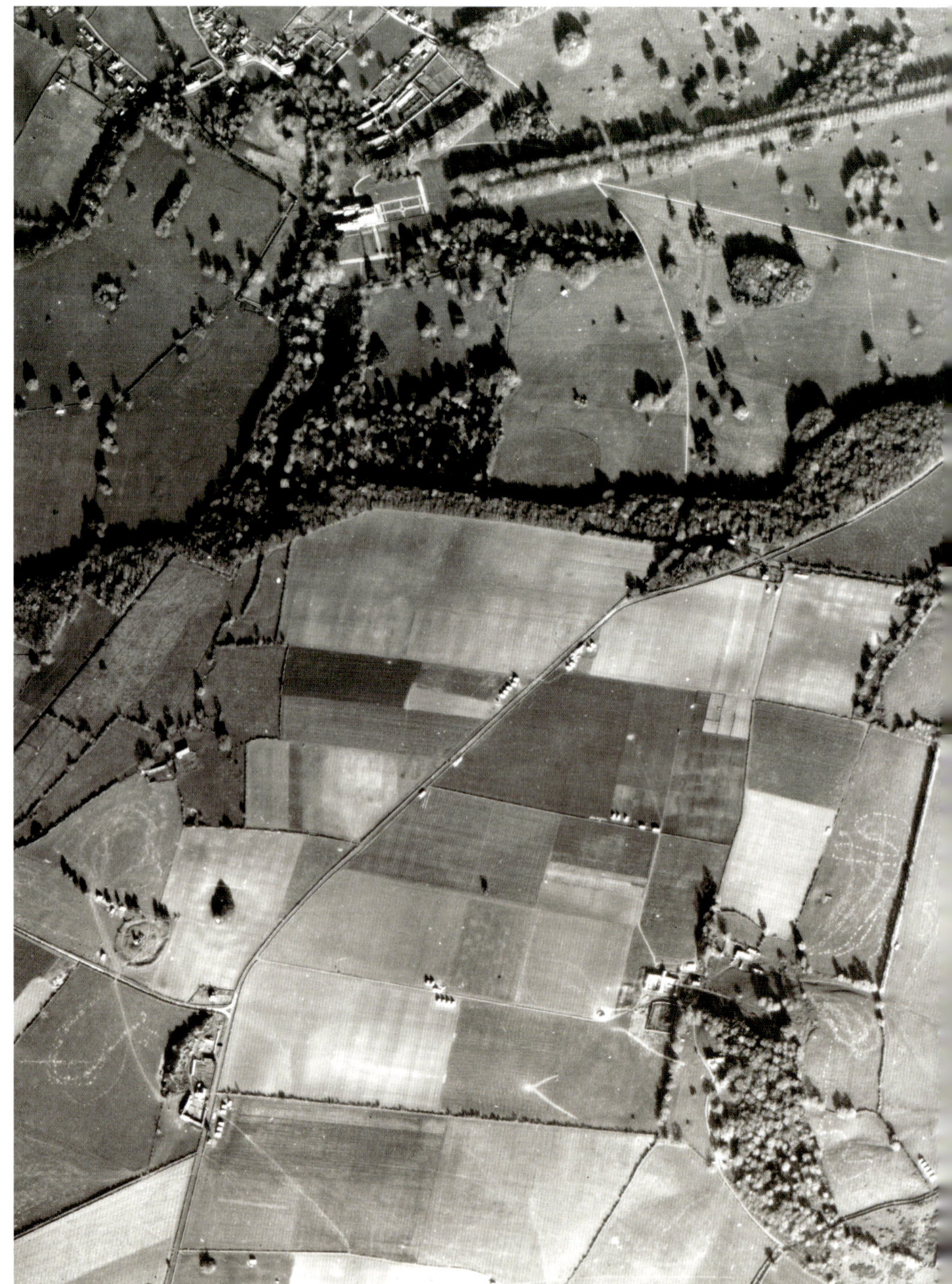

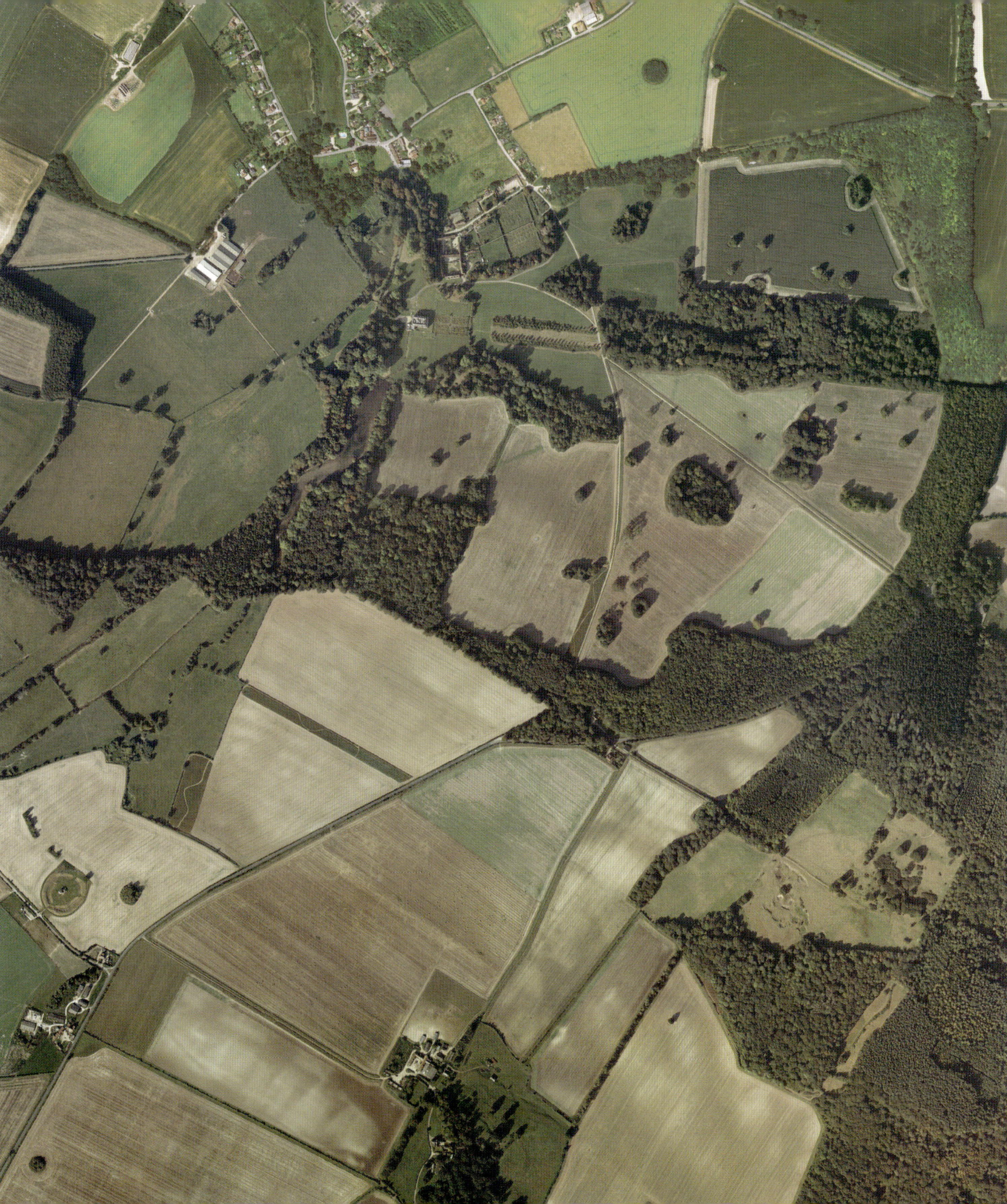

Lyme Regis 1947 photograph reference 2475-3345, centred on grid reference SY 344 917

The ancient port of Lyme Regis with its harbour of the Cobb is a remarkable survivor. At first glance the pictures seem to show a typical example of post war expansion. Within the town open spaces have been in-filled, on the eastern side of the town an area of allotments has been turned into a large car park, whilst on the west large housing estates have been built. Woodland has also increased, both inside and around the town.

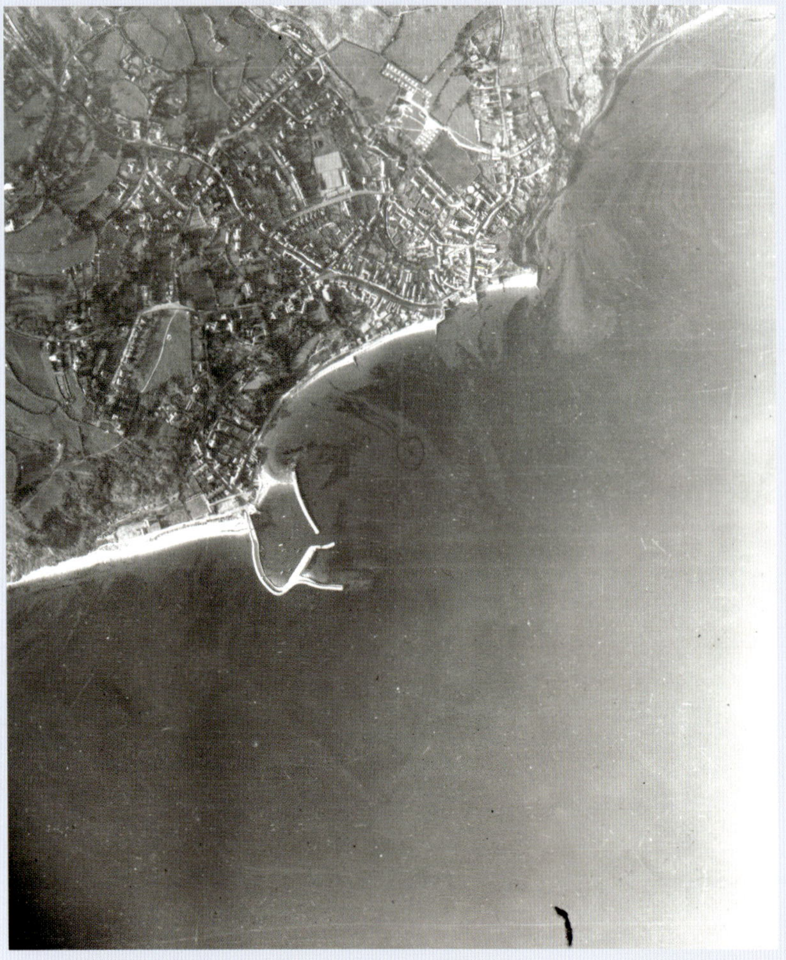

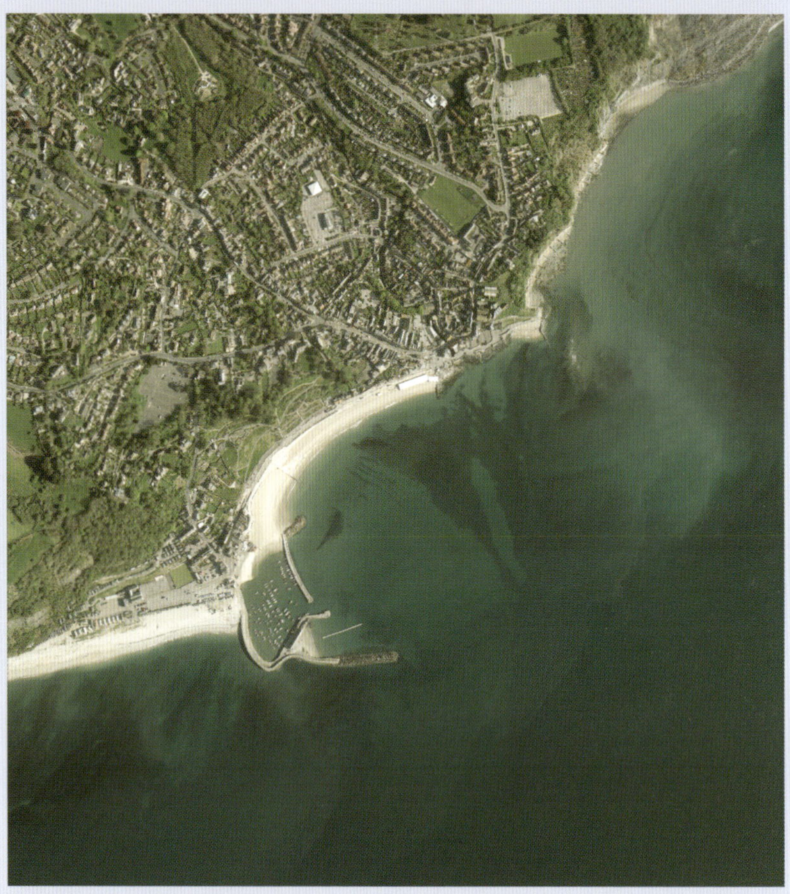

But the most interesting area is that around the Cobb. The harbour piers have been lengthened with a mass of blocks of stone 'rock armour'. Whilst the houses of Cobb Hamlet, immediately beside the Cobb, seem to have hardly increased at all, in fact careful examination of the pictures will show some have gone. This is due to landslips and subsidence, a result of both the natural instability of the ground and some ill-advised building works, causing the land to start moving. The gardens to the east of the Cobb have also had to be stabilised, in the hope of stopping Lyme Regis from slipping into the sea.

Lyscombe Bottom 1947 photograph reference 1934-5102, centred on grid reference ST 735 013

Lyscombe Bottom, a remarkable natural amphitheatre between Cheselbourne and Piddlehinton, is notable for the remarkably well-preserved prehistoric settlement and field system. The size and quality of preservation of the remains was first recognised on the 1947 aerial photographs. Subsequently much of the area has been designated as a Scheduled Monument and is now protected.

The curving shape of Lyscombe Bottom can be seen to the north of the photographs. On either side are prominent rectangular earthworks which mark the prehistoric field systems. On one field on the eastern side of the Bottom the area had recently been ploughed in 1947, so the remains of the fields are visible here as differently coloured patches in the soil. Immediately to the north of this field smaller earthworks mark a prehistoric, probably Iron Age, settlement.

Apart from those that had been ploughed in 1947, the earthworks are still present today though they are clearest on the 1947 photograph as the lighting was better for revealing low banks and ditches when the picture was taken.

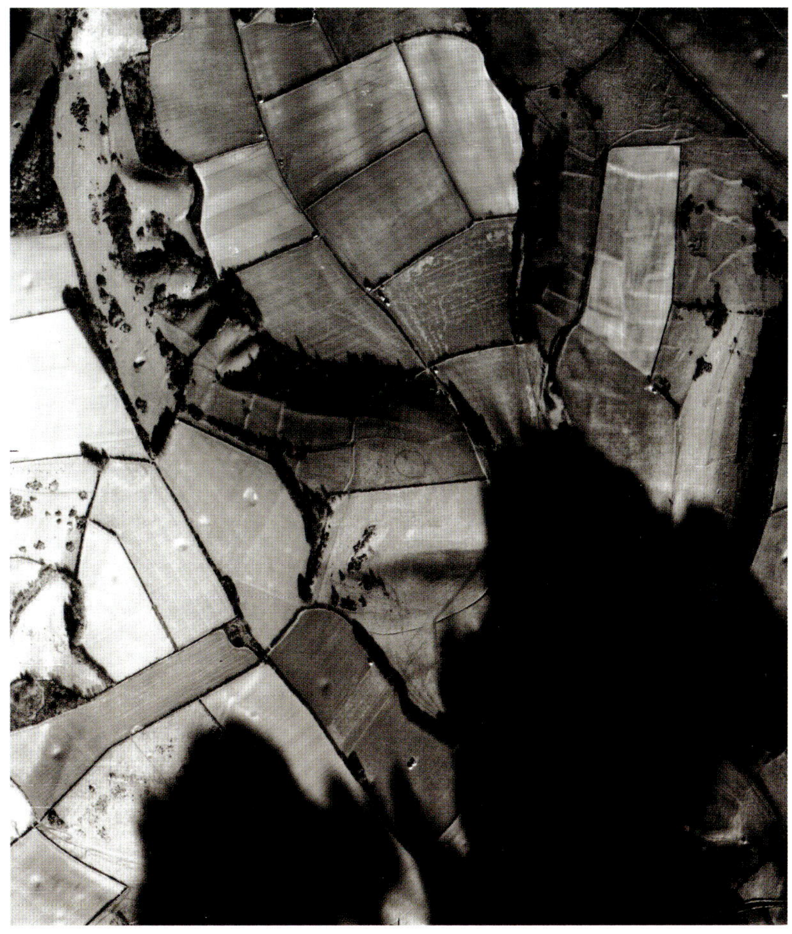

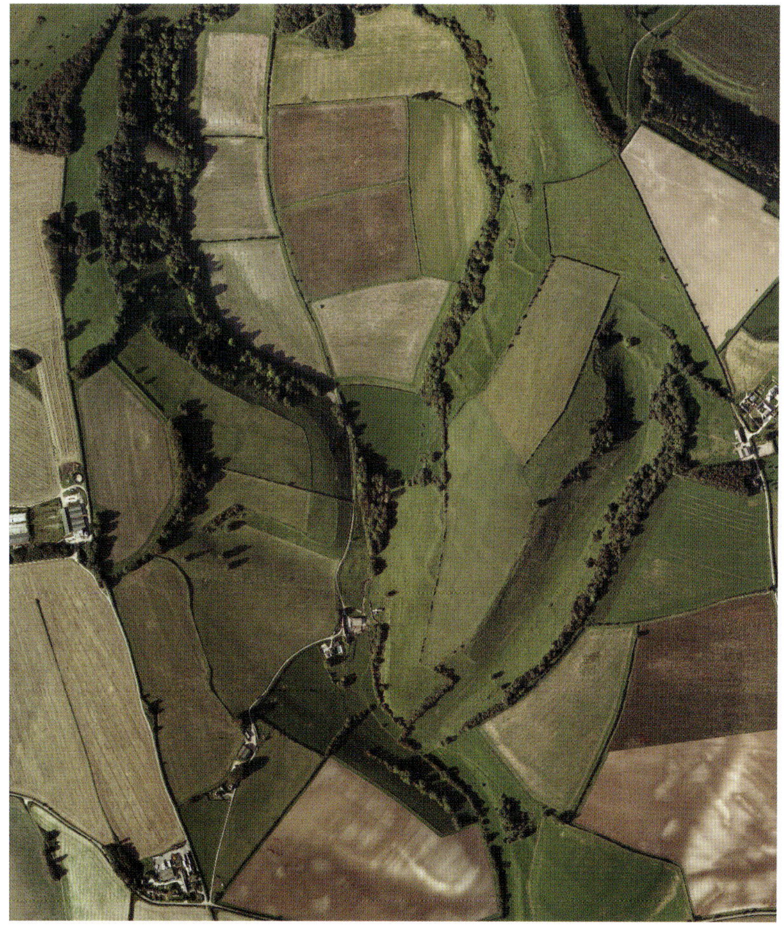

Maiden Castle 1947 photograph reference 1934-3088, centred on grid reference SY 672 883

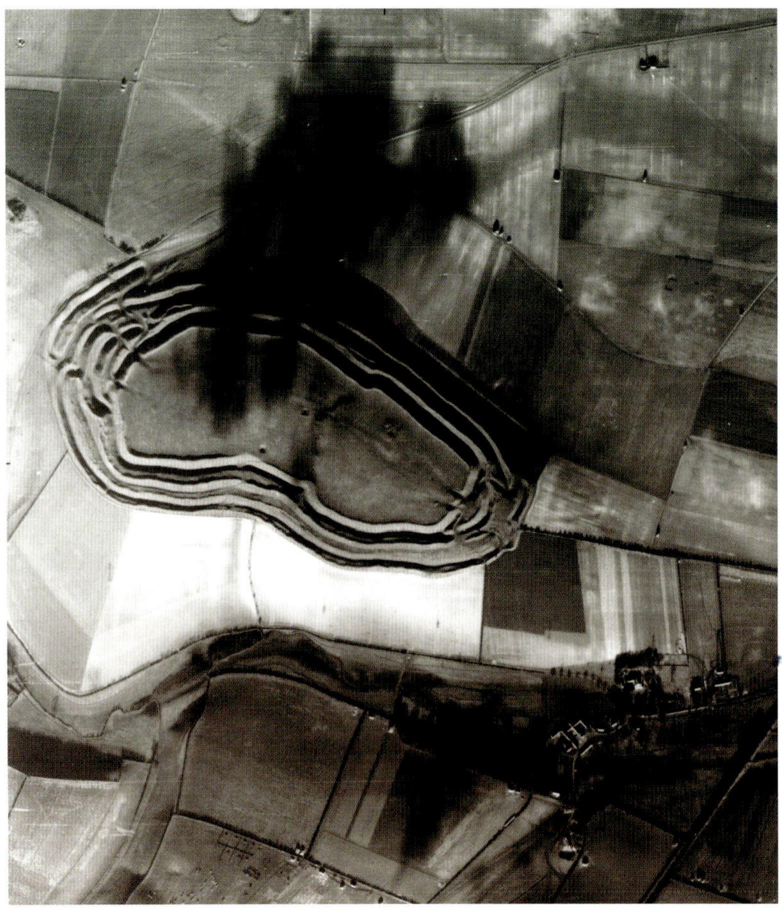

Looking in the fields around Maiden Castle traces of prehistoric activity can be seen, for example two 'ring ditches', remains of burial mounds, to the east of the Castle on the modern picture. What is perhaps more interesting is what can be discerned within Maiden Castle, particularly on the 1947 picture. The shape of an earlier hill fort can be seen at the eastern end, while running along the middle of the fort is a Neolithic bank barrow, a curious monument whose function is still unclear.

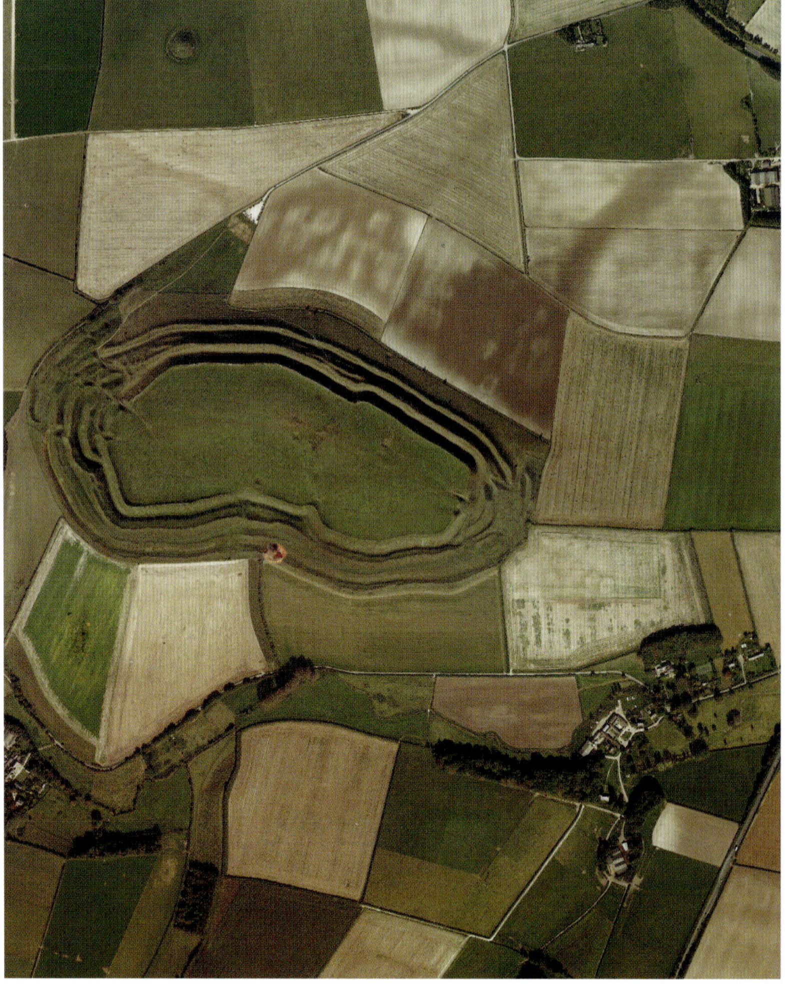

There is little to say about these pictures of the magnificent Maiden Castle, the largest Iron Age hill fort in Britain. Since 1947 there has been very little change for two reasons, the hill fort itself is strongly protected and, apart from a small car park to the north, very little has happened here to alter the appearance of the monument. The surrounding fields too are little altered; they were only laid out in 1874, when the land belonging to the Duchy of Cornwall was enclosed, and are large and suitable for modern farm machinery. Even the tiny village of Winterborne Monkton (little more than a single farm and an ancient church) has hardly grown.

Maiden Newton 1947 photograph reference 1974-1383, centred on grid reference SY 602 979

In 1940, military planners considered how best to defend Britain against a possible German invasion. It was realised that it would be very difficult to prevent a landing, as Britain did not have enough troops or equipment to defend every part of the coast. What was decided was to set up a series of defences inland to slow any invaders down so that troops could be moved to attack them. These defences ran right across the country and were called 'Stop Lines'. Along each stop line were more heavily defended points known as 'Tank Islands', and the village of Maiden Newton was one of these.

Close examination of the 1947 photograph reveals traces of these defences. White dots which seem to be scatted over the whole village, are dragons teeth or tank traps, large concrete blocks designed to stop armoured vehicles, which can be seen between cottages. It was thought that a tank would probably be stopped well enough by a house! Otherwise there are small groups of wooden huts, accommodation for troops stationed there in the run up to D-Day when the threat of invasion had receded.

Today the huts have gone, though a number of the dragons teeth still stand around the village. There has been some new housing, the railway branch line running westwards has gone, though the main line remains, and even one area of allotments remains in use, the last remnant of the time when Maiden Newton was at the forefront of the defence of Britain.

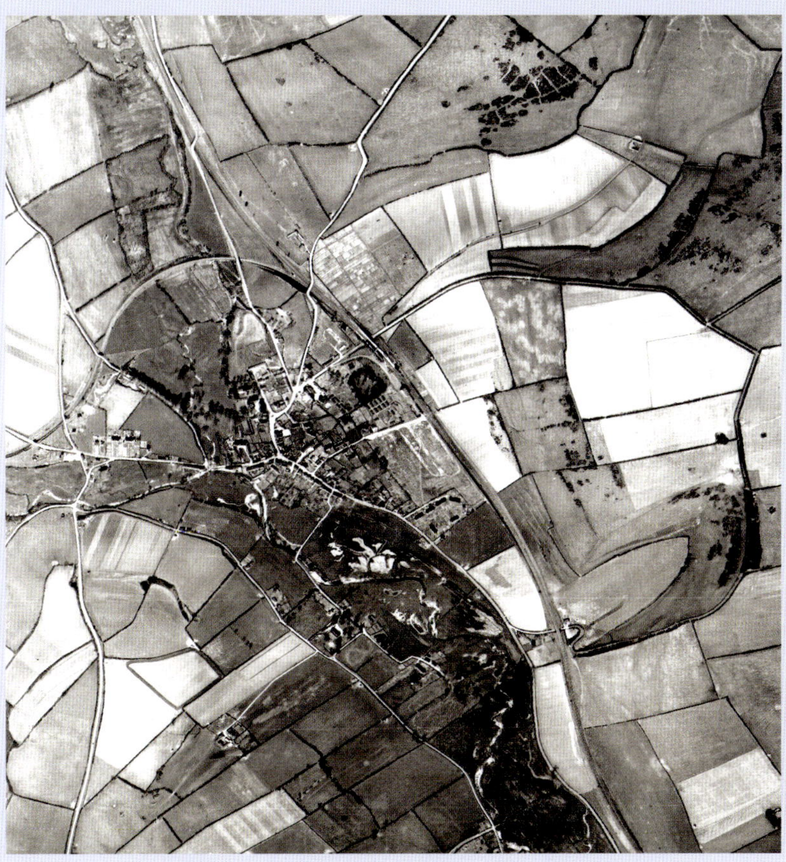

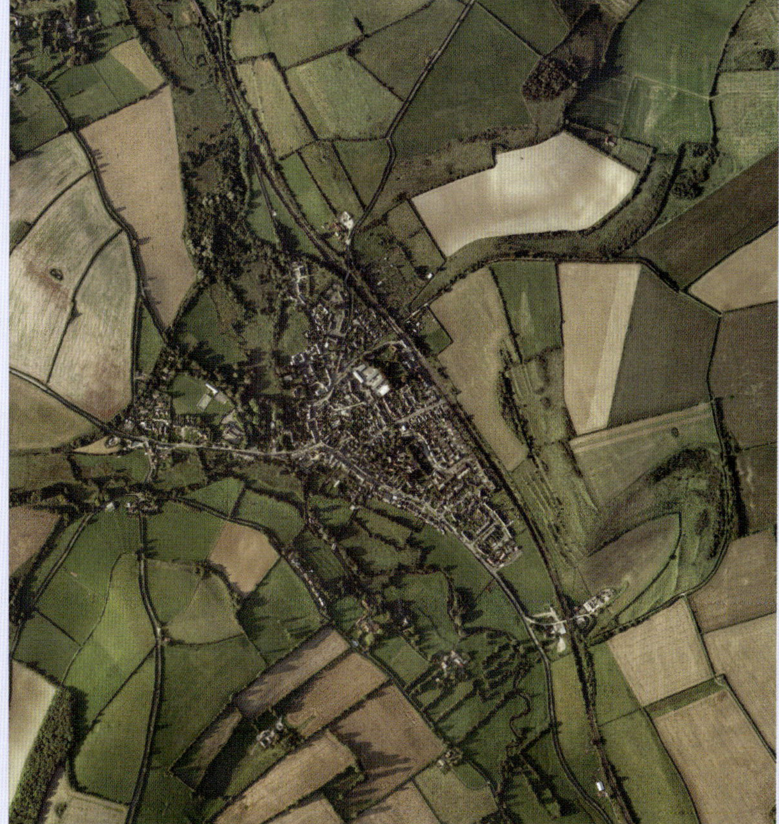

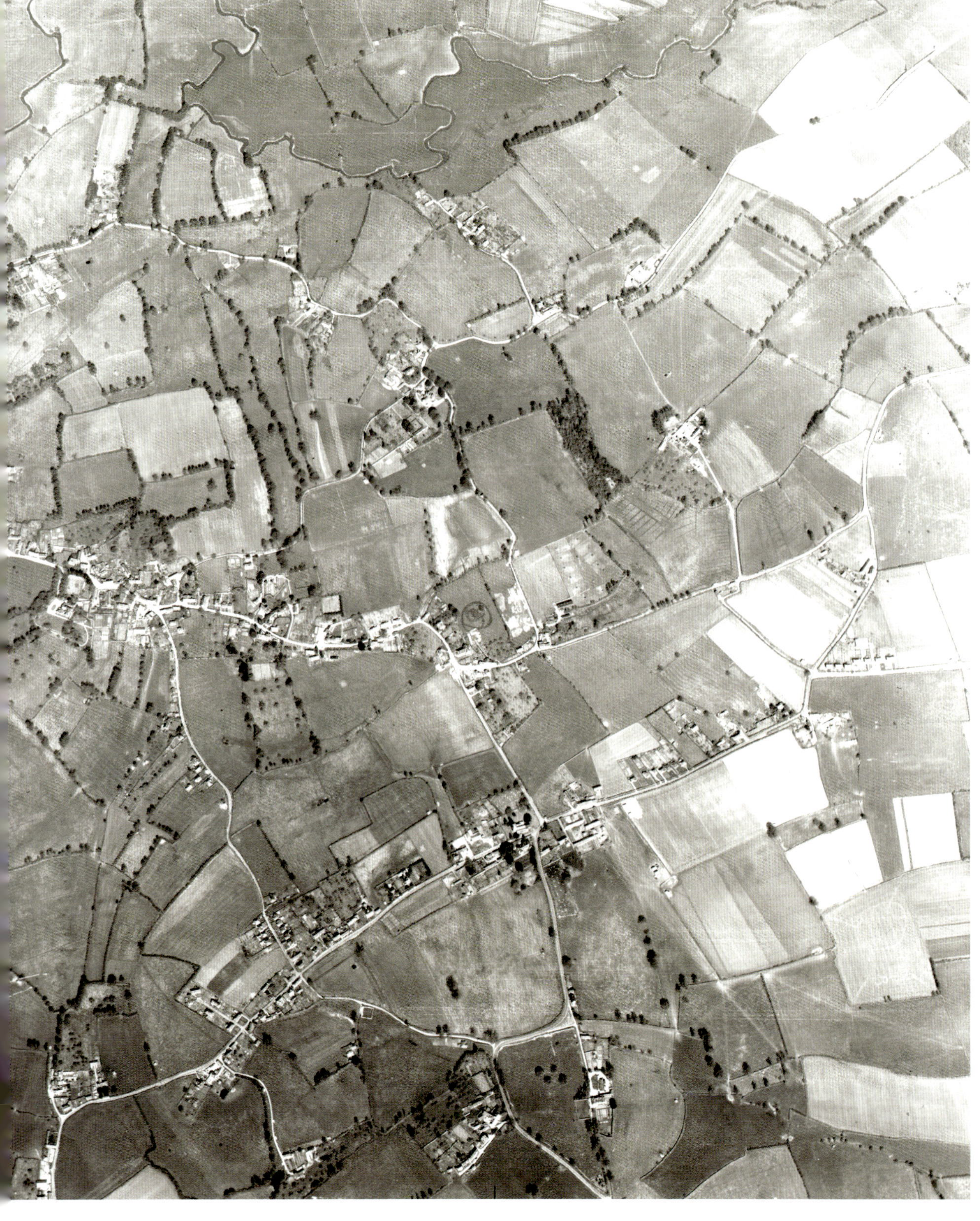

Marnhull

1947 photograph reference 1974-4165, centred on grid reference ST 782 194

In 1947 the village of Marnhull was very dispersed, scattered over a wide area of countryside following narrow country roads through a landscape of small fields.

Today the village is more concentrated in a single area, centred on the church, the original focus of the village. Other developments have followed some of the roads and the village is still spread over a wide area. Although there are still a large number of small fields, many field boundaries have gone. There have been smaller areas of woodland growth though the small orchards visible at the back of some of the cottages in 1947, no longer seem to exist.

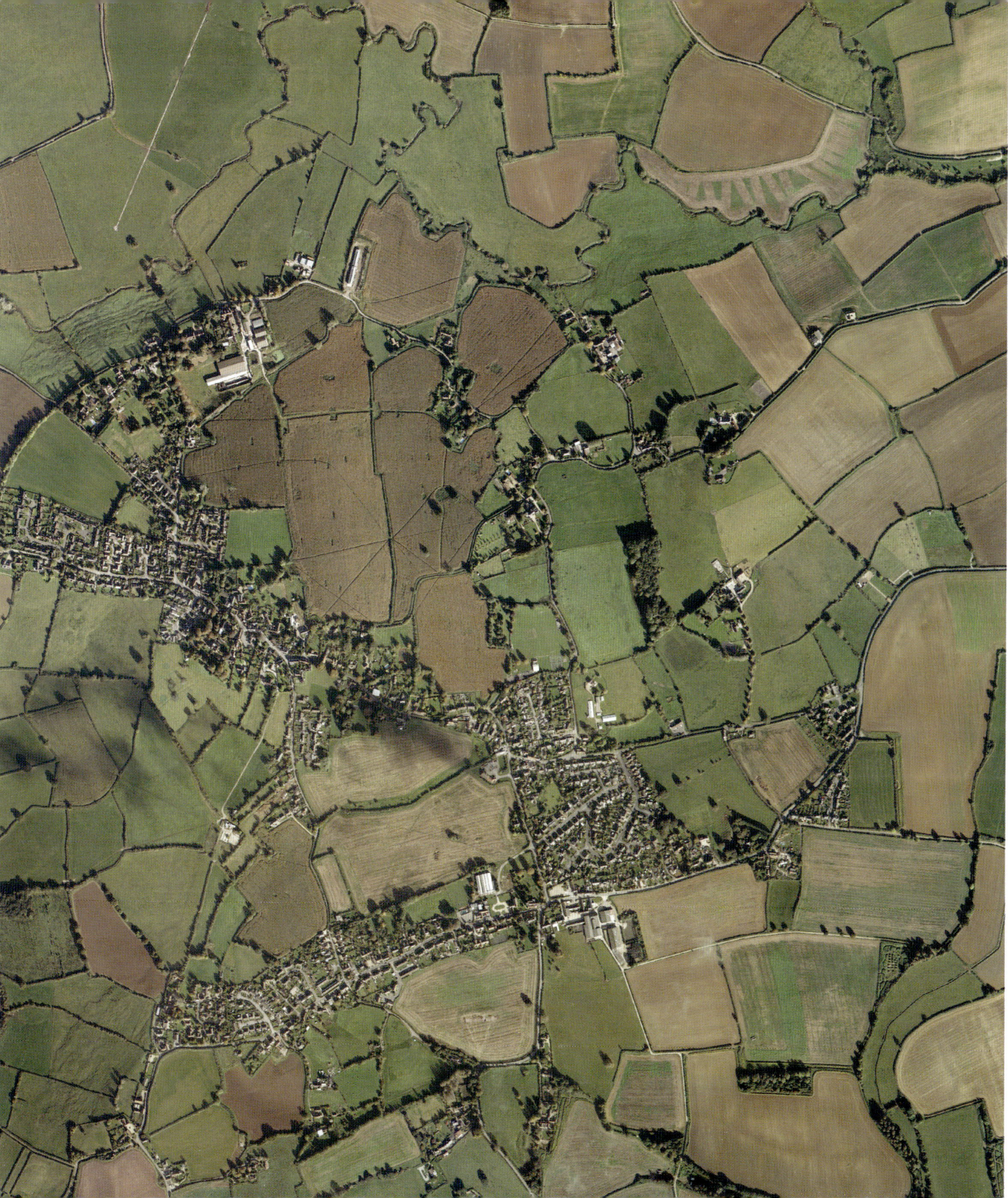

Marshwood Vale

1947 photograph reference 2431-4212, centred on grid reference SY 406 976

Marshwood is now a scatter of farms, but as one might guess it was once much more important, for it has given its name to the Marshwood Vale which covers a large area of western Dorset. The photographs show the reason: immediately to the north of the farm in the centre of the photographs can be seen the earthworks of Marshwood Castle. This was probably built in the twelfth century and was still in use in the fourteenth. Surrounding the castle was a network of irregular shaped small fields, which had been enclosed many centuries ago, dividing up the land between the small sinuous streams. The pattern shown on the 1947 photograph was quite possibly the same that could have been seen when the castle was occupied.

Today many of the hedgerows have gone, and round the castle are large open fields.

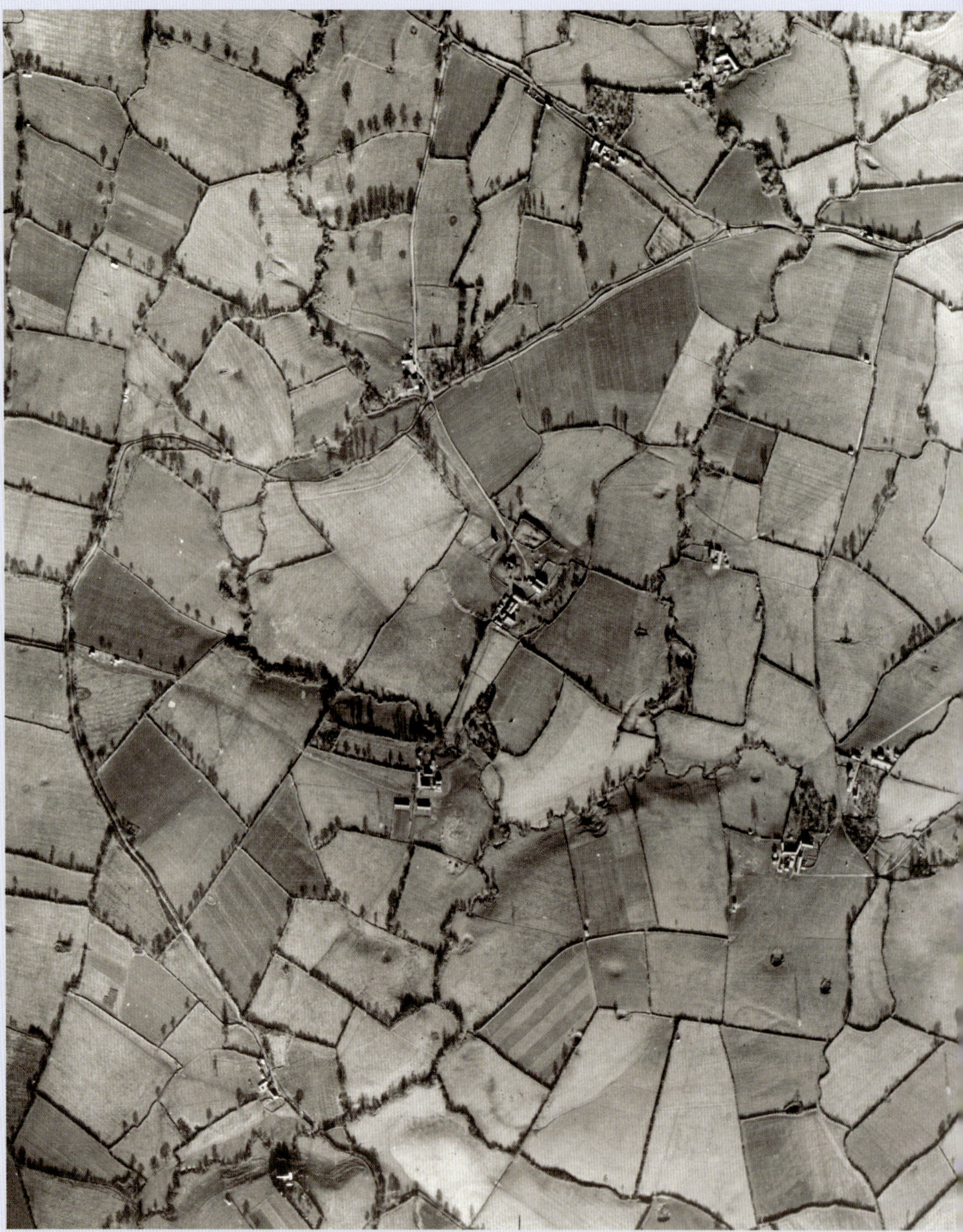

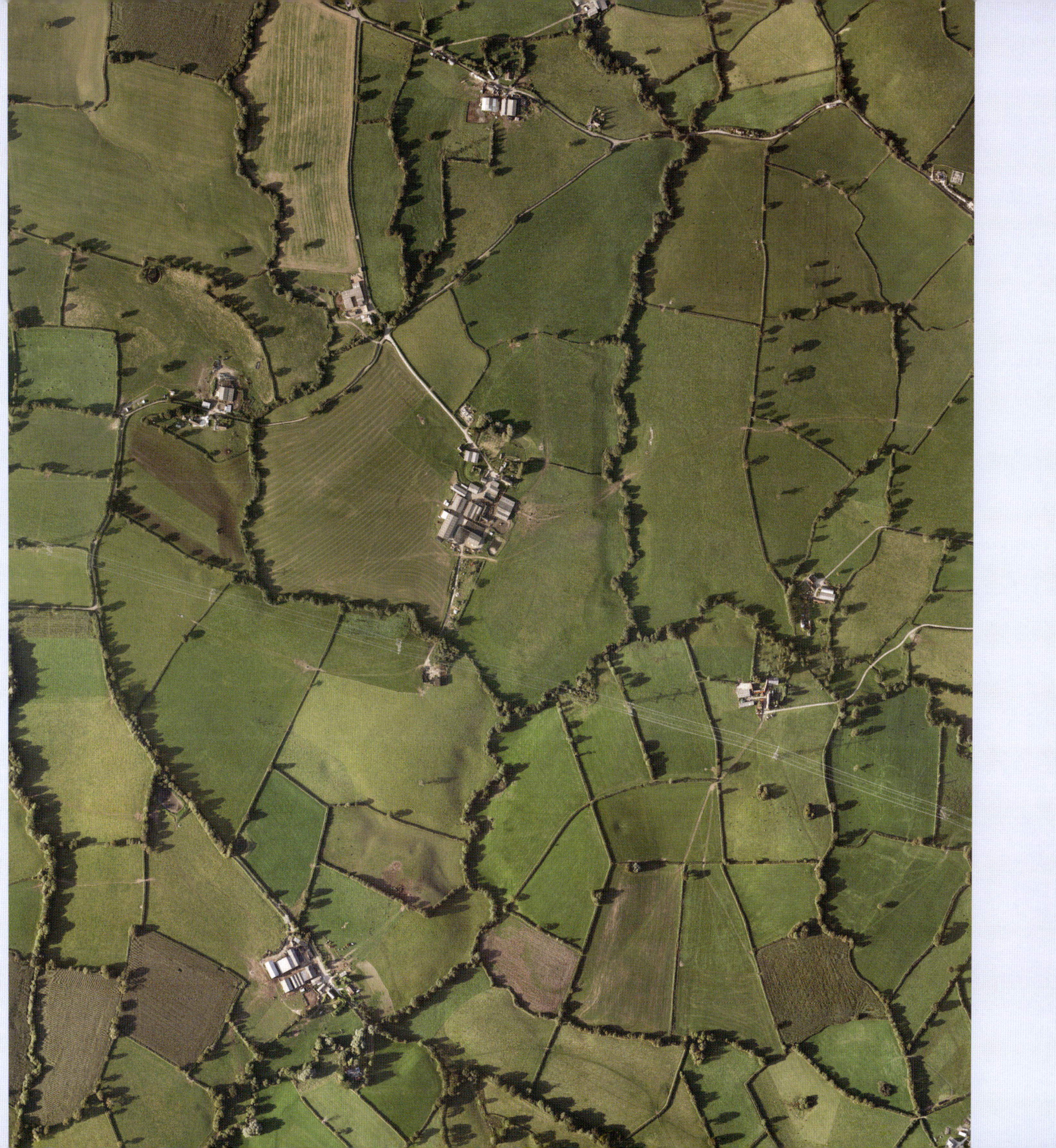

Melbury Park 1947 photograph reference1974-2061, centred on grid reference ST 572 069

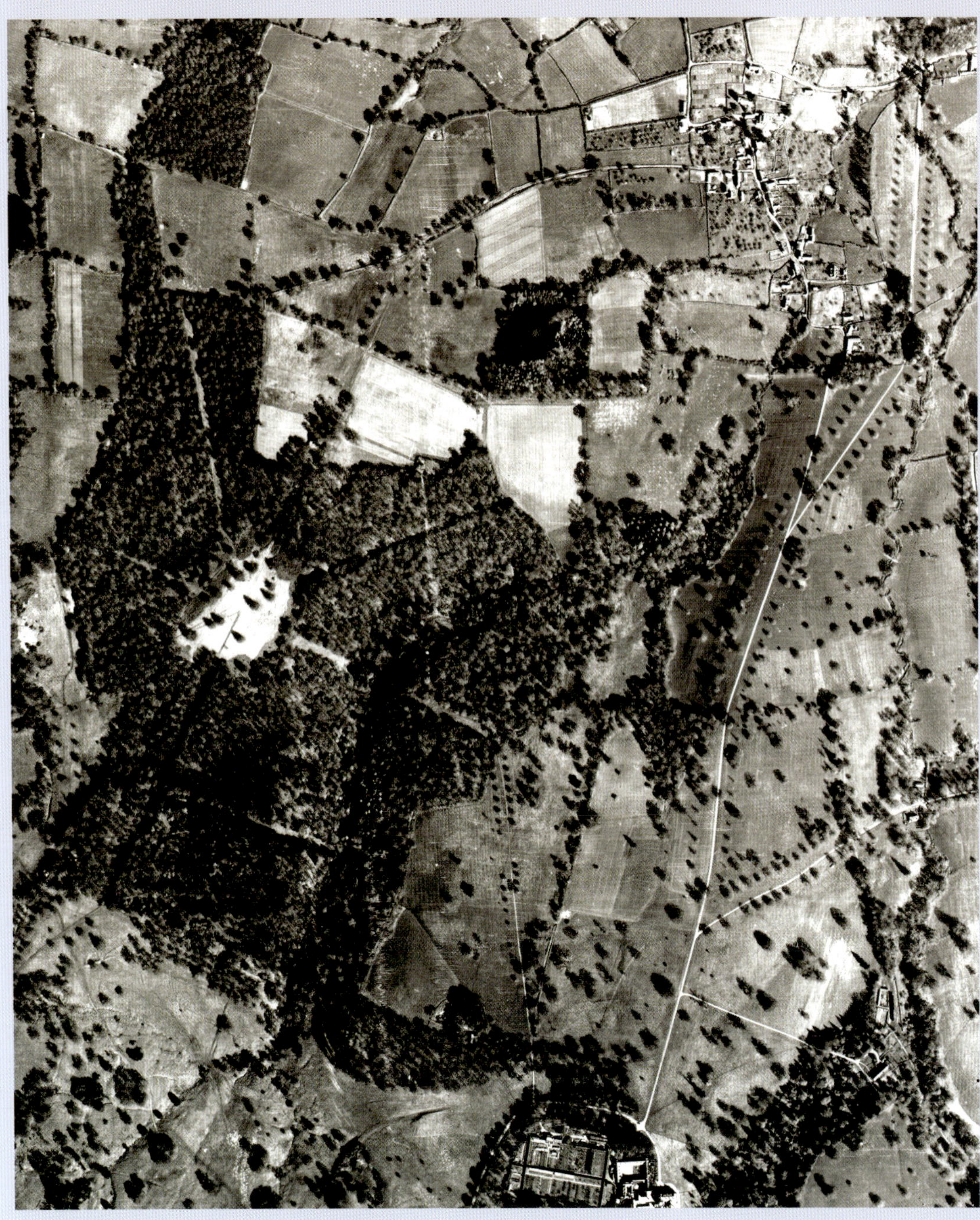

Unlike many of Dorset's county houses, Melbury is still occupied and maintained as a great house in its park. This can clearly be seen on the photographs, as land in the park that was ploughed in 1947, when there was a need for Britain to grow as much of its own food as possible, has now been returned to parkland. Avenues have been maintained – some have gone as trees have come to the end of their lives but others have been planted.

The mass of woodland shows evidence of an early type of landscape gardening when complex geometric shapes were laid out in the countryside. This is a planned landscape on a massive sale which remarkably still survives into the twenty-first century.

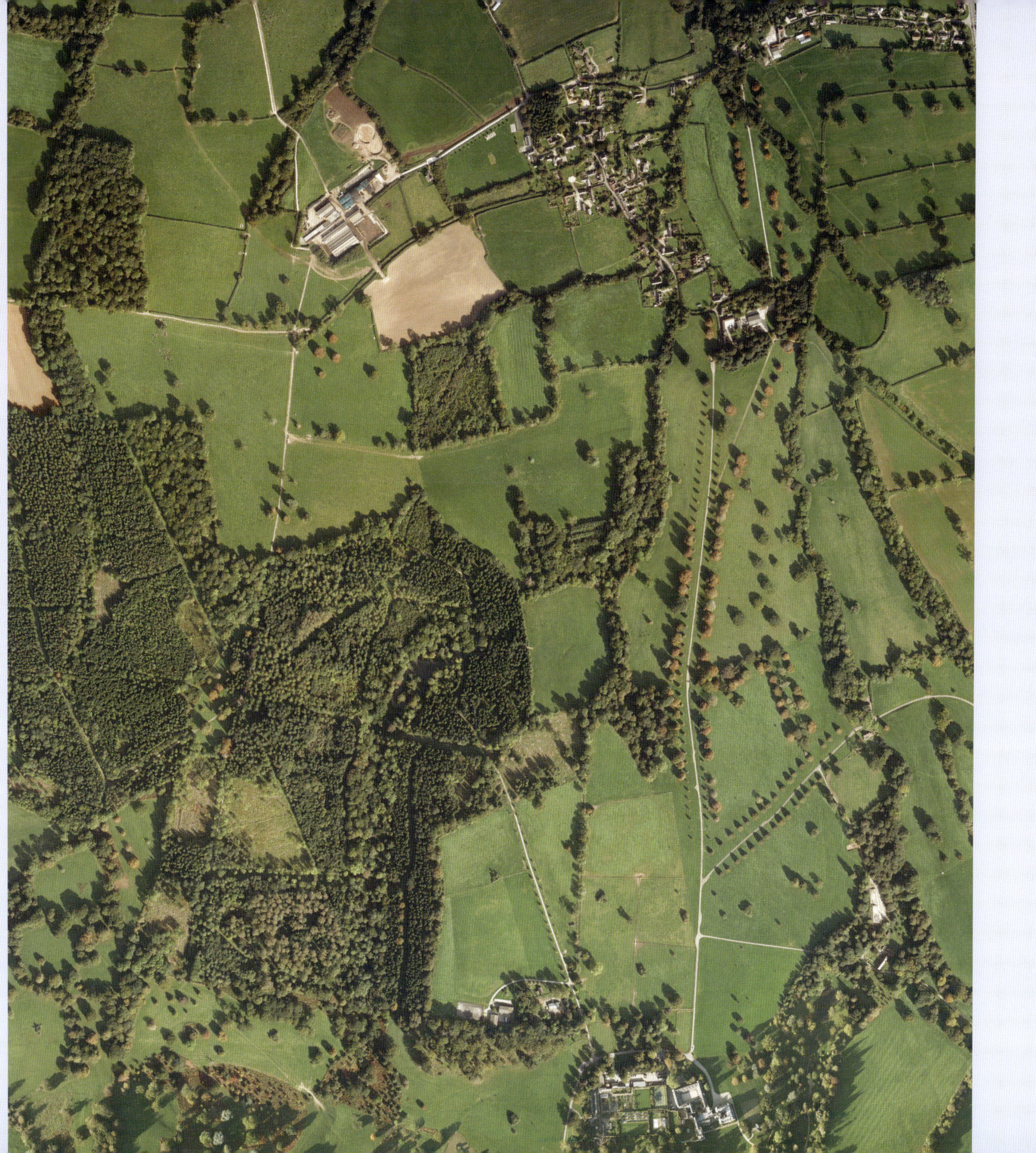

Milborne St Andrew 1947 photograph reference 1934-4115, centred on grid reference SY 803 970

In 1947 the village of Milborne St Andrew was still fairly small. However the photograph shows a small terrace of houses and a large building on the very northern edge of the photograph. This was a state of the art dairy built in the 1920s. To the south lies the Iron Age hill fort of Weatherbury Camp.

Today the village has grown with several small estates. The road through the village is the main road from Dorchester to Blandford and many of the people who live here now work in one of the two towns. The surrounding field system is essentially unchanged and only a few areas are more wooded.

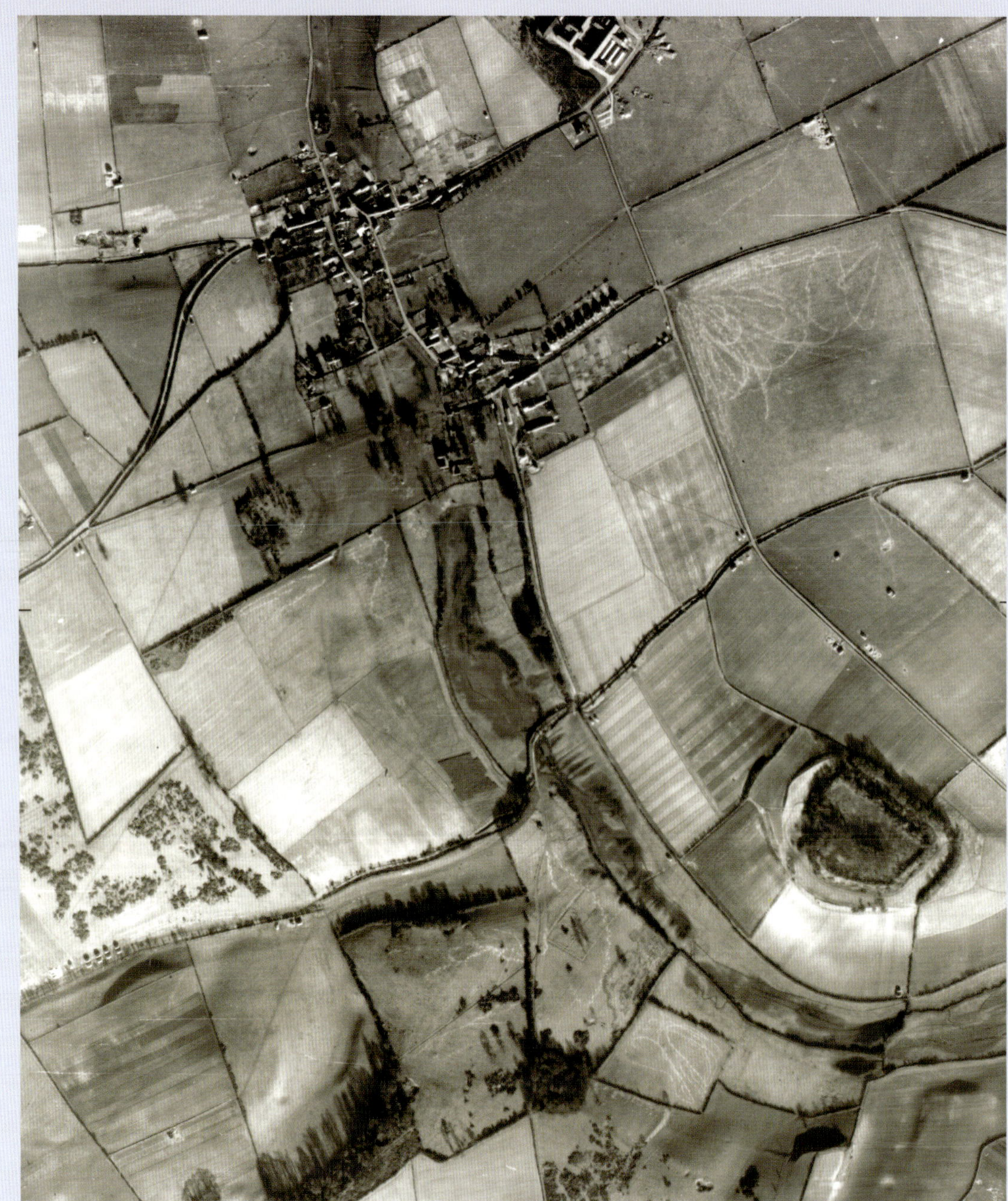

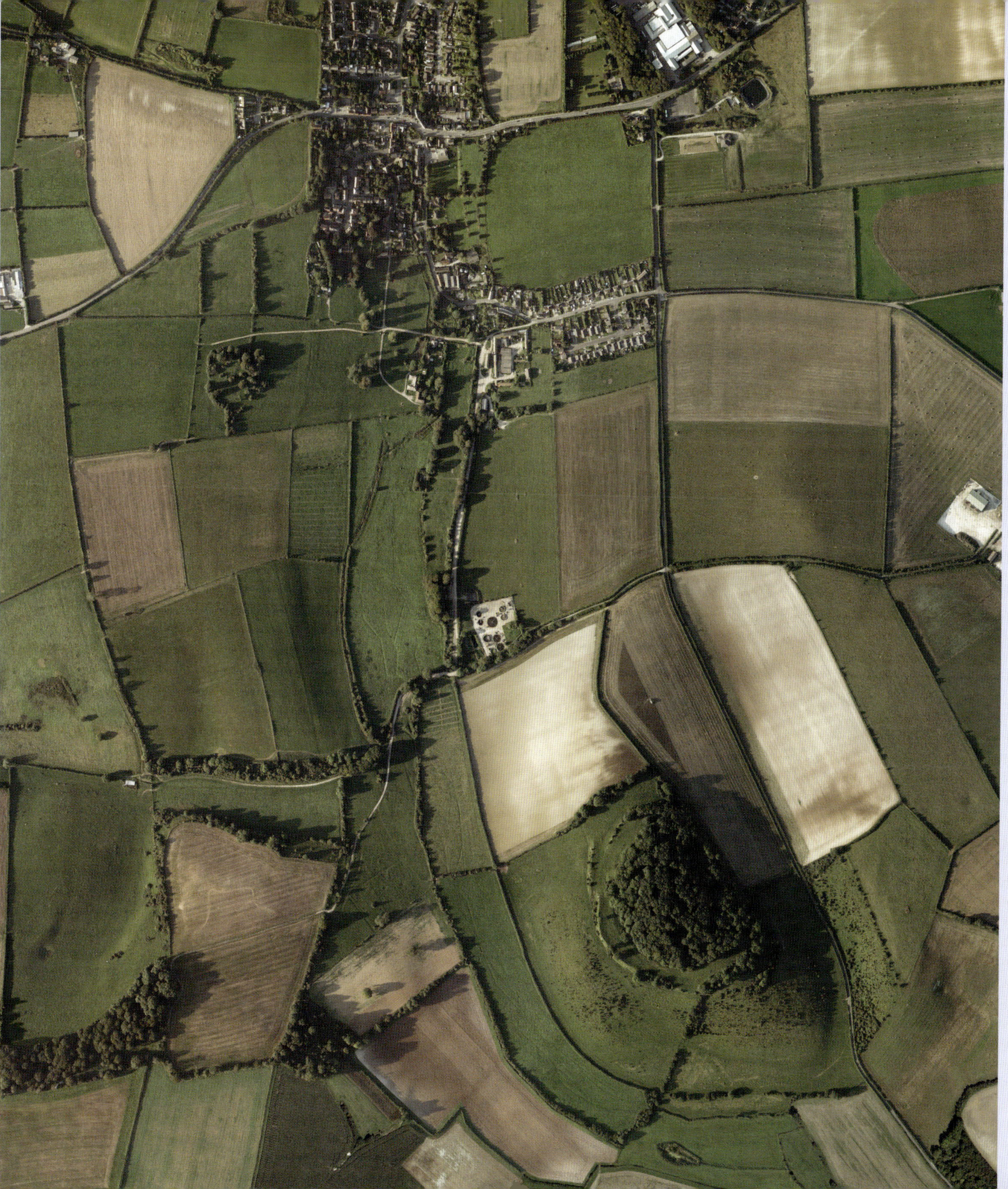

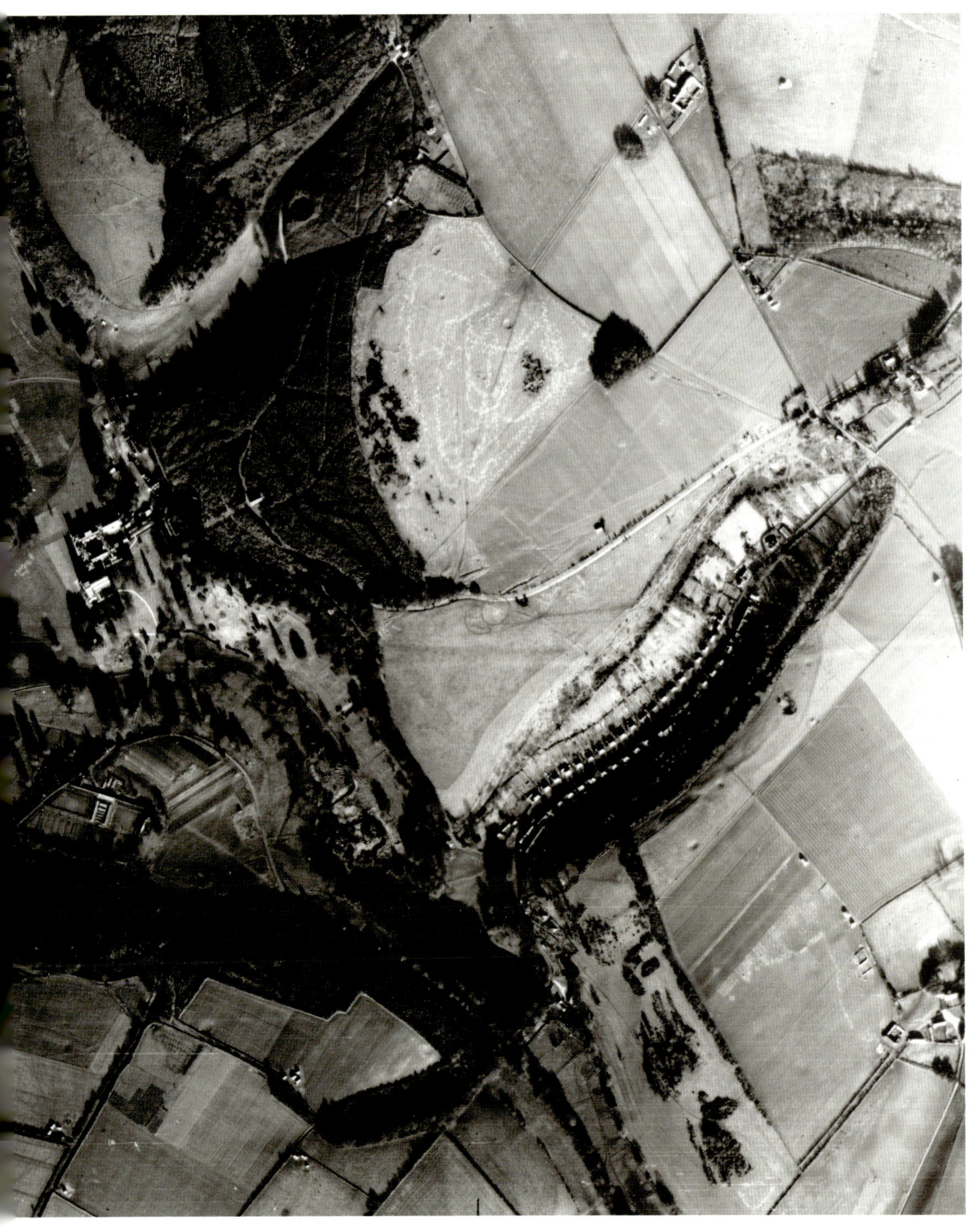

Milton Abbas

1947 photograph reference 1934-3113, centred on grid reference ST 805 020

Milton Abbas must be one of the most famous villages in Dorset, because of the story of how Lord Milton moved the entire village, which he felt was too close to his home, so he could create a fine landscape park in the eighteenth century.

The 1947 shows the village almost as Lord Milton had created it, with a line of cottages running up each side of the road. Milton Abbey lies in the park, with the bulk of the Abbey church immediately to the south of it. Careful examination of the photograph shows faint traces of earthworks south east of the Abbey, which are the remains of the town of Middleton which was destroyed to make way for the park. Clearer are the earthworks of prehistoric fields immediately north of the village.

Today the village has grown, but very carefully. The streetscape Lord Milton created is seen as too important historically to change with the addition of modern buildings, so the new houses in Milton Abbas have been built on a road parallel to that of the original village. Milton Abbey is now a school, and additional buildings have been built in its grounds, but the park is carefully preserved. One unusual feature of the garden can clearly be seen in both photographs. Running west from Milton Abbey a straight line runs through the wood; these are the 'grass steps', which link the Abbey to the tiny chapel of St Catherine on the hill top.

Woodland has spread quite extensively, and the number of trees in the gardens behind the older cottages is particularly noticeable.

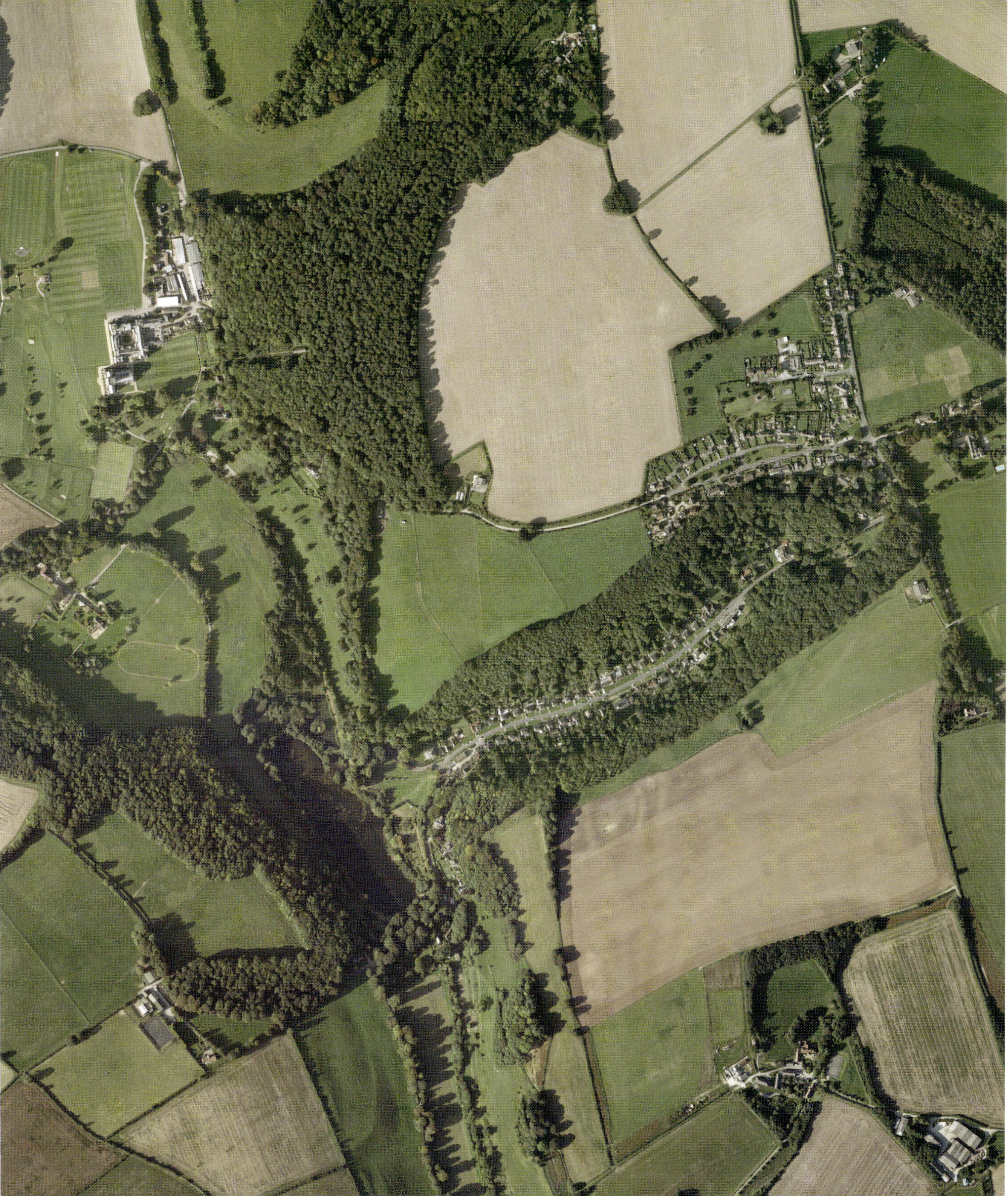

Oakley Down 1947 photograph reference 2038-1062, centred on grid reference SU 023 185

These pictures show an area of Dorset that has changed remarkably little, the fields are almost unaltered and the small settlement of Woodyates, towards the north of the picture, has grown very little.

Particularly important in these pictures is the archaeology. The Roman Road from Sorviodunum (Old Sarum) to Vindocladia (Badbury Rings) runs diagonally across the pictures. The northern two thirds is still the

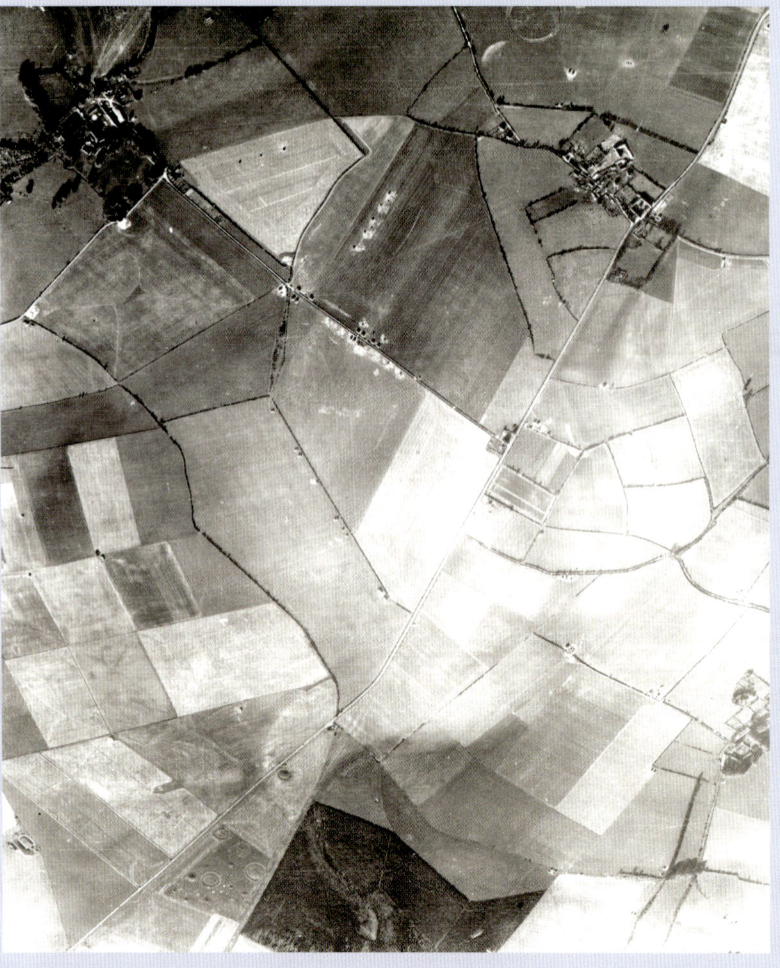

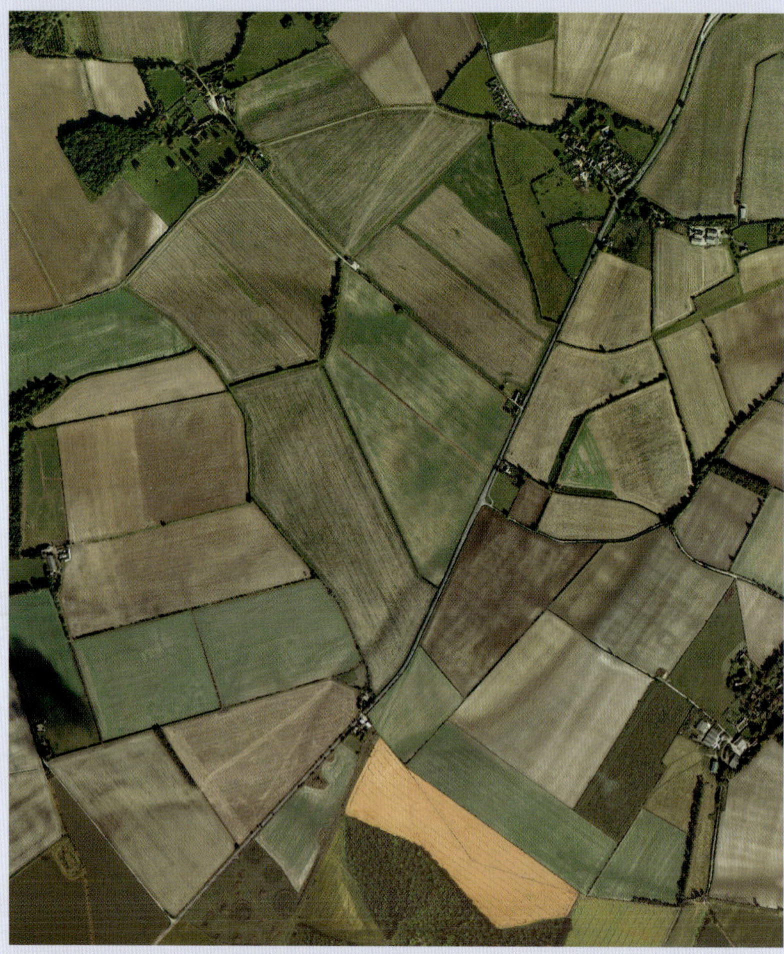

main road to Salisbury, but then the road swings westwards whilst the Roman Road continues arrow straight, to be seen first as a pair of parallel lines in the field, then as a massive bank. At the southern edge of picture lies the Oakley Down barrow cemetery. One of the barrows has been cut by the Roman Road, which was first noticed in the early eighteenth century and showed that the round barrows were more than two thousand years old (we now know they are much older).

Osmington White Horse

1947 photograph reference 1821-6441, centred on grid reference SY 715 851

The main interest of this picture lies in the white horse, originally built in 1808 as a patriotic gesture, but by 1940 this expression of patriotism had become a security risk. It made the hills, just eastward of the major naval base of Portland too easy to identify by enemy aircraft, so in company with all the other hill figures in Britain it was camouflaged. By 1947 this was still in place.

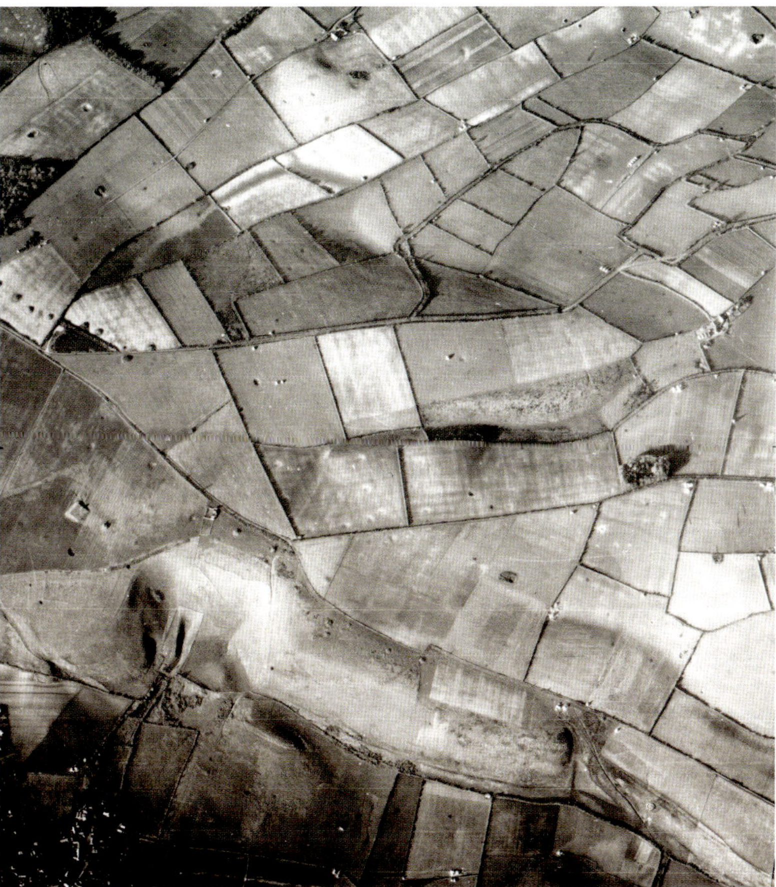

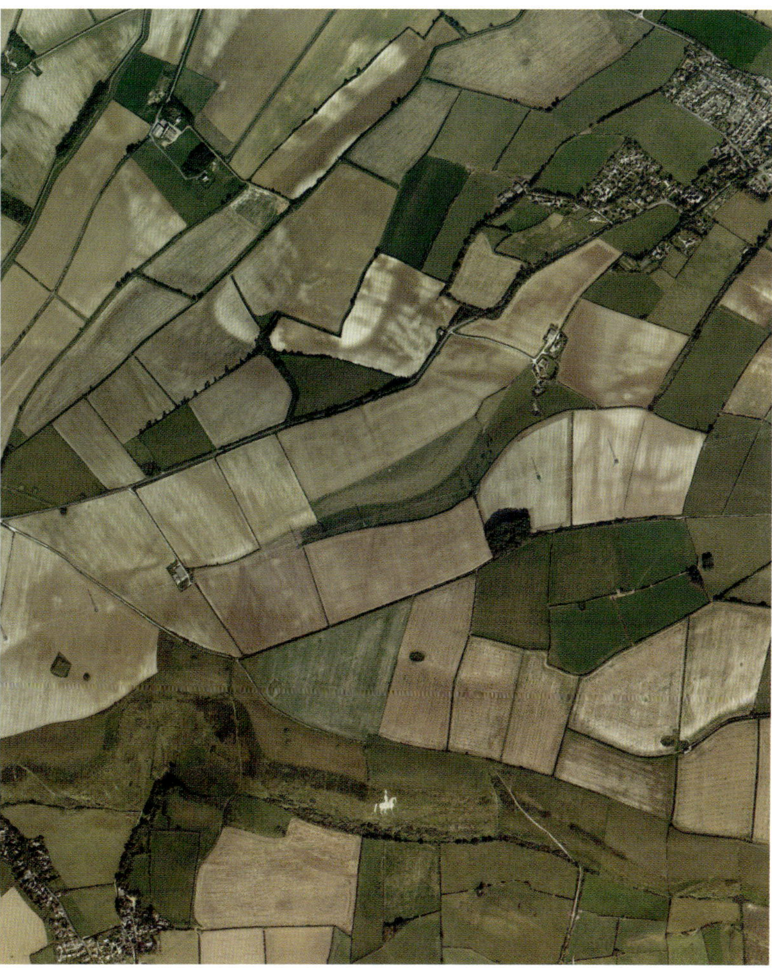

Above the horse, running along the ridge are a number of round barrows. These are part of the huge barrow group of the South Dorset ridgeway.

Parkstone 1947 photograph reference 1934-5038, centred on grid reference SZ 025 908

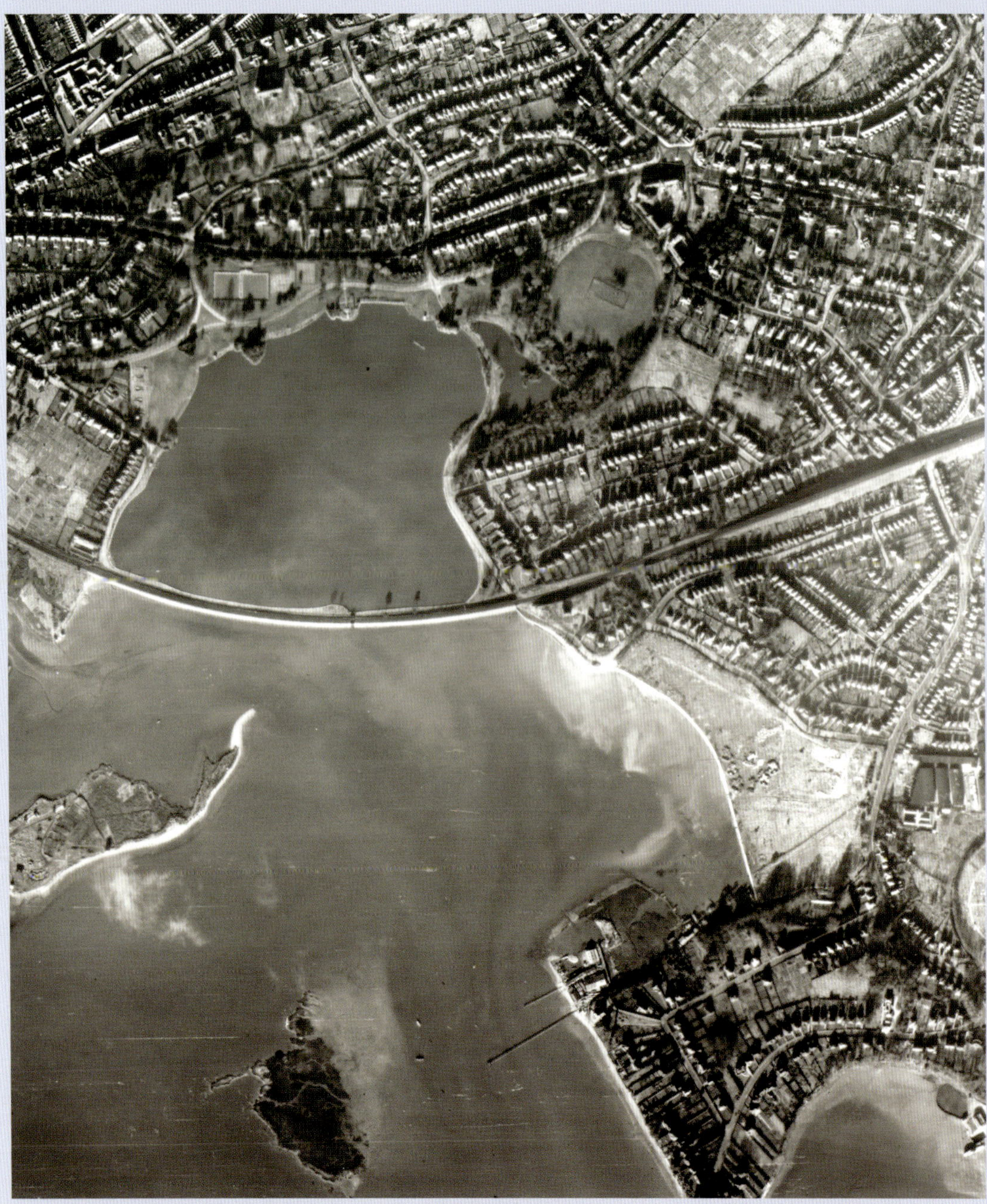

Parkstone, now part of Poole, shows the expansion of the town in a spectacular fashion. The Boating Lake was once a large bay, called Holes Bay before it was cut off by the railway, and the name was transferred to the large lagoon to the north of Poole. In 1947, the thin peninsula of Baiter Point still ran out into the harbour. For generations this had been the part of Poole where facilities had been placed that were needed, but not too close to the town: this had included a gallows, a gunpowder store and an Isolation Hospital.

Today the land around Baiter Point has been reclaimed, and is a popular area for recreation. In the harbour Parkstone Marina has grown, incorporating the big industrial piers that were built just before the Second World War.

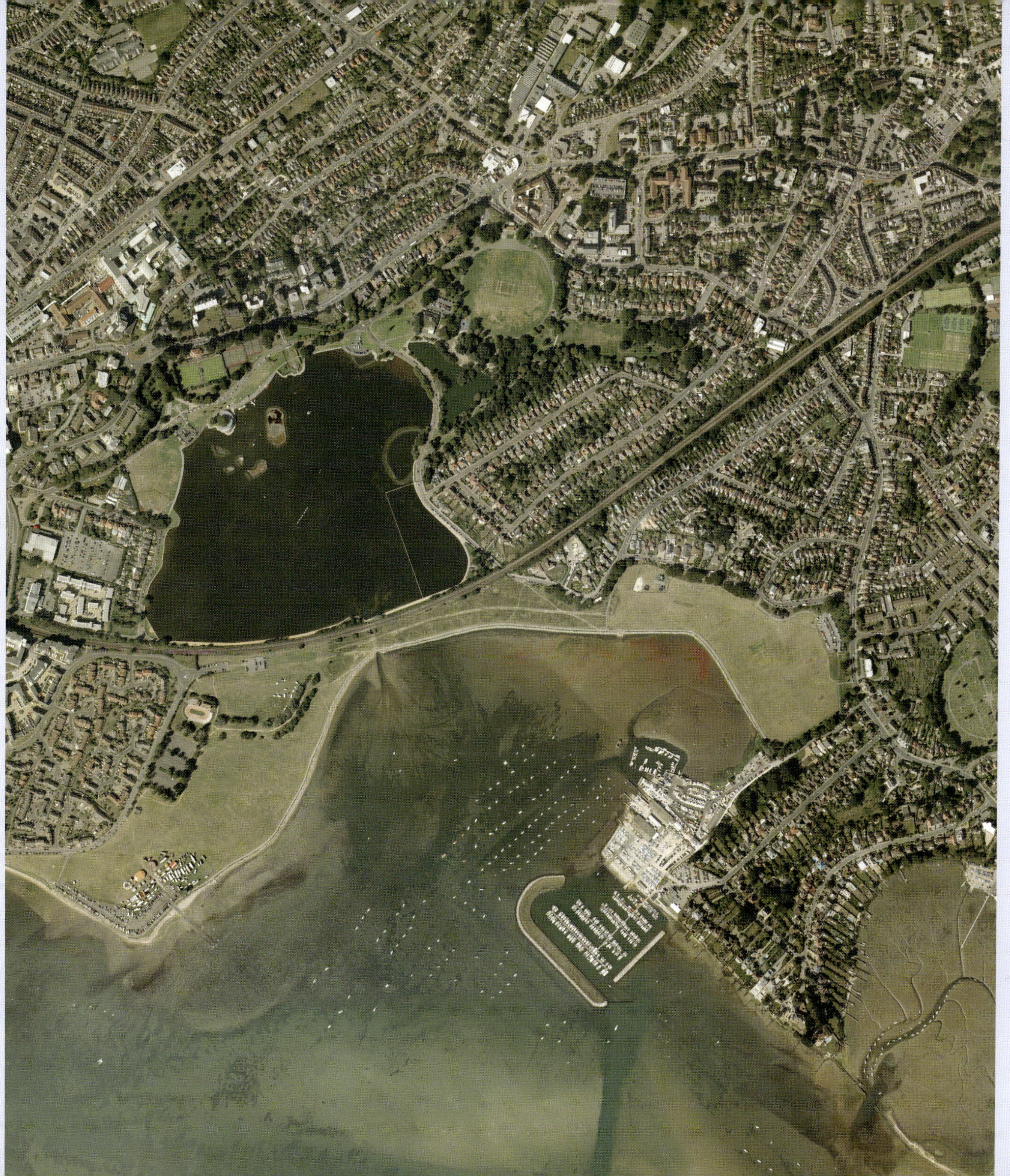

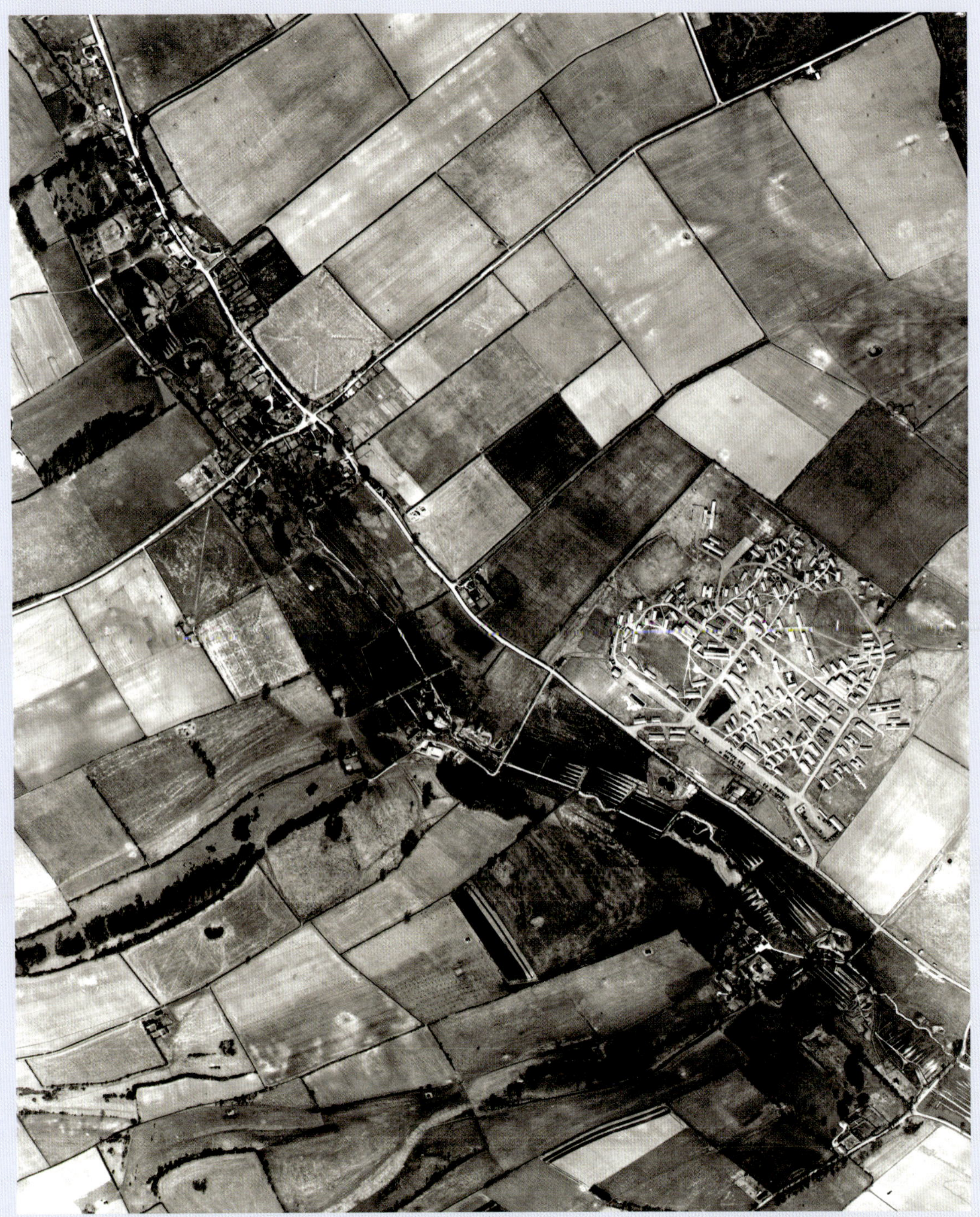

Piddlehinton

1947 photograph reference 1974-1366, centred on grid reference SY 719 968

The village of Piddlehinton is long and thin running up a narrow valley beside the River Piddle which gives the village its name. In 1947 the village was much as it is today with fields laid out at 90° to the river. The most obvious feature on the 1947 picture is a large army camp to the east of the village. After the war it was used for several different purposes, housing for the homeless and a council store, before it was developed as an industrial site. Now it is one of the main employers of the area.

The field boundaries have been considerably reduced and very few of the fields are the same size that they were in 1947. Woodland has spread along the river valley with the result that the valley feels wooded but as soon as one rises on either side the landscape is open and unenclosed.

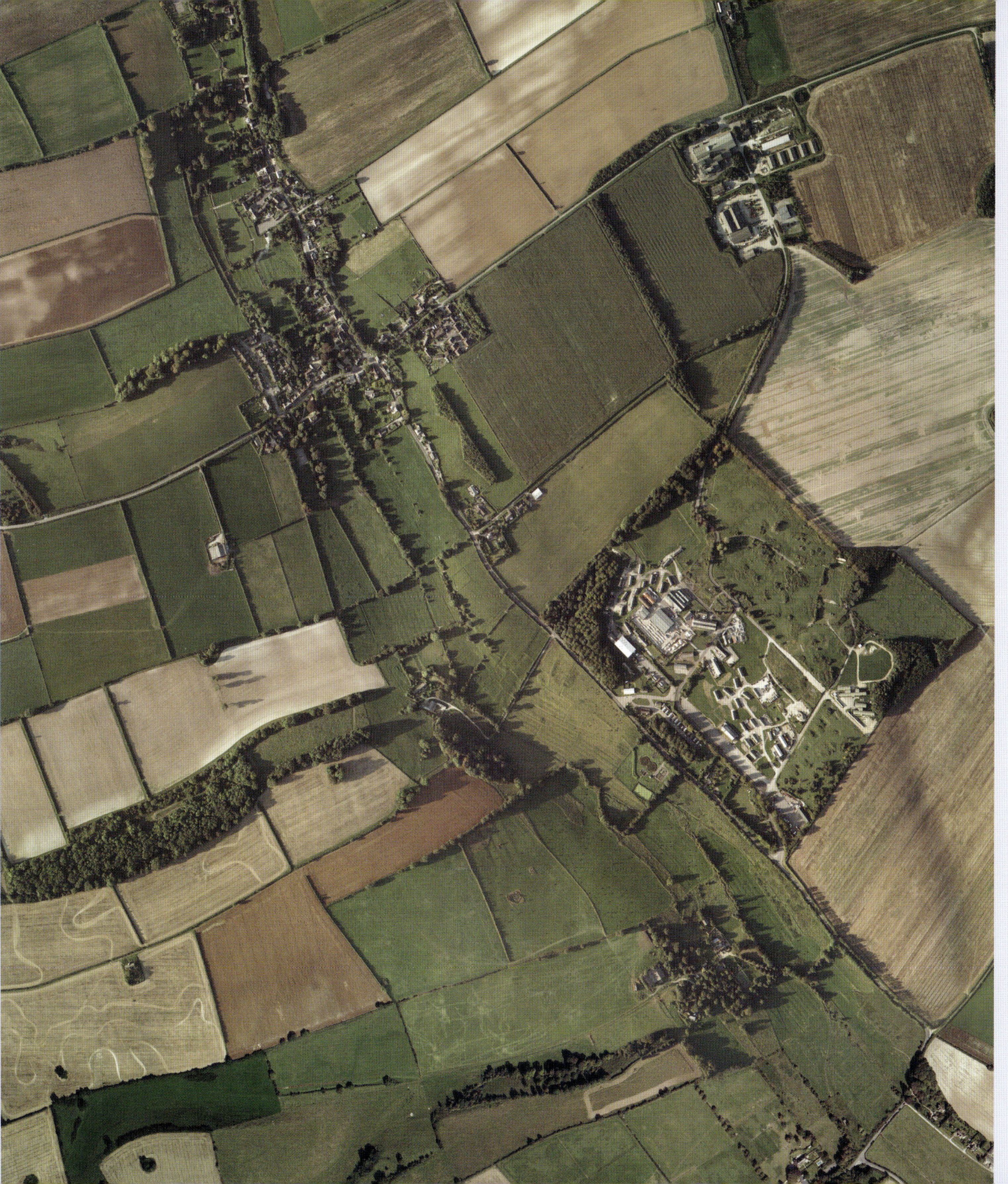

Pilsdon

1947 photograph reference 1974-4335, centred on grid reference SY 418 999

This landscape, to the north of the Marshwood Vale in western Dorset is remarkable. The network of winding hedges and irregular fields has remained virtually unaltered over the past sixty years. The main change has been the extensive spread of woodland, many of the hedgerows are now thin strips of woodland and some small fields are now woods.

To the north are the oval earthworks of Pilsdon Pen, an Iron Age hill fort, and inside it can be seen smaller earthworks. These are the remains of a medieval rabbit farm! When rabbits were introduced to England they were delicate animals that couldn't survive in the wild, so they even had to have their burrows dug for them! The earthworks are the remains of artificial warrens and a Warrener's house; even the 'Pen' of Pilsdon Pen was a rabbit pen.

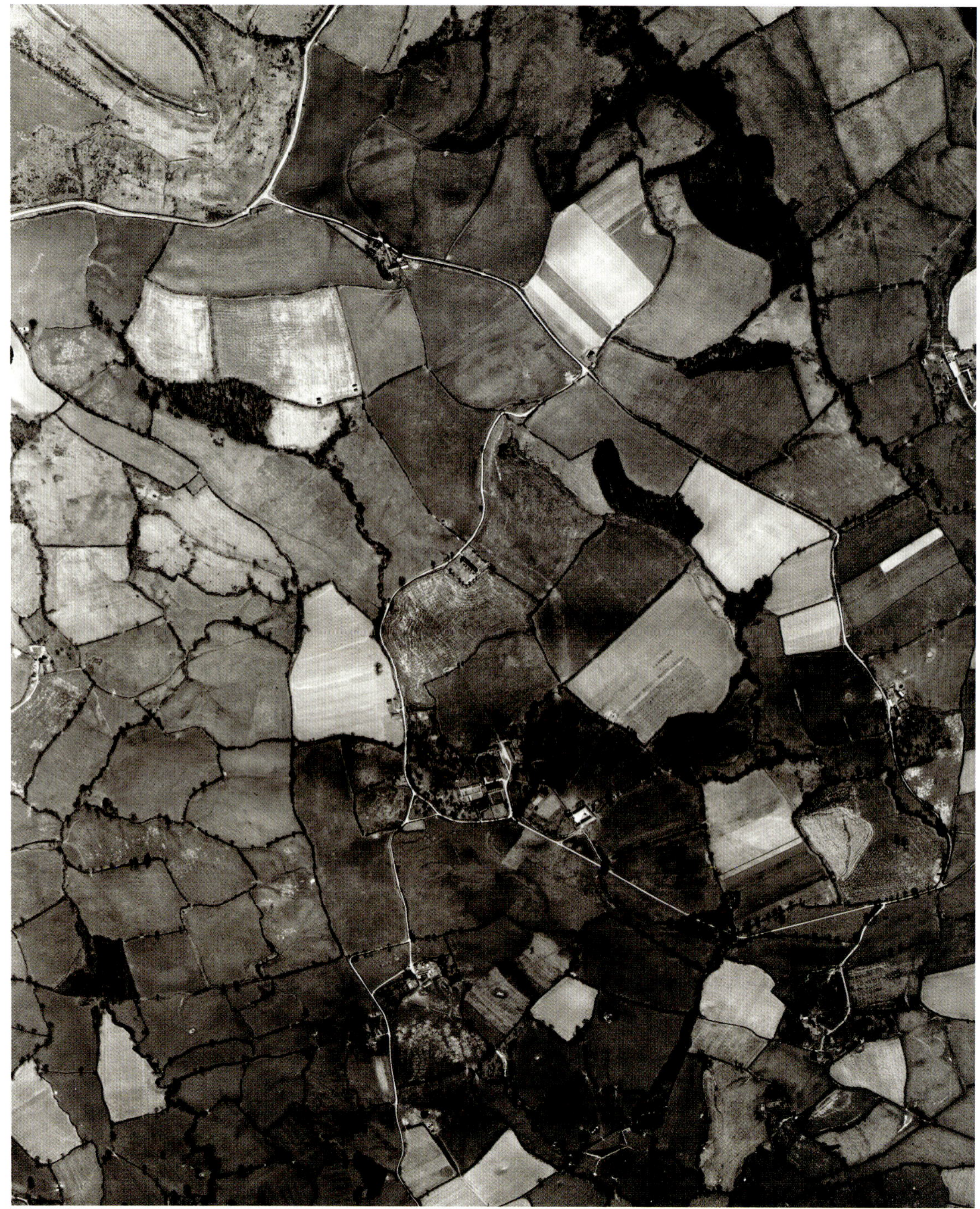

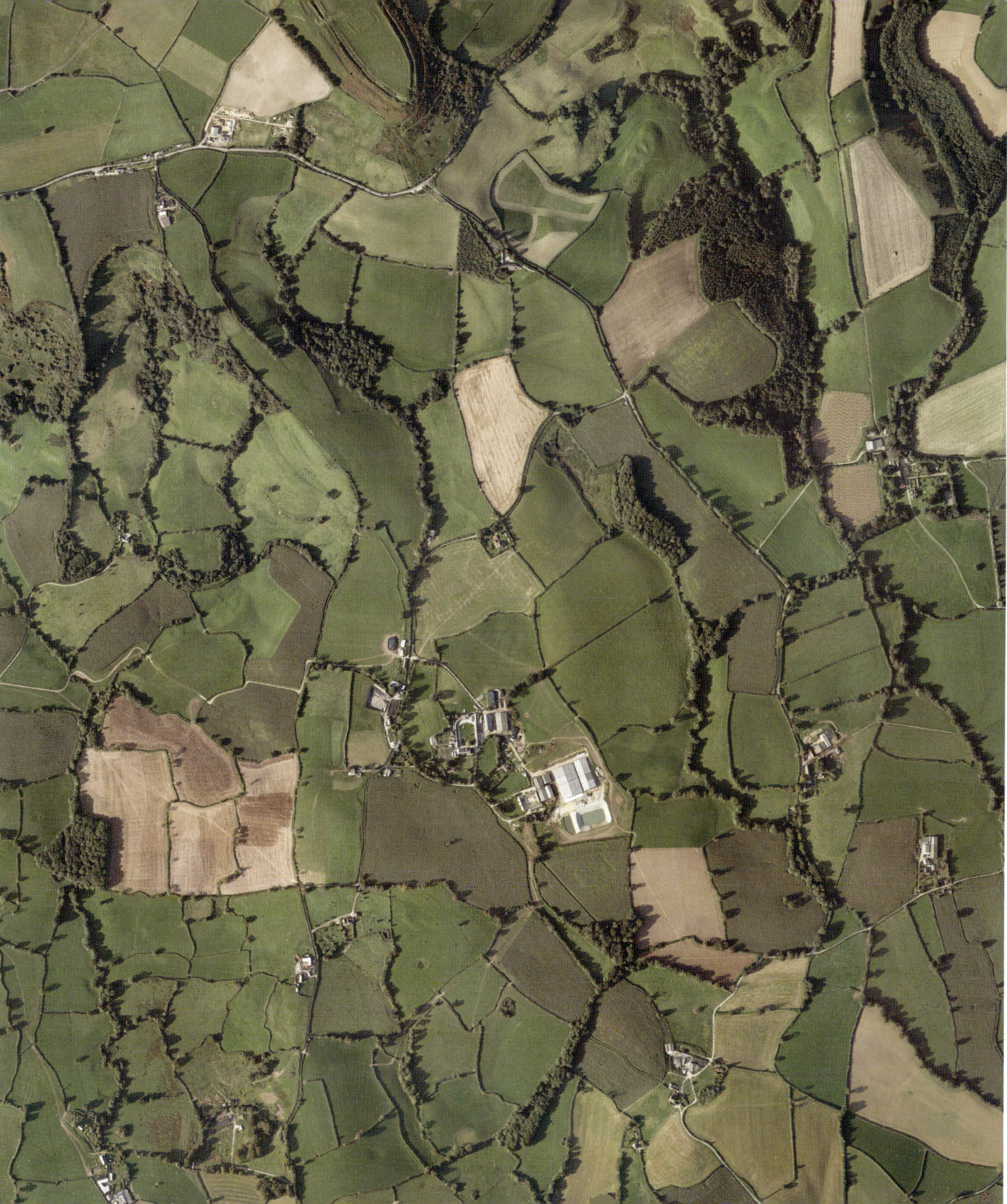

Poole 1947 photograph reference 1934-5041, centred on grid reference SZ 005 907

The town of Poole has been an important port for centuries, and the greatest change visible between these two photographs shows the changes made to enable Poole to maintain its position as a port throughout the late twentieth century.

The Hamworthy peninsula, to the west of the pictures, has expanded southwards, with huge car and lorry parks and the facilities for the cross channel ferries. On the extreme south east of the reclaimed land can be seen the sunken remains of two landing craft, similar to those seen moored in Holes Bay (on the northern side of the picture) in 1947. These

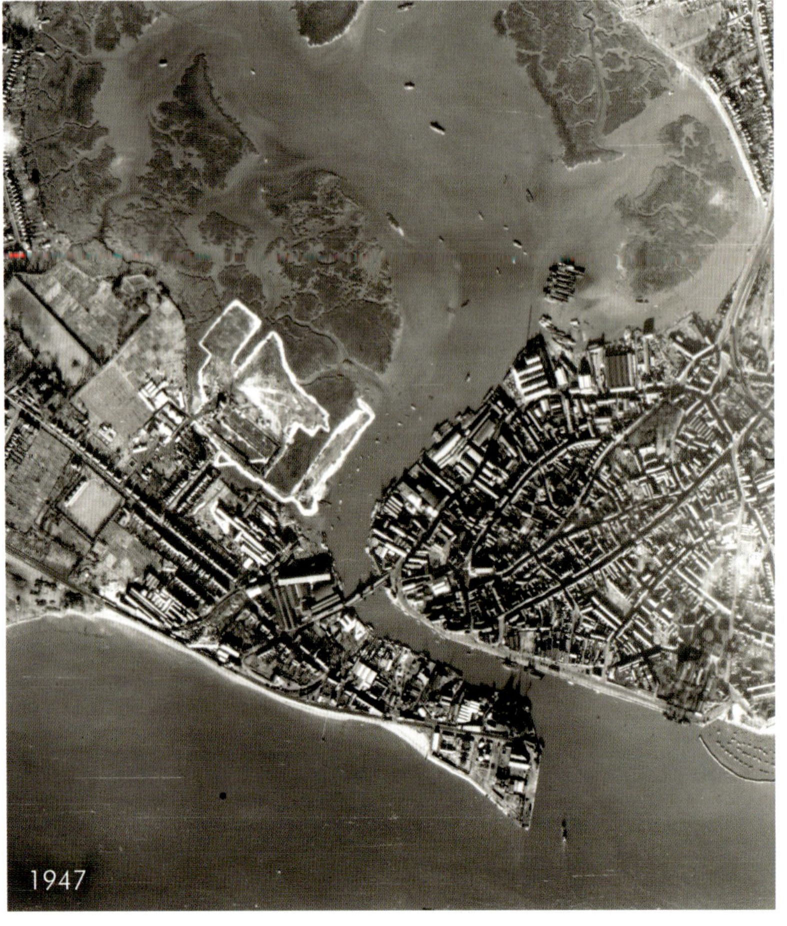

1947

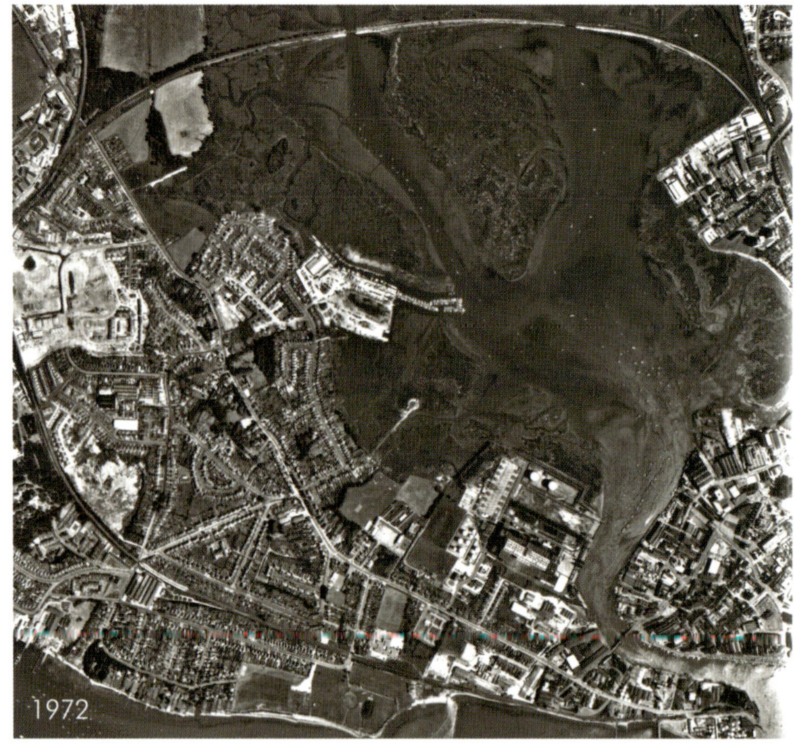

1972

were sunk to protect the developing harbour as work on building it began, and they are still there.

The town of Poole, on the other side of the channel, has changed remarkably. Other old towns have grown but have retained their historic core; in Poole there was a deliberate policy of rebuilding much of the centre of the town. Street after street of seventeenth and eighteenth century houses were demolished by the council. The changed road layout and vanished masses of houses bears witness to that.

Finally there is the curious case of Poole power station; in 1947 the land reclamation project was underway on the south-west side of Holes Bay to build a new power station. For decades the chimneys of the power station were a prominent landmark, but now the power station has gone and the reclaimed land is waiting for the next grand building, a new bridge.

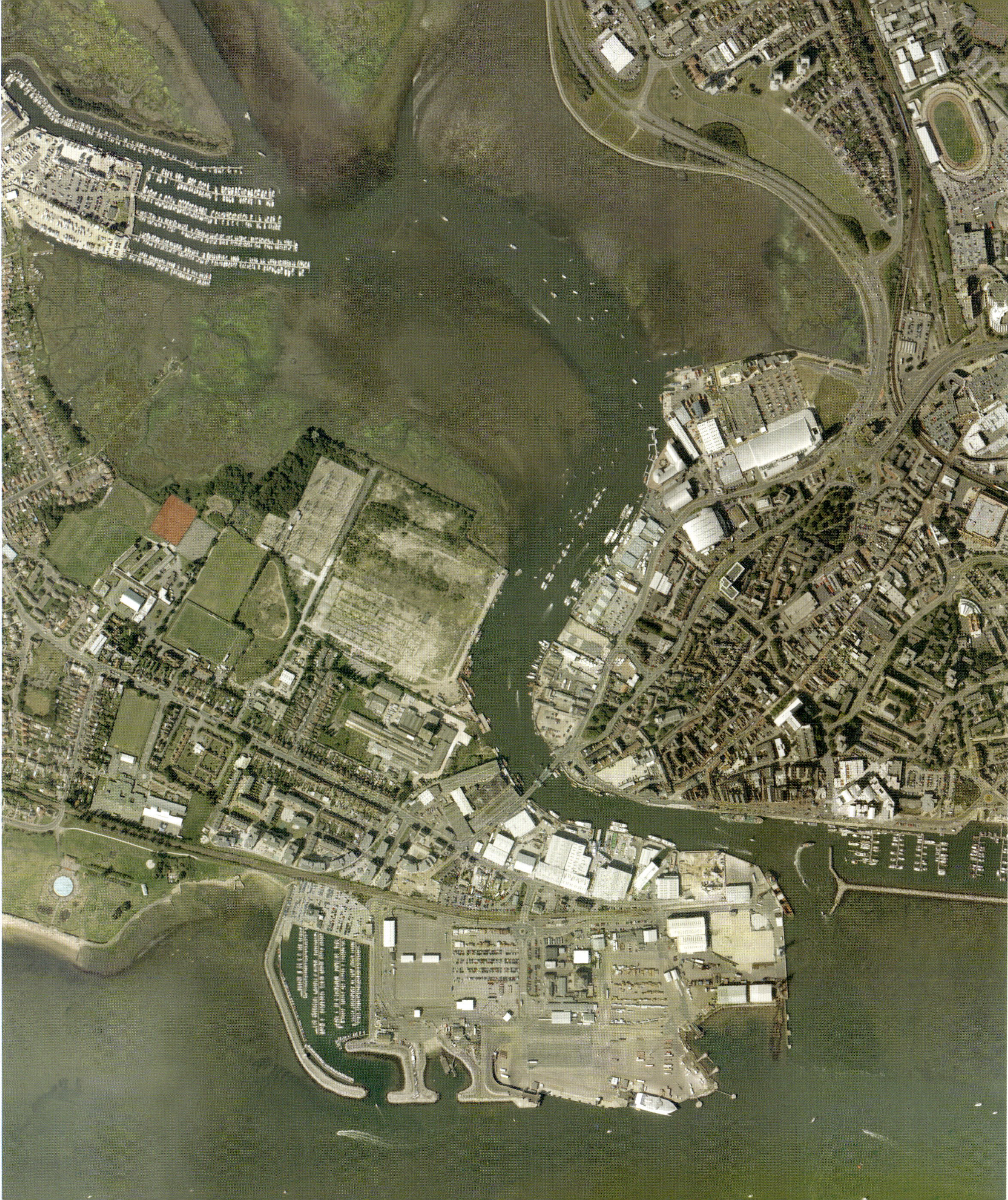

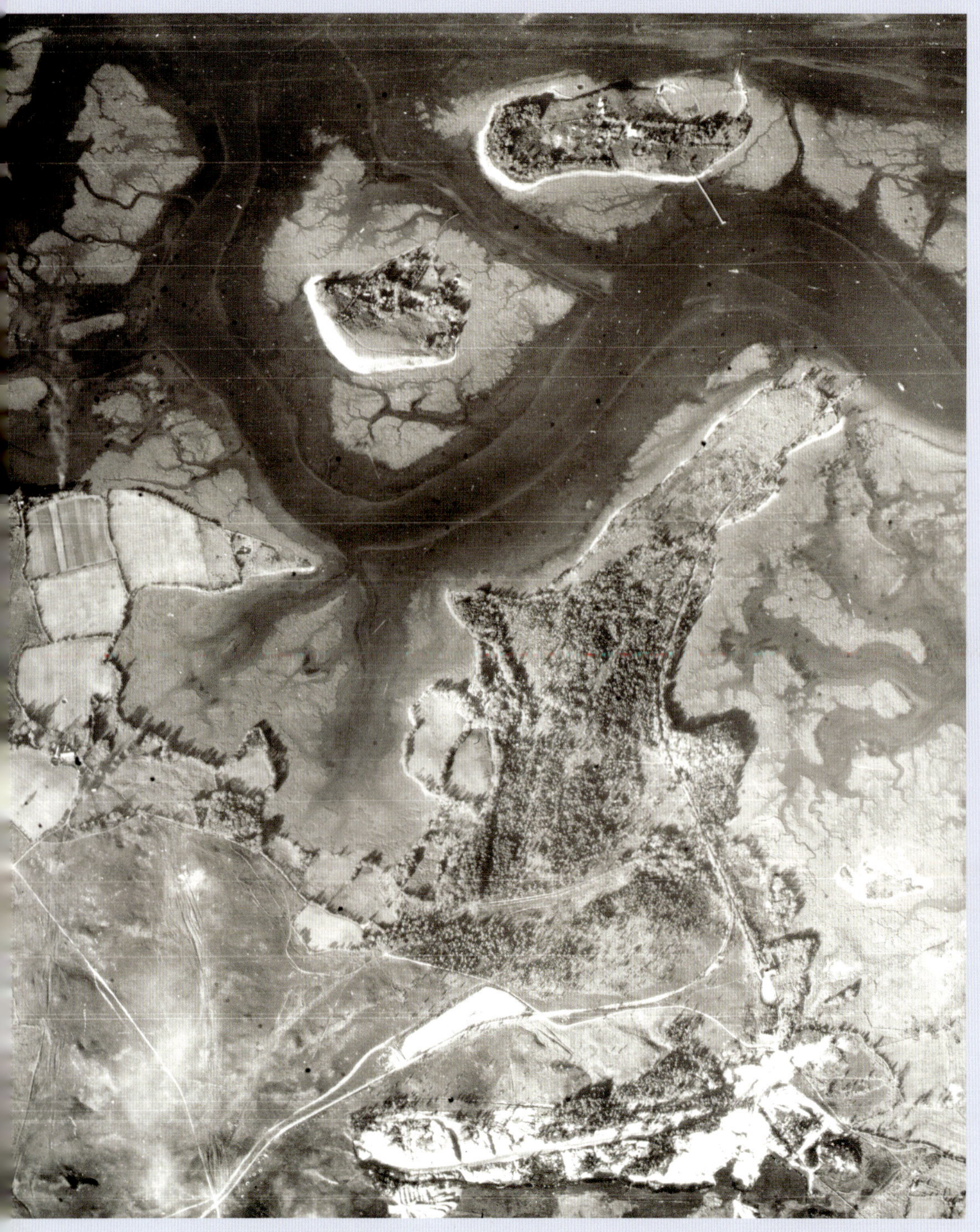

Poole Harbour – South West Corner

1947 photograph reference 1821-6389, centred on grid reference SZ 007 859

The south-west corner of Poole Harbour is regarded as the scenic part of the harbour, 'Dorset's Lakeland' admired for its natural beauty. But, as these photographs show, industry had, and still has, an important role to play in the development of this area.

The earliest traces of industry are the tracks that cross the heathland in the south-west part of the pictures; these were originally established to take Purbeck Marble from its quarries near Corfe to the quay at Ower, just to the west of the picture. During the nineteenth and early twentieth centuries the clay industry was very important here, but by 1947 it was in decline. The massive clay pit to the south of the picture had closed but the lines of the industrial railways were still clear, running across the heath and towards the quay at the end of the Goathorn Peninsula.

Today woodland has covered the clay works and been planted on much of the heathland, but a new industry has replaced clay – oil. On the Goathorn Peninsula is a large oil well, whilst a large pumping station hides in the woodland on Furzey Island at the top of the photograph.

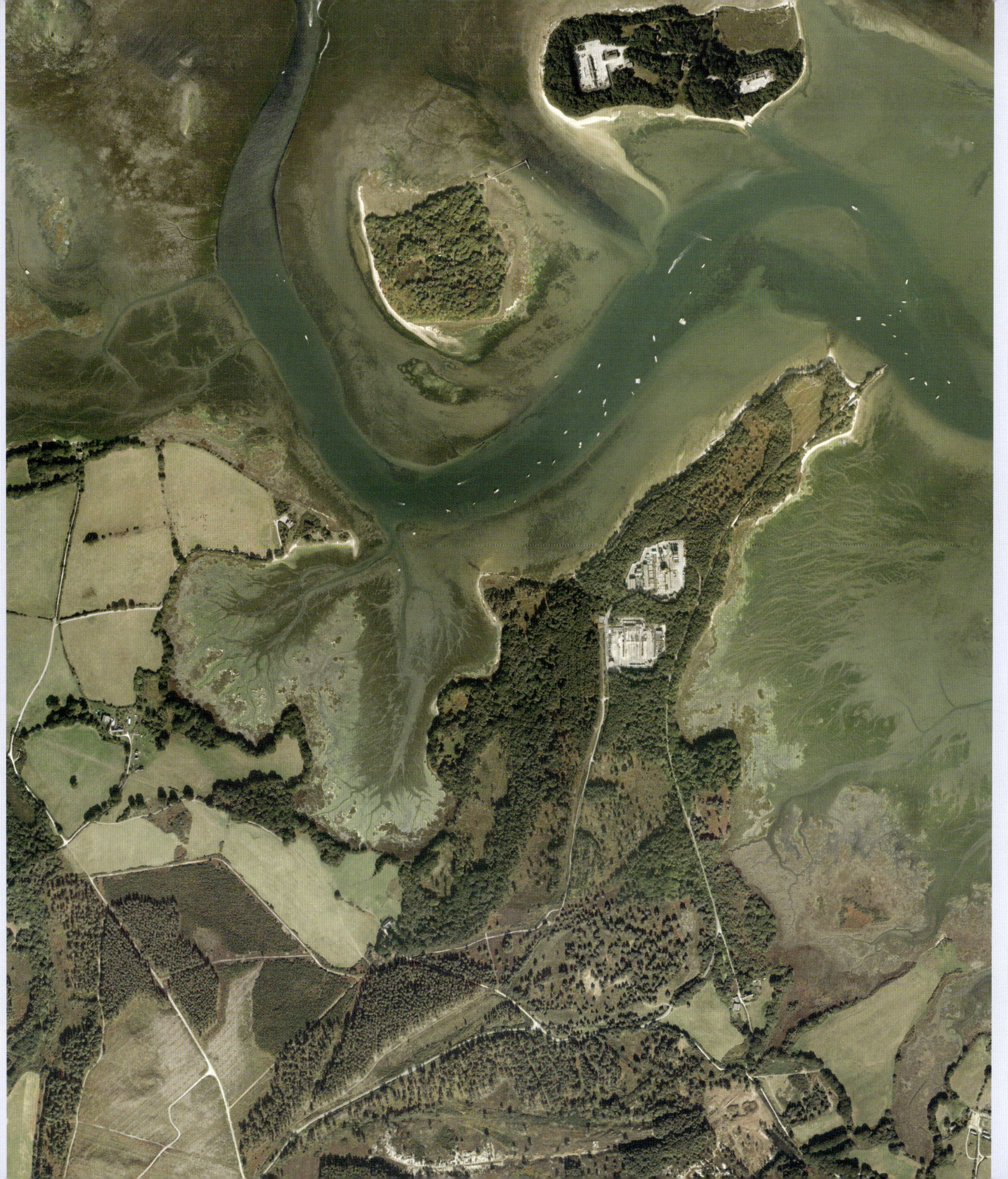

Portland Bill 1947 photograph reference 1821-4051, centred on grid reference SY 684 693

The landscape of Portland Bill is a remarkable one. Looking at both the modern and 1947 pictures the fields can be seen to be divided into long, thin and sometimes sinuous strips. These are strip fields, laid out in one of very few remaining working strip field systems in Britain. This was a common medieval practice, but changing agricultural methods from the sixteenth century onwards led to its gradual disappearance, apart from Portland Bill.

The coast, particularly on the eastern edge is lined with small quarries, which had fallen out of use by 1947. At the Bill, the lighthouse stands. This is the third location for a lighthouse on Portland. The two earlier ones can be seen on either side of the peninsula, the old Lower Light is now the Portland Bird Observatory, and can easily be identified on the modern picture as it is surrounded by scrub and low woodland. There has been only little development of woodland here, but as the landscape was essentially treeless in 1947 the change has been substantial.

The complexes of buildings just north of the Bill, and at the northern edge of the modern picture were military research and development sites. They developed during the Cold War, after the 1947 picture was taken. Indeed if the modern photograph is examined closely, in the grassland on the western side of the Bill, just north of the former military buildings, several circles can be seen looking like very neat Disc Barrows. These are the bases of massive radio masts, erected during the 1970s and 1980s, and now long gone leaving yet another layer to Dorset's historic landscape.

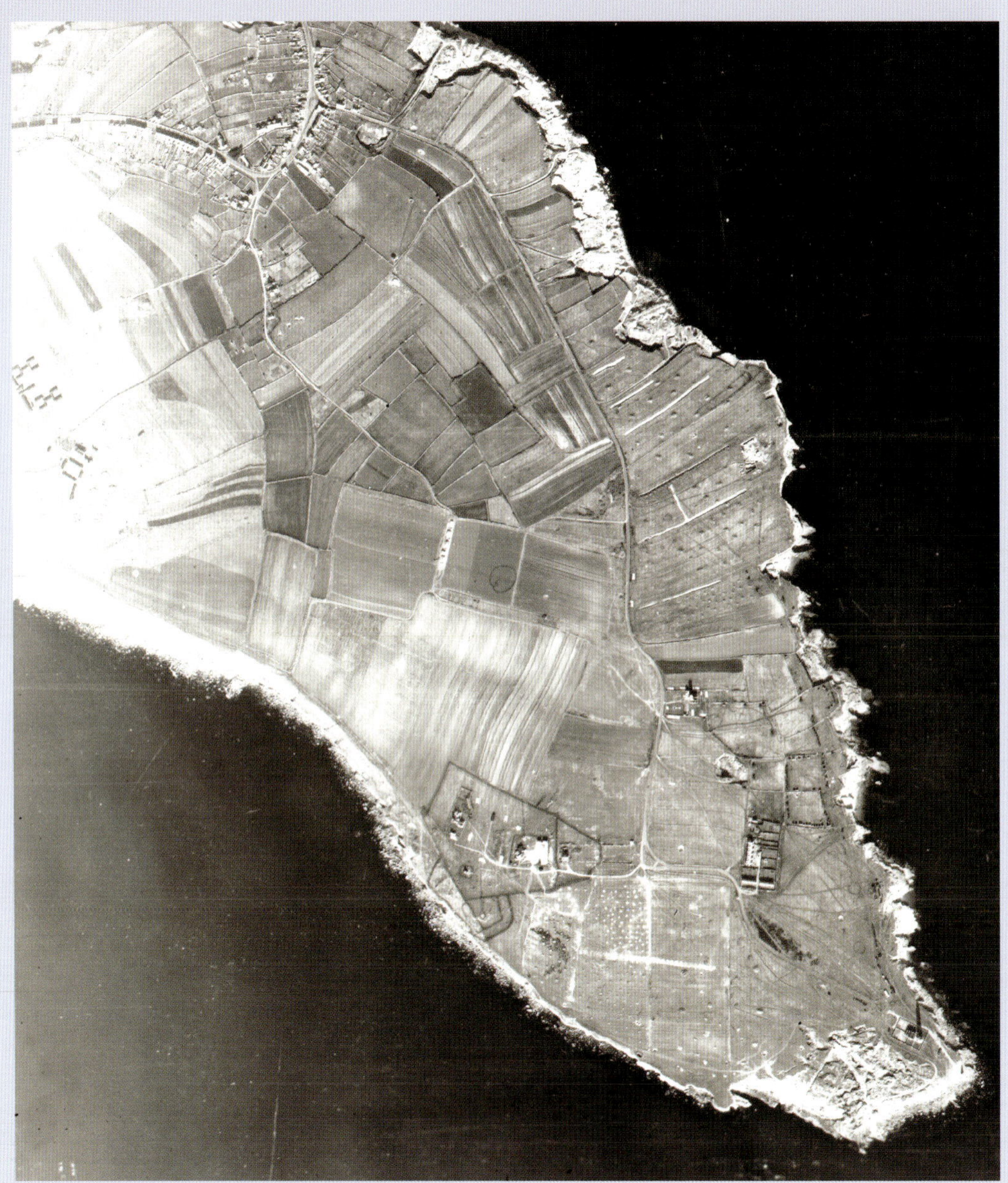

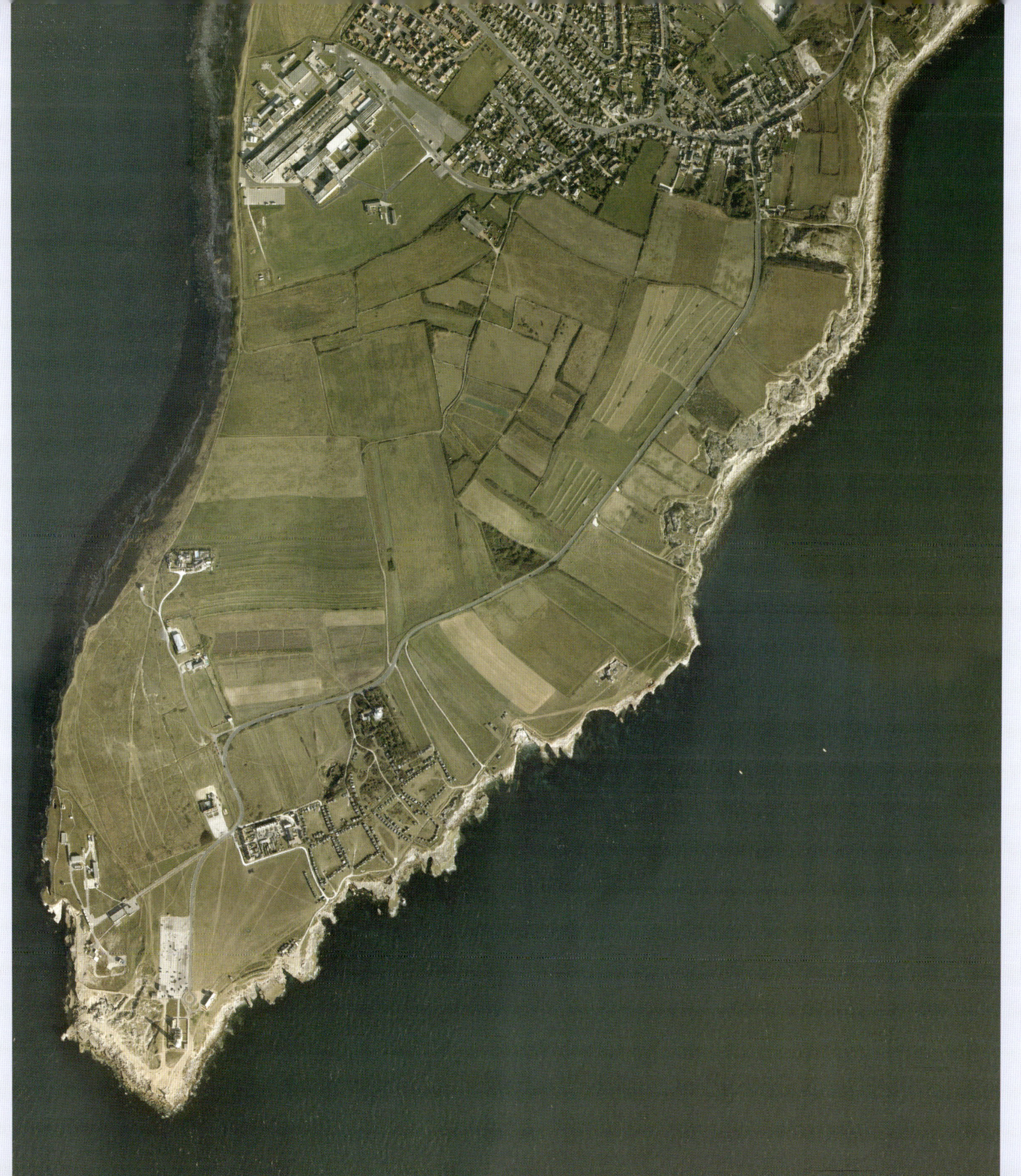

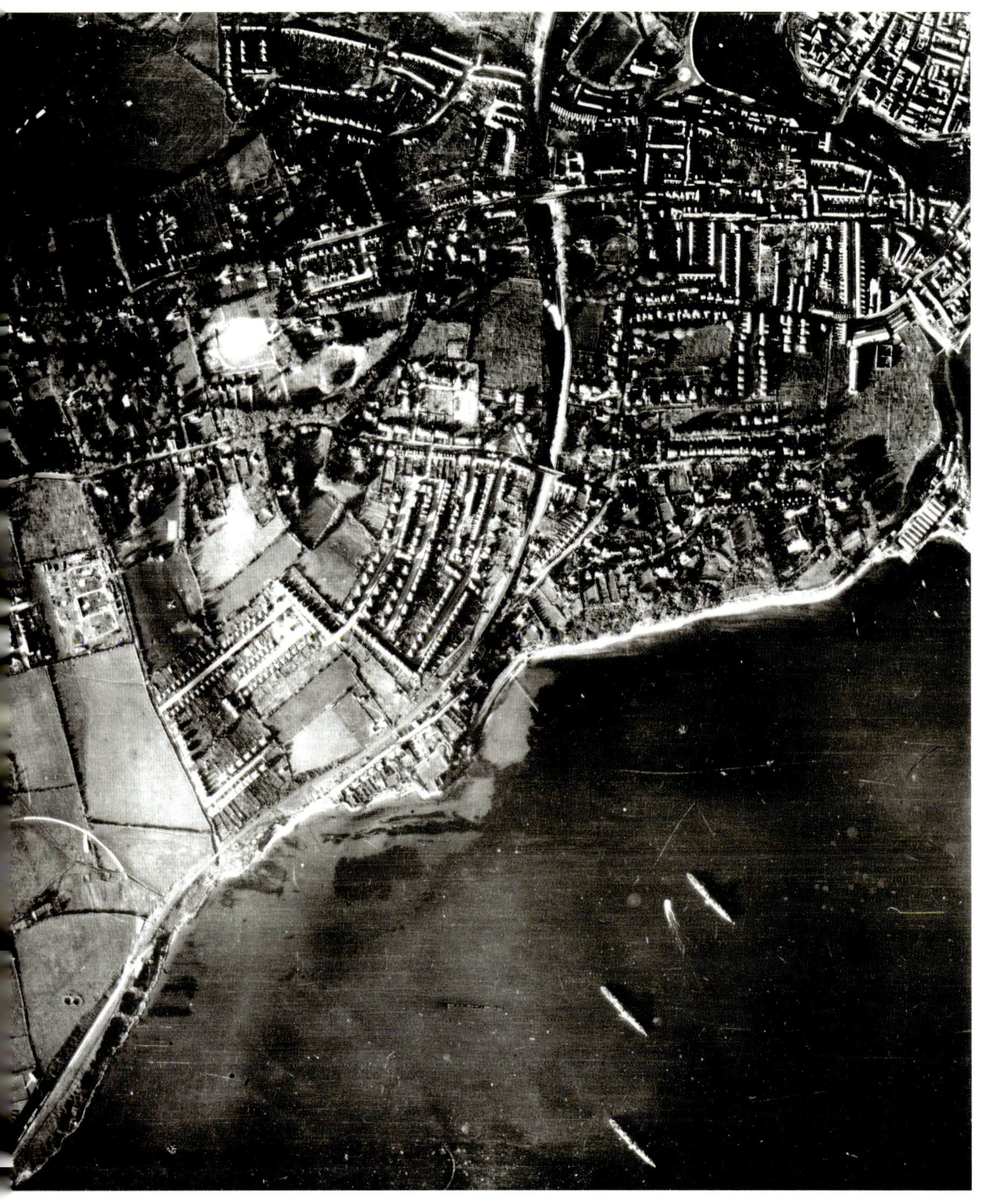

Portland Harbour and Sandsfoot Castle

1947 photograph reference 1821-5446, centred on grid reference SY 676 775

In 1947 Weymouth (to the north of the photographs) had already spread south with terraces of late Victorian and twentieth century houses together with occasional larger villas, particularly along the harbour shore. These had, for the most part, been fitted into the pre-existing field pattern and the mixture of fields and housing developments can clearly be seen. Today houses have spread over most of the area, often ignoring the older boundaries.

Crossing the 1947 picture is the Weymouth to Portland Railway. This has long gone, but it is still clearly visible, and used as a medium distance foot-path – the Rodwell Trail – and has become very well wooded.

On the shoreline lie the ruins of Sandsfoot Castle. Built in the sixteenth century it has long been ruined, and during the 1930s had been surrounded by gardens. The gardens still survive as does the castle, though more has been lost to erosion since 1947.

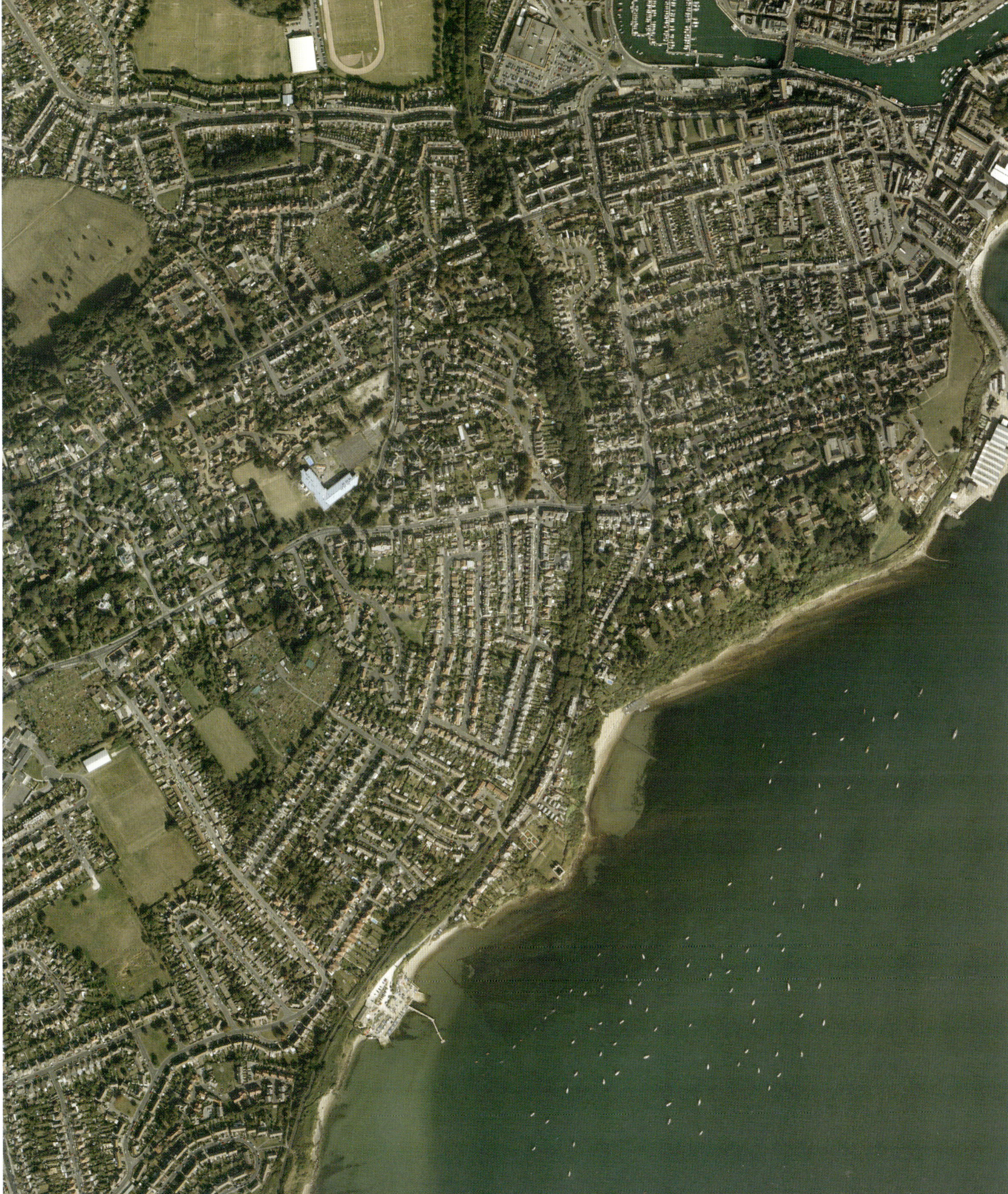

Portland Verne 1947 photograph reference 1821-1408, centred on grid reference SY 693 737

The Verne is the massive Victorian fort built on the heights overlooking Portland Harbour, as part of the defences of this important naval base. Its distinctive shape, with mid-nineteenth-century state-of-the-art defences is clearly recognisable in the middle of the pictures.

The differences between the two sets of pictures are considerable, and are best considered moving from south to north.

To the south, in 1947 there was a considerable area of quarrying, which has now moved to a different location but is continuing. Quarrying is, after all, the main industry of Portland and has been for centuries. Just north of the quarries lie the High Angle Batteries, which were part of the nineteenth century defences of the island, but were already obsolete by 1947 and had no military function. Then there is the Verne Citadel, the massive Victorian fort. During the war it had been used for accommodation and administration; today it is a prison, the walls originally designed to keep the French out now keep British prisoners in.

West of the Verne the zigzag track leading down to Castletown is testament to the steepness of the slope. This is crossed by a straight line leading down to the port. In 1947 this was an inclined railway, the Merchants' Railway originally built to take stone off the island, which closed shortly after the picture was taken. Curving round the north of the island and along the cliffs to the east of the Verne the Portland Railway ran in 1947 – the smoke from a train can be seen rising into the still air – this too has gone though much of its route can still be traced on the ground.

North of the Verne the slopes were open in 1947, though are now covered with dense scrubby woodland dropping down into Portland Port. Now a civilian port in 1947 it was an important naval base, and a large warship can be seen moored north of the breakwater. At the very top of the 1947 picture are rectangular objects. These are concrete caissons of the Mulberry Harbours, which had been designed to be towed across the Channel to create artificial harbours for the offloading of equipment in the immediate aftermath of D-Day. These units were surplus to requirement and were being kept to see if there was a use for them. Amazingly there was. In 1953 a disastrous flood hit the countries around the North Sea. In Holland many of the dykes were breached, and many of the unused Mulberry Harbour caissons were towed across the North Sea and used to help repair the damage. Two were not used and were moored in a different position. They are still there and are now two of Dorset's strangest listed buildings.

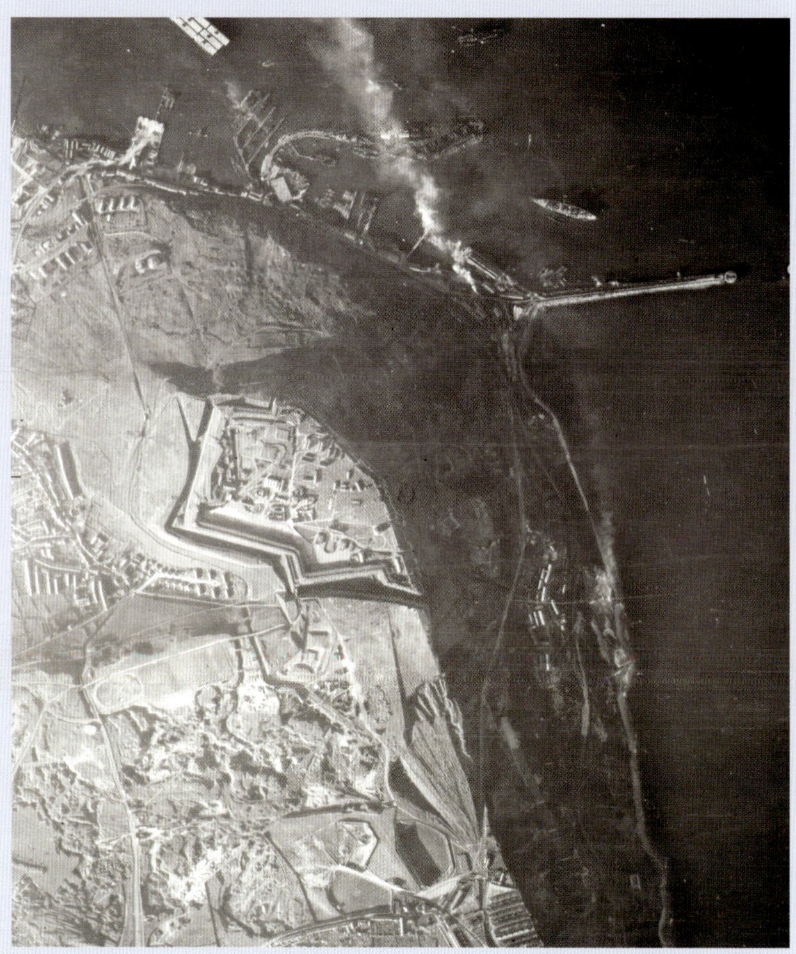

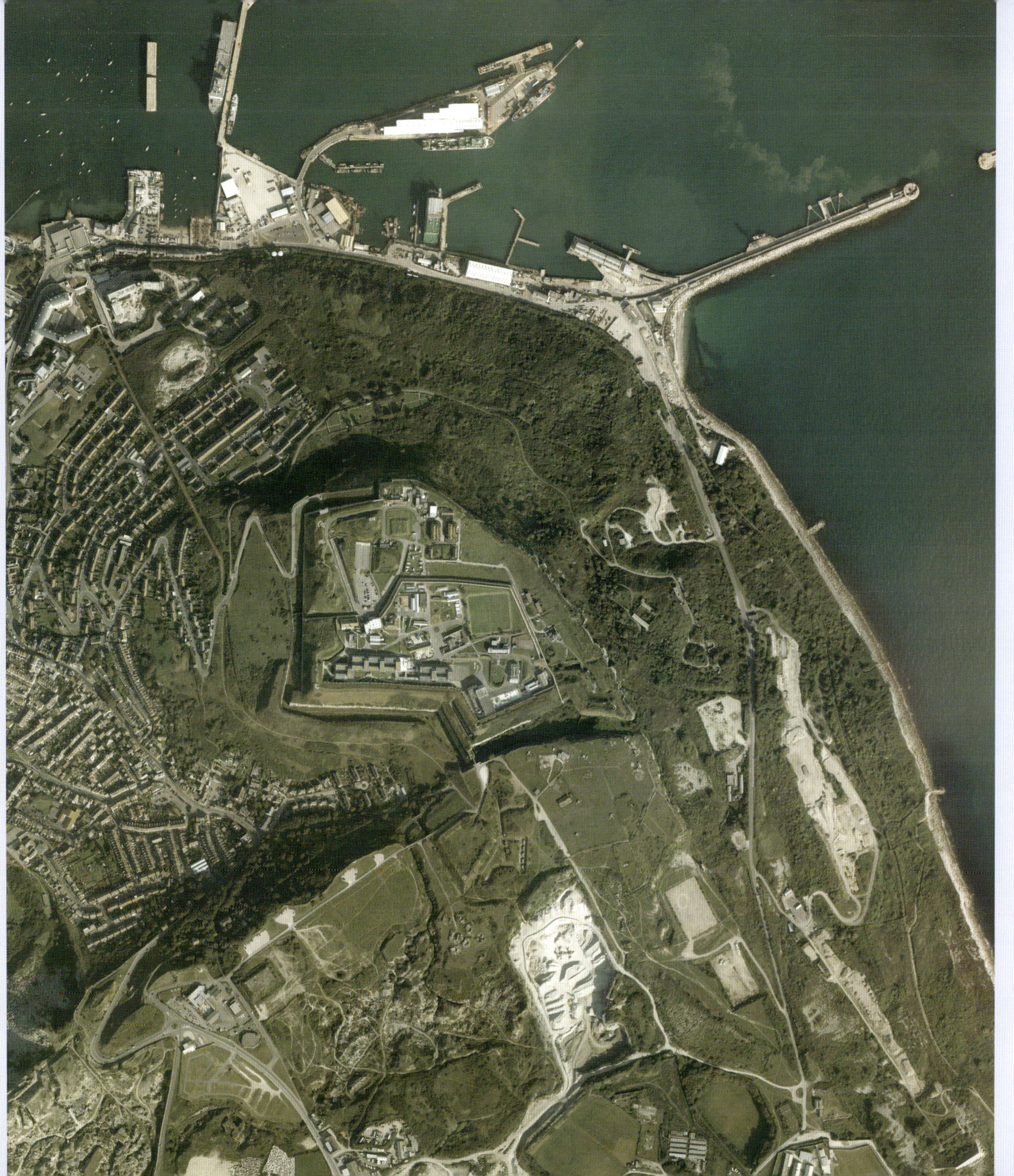

Rampisham Down Radio Masts

1947 photograph reference 1974-2393, centred on grid reference ST 539 018

Rampisham Down is a notable, and perhaps surprising, landmark of western Dorset. For many miles around the complex of radio aerials

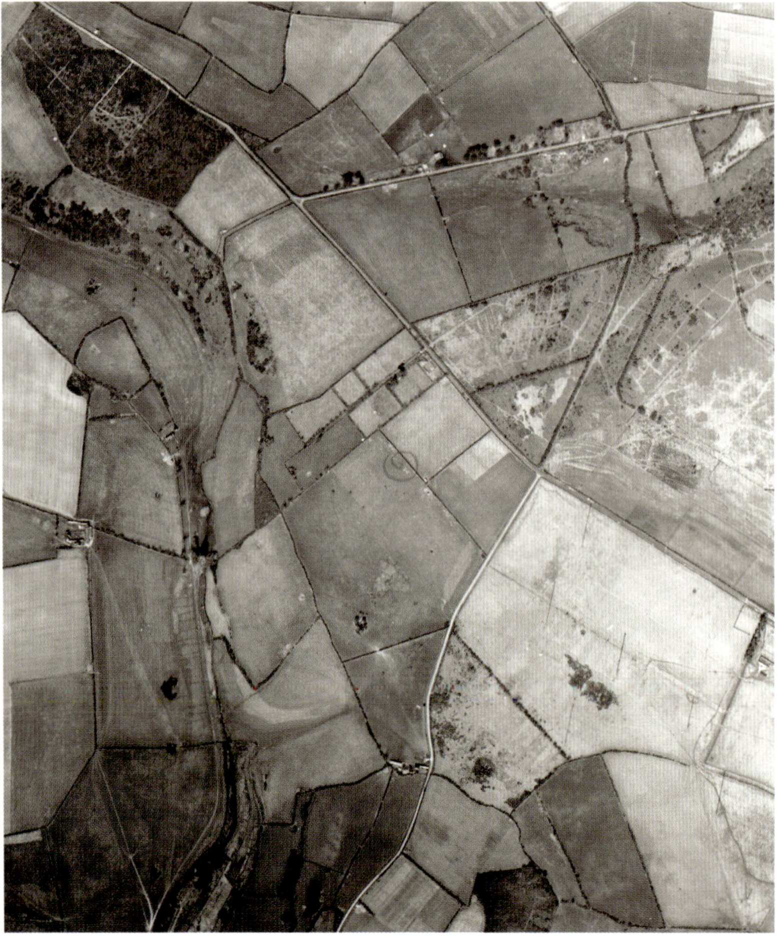

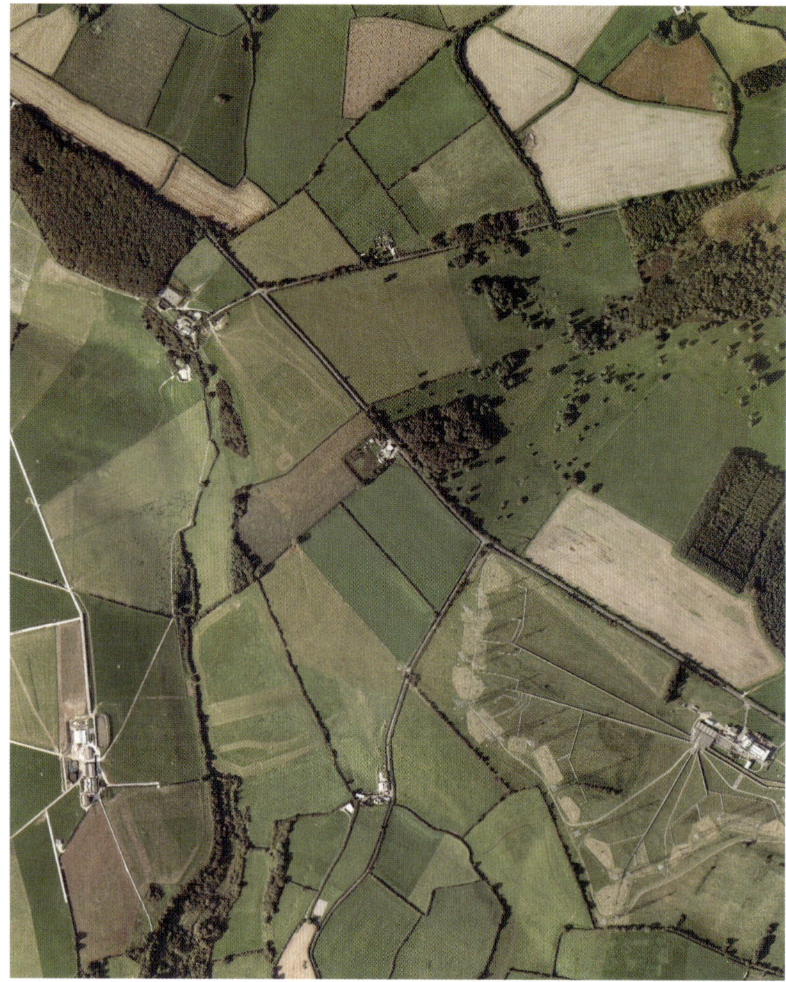

dominates the skyline. In 1947 there were only a few aerials in position, but today the station, on the eastern edge of the photographs, is one of the main transmitters for the BBC World Service.

Elsewhere the differences between the two pictures are typical of much of rural Dorset, some loss of field boundaries, and quite a considerable increase in woodland.

Sandbanks 1947 photograph reference 1821-1009, centred on grid reference SZ 044 872

In 1947 Sandbanks was just beginning to recover from the war; before 1939 it had only begun to be developed. In the days before cheap motor transport it was at the end of a long bus ride from Poole or Bournemouth and so was still fairly quiet and remote.

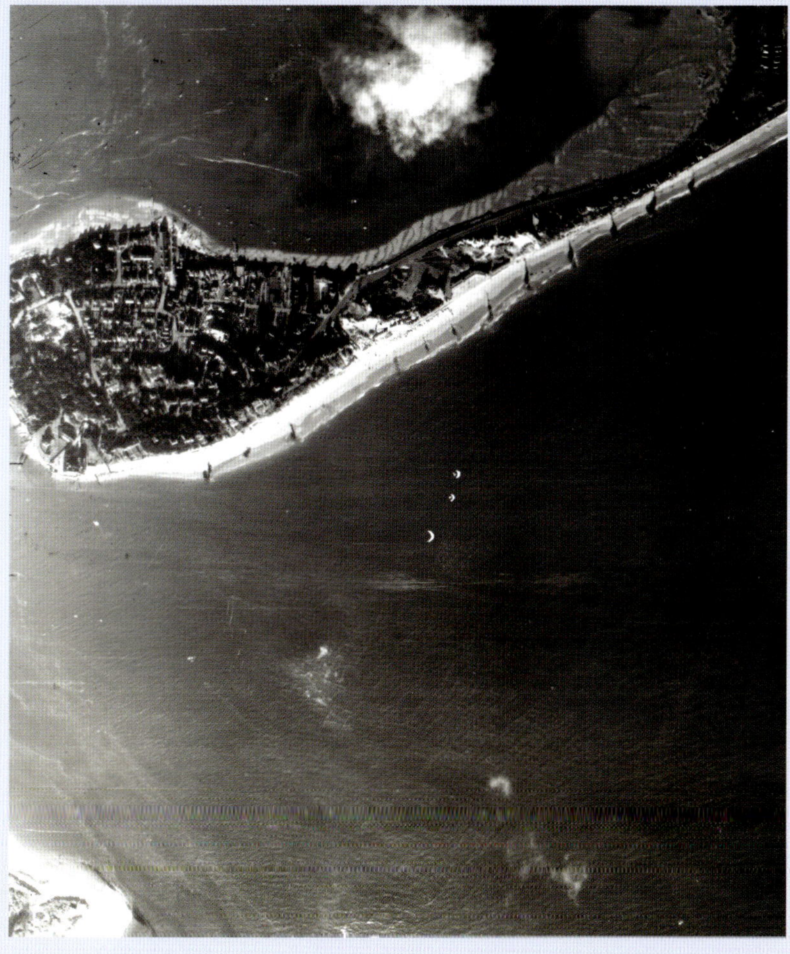

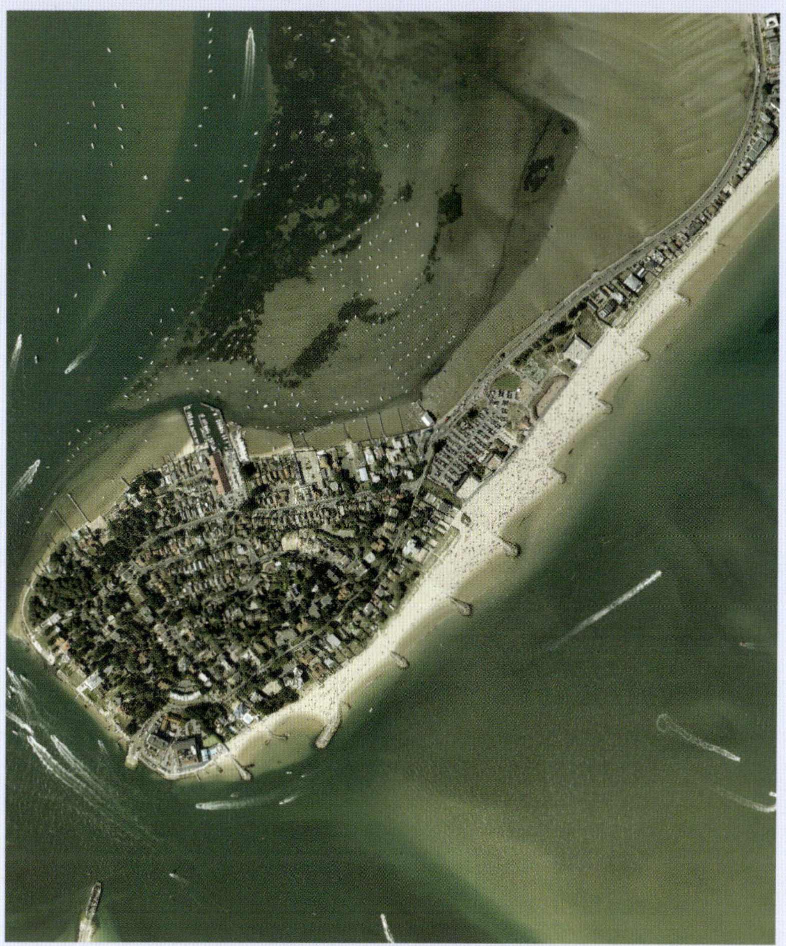

This has now all changed, with large car parks, the marina of the Poole Royal Motor Yacht Club and above all the house prices have soared: for many years this area has had the dubious honour of having some of the highest property prices in England

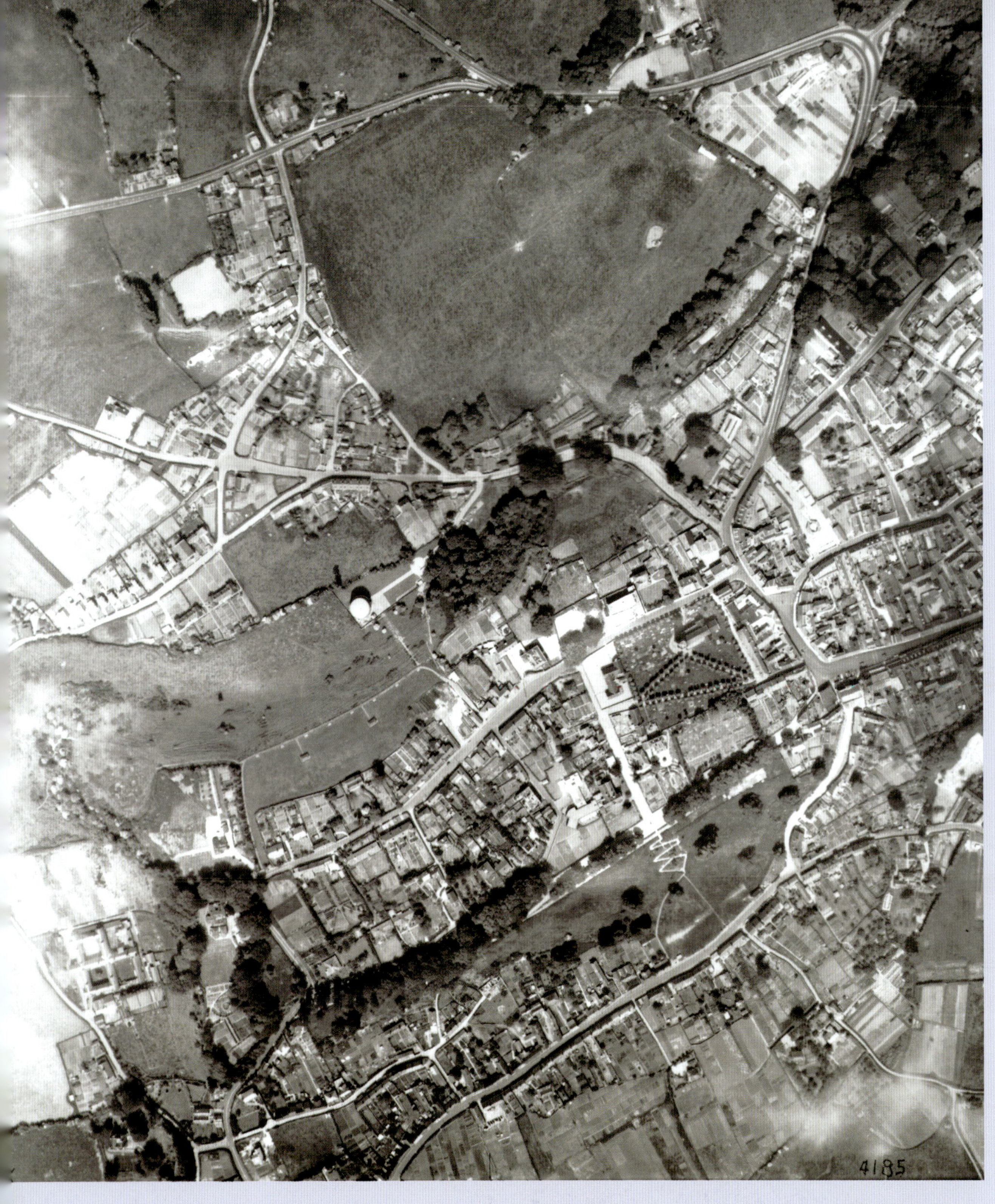

Shaftesbury

1947-9 photograph reference 4-6-50 5029, centred on grid reference ST 860 230

The hilltop town of Shaftesbury runs along a narrow, steep-sided, ridge. This gave the town a linear shape, clearly visible on the 1947 photograph, and still visible today. The town might have grown but it is virtually impossible (and very unwise) to build on the steep slopes so these have been left. The zigzag path clearly visible on the southern side of the town is an obvious clue to the steepness of the slope.

Today Shaftesbury has grown, to the north and south, leaving the historic town isolated on its hill top. Unusually within a town woodland has spread, trees have grown up in gardens and particularly around Castle Hill on the western edge of the old town, where the tree roots are damaging the archaeology and conservation work has taken place to remove some of them.

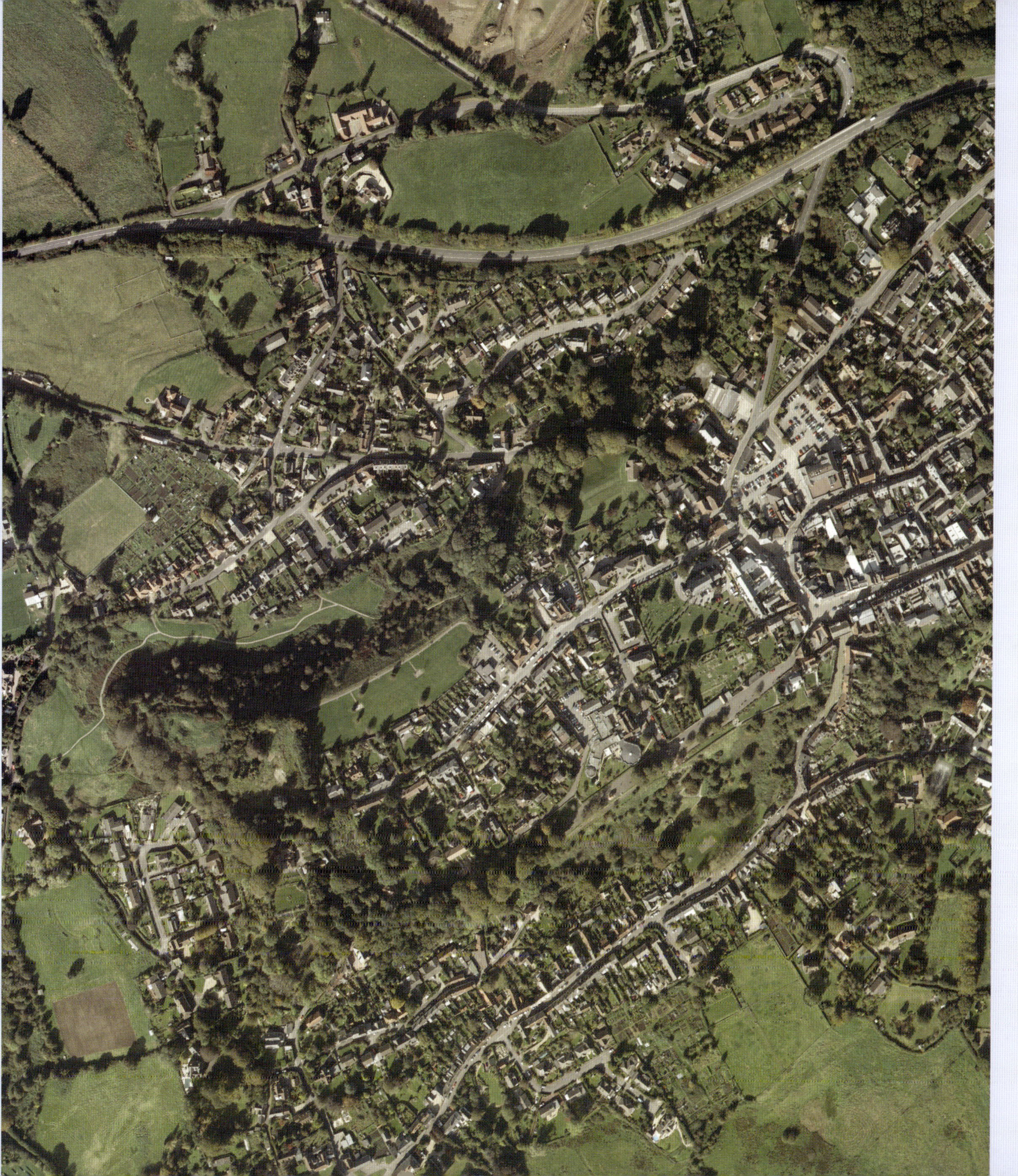

Sherborne 1947 photograph reference 1974-2145, centred on grid reference ST 637 169

The core of the historic town of Sherborne has changed very little in the past sixty years. The pleasing architecture of the town seems to have had an effect on all those who come to build here: they have tried to emulate rather than destroy. Even the Victorian gas works, still in use in 1947 and visible on the southern side of the town, are attractive buildings.

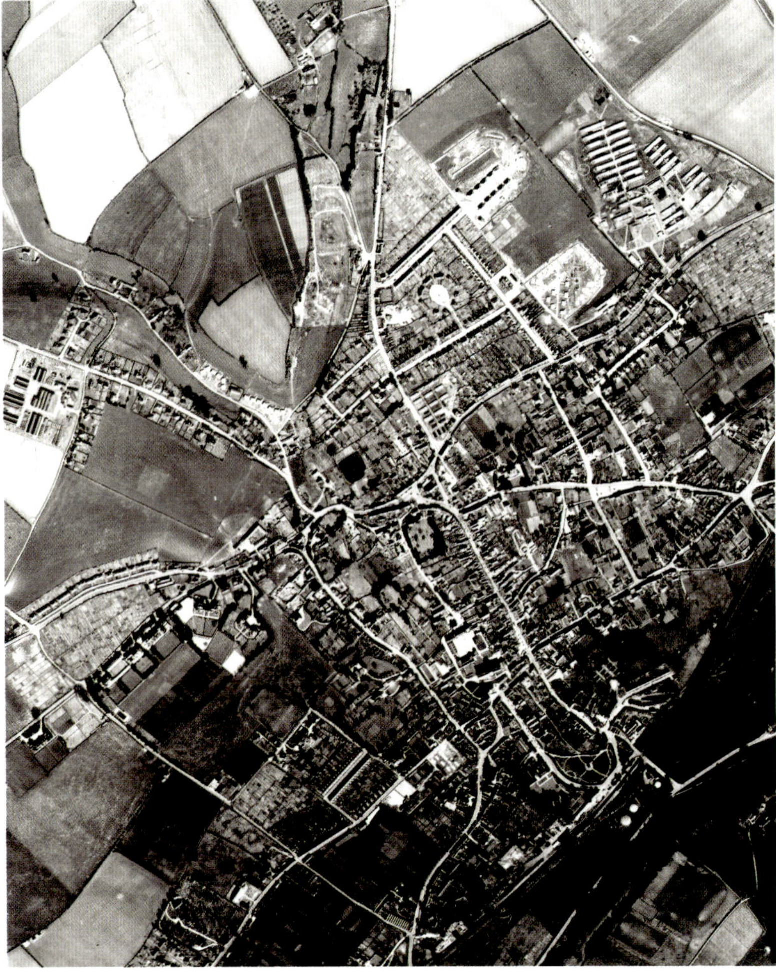

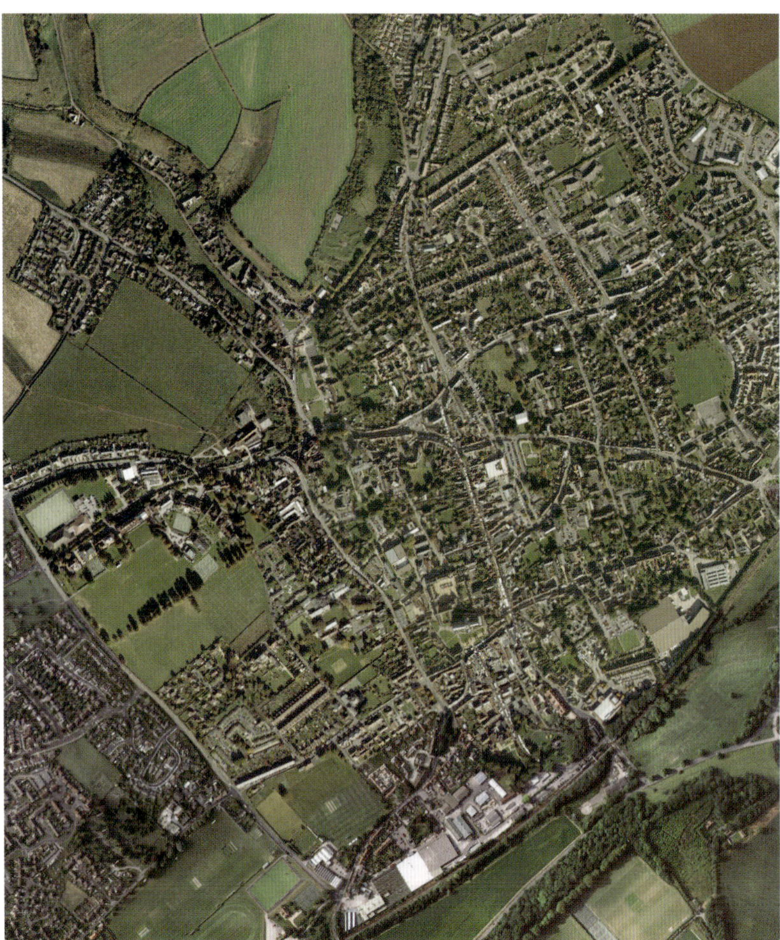

Around the edges of the town there has been extensive development. The large areas of allotments have mostly been built over, as have the numerous military buildings. To the north east of the town, in 1947, was a large military hospital. Beside the hospital can be seen the beginning of the development of post-war Sherborne, the light colours of the new roads and buildings very clear.

Shillingstone

1947 photograph reference 1974-2172, centred on grid reference ST 824 106

The village of Shillingstone has changed in a way typical of many Dorset villages. In 1947 it was essentially a linear village, with most of the houses fronting onto the main road running between Blandford and Sturminster Newton. The only houses away from the road were those towards the ancient church, which had been built on a low mound, just south of the road and above the river. Immediately north of the village ran the railway, and beyond that the River Stour. But change was coming and at the eastern edge of the village new houses were being built; the picture even shows the foundations of two which were under construction.

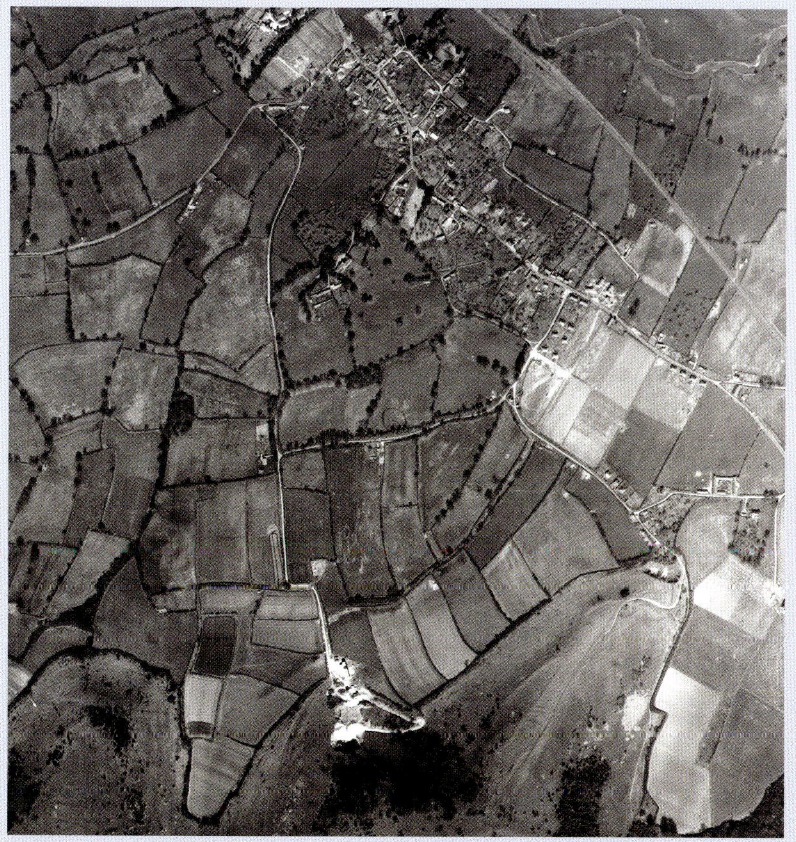

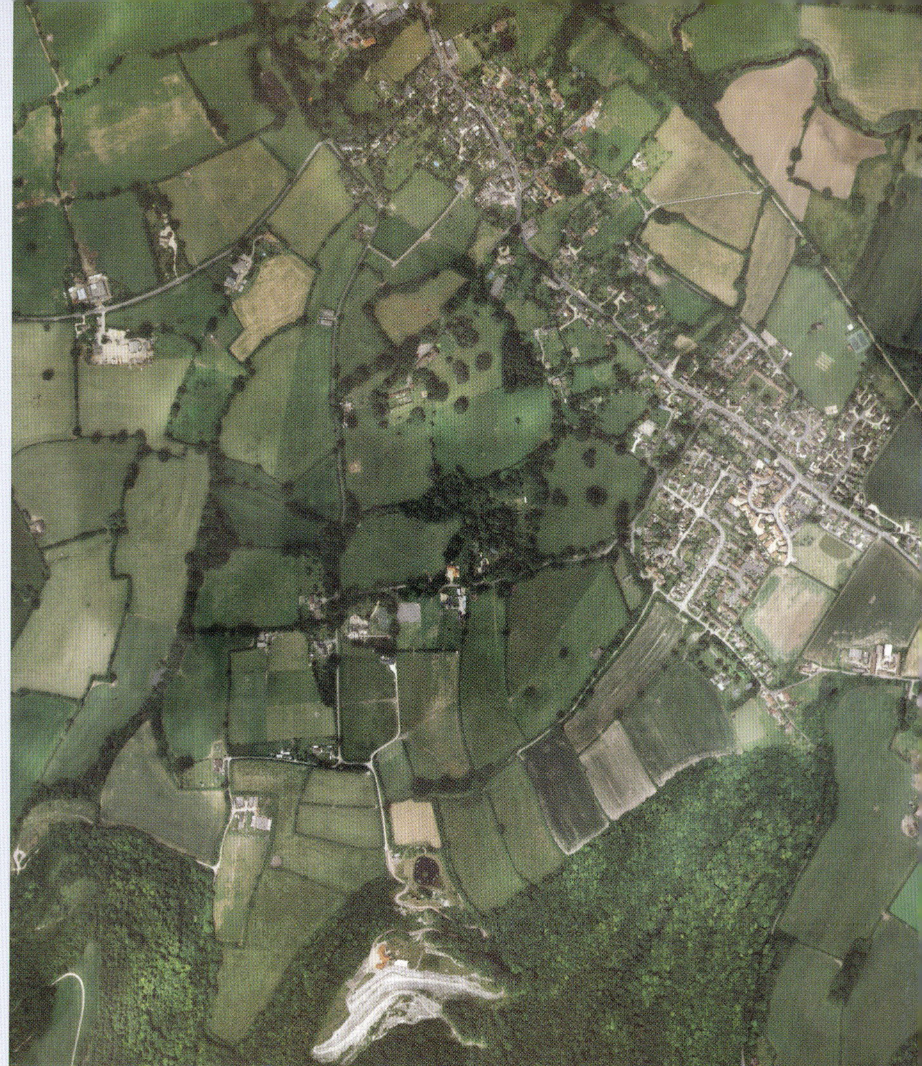

Today those houses have formed the nucleus of the main area of newer housing. The railway has gone, but the surrounding field pattern is essentially unaltered. Some fields, particularly to the south of the pictures have a distinctive S shape, suggesting that they were formed by enclosing strip fields, the shape of the modern field echoing the shape of the medieval strips.

The spread of woodland has been extensive. The downland to the south, essentially open in 1947 is now covered with trees, and woodland has spread along the former railway line and covered several small fields. However there have been losses too. Around the village, the small fields behind the cottages were dotted with trees, almost certainly orchards, frequent in early twentieth century Dorset when cider was a common drink, sadly rare today.

Spetisbury 1947 photograph reference 1934-1101, centred on grid reference ST 910 029

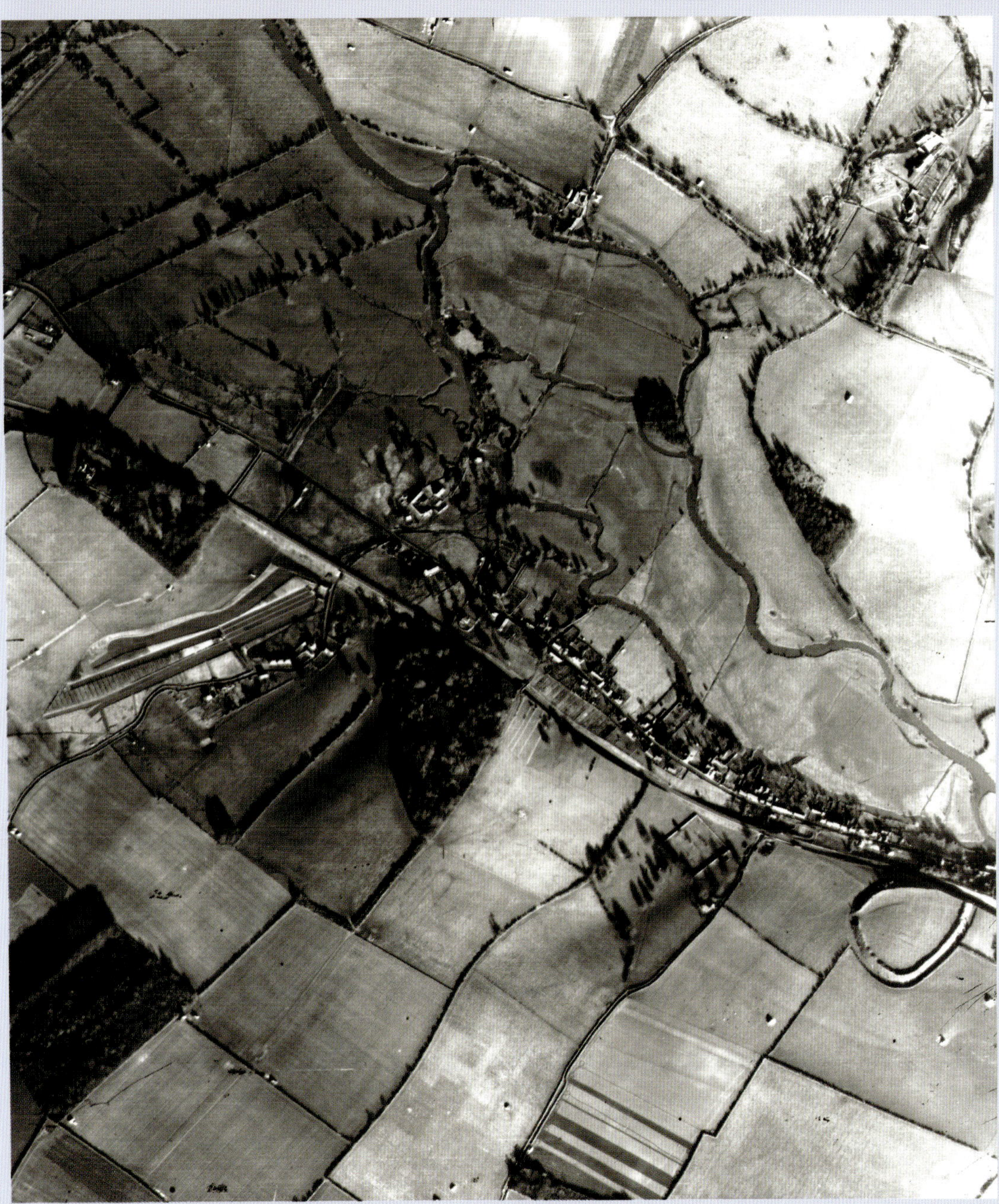

The village of Spetisbury lies beside the River Stour a few miles south of Blandford. Immediately south of the village, and overlooking the river, is the Iron Age hill fort of Spettisbury Rings.

In 1947 the railway ran up the river valley paralleling the road and the river. The village lay between the railway and the river, whilst to the south was a large watercress farm.

Today whilst the village has grown, growth has been confined to the area between the river and the embankment of the former railway. The only development on the other side of the old railway line is a group of houses beside the watercress farm, which is still in production. The field pattern is generally unchanged and there has been comparatively little woodland development apart from along the old railway embankment, which is now essentially a linear woodland.

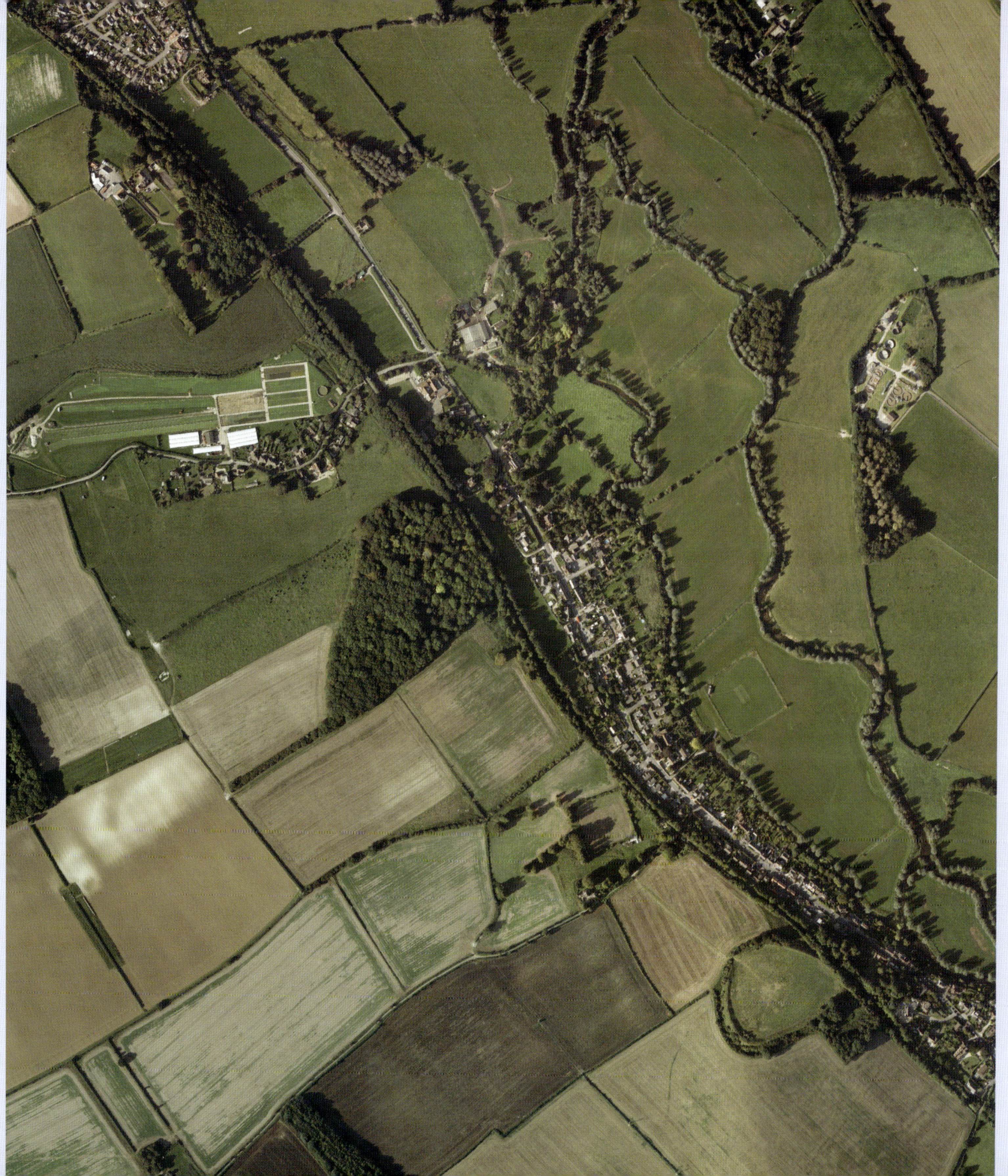

Stoborough Heath

1947 photograph reference 1821-4411, centred on grid reference SY 930 842

Stoborough Heath to the south of Wareham is a fragment of the great heathlands that once covered a good deal of eastern Dorset. Created by the agricultural practices of Bronze Age farmers, and maintained by rough grazing they were generally little valued until the late twentieth century when the importance of their remarkable wildlife was recognised. As a result many of the large surviving areas of heathland, like Stoborough Heath have been designated as nature reserves.

The soils are very poor and had not been ploughed for centuries. As a result features survive here that have disappeared elsewhere. The 1947 photograph shows what appear to be hundreds of thin ditches crossing the heathland, but in fact these are all ancient tracks. It will be seen that they are paralleling the road from Wareham to Corfe Castle that crosses the picture from north west to south east. These are essentially the medieval roads from the important port at Wareham to the great castle at Corfe. They were formed when one track across the heathland became too eroded to be easily used, then a new track was made alongside and so parallel tracks were formed. Only at places like fords, did these parallel tracks converge, often eroding very deep sunken ways or holloways at these point. These tracks still exist – nothing has been done to damage most of them, it is just that the heather is longer and they are more difficult to see.

There is evidence of other transport methods visible as well as the roads. The railway crosses the heath: over the past sixty years it has been open, closed, used as an industrial line, and now open again, but there are other railways visible as well. Running due north was an industrial line, the Middlebere Plateway, built in 1805 to carry ball clay to Middlebere

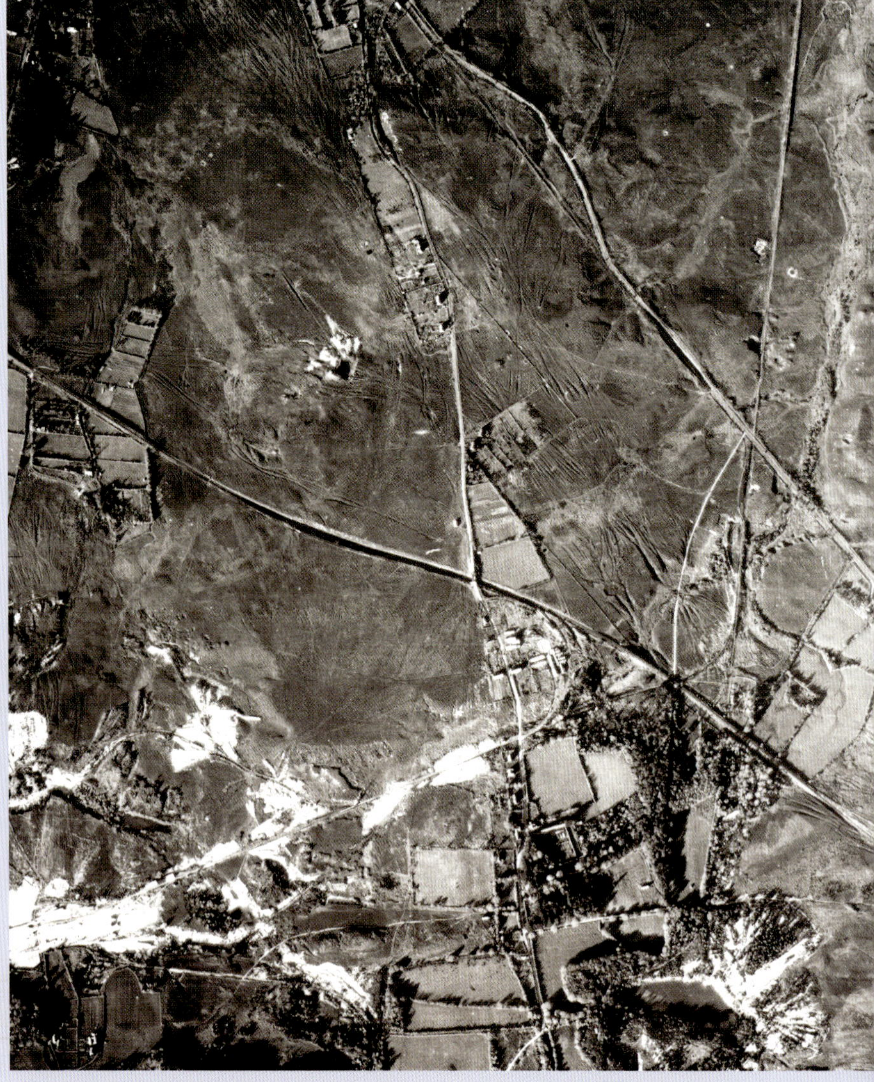

Quay in Poole Harbour. Other industrial lines can be seen on the 1947 photograph, but they have all gone now and can be traced on the photographs and across the heathland like the medieval roads before.

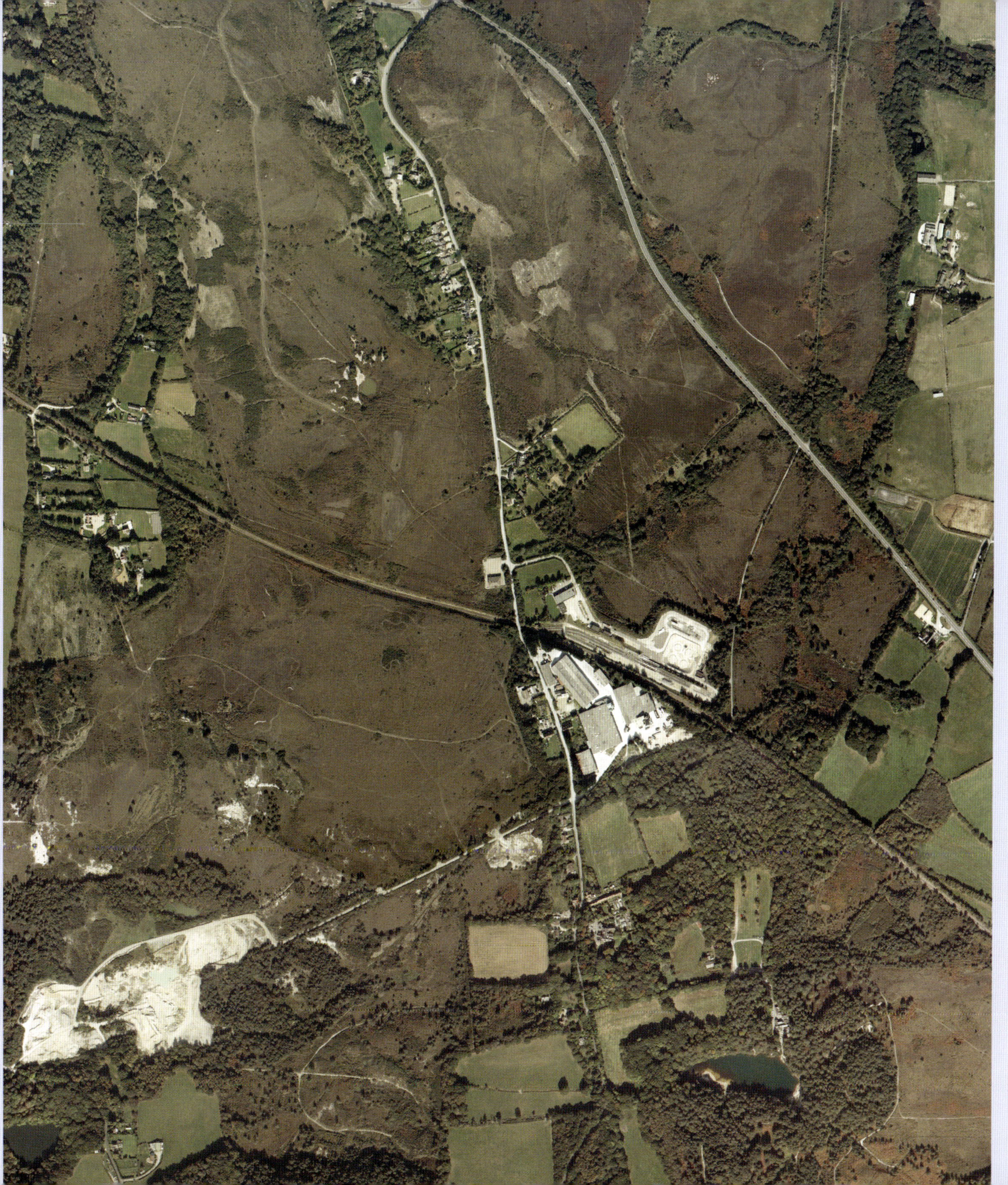

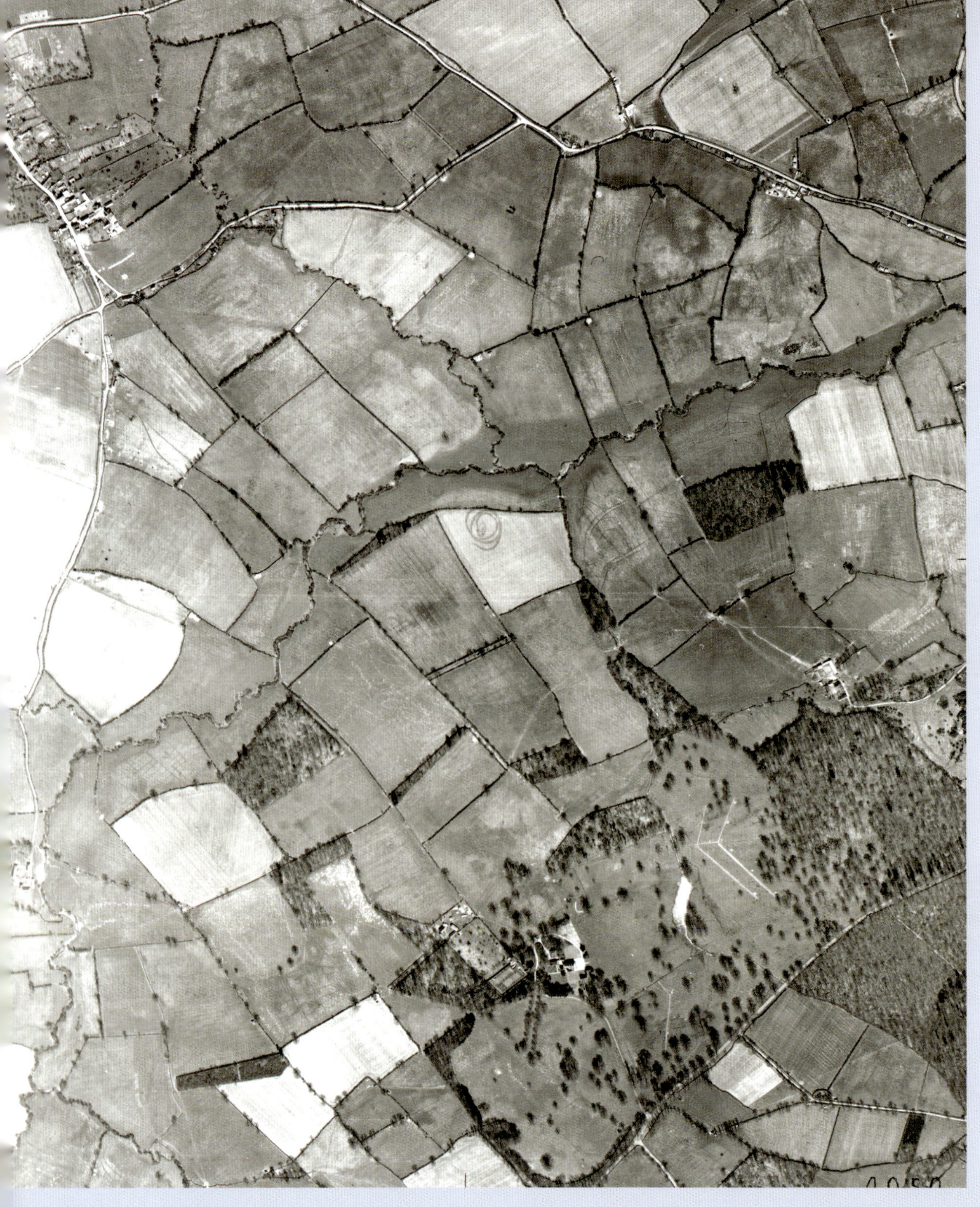

Stourton Caundle and Stock Gaylard

1947 photograph reference 1974-4157, centred on grid reference ST 722 140

The small village of Stourton Caundle, in central Dorset, was a small linear village in 1947. It has grown slightly with new housing at the southern end of the village. But the field pattern surrounding the village is essentially unchanged. The same is true of the southern part of the picture, which is dominated by Stock Gaylard house and park.

Stock Gaylard park was used by the military during the Second World War, and this picture shows the park in the process of being returned to civilian use. Away from the house parallel lines can be seen crossing the grass, which marked the roadways of the camp. They can still be traced on the modern picture, archaeological traces in a park better known today for its herd of deer and fine trees.

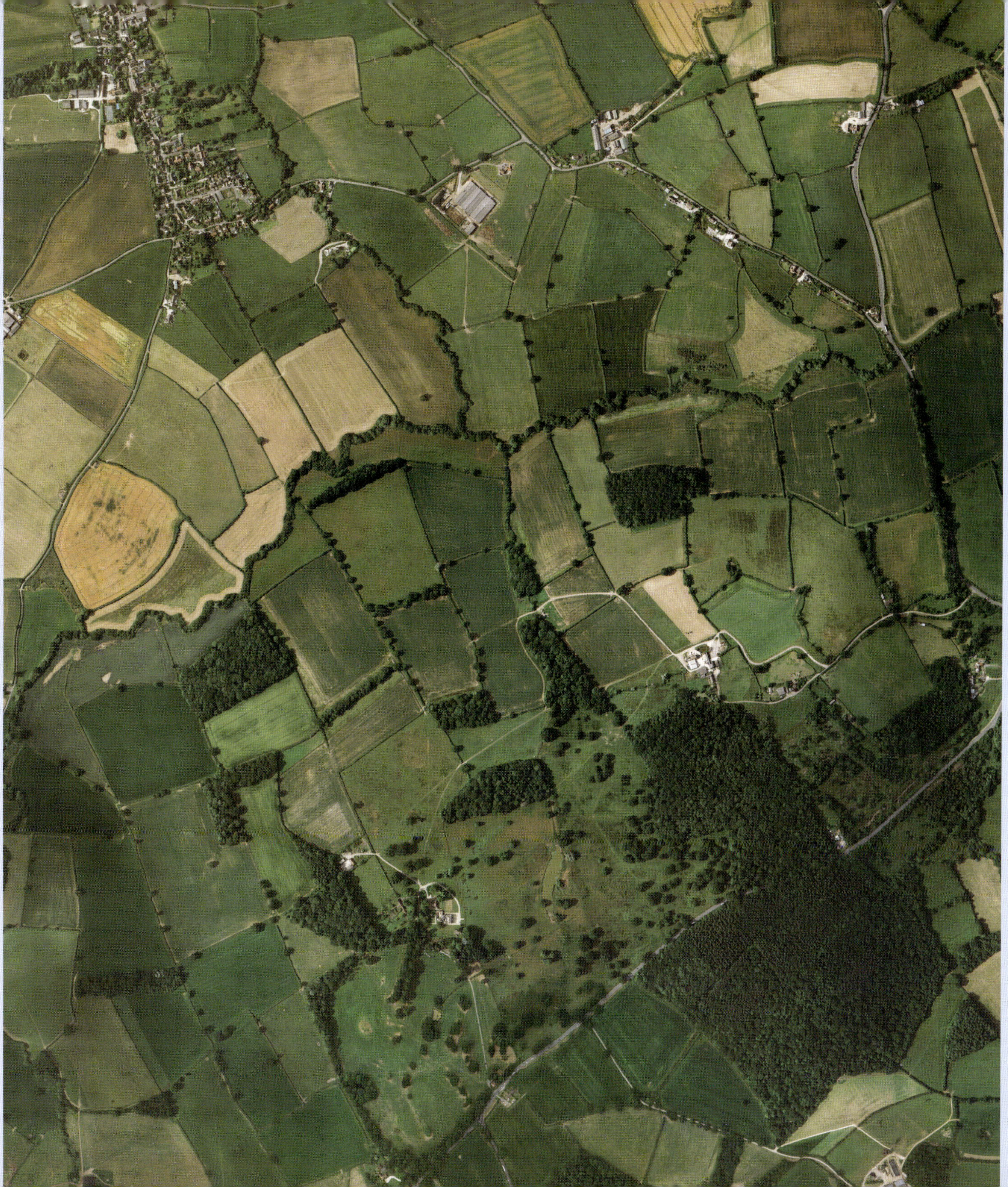

Sturminster Newton

1947 photograph reference 1974-1162, centred on grid reference ST 791 136

The town of Sturminster Newton grew substantially when the railway arrived, as it acted as an important depot for agricultural produce. In 1947 there was a large goods yard and associated railway buildings. Today all that has gone, in some places the railway line is a footpath, in others it has almost vanished. The goods yard is now a retail area and the town has grown substantially to the north. Evidence of the first new houses after the war can be seen to the north east of the town, expansion to the south being limited by the flood plain of the River Stour.

South of the river the small village of Broad Oak has also grown, perhaps more than similar areas elsewhere in the county, probably due to the proximity of Sturminster Newton. This is an area where trees have done extremely well.

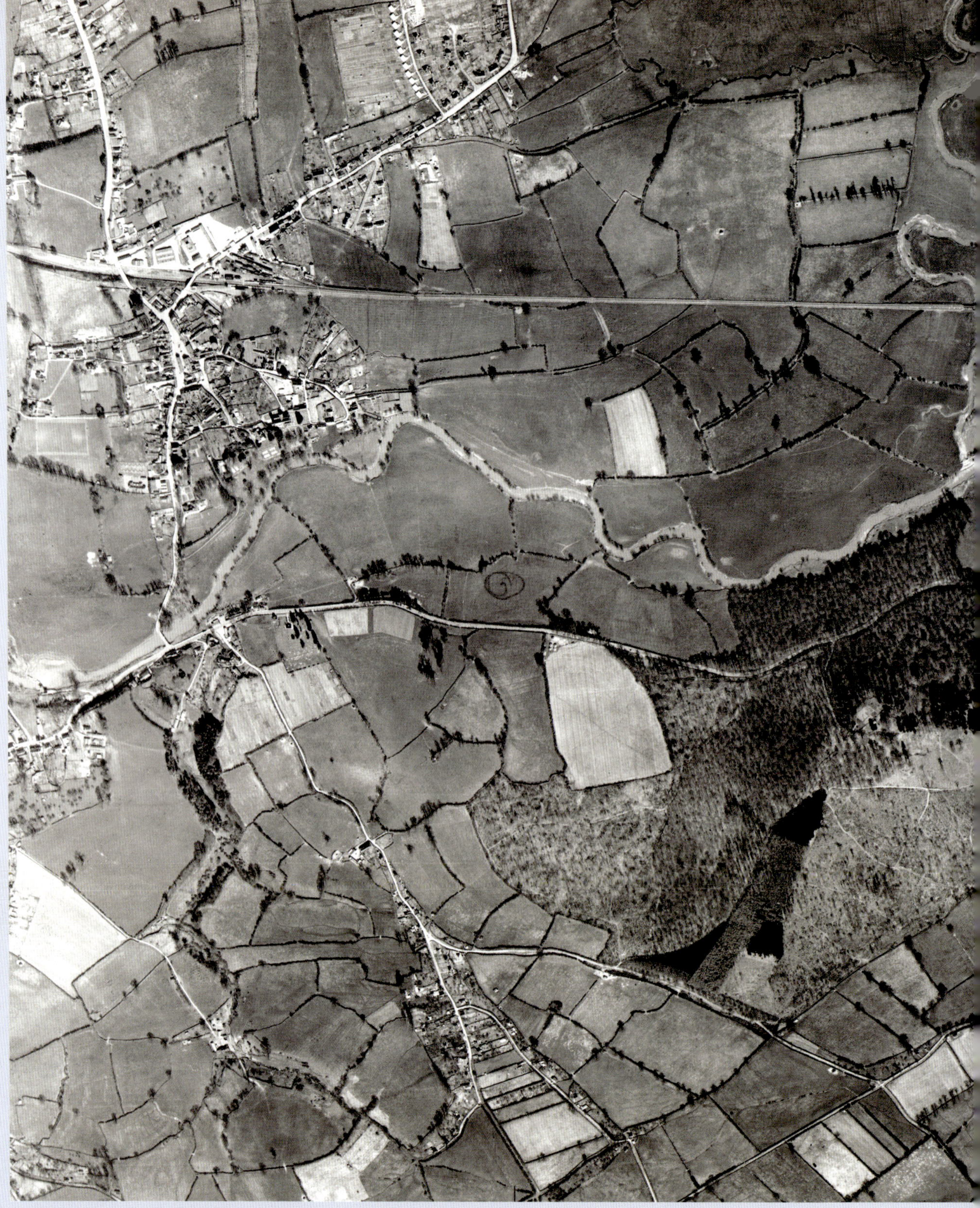

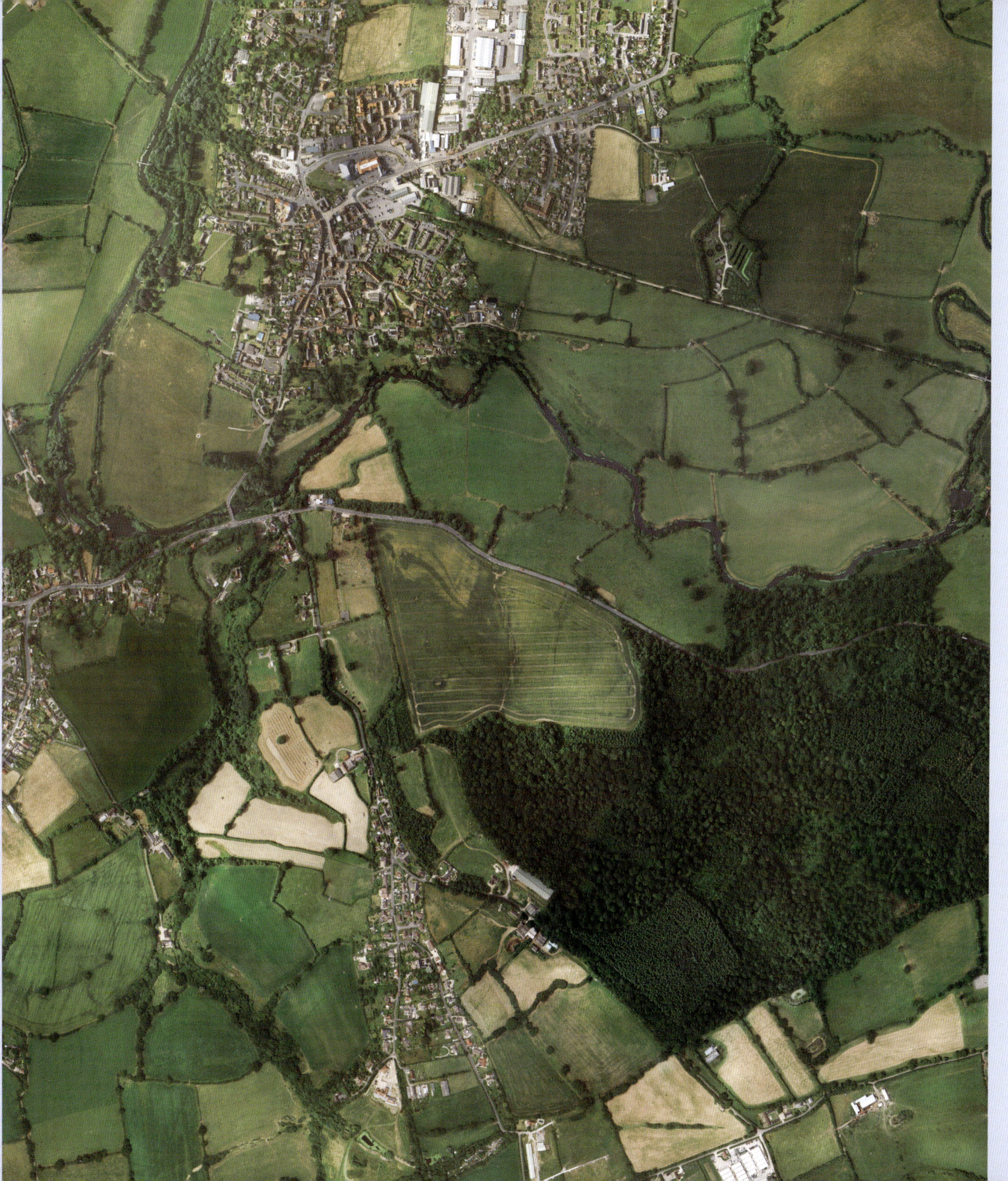

Tarrant Rushton 1947 photograph reference 1934-3153, centred on grid reference ST 942 069

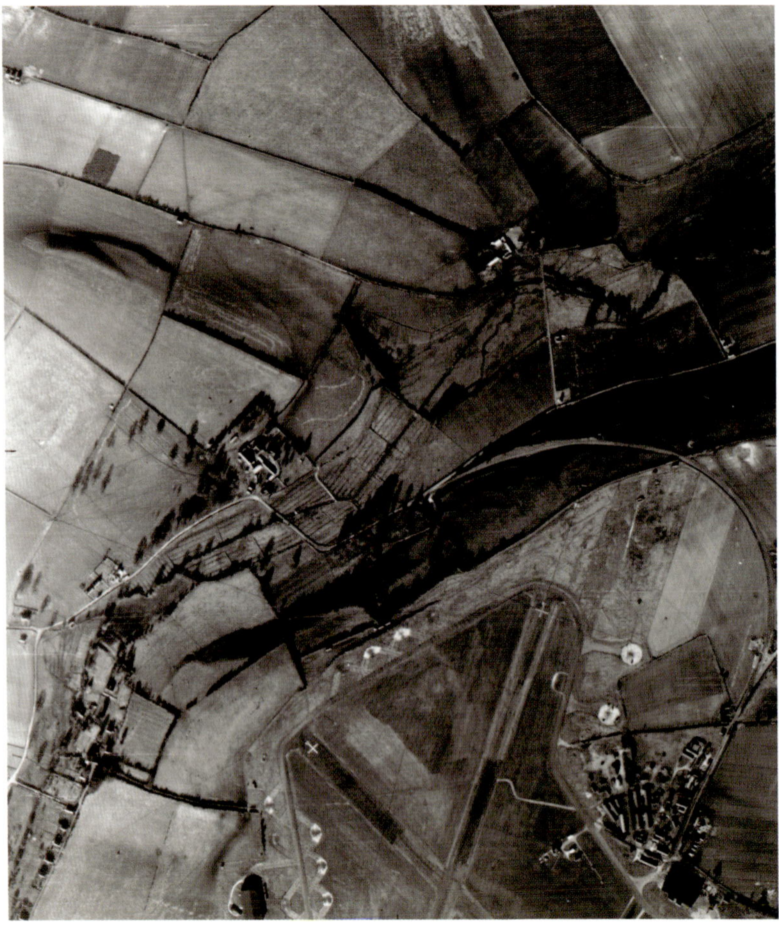

In 1947 Tarrant Rushton was an important air base. It had played a key role in the liberation of Europe, as it was from here that towed gliders left carrying airborne troops. In 1947 the airfield was still intact, with a complex of buildings in the south west corner.

To the north and west of the airfield the land dropped down to the river, where there was a water meadow system. Today this has gone out of use and the channels are difficult to see. The airfield has also gone, its runways appearing as crop marks in the field, like Roman roads. Only the perimeter track and one hangar survives, used by the farmer as a barn. Swords have been turned into ploughshares.

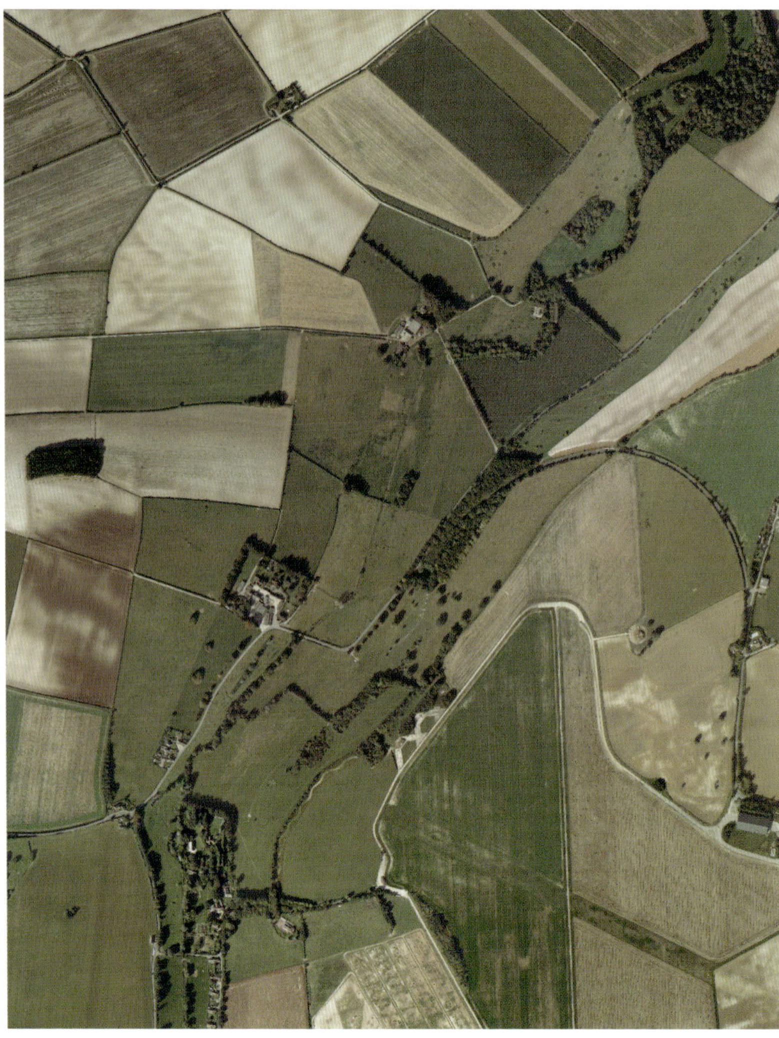

Throop 1947 photograph reference 1934-4025, centred on grid reference SZ 107 961

Throop now lies on the eastern edge of Bournemouth. In 1947 Throop was a tiny village surrounded by farmland, where small fields ran down to the river.

The changes over the past sixty years have been curious. Throop is still a separate village, as there is still a little undeveloped farm land between it and the developing urban mass of Bournemouth. It has grown like any other Dorset village: whilst there has been considerable loss of field boundaries, the riverside fields are now large, suitable for modern machinery to cut hay and silage.

One adjunct that is not often found at other villages, but is essential to the large town, is a sewage treatment works just to the north of the village, set within one of the older fields.

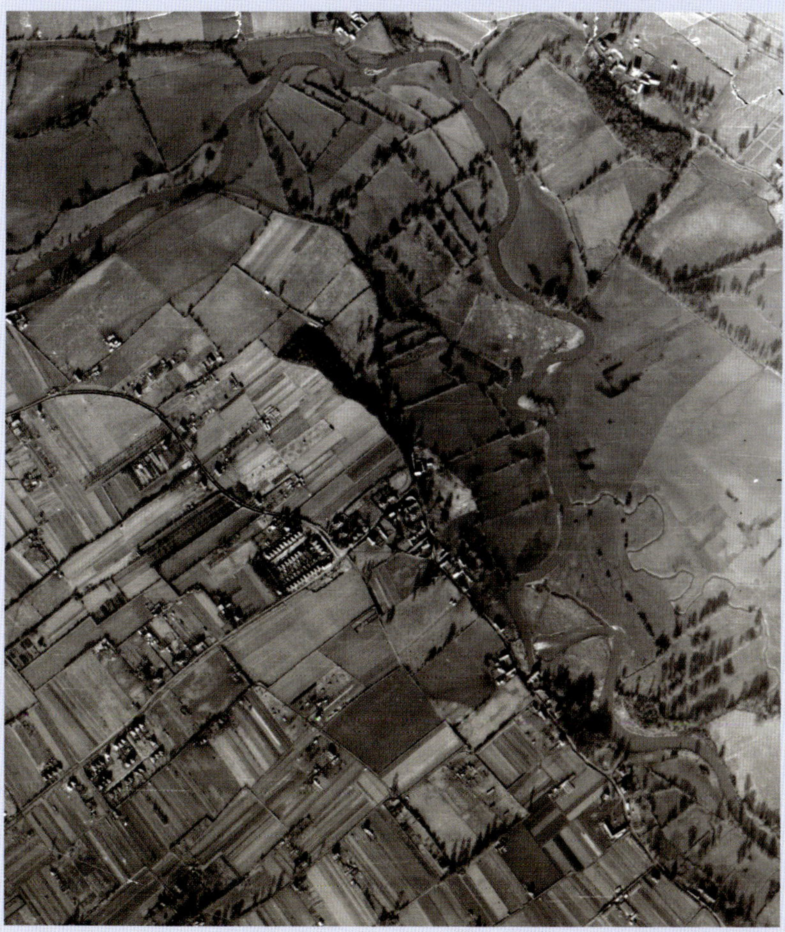

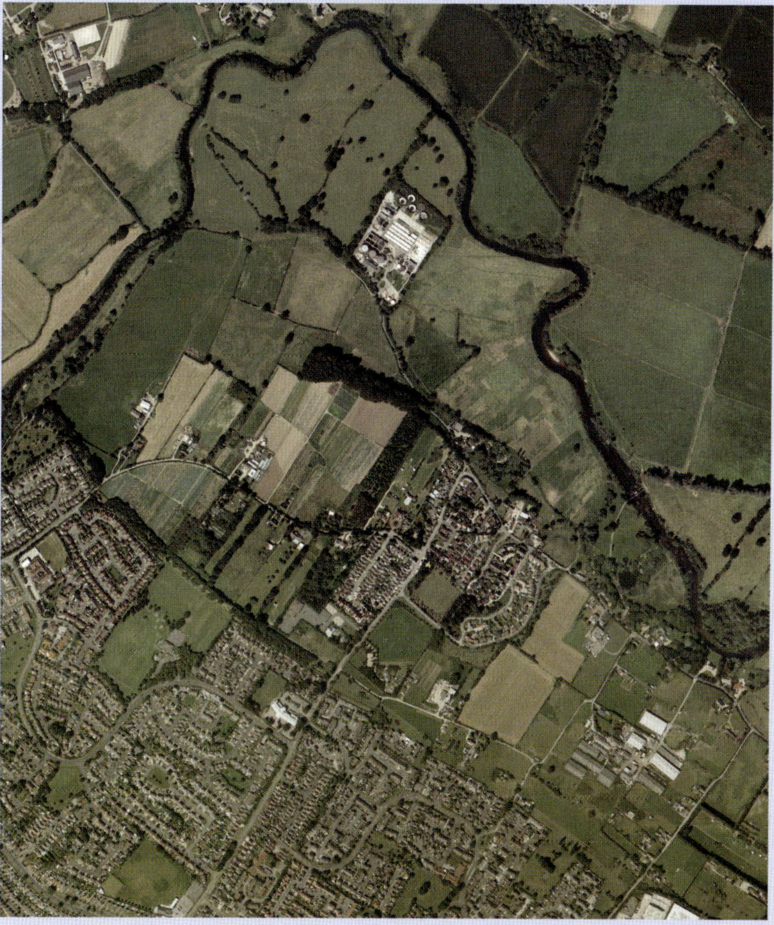

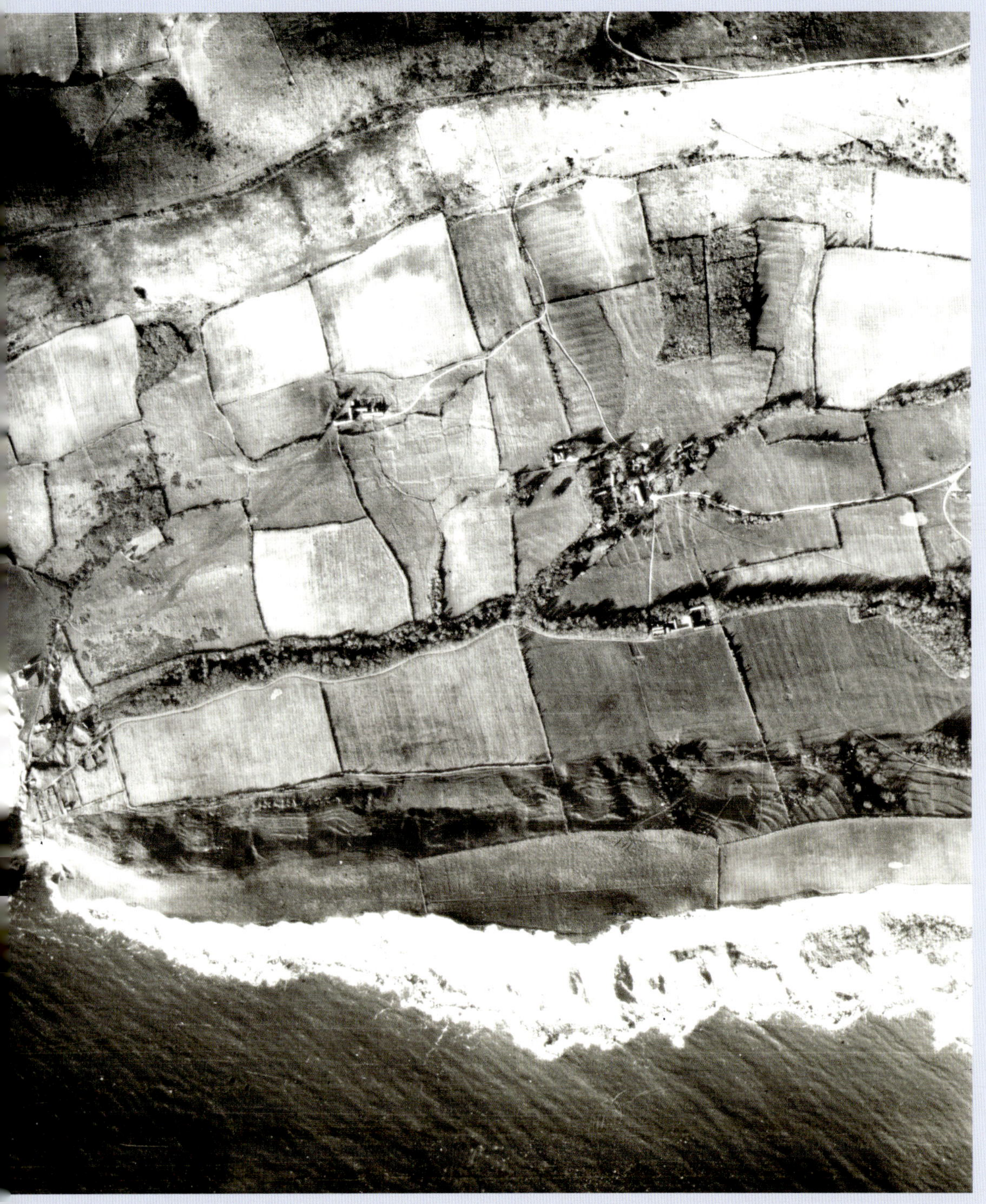

Tyneham

1947 photograph reference 1821-5424, centred on grid reference SY 877 802

Tyneham is Dorset's most famous 'lost village'. It was taken over by the army for training purposes in 1943 and purchased some while later. The 1947 picture shows it almost as it was when it was deserted, the cluster of houses by the church and the few fishermen's cottages on the shores of Worbarrow Bay. Across several of the fields around the village can be seen 'ridge and furrow', long strips marking the medieval strip fields that had fallen out of use generations before the villagers left.

Today the ridge and furrow still remains, though it is not as easy to see on the photograph, but the field boundaries have gone, not destroyed but abandoned, with no one to maintain them, and with the area being grazed they have faded to the thin ghosts visible today. Woodland has spread, though the extensive grazing used to keep the area open as a firing range has limited its growth. To the west of the village the Y shaped bank is an automatic target railway, similar to the one that once existed at Kimmeridge.

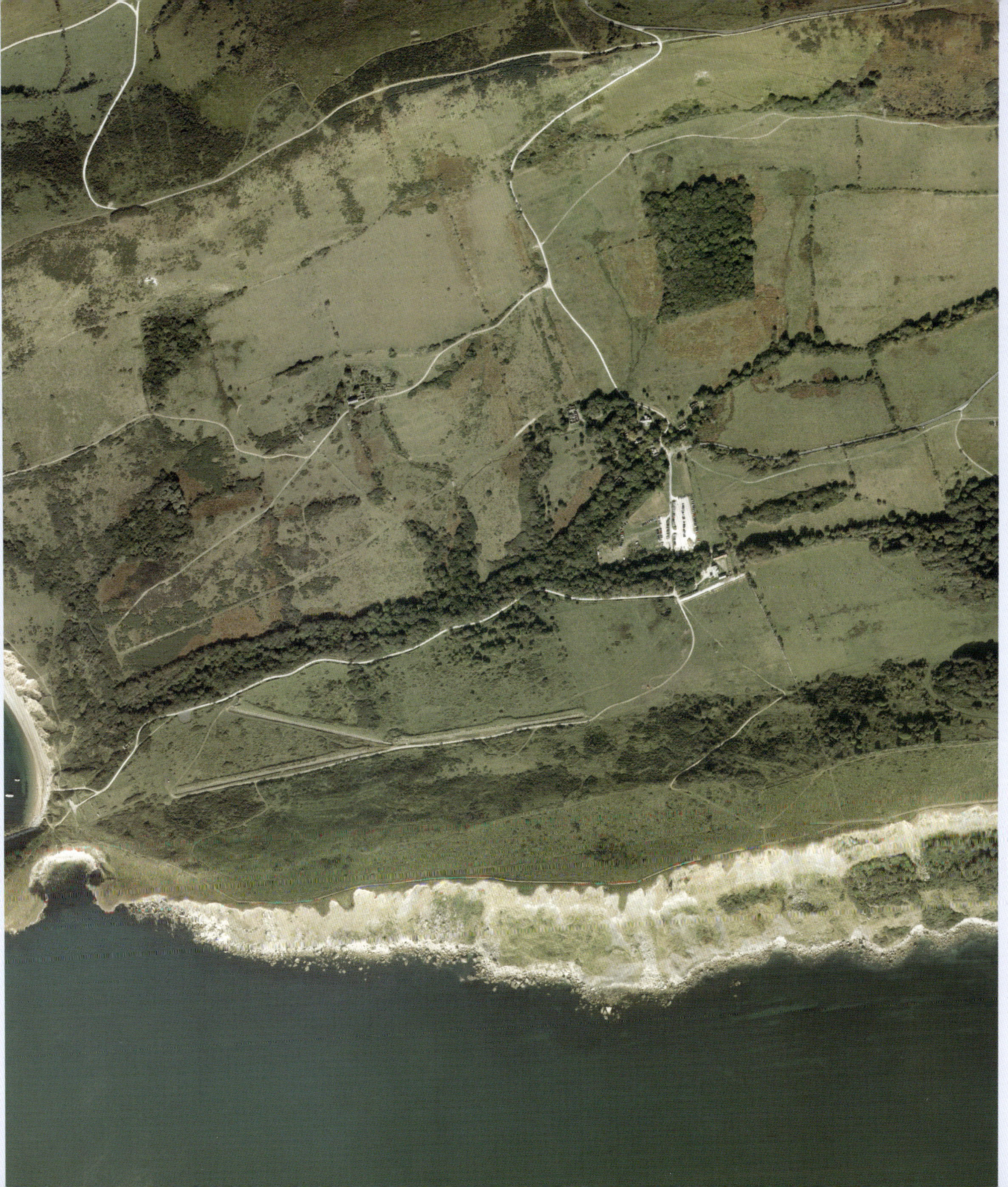

Verwood 1947 photograph reference 1845-4022, centred on grid reference SU 096 075

The changes that have taken place to Verwood in the past sixty years have been remarkable. In 1947 Verwood was a scattered settlement, there were a few large modern houses, but mostly it was made up of cottages that were almost smallholdings, with a paddock and often an orchard attached. To the north of the picture you can see the clay pit that served the Cross Roads Pottery, the last of the East Dorset Potteries which dated back to the sixteenth century. It was to finally close a few years after the picture was taken. To the south there are some fields and large areas of heathland with a single, small, plantation that had been planted as an experiment to see how pine trees would do in the thin, heathland soil.

Today Verwood no longer considers itself a village, rather a town. It has spread, not only infilling the gaps between the existing cottages but expanding onto the adjacent heathland. To the south the heathland has almost disappeared under the spreading woodland – the experiment has worked only too well. Today much of the heathland of eastern Dorset that existed only a generation or two ago, has disappeared under pine woods, and active conservation is needed to protect those areas of heathland that survive.

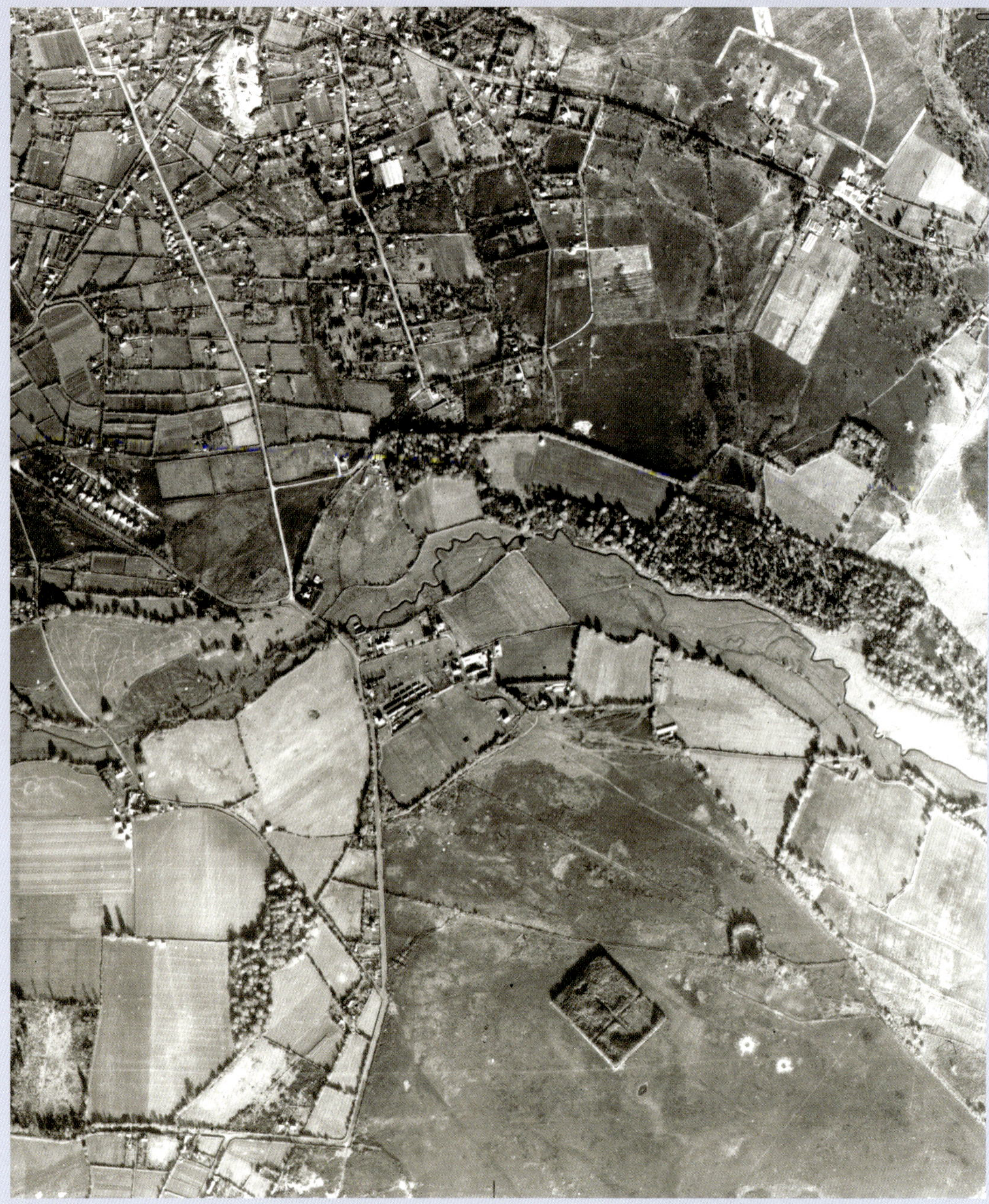

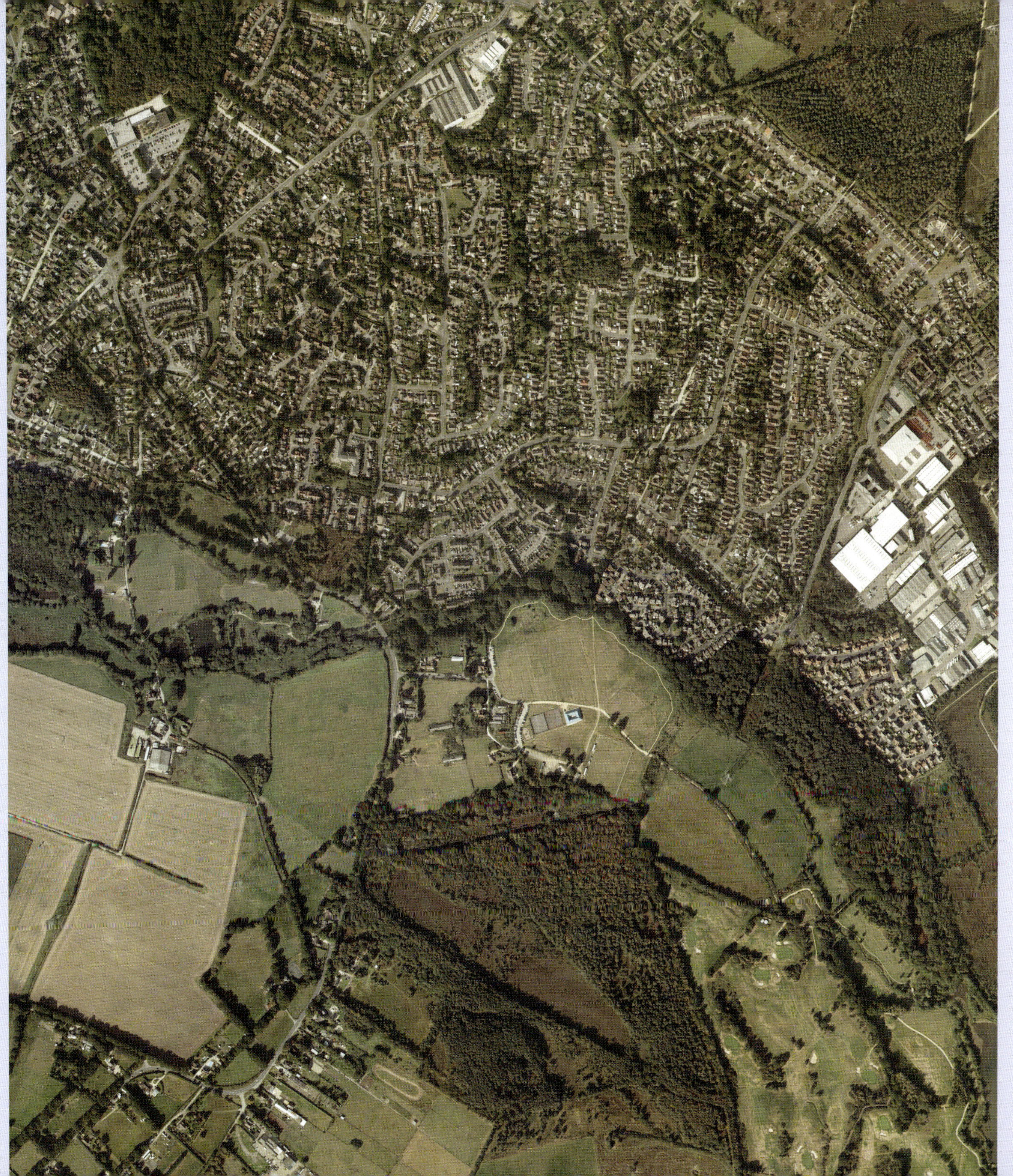

Wareham 1947 photograph reference 1821-1026, centred on grid reference SY 923 867

In 1947 Wareham was still almost confined within the old Saxon walls, indeed the town had declined so much during the Middle Ages that much of the space had been given over to agriculture. There was still open ground inside the walls. Expansion had begun but it was still slight.

Today the town has expanded, but much less than others in Dorset as the topography of the town has prevented development on the low lying ground to the south and north. Only along the ridge to the east has

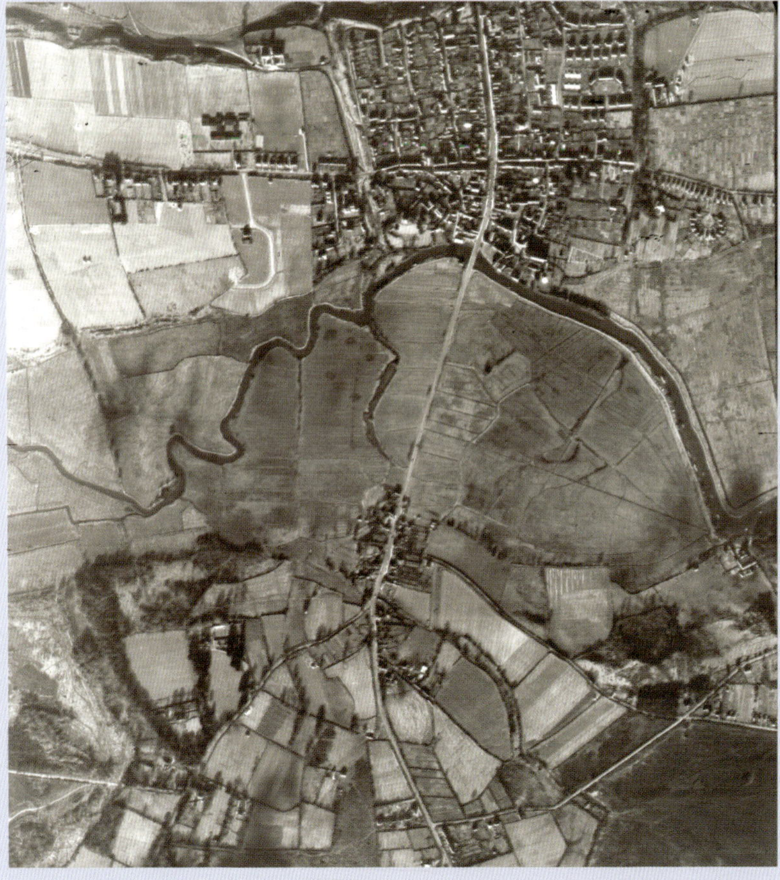

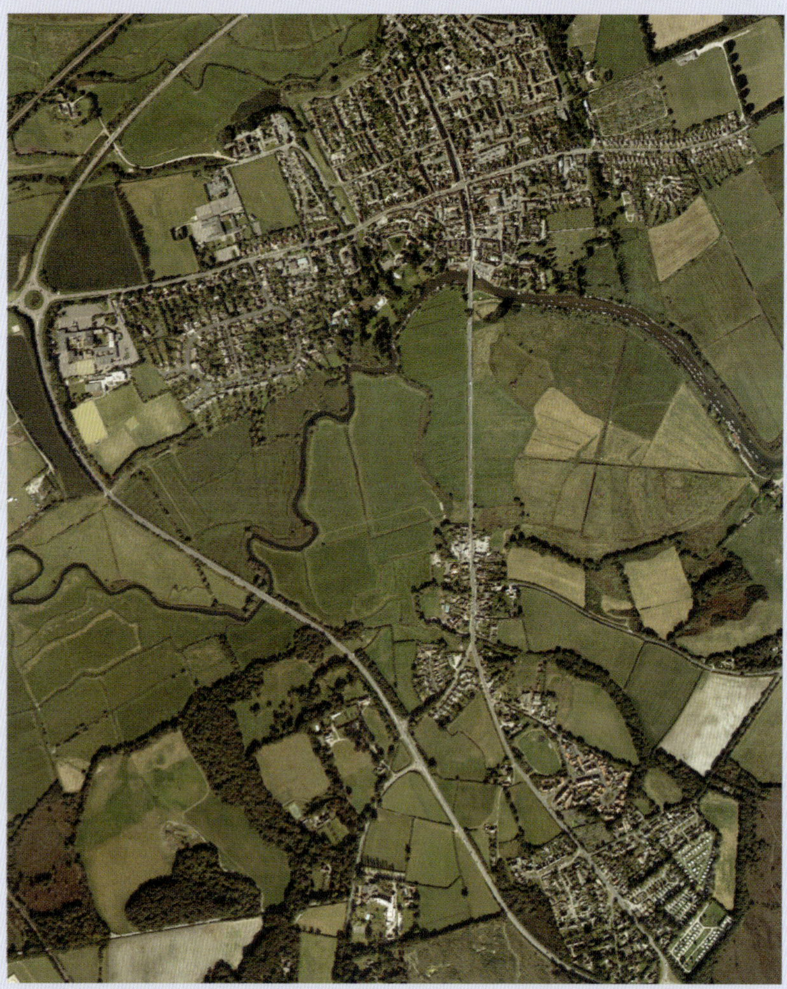

development been possible, though even here it has not been particularly dense. The roads running through the town were once a major bottleneck leading to the building of the by-pass in the late twentieth century.

Warmwell – Crossways

1947 photograph reference 1934-3076, centred on grid reference SY 765 875

In 1937 an airfield was built between Woodsford and Warmwell. First called RAF Woodsford, the name was changed to RAF Warmwell after there was unfortunate confusion with RAF Woodford near Birmingham! During the Battle of Britain it was a key base for the defence of Portland Harbour.

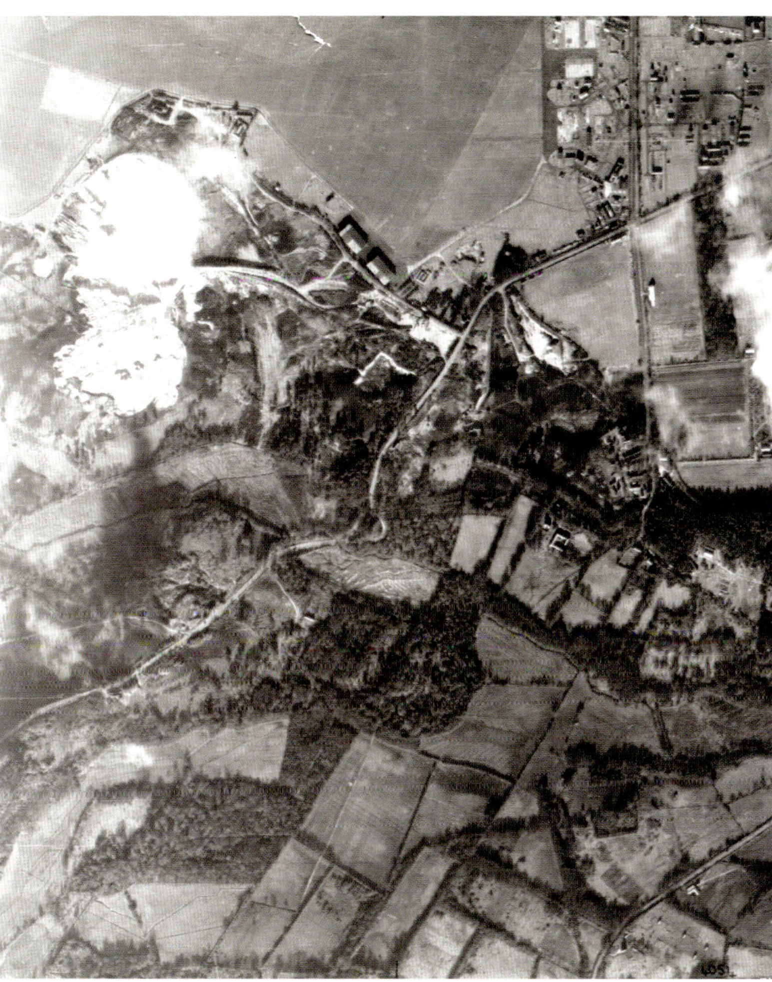

In 1947 the base was still in use, and can be seen at the north of the photograph. To the south there was a mixture of farmland, heathland woodland and a gravel pit.

Today the airfield has gone, most of it has been taken up by a completely new settlement of Crossways, whilst other areas have been given over to gravel extraction. To the south woodland has spread and caravans and mobile homes have proliferated.

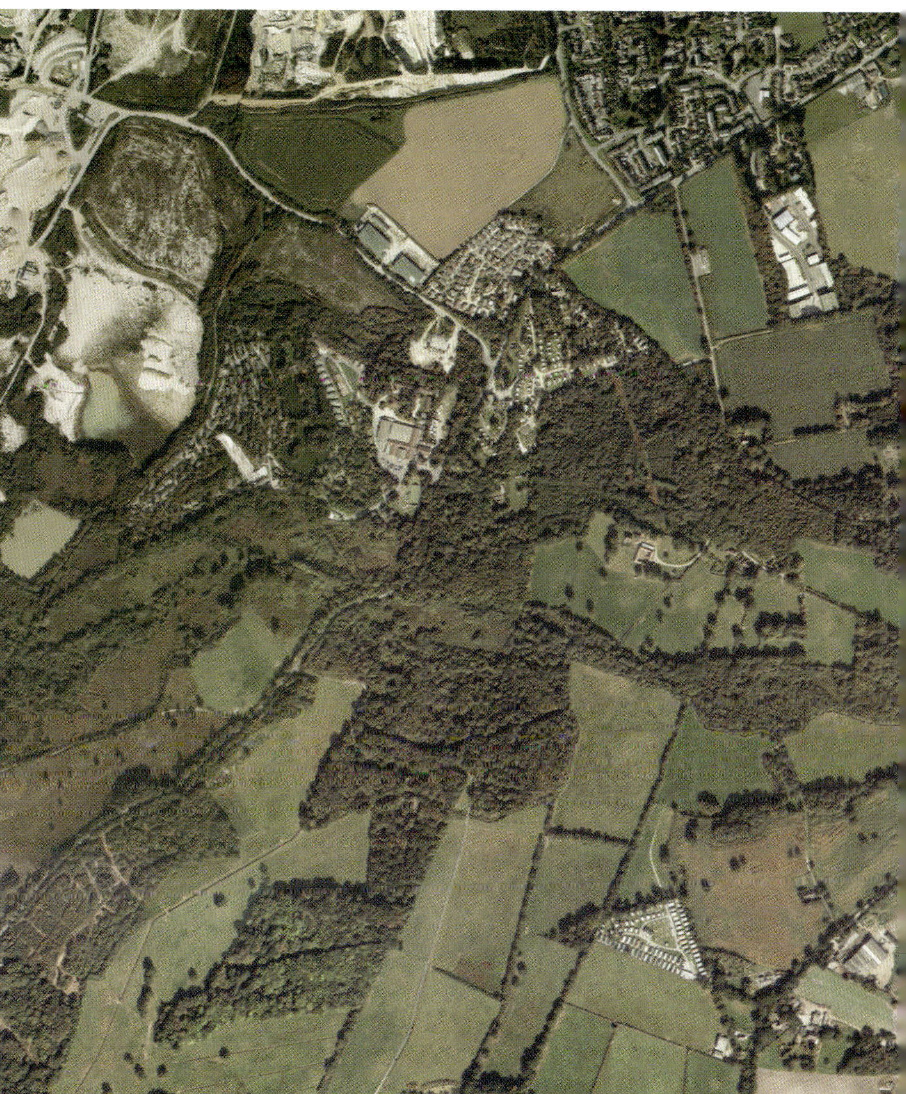

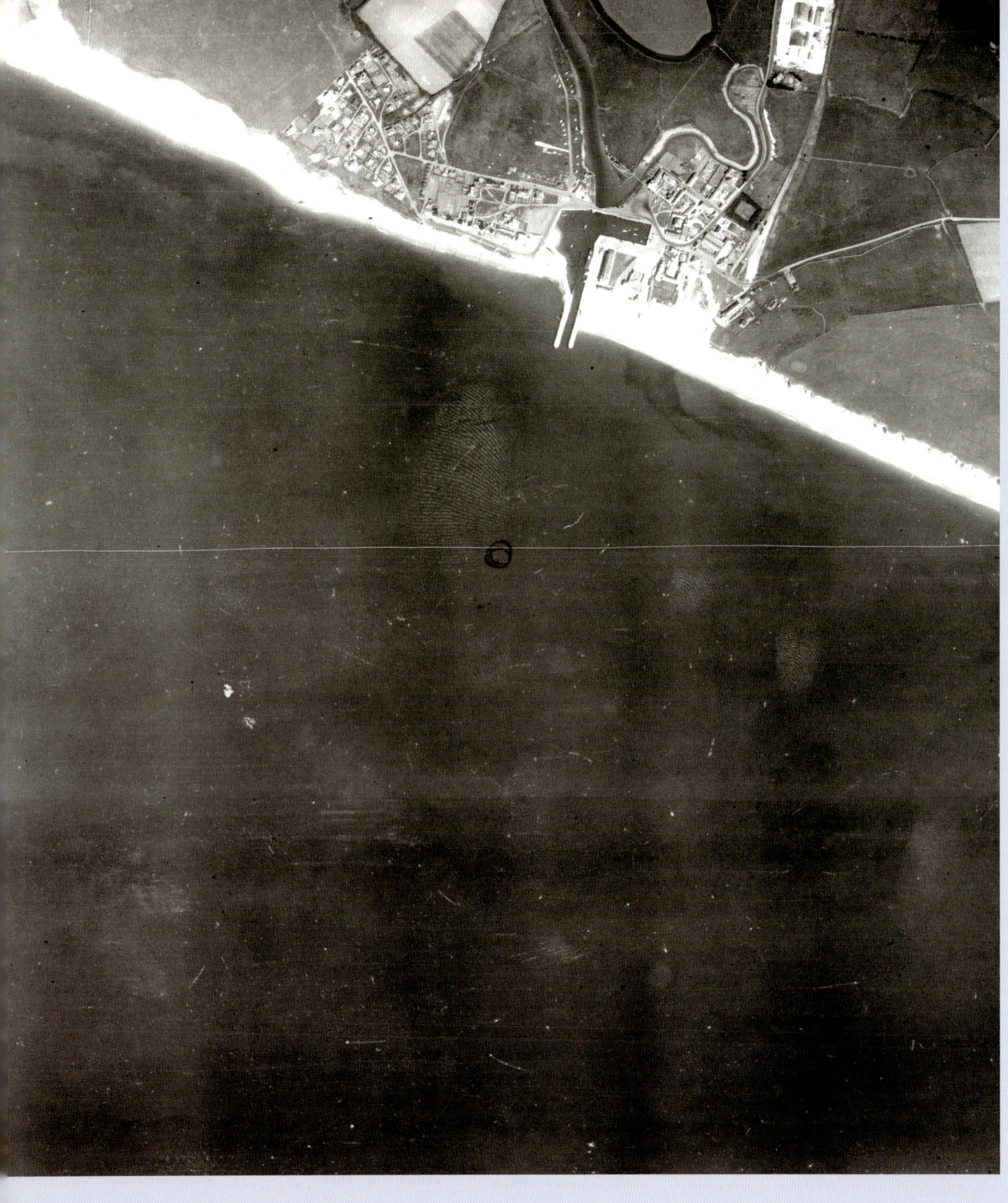

West Bay

1947 photograph reference 2475-3069, centred on grid reference SY 461 899

Bridport Harbour had become West Bay in the nineteenth century when the railway arrived. The railway company wanted to create a new holiday resort and felt a change of name would help. It didn't and, as can be seen, West Bay was still very small in 1947. The railway ran down the eastern side and there were a few buildings around the nineteenth century harbour; to the west a few houses had been built in an attempt to expand the town.

Today the most obvious change is the new harbour pier, built in order to improve the harbour and to make it usable in all weather conditions. West of the harbour there are large caravan parks and some new houses, but there have been losses too, as houses have been lost to the cliff erosion, and defences have been built at the base of the cliffs. Probably if a photograph was taken of West Bay in twenty or thirty years it might look very different.

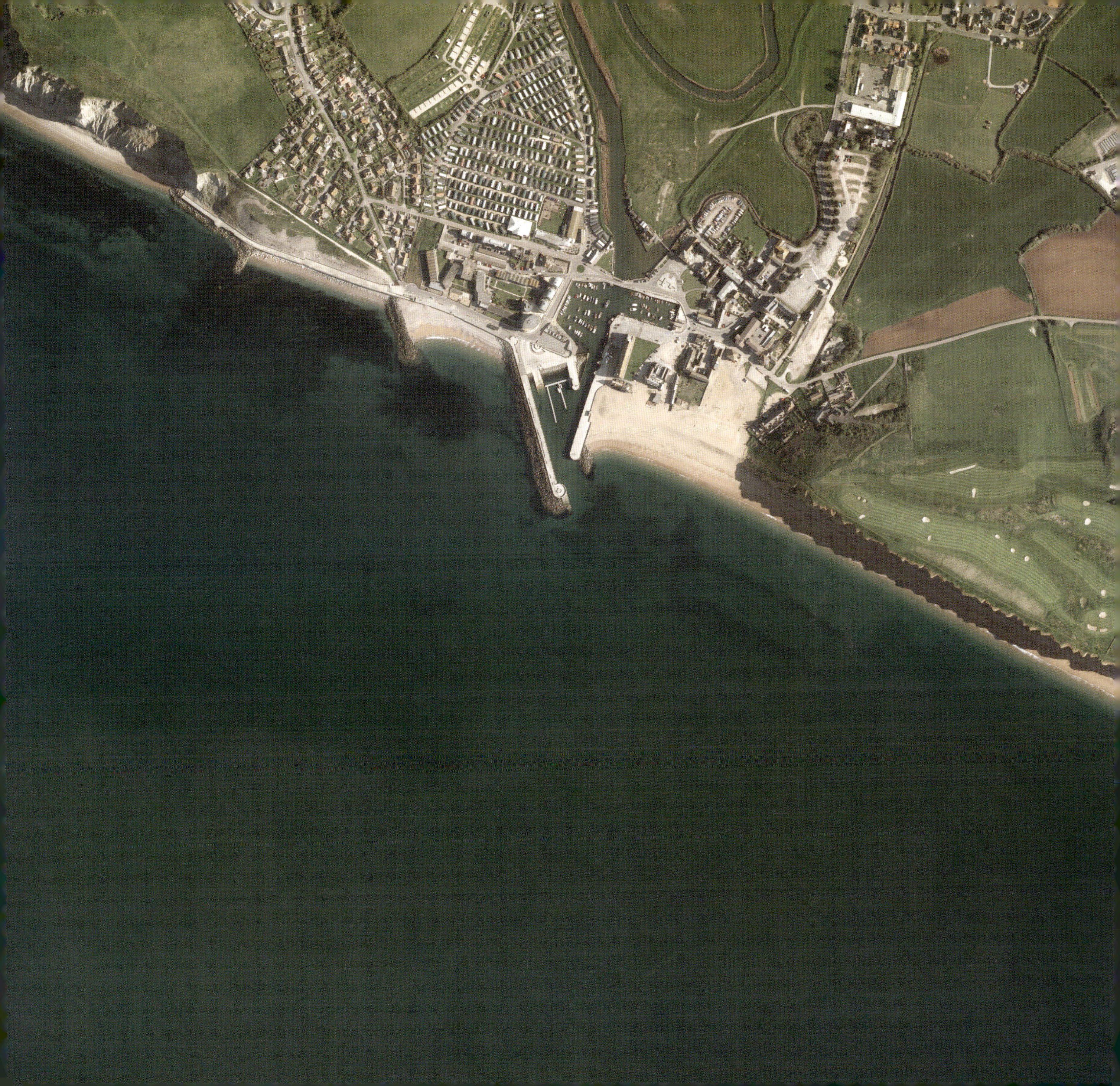

West Moors

1947 photograph reference 1845-5022, centred on grid reference SU 084 039

In 1939 land outside the village of West Moors in eastern Dorset was acquired by the army for use as an armaments store. In 1943 the land was handed over to the US Army who began to build a fuel store, its location chosen because it was in a fairly isolated spot yet with good rail links. After the war it was taken over by the British Army, and it is still in use today as Petroleum Centre RLC (Royal Logistic Corps).

The photograph of 1947 shows the camp as the British Army was in the process of taking it over. On the northern side of the camp are a row of Nissen huts; these had previously been used as a POW camp for low risk German prisoners. It is said that the armed guards and patrolling dogs were there to protect the fuel rather than keep the prisoners in.

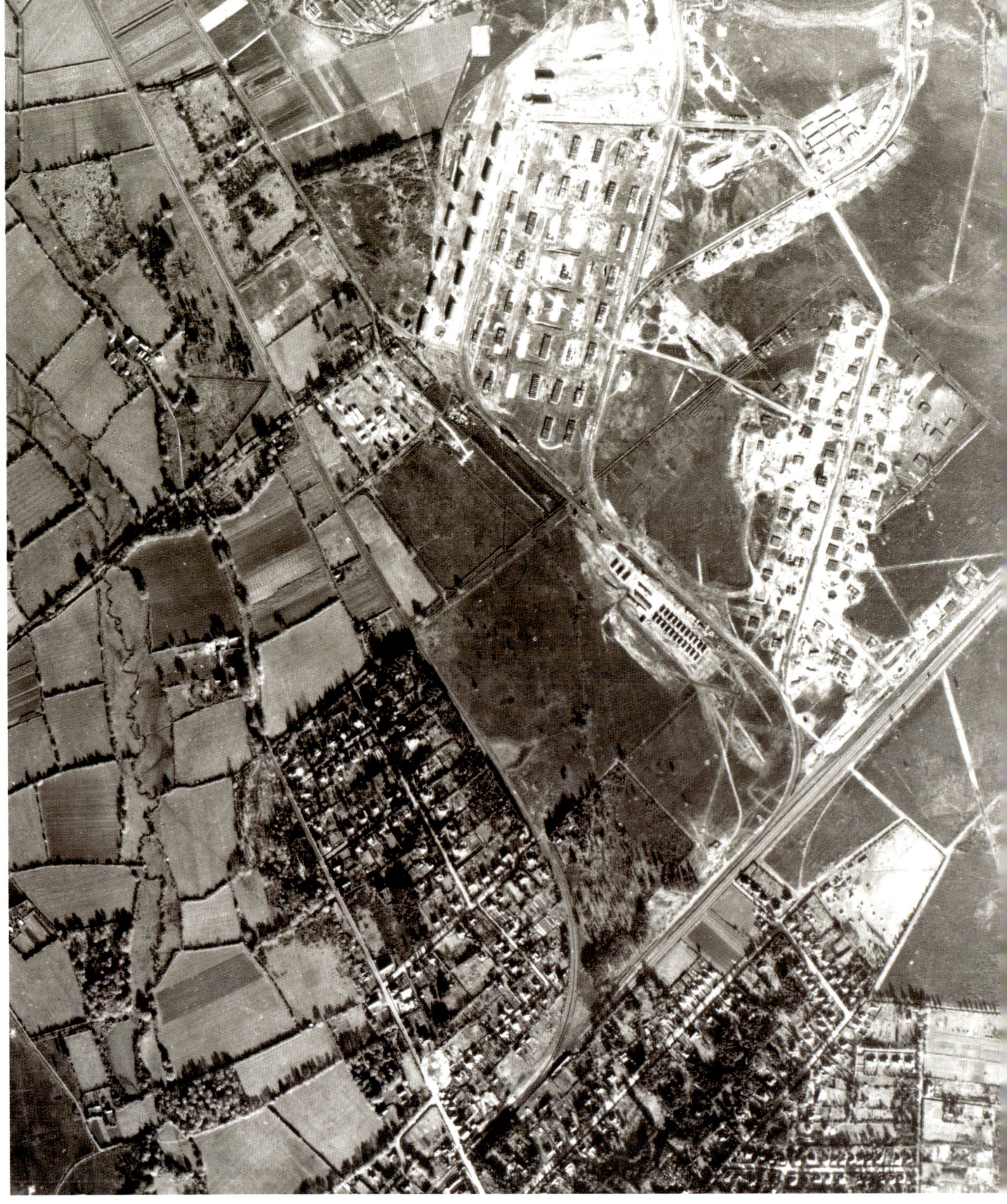

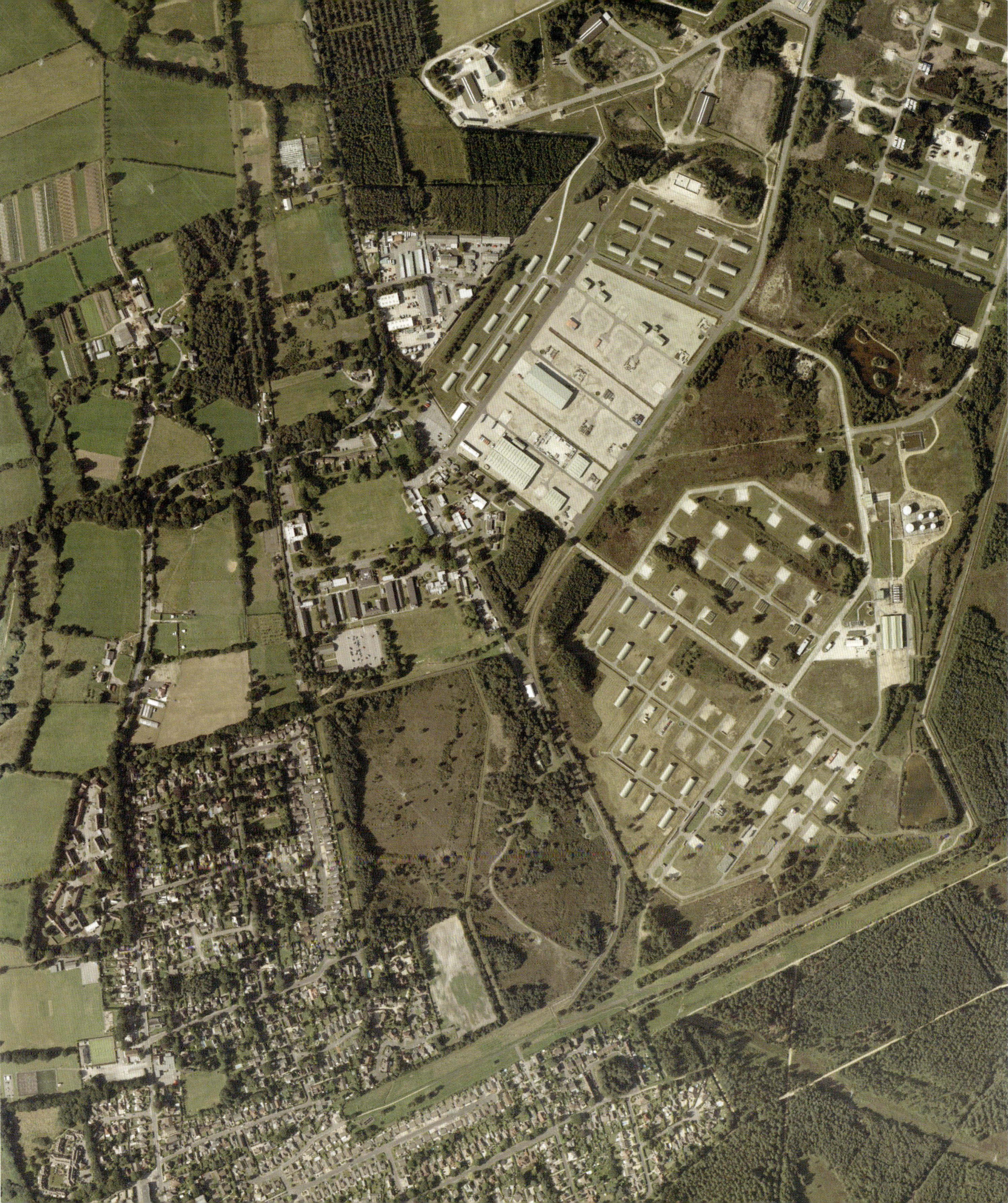

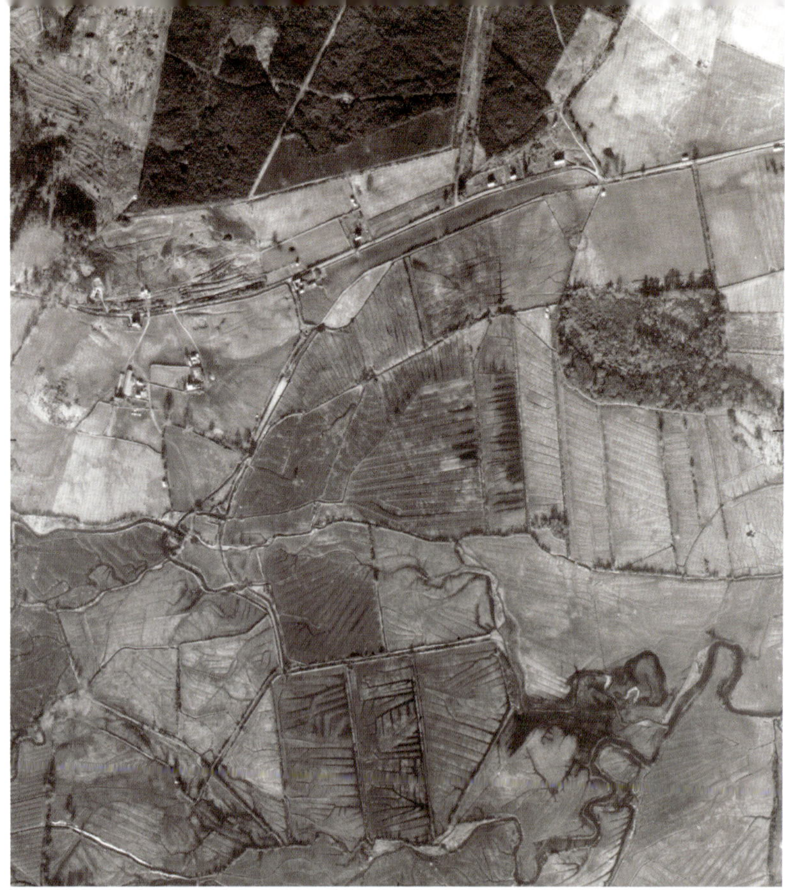

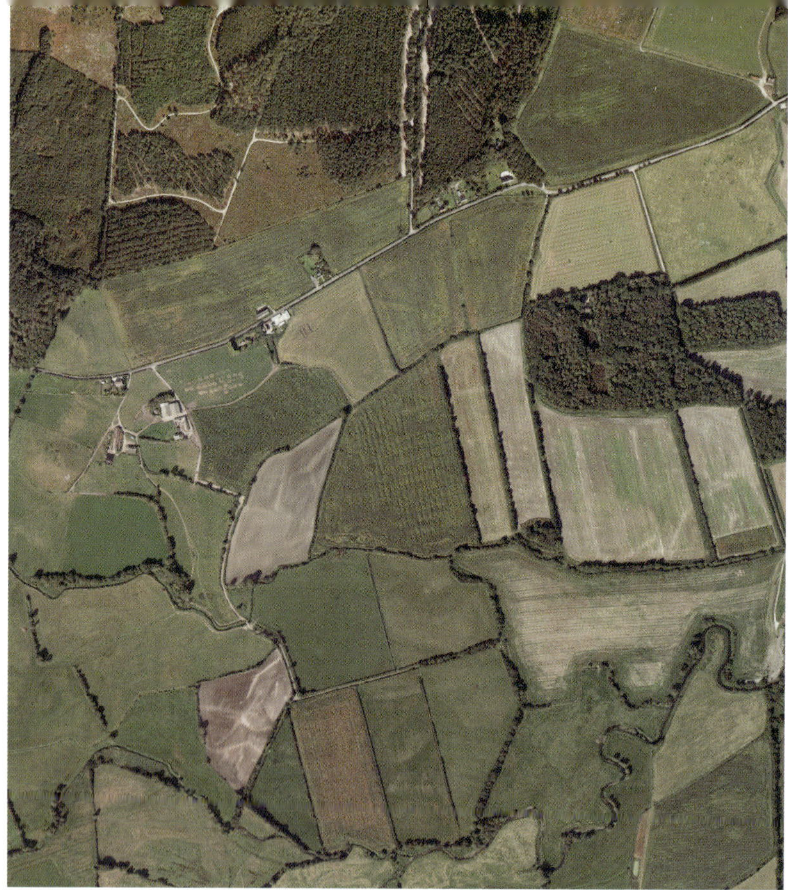

West Stafford Watermeadows

1947 photograph reference 1934-2078, centred on grid reference SY 743 911

These photographs, of land near West Stafford lying to the east of Dorchester, have been included not so much to show change or lack of it, though there hasn't been very much in this area, rather they have been chosen to show the remarkable development of a lost agricultural system, that of watermeadows.

Watermeadows were introduced to Dorset in the seventeenth century and reached their apogee in the nineteenth. These can be seen in the photographs, particularly that of 1947, as a network of channels crossing the fields in the southern half of the photographs. These are nothing to do with drainage or irrigation, as is sometimes thought, rather they are designed to regulate temperature, with some fertilization as a side benefit.

During the late winter and early spring water was allowed to flow gently over the surface of the fields, this would keep the ground unfrozen as it takes a very severe frost to freeze flowing water. As a side benefit the field would gain extra nutrients from the water, especially if the fields were downstream of a town which dumped its sewage into the river. This would give an early boost to the grass and so give a richer hay crop or grazing for animals. The main problem was that the system was extremely labour intensive. The fields had to be watched twenty four hours a day when the system was running, to make sure water was flowing when frost might be expected and to make sure it never stopped and stood over the field. Still water would freeze and wouldn't have enough oxygen for the grass, and so kill it.

The systems went into a decline during and after the First World War, and were virtually unused by 1947, but their remains make an amazing picture when seen from the air.

Weymouth 1947 photograph reference 1821-2453, centred on grid reference SY 667 802

The town of Weymouth has changed considerably since 1947: these changes involve transport, development and land reclamation. In 1947 as today Weymouth was both a port and a holiday destination.

In 1947 most visitors and goods would have arrived and left by train. The railway entered the town from the north. Beside the station was a large goods yard. Two lines then went further on, one alongside the harbour, running along the road, to the terminal for the cross channel ferries, the other crossed the harbour and continued to Portland. Whilst the railway still runs to Weymouth, it terminates at the station; the line to Portland is now a footpath, whilst the tracks along the road survive but can no longer be used. The large goods yard is a retail park.

Today most people come by road. There is a new road to the west of Radipole Lake, and a new bridge across the harbour close to where the railway bridge once ran. New car parks have been built, the biggest on reclaimed land at the southern end of Radipole Lake.

Much of the open land on the 1947 photograph has been developed with new housing, whilst in the centre of the town large areas of housing and small shops have been removed to make way for larger commercial premises. There is the large car park on Radipole Lake, whilst the new road has led to the reclamation of land and subsequent development. Finally a large area has been reclaimed for the ferry terminal and the car parks by the Pavilion.

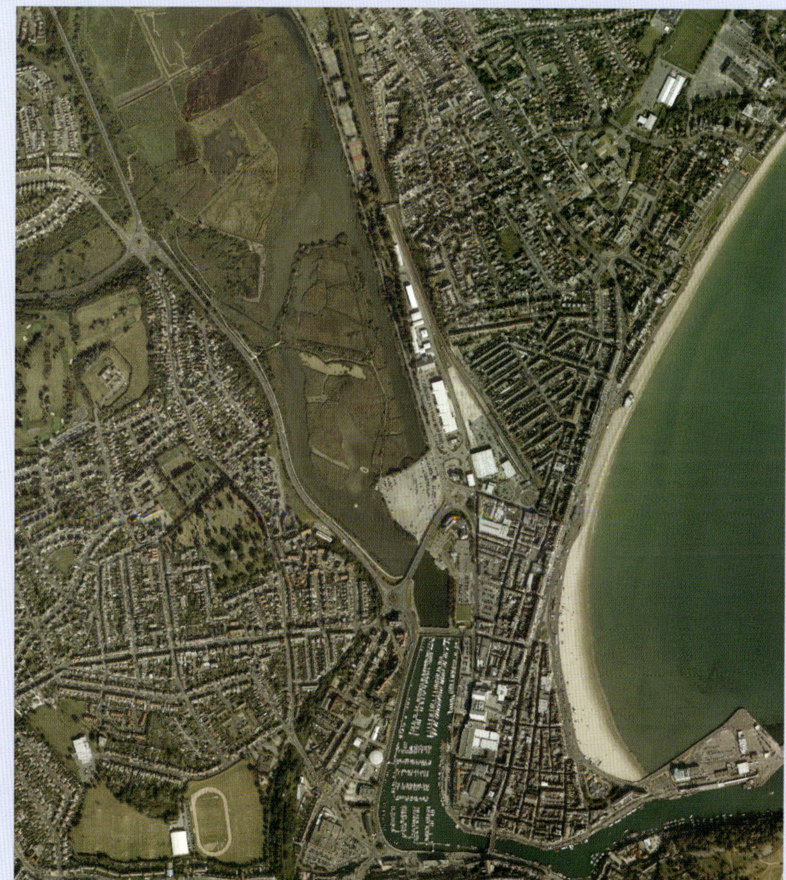

Whitchurch Canonicorum

1947 photograph reference 2431-4178, centred on grid reference SY 389 955

The ancient village of Whitchurch Canonicorum has changed remarkably little in the past sixty years. There has been little new housing, on the minor roads around the church. The same cannot be said for the surrounding countryside. In 1947 there were numerous small fields, divided by hedgerows full of hedgerow trees and occasional small woods.

Today the fields are much bigger, many hedgerows have gone, though those that do survive have more hedgerow trees in them and there are more areas of small woodland.

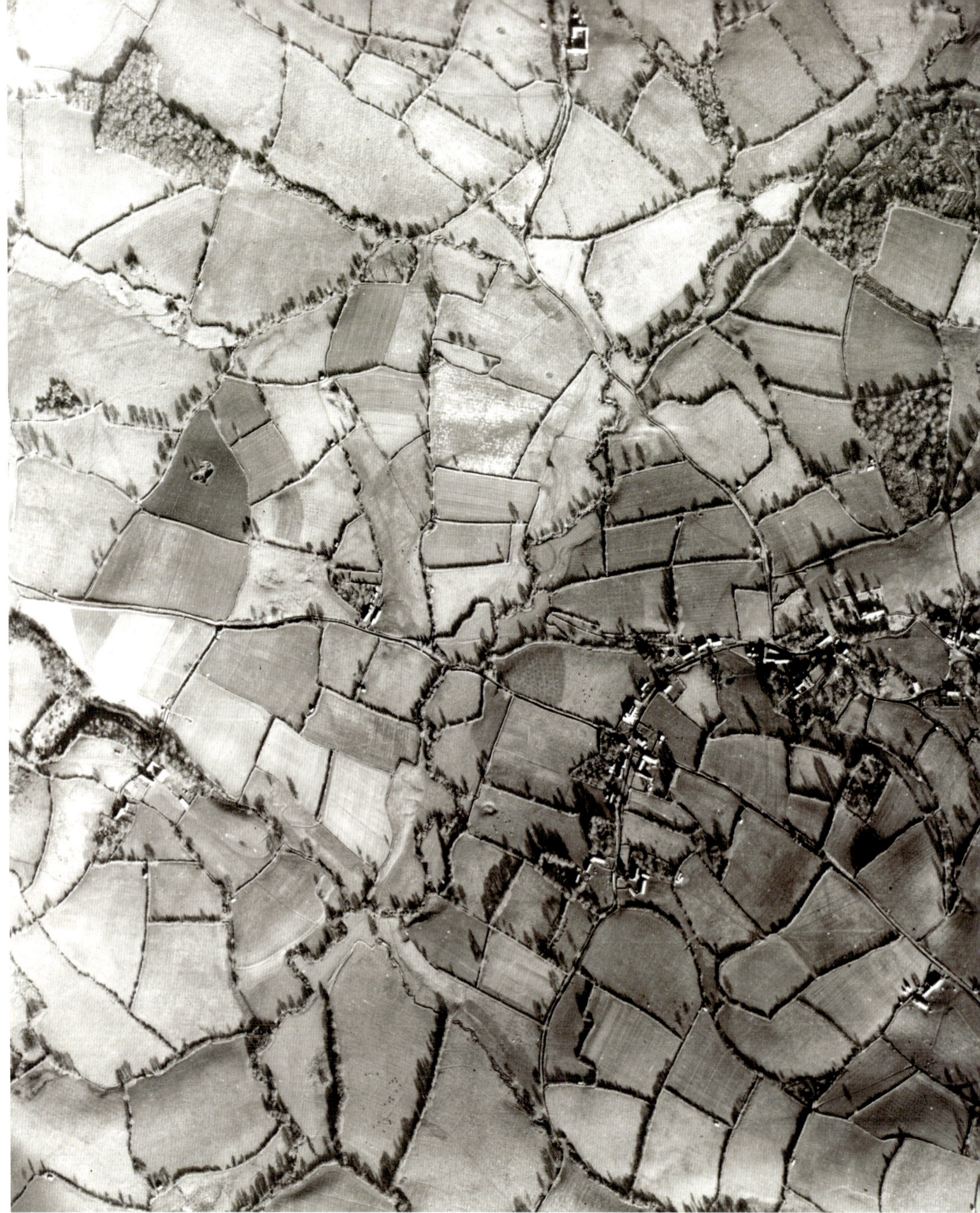

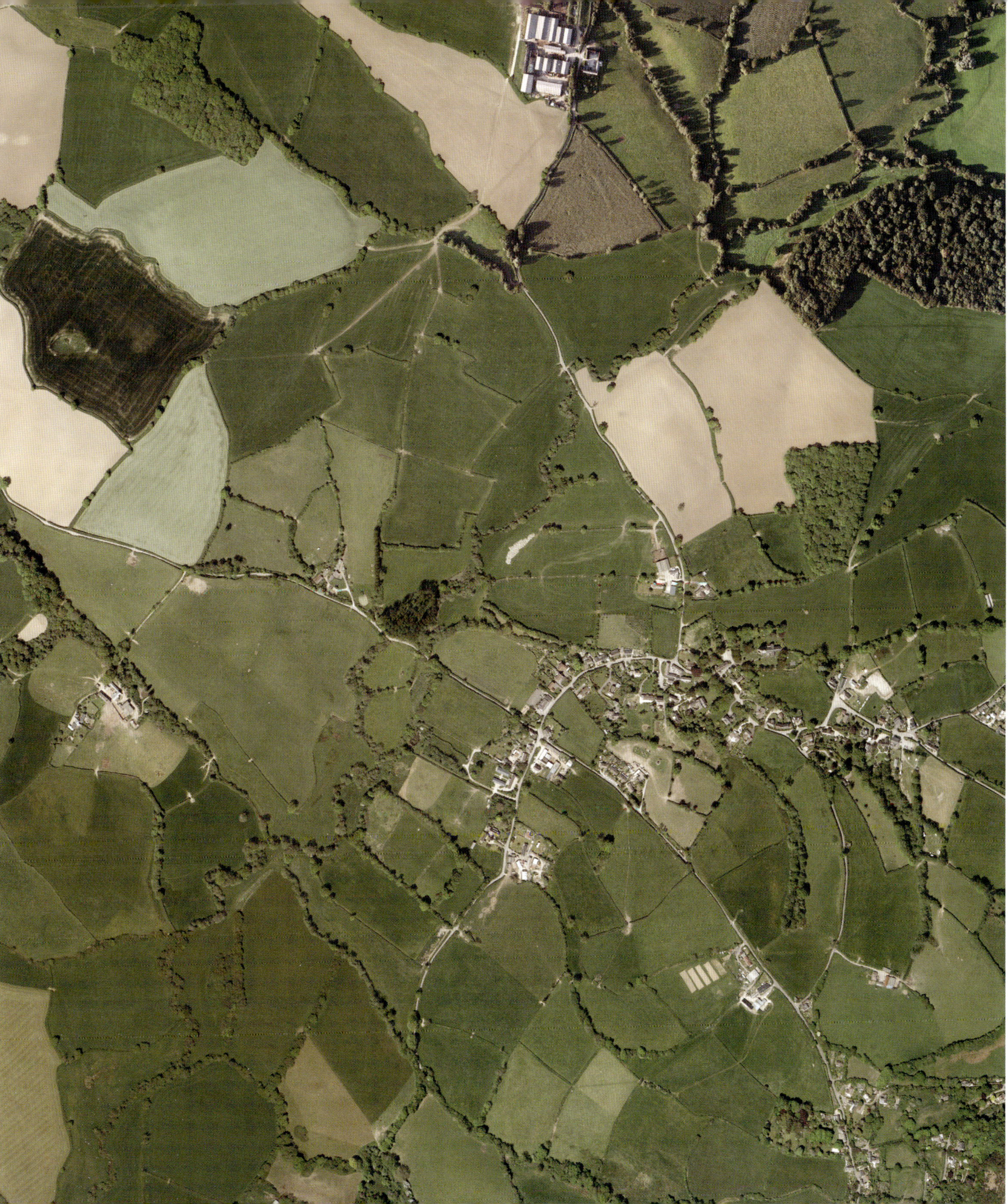

Wimborne Minster 1947 photograph reference 1934-5190, centred on grid reference SZ 011 998

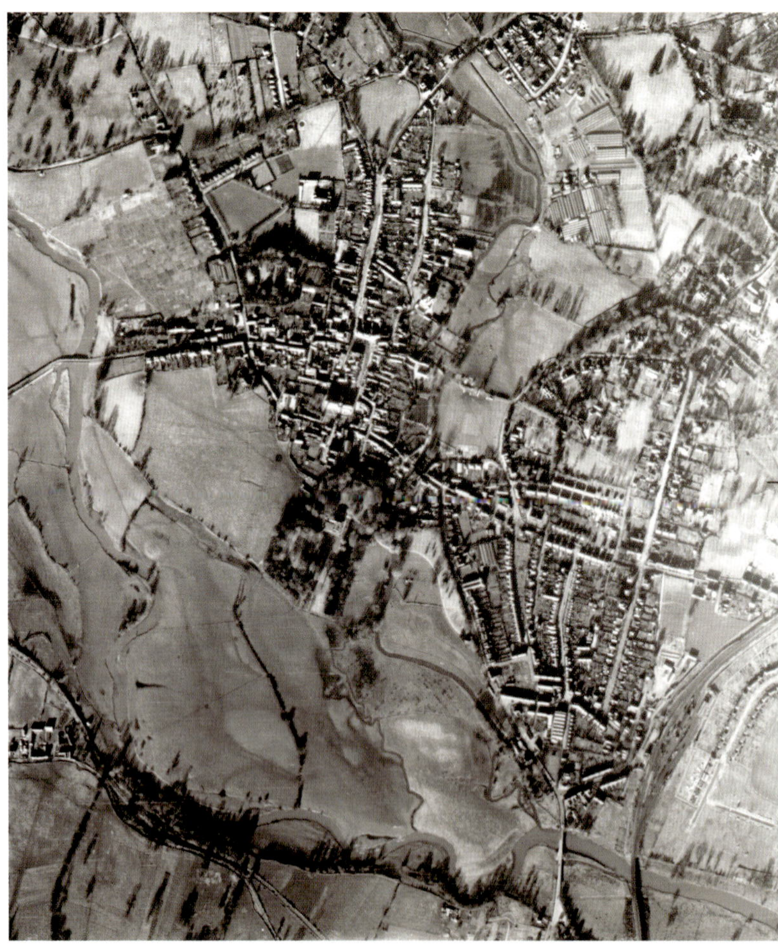

Wimborne Minster had grown considerably during the late nineteenth and early twentieth centuries following the coming of the railway. For various reasons the station was situated some way east of the town and a suburb grew up between the railway and the old town. In 1947 the old town of Wimborne Minster was still separated from this suburb by lower ground beside the River Allen.

Today the railway has gone, and the site of the station is now an industrial area. Houses have spread, infilling gaps between existing houses and terraces and new estates built, particularly on the lower land. The difference in layout between the older and newer estates is clear, older estates tended to be very regular and geometric whilst the more recent developments are irregular and sinuous.

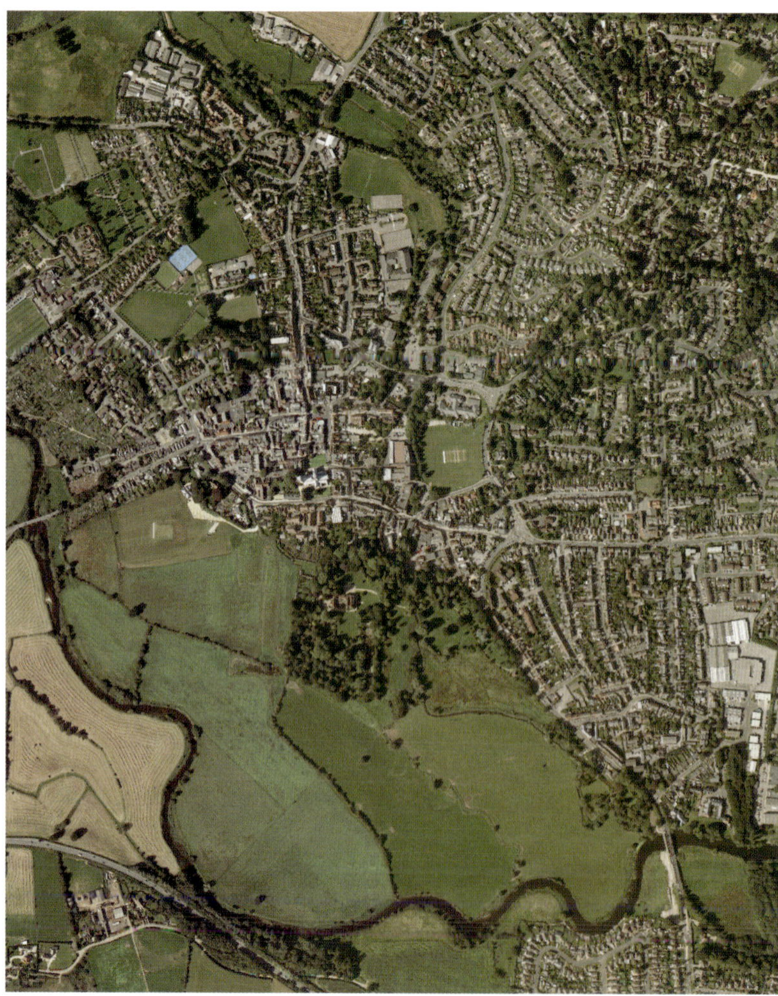

To the south the Wimborne by-pass cuts across the fields. This, by removing a great deal of the traffic that formerly ran through the town, has enabled more development alongside the main road to the east.

Woodlands

1947 photograph reference 1845-4031, centred on grid reference SU 056 079

This area, just to the south of Woodlands in eastern Dorset has had a most curious history.

In 1947 there was a large area of heathland being turned into managed woodland. There were already several blocks of trees of varying degrees of maturity and, in the normal course of things, it might have been expected that the modern view would show a solid mass of timber. Instead the wood has been turned into a golf course.

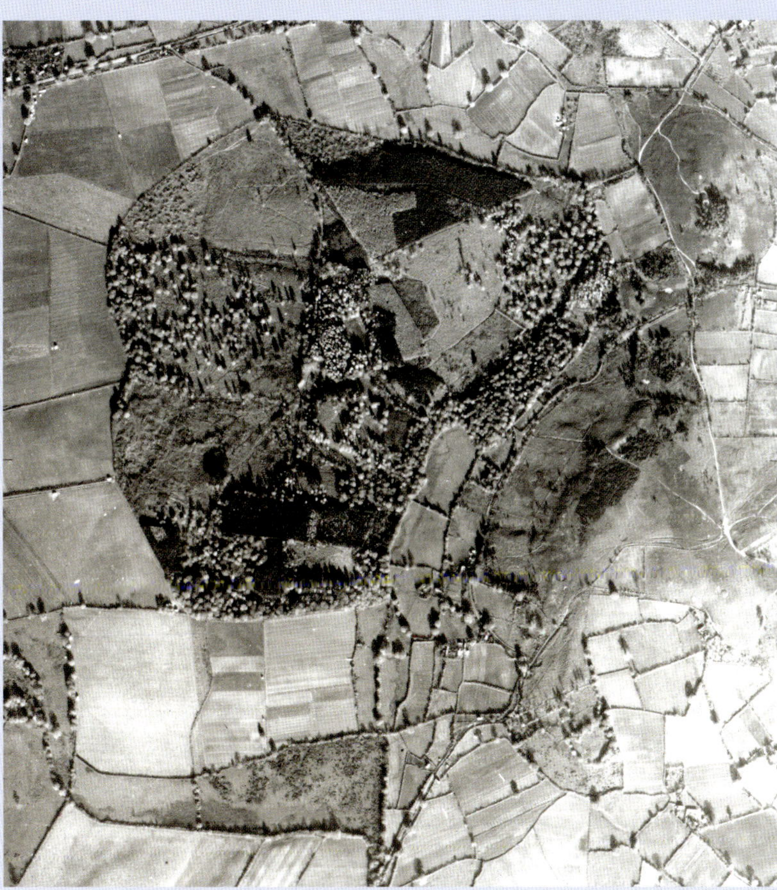

When the parks of large country houses were being laid out it was common for them to be surrounded by a shelter belt of trees to give the owners privacy. This has now been applied to the golf course, an unusual affair.

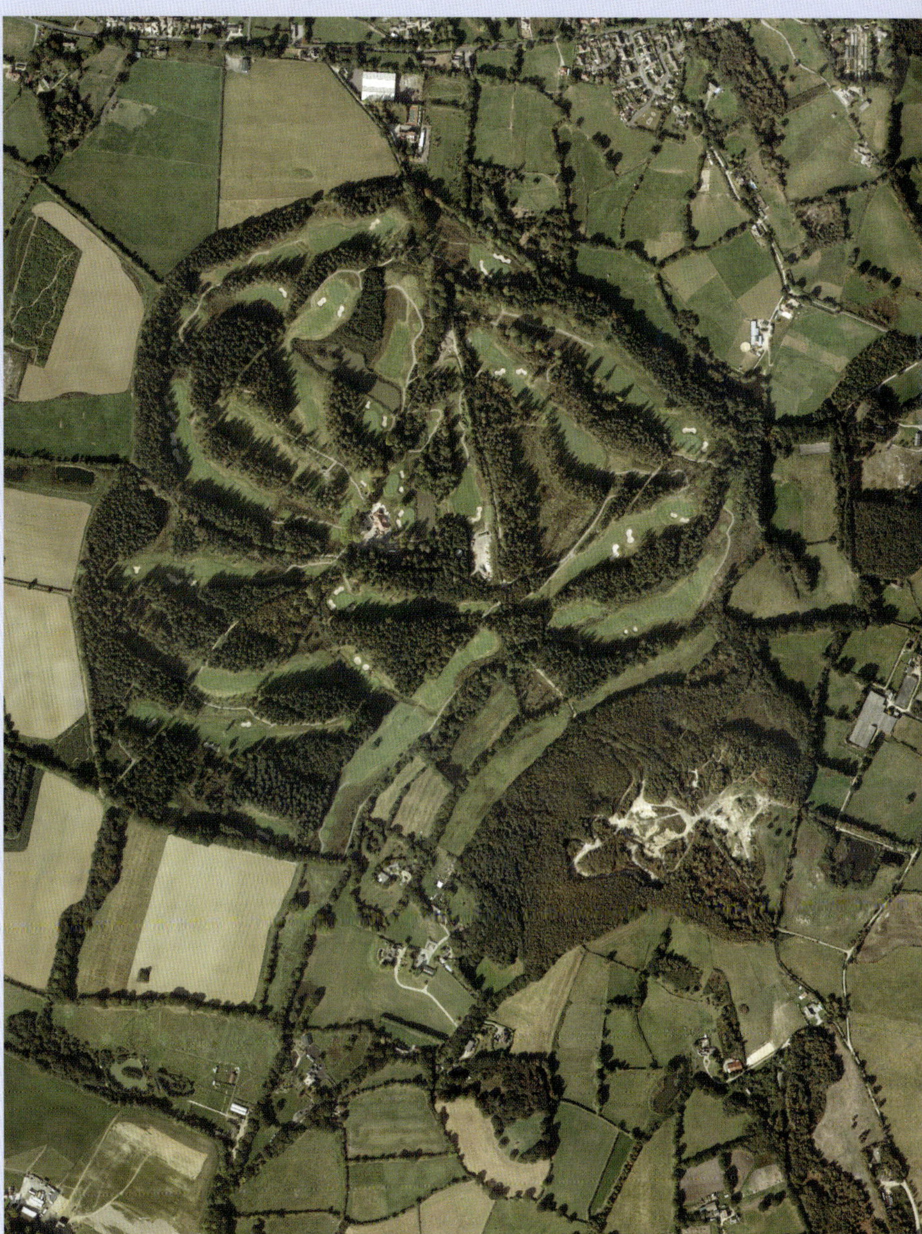

Worth Matravers 1947 photograph reference 1821-3402, centred on grid reference SY 974 776

The changes around the village of Worth Matravers have been comparatively slight but interesting. The village itself has grown, albeit not substantially and the developments have been confined to pre-existing fields. Indeed the field systems are some of the most interesting things around Worth Matravers. To the south of the village are numerous medieval terraced fields, or lynchets. These had been created to enable the steep slopes of the downs to be ploughed. These had fallen out of use in the late medieval period due to changes in population and agricultural practices. The lynchets at Worth Matravers, interestingly more clearly visible on the modern picture that on that of 1947, are considered some of the best examples in the country. In addition the pattern of fields, mostly marked out by dry-stone walls is virtually unchanged since 1947.

West of Worth Matravers, in 1947, is a large encampment of small buildings, which have all gone today. Between 1940 and '42 these housed one of the key teams developing radar, but the research scientists were moved Malvern in 1942, for security reasons. The buildings remained to serve a radar station. The thin shadow of one of the radar towers can clearly be seen; this was demolished in the 1970s.

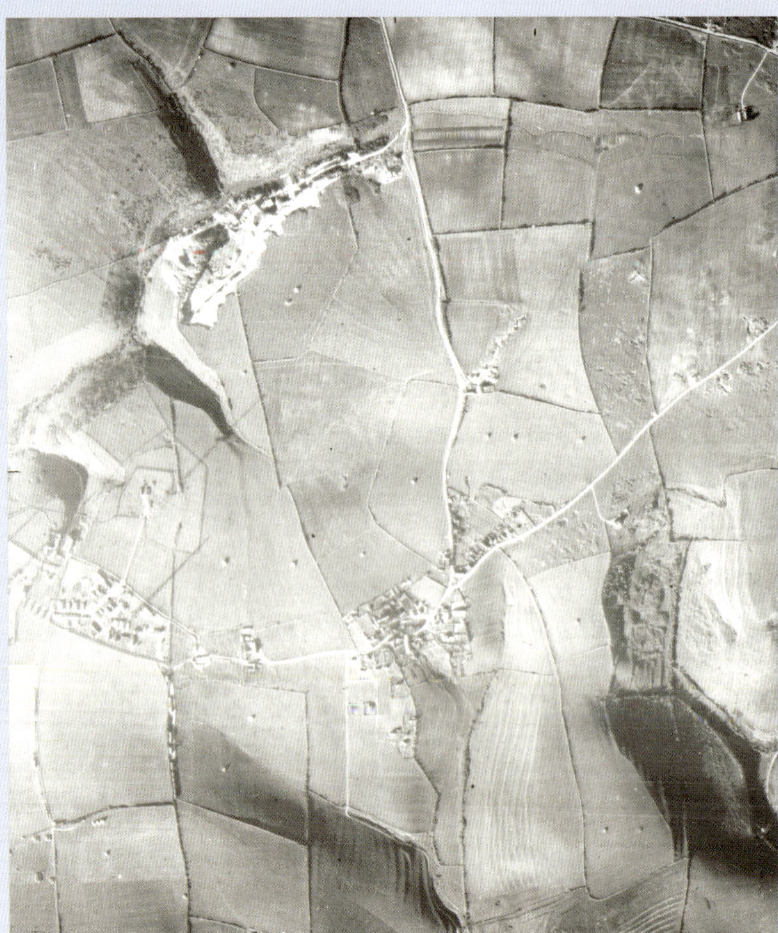

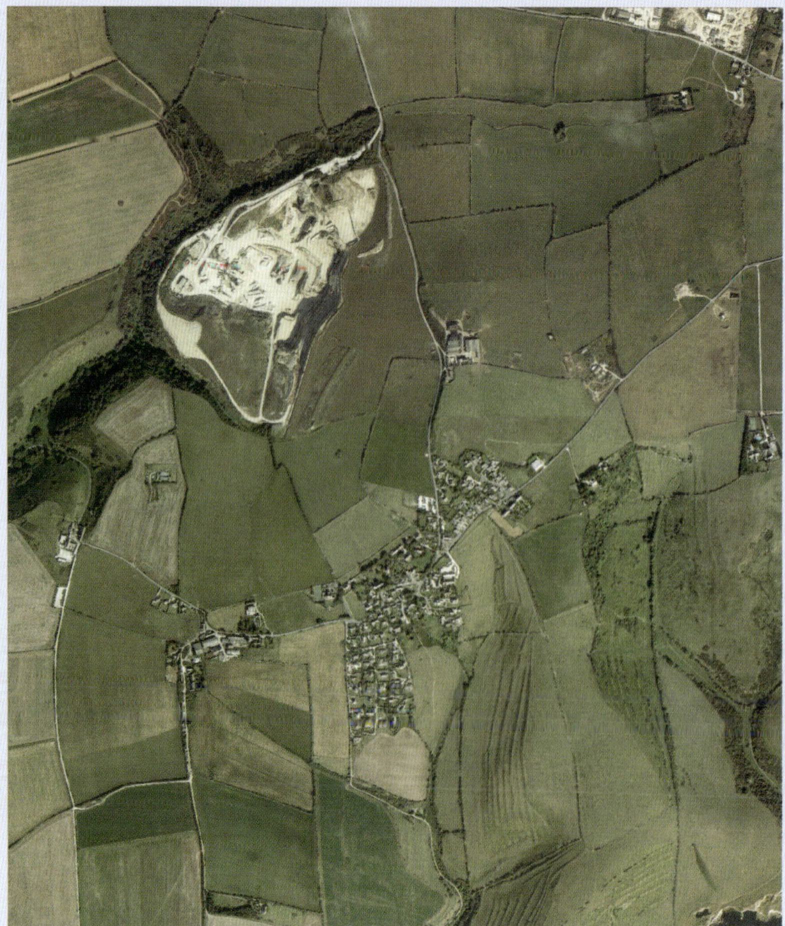